SCHOOL BOARD MINUTES
ENUMERATION LISTS
AND
ACCOUNT RECORDS

BARBOUR COUNTY
WEST VIRGINIA

Township of Barker
1870–1890

Independent District
of Belington
1893–1899

☙

Sharon Wilmoth Harsh

HERITAGE BOOKS
2012

HERITAGE BOOKS
AN IMPRINT OF HERITAGE BOOKS, INC.

Books, CDs, and more—Worldwide

For our listing of thousands of titles see our website
at
www.HeritageBooks.com

Published 2012 by
HERITAGE BOOKS, INC.
Publishing Division
100 Railroad Ave. #104
Westminster, Maryland 21157

Copyright © 2000 Sharon Wilmoth Harsh

Other Heritage Books by the author:

School Board Minutes, Enumerations Lists and Account Records, Barbour County, West Virginia: Philippi Independent District, July 1870–December 1899
Philippi District, September 1871–November 1899

All rights reserved. No part of this book may be reproduced or transmitted in any form or by any means, electronic or mechanical, including photocopying, recording or by any information storage and retrieval system without written permission from the author, except for the inclusion of brief quotations in a review.

International Standard Book Numbers
Paperbound: 978-0-7884-1676-7
Clothbound: 978-0-7884-9400-0

CONTENTS

INTRODUCTION...1
    Historical Background
    School Board Minutes
    Enumeration of Youth
    Independent and Township Districts
    School Commissioners and Trustees
    School Term
    School Funding and Expenditures
    School Teachers
    School Buildings

TOWNSHIP OF BARKER
    School Board Minutes
    1870..9
    1871..21
    1872..37
    1873..51
    1874..61
    1875..74
    1876..89
    1877..104
    1878..121
    1879..135
    1880..155
    1881..167
    1882..178
    1883..186
    1884..193
    1885..205
    1886..215
    1887..225
    1888..235
    1889..246
    1890..255

    Barker District Enumeration of Youth
    1870..261
    1871..274
    1872..275

1873	278
1874	279
1875	280
1876	281
1877	282
1878	283
1979	284
1880	284
1881	285
1882	286
1883	286
1884	286
1885	286
1886	286
1887	287
1888	287
1889	287
1890	287

BELINGTON INDEPENDENT DISTRICT
School Board Minutes

1893	289
1894	294
1895	301
1896	307
1897	317
1898	328
1899	341

NAME INDEX	365

PREFACE

School board minutes for the Township of Barker and The Independent School District of Belington are transcribed verbatim from the handwritten records. The transcribed minutes include the irregularities in grammar and spelling that were contained in the records. Meeting dates and names are printed in boldface type to facilitate the search for individual persons.

The original minutes are housed at the Barbour County Board of Education office in Philippi, West Virginia.

INTRODUCTION

HISTORICAL BACKGROUND

Prior to the Civil War, the territory that encompassed present day West Virginia operated schools according to the laws established by the colonial Virginia government. In the early years of Virginia history, the government did not mandate or fund elementary or secondary schools, and left the responsibility for educating children to the family. In many cases, wealthy plantation owners hired independent tutors and private schoolmasters to educate their children.

Virginia's first attempt to provide a state funded education was in the development of schools for the poor. However, schools for the poor were not designed to include children of slaves, therefore, over time, wealthy land owners began to include children of their slaves in the private plantation schools. In the years preceding the Civil War, private education arrangements evolved into common schools where children of plantation owners along with children of laborers and indigent children were taught together in buildings known as Field Schools. By 1846, the Virginia legislature permitted the establishment of district public school systems on petition of one-third of the local qualified voters. But because of sparse population in most of western Virginia, the district free school system evolved more slowly than in eastern Virginia, and itinerant school masters and subscription schools remained the common form of schooling in western Virginia through most of the pre Civil War years.

During the Civil War, education was suspended for the majority of the western Virginia counties. Across the state, public buildings, churches, and schools were burned, and raids by home guard groups, as well as skirmishes involving Union and Confederate soldiers made it dangerous for groups of students to congregate in conspicuous places. In many of the north western counties, dangerous conditions were exacerbated as divided loyalties created additional tension among families and local citizenry, and even in areas where public sentiment was united, education was suspended as students and teachers alike often volunteered for active duty, preferring to fight rather than to study or teach.

When West Virginia declared separate statehood in 1863, members of the first state legislature were charged with designing a new state government, including a new educational system. In keeping with the purpose for separate statehood, the legislature was expected to design a public education system modeled after the public schools that were operated in northern states. Ironically, the majority of the elected representatives in the early years of statehood were more familiar with southern schools and traditions than northern education systems, and as a result, early legislative enactments were heavily modeled after colonial Virginia schools. As a result, the Virginia model of common primary schools became the typical education format for schools throughout the state.

After the Civil War, West Virginia's newly formed education system was implemented unevenly across the state. In counties where Union loyalties prevailed, school levies were collected and state support for schools was distributed. In counties where large numbers of soldiers enlisted in the Confederate army or where southern sympathizers lived, school levies were often not collected and enumeration of the school age population was frequently not taken or submitted to the state. In these cases, state funds to operate schools were not distributed to the non cooperating counties, delaying the implementation of public schools in these areas. But by 1870, most of the legislative enactments establishing the procedures for school funding was in place and schools were established in even the most rural areas of the state.

The years following statehood through the turn of the century may arguably be the most controversial years in the history of public education in West Virginia. During this span of time, public criticism about taxation, teachers, and the operation of schools provided the basis for legislative changes that altered or modified the course of the state's emerging educational system. Various aspects of the public education system enacted during the early years of statehood provided the points of controversy for the public criticism, with school funding among the most frequently criticized aspects. Citizens complained that state and district tax levies generated sufficient funds for school operation in larger towns and cities but created financial burdens and limited operational resources in the sparsely populated majority of the state. Citizens additionally complained that the control of school districts was centered in select local citizens who had little accountability for the expenditure of school funds.

Against this backdrop, the educational system in West Virginia developed and changed in response to public reaction to the operation of the local schools. During the early years of statehood, particularly from 1870 to 1899, the education system was in the hands of powerful and influential local leaders who wielded great control over the operation of the schools.

SCHOOL BOARD MINUTES

School board minutes established a written record of all transactions made by the school board commissioners. The records were hand written by a board appointed or elected secretary who attended the board meetings and recorded the transactions in a permanently bound minute book. The minutes describe each transaction made by the board and identify by name each person with whom the board transacted business.

Early school board minutes during this time provide a rich store of information on the evolution of district schools. The minutes identify the family groups living in the area, the local communities served by the schools, and the local citizen leaders who controlled the schools. In documenting the process of operating schools, the early board minutes identify which citizens were entrusted to teach and which citizens were given the authority to serve as school commissioners and trustees. The minutes identify which local businesses were in operation and which ones benefitted from school board expenditures. The minutes also identify the local citizens who were employed to construct or repair existing schools.

In areas where demographic data and court records are incomplete, school board minutes during these early years of statehood provide valuable sources of community and family history.

ENUMERATION OF YOUTH

Beginning in 1863, state revenue funds were redistributed to counties for the operation of public schools based on an annual enumeration of youth.

The enumeration of school aged population was conducted annually, certified, and reported to the state. State school funds were then redistributed to the counties based on the enumeration reports.

The enumeration of youth reported to the state showed the total number of youth ages 6-21 who were eligible to attend school. For most years, the enumeration lists indicated the number of youth residing in each school district area. In 1870 and 1872, the enumeration lists identify by name each family with school age youth living in the district. Enumeration data during the early years of statehood show that not all school age youth were enrolled in school, and that those who were enrolled did not attend regularly. State

Department of Education statistics for 1870 show that in West Virginia, there were over 157,000 school age youth. In 1870, just over half of the identified youth (87,330) were enrolled in school and only 55,083 were in school on a daily basis.

By law, the township school boards were given the responsibility for the annual enumeration. In each township, the responsibility for conducting the actual enumeration was delegated to the teachers who were employed in the subdistrict schools. By 1867, the responsibility for enumeration of the school age population was given to the county superintendent, who in turn delegated the responsibility to school trustees and teachers. In 1873, the state legislature placed the responsibility for enumeration on township commission boards. Although the responsibility for annual enumerations was commonly delegated to teachers in most districts, it was not until 1879 that the state legislature enacted a bill that officially permitted sub district teachers to take the annual enumeration. To ensure accuracy of the enumeration data, the 1879 legislature required teachers completing the enumeration to take an oath stating that the report was correct.

INDEPENDENT AND TOWNSHIP DISTRICTS

Within weeks of the formation of the state, a series of local mass meetings were held in every geographical area. Citizens attending these mass meetings voted on a number of issues that were critical to the initial operation of the state. Along with other issues, voters approved the division of the county into townships and elected school commissioners to oversee the operation of schools. In central and eastern counties where civil strife continued, mass meetings had to be postponed and decisions regarding township divisions and school districts were delayed for several months, and in some areas, for several years.

An act passed by the first state legislature in 1863 permitted local school districts to be divided into township districts or to operate as independent school districts. Throughout the remainder of the 19th century, school districts often operated as independent districts, hiring their own teachers and operating their own school facilities. Records for these independent districts were maintained by elected school board members and commissioners.

SCHOOL COMMISSIONERS AND TRUSTEES

In 1863, the public education system in West Virginia was

organized around townships. The township was designated as the unit of control for administering the public schools. In each township, qualified voters annually elected three commissioners who were vested with the authority to operate the schools. The school commissioners and the secretary constituted the township board of education.

The duties of elected school commissioners were established by state law. The three school commissioners had the authority to employ qualified teachers, establish teacher salaries, approve subjects to be taught in the schools, build and maintain school facilities, collect school taxes, and authorize the expenditure of school funds.

During the first three years of statehood, members of the public complained that school commissioners were not fulfilling their statutory duties specified under law. In many areas of the state, citizens reported that commissioners neglected to take or report annual enumerations, that when reports were made they were often inaccurate, and that commissioners spent school funds in questionable ways. In response to the criticism, the 1866 legislature authorized the voters in each sub district to annually elect three trustees. The legislature gave the trustees authority to hire and fire teachers, establish teacher salaries, visit subdistrict schools and submit reports to the township commission boards.

The elected trustee model was implemented by the state in 1866, but after one year, the 1867 legislature modified the law to make the trustees appointed by the township board instead of elected by the local voters. By law, trustees were given the authority to hire and dismiss teachers, fix salaries, and expel or suspend students for misbehavior. Trustees were required by law to visit every school within two weeks of the opening of the school term and again within two weeks of the closing of the term to inspect the school building, check the records maintained by the teachers, and make inquiries about the educational program. In many subdistricts, the appointed trustees were responsible citizens who took their duties very seriously.

SCHOOL TERM

The first West Virginia legislature established a six month instructional term for public schools within the state. Although the school term was to be six months in length, local township levies often did not generate enough revenue to operate the schools for a full six month term.

6 School Board Minutes

SCHOOL FUNDING AND EXPENDITURES

Funds for the operation of the public schools were generated through township levies. During the first year of statehood, township levies were established by state law at ten cents on the hundred dollars valuation. During the second year of statehood, voters attending annual township mass meetings recognized that additional school buildings were needed to house the increased number of students enrolling in school and that the ten cent levy did not general sufficient funds to operate the schools and construct new buildings. By 1865, township school commissioners were authorized to levy two separate school taxes. If approved by township voters, local school commissioners could levy up to twenty-five cents on the hundred dollars for the district's teacher fund, and without voter approval, the commissioners could levy twenty cents on the hundred dollars for a building fund. When tax collections remained insufficient to operate, the state legislature in 1867 reduced the legal term of school to four months.

The local sheriff, by law, was the officer in charge of collecting school taxes and disbursing school funds received by the state. The sheriff maintained records of expenditures and receipts, and where a discrepancy in financial records existed between the local school district statement and the sheriff statement, notations of the discrepancy or difference was noted in the board minutes.

SCHOOL TEACHERS

The primary criteria for hiring teachers was that the individual had to be of good moral character. While teachers could be dismissed for academic incompetency, the majority of teacher dismissals were based on allegations of immoral conduct. Local trustees and commissioners were responsible for hiring teachers of good moral character and were given the authority to dismiss teachers who did not maintain acceptable standards of conduct.

Teacher salaries were not standardized across all school districts and varied according to the amount established by local school board commissioners and the amount of local levy money generated by taxpayers. During the first year of statehood, the average teacher salary was $34 for male teachers and $27 for females. The highest paid teachers during this first year was in the Wheeling Independent District where male teachers were paid an average of $139 per month and female teachers were paid an average of $42 per month.

Since teacher salaries were low in most areas of the state, teachers often supplemented their income with other vocational pursuits. Teachers frequently were farmers, preachers, and proprietors or joint owners of local businesses. When the two careers were kept separate, teacher activities were generally not questioned. In some areas, teachers could purchase supplies from family owned stores, hire relatives to conduct the annual enumeration, or cancel school for the operation of Sunday Schools without reprisal from local trustees or commissioners, while other teachers were dismissed for similar actions.

During the early years of the public education system, teachers received little supervision and were permitted to instruct students according to their own methods. This lack of professional supervision allowed considerable diversity in the quality of instruction across schools. Teachers who were skilled in basic subjects designed instruction around recitation and practice. Less capable school teachers who permitted students to be unruly or who provided monotonous or inadequate instruction could be dismissed based on the recommendation of a trustee who may or may not have visited the school to observe the instructional program.

SCHOOL BUILDINGS

During the early years of statehood, school buildings were usually single story log structures. Logs for school buildings were cut on property owned by local taxpayers or were purchased from parents within the enumeration district. The roof of the school buildings was made of clap boards, the floor was made from planked boards, and the windows were made from greased paper or single panes of glass. The buildings were heated by fireplaces or wood burning stoves, light was provided by oil lamps, and drinking water was carried inside by bucket and consumed using a common dipper.

School buildings stood empty for months at a time. When school was not in session, the building was often used for religious services or community activities.

School Board Minutes

Sources of Information

Ambler, Charles H. A History of Education in West Virginia. 1951. Standard Printing & Publishing Company, Huntington, West Virginia.

Best, J.H. And Sidwell, R.T. Eds. The American Legacy of Learning. 1967. J.B. Lippincott Co., New York.

Butts, R. Freeman. A Cultural History of Education. 1947. McGraw-Hill Book Company, New York.

Cubberley, Ellwood, P. The History of Education. 1920. The Riverside Press, Cambridge, Mass.

The History of Education in West Virginia. 1907. Tribune Printing Company, Charleston.

West Virginia Code. Acts of the Legislature 1863, 1866, 1867, 1868, 1870. Chapter XLV of Education.

TOWNSHIP OF BARKER
1870-1890

At a meeting of the Board of Education of the Township of Barker held at the School house in District No. 8 on the **15th of July 1870** the following members were present. Viz: **Wm. J. Right** President, **Major Fenelon Howes**, and **Thomas Williams**, and **John L. Hilkey**, Secretary.

1st. The Board proceeded to hear the evidence and decide on the petition, charges, and specifications below set forth being a petition of citizens of the 14th school district of Barker Tp. asking the removal of the Trustees of said district for refusing to remove **V. N. Gribble** teacher of said district and also for refusing to open the schoolhouse of said district for the purpose of Holding Singing School, Religious worship, Sabbath Schools &c. after being notified by the Board of Education to do so. The defendants moved the Board to refuse to hear any evidence on the charge of refusing to open the said schoolhouse for other purposes than the use of primary schools, but were overruled by said Board of Education; after hearing the evidence the Board decided to remove said Trustees. The Defts. thereupon gave notice that they would appeal from said decision and would apply to the Circuit Court of Barbour County for a writ of certiorari, and ask to have said judgment suspended.

2nd. **V. N. Gribble** this day presented to this Board a certificate from the Trustees of school district No. 14 showing that he is entitled to the sum of $64.00 for two months services as teacher in said dstrict, commencing on the day and ending on the 14th of July 1870 - the same is allowed, and it is ordered that a draft be drawn in his favor for that amount payable out of the school fund allotted to said district.

The Board adjourned to meet on 30th July 1870.
Wm. J. Right, President Bd Ed
J. L. Hilkey, Secretary

At a meeting of the Board of Education of the Township of Barker held at the Storehouse **Newlon** & **Stalnaker** in Belington on the **30th day of July 1870**. The following members were present. Viz: **Wm. J. Right**, President, **Maj. F. Howes** & **Thos. Williams**, and

10 School Board Minutes

John L. Hilkey, Secretary.

The appointment of Trustees in each District showing the time each one has to serve from Sept. 1st, 1870.

District No.1	Wm. P. Wilson	3 years
	Simon Swick	2 years
	Geo. Thorn	1 year
District No.2	A. J. Williams	3 years
	A. J. Wilmoth	2 years
	James Booth	1 year
District No.3	R. R. Talbott	3 years
	Francis Hathaway	2 years
	Matthew Edmond	1 year
District No.4	Patrick McGuiness	3 years
	R. D. Kerr	2 years
	Hysam Yeager	1 year
District No.5	Jacob Sipe	3 years
	James W. George	2 years
	Richard Werner	1 year
District No.6	Hiram Rineheart	3 years
	Jesse Teter	2 years
	J. W. Harper	1 year
District No.7	Solomon Coffman	3 years
	E. Viquesney	2 years
	A. J. Row	1 year
District No.8	W. S. Phares	3 years
	Granville Stalnaker	2 years
	John L. Hilkey	1 year
District No. 9	J. J. Ramsey	3 years
	Levi Cross	2 years
	Laben Moore	1 year

School Board Minutes 11

District No.10	Wm. G. W. Price	3 years
	James England	2 years
	John M. Ramsey	1 year
District No.11	Daniel Moore	3 years
	Dyer Kelly	2 years
	J. R. W. Smith	1 year
District No.12	Francis Shockey	3 years
	John M. Corley	2 years
	Randolph Coberly	1 year
District No.13	Isaac Price	3 years
	A. Right	2 years
	Wm. R. Moore	1 year
District No.14	George Digman	3 years
	John D. Ball	2 years
	Lloyd Davis	1 year

2nd

Wm. P. Keys assessor of the county this day furnished this Board a copy of his book for this Township shewing the valuations of the real & personal estate therein to be as follows. Viz. Real estate $ B 765.04 T 305.66   Personal Estate $ B 299.48 T 119.39   This Board doth order that a levy of Two Mills on the dollar for school fund and five Mills for building purposes, be laid and assessed upon said valuation for the current year.

Ordered that the Board now adjourn to meet at the Schoolhouse in District No.8 on Saturday the 27th day of August 1870.
Wm.J. Right President
John L. Hilkey Secretary

At a meeting of the Board of Education of the Township of Barker held at the School house in Belington District No.8 on Saturday the **27th August 1870**. The following members were present, Viz: **Wm. J. Right** - President, **Maj. F. Howes** & **Thomas Williams**, and

School Board Minutes

John L. Hilkey, Secretary.

1st

The Board of Education gives their consent to the Trustees of District No.5 to use their Schoolhouse for other purposes than primary schools (when not occupied or in use for such schools) such as Debating Societies, Singing Schools, Sabbath Schools, Religious Worship &C.

Ordered that the Board adjourn to meet at the Schoolhouse in District No.8 on Saturday September 24th 1870 at 9 o'clock A.M.

Wm J. Right   Pres
John L. Hilkey, Secretary

At a meeting of the Board of Education of the Township of Barker held at **R. A. McCutcheons** store in Belington on Monday **31st October 1870.** The following members were present, Viz: **Wm. J. Right** President, **F. Howes** and **J. L. Hilkey**, Secretary.

This Board being indebted **Levi Cross** in the sum of $596 - for the construction of a schoolhouse in District No.13 for which he is entitled to receive Two Drafts on treasurer payable at sight & four several bonds of $96.50 each payable as followes, one due November 1st 1870 the others payable in one, Two and Three years from January 1st 1870, it is ordered Two Drafts & 4 Bonds for that sum payable as aforesaid by given to him signed by the President & Countersigned by the Secretary on behalf of this Board.

R. A. McCutcheon, this day presented to this Board a certificate from the Trustees of school District No.6 showing that he is entitiled to the sum of $1.35 for one Bucket, one cup & one Broom, the same is allowed and it is ordered that a Draft be drawn in his favor for that amount payable out of the School fund allowed to said District.

R. A. McCutcheon, this day presented to this Board a certificate from the Trustees of School district No.13 showing that he is entitled to the sum of $1.30 for value rec'd the same is allowed and it is ordered that a Draft be drawn in his favor for that amount payable out of the School fund allowed to said District.

On motion the Board adjourned to meet at **R. A. McCutcheon's** Storehouse on Saturday the 12th of November 1870.

Wm. J. Right President
W. J. Drummond Secretary Protem

At a meeting of the Board of Education of the Township of Barker held at the Storehouse of **R. A. McCutcheon** on Saturday **12th Nov - 1870** the following members were present, Viz: **Wm. J. Right** President, **Fenelon Howes** & **Daniel Moore**, and **John L. Hilkey**, Secretary.

1st

T. J. Anderson this day presented to this Board a certificate from the Trustees of School District No.4 showing that he is entitled to the sum of $2 - for services rendered (Boarding Teacher) in said District, the same is allowed and it is ordered that a draft be drawn in his favor for that amount payable out of the school fund allotted to said District.

2nd

Fenelon Howes, this day presented to this board a certificate from the Trustees of school district No.6 showing that he is entitled to the sum of $10.- for furnishing one hundred Bushels of Coal in said district the same is allowed &it is ordered that a draft be drawn in his favor for that amount payable out of the school fund allotted to said District.

3

Celia Wilson, this day presented to this Board a certificate from the Trustees of School District No.12 showing that she is entitled to the sum of $34 - for Teaching School in said District one month & 10 days the same is allowed and it is ordered that a draft be drawn in her favor for that amount payable out of the School fund allotted to said District.

4

John M. Corley, this day presented to this board a certificate from the Trustees of School district No.12 showing that he is entitled to the sum of $15 - for services (Boarding Teacher) in said District the same is allowed and it is ordered that a draft be drawn in his favor for that amount payable out of the school fund allotted to said District.

School Board Minutes

5

Ordered that **Levi Cross** be paid $2 - out of Building fund, for which a draft has been drawn in his favor.

Apportionment Nov. 12th 1870

District	3 fifths	2 fifths & Levy	Total of new	Old	Whole amount $	Cts
No.1	42.50	59.53	102.03	201.14	303	17
No.2	55.25	59.53	114.78	54.62	169	40
No.3	62.90	59.53	122.43	128.08	250	51
No.4	33.15	59.53	92.68	42.74	135	42
No.5	53.55	59.53	113.08	25.07	138	15
No.6	44.20	59.53	103.73	48.12	151	45
No.7	28.90	59.53	88.43	17.60	106	03
No.8	49.30	59.53	108.83	25.51	134	34
No.9	45.05	59.53	104.58	45.53	150	11
No.10	57.60	59.53	117.13	In debt 48.49	68	64
No.11	28.05	59.53	87.58	6.08	93	66
No.12	55.25	59.53	114.78	64.69	179	47
No.13	55.05	59.53	114.58	61.52	176	10
No.14	28.90	59.53	88.43	89.94	178	37

Ordered that **James W. George** be charged with
State School fund $1095.61
Tuition fund Levy of 70 425.05
Building fund Levy of 70 1064.52

Ordered that the homestead of **John Price** be included in District No.13.

Ordered that the Board now adjourn to meet again on Nov. 18th 1870 at **R. A. McCutcheon**'s Storehouse.

Wm. J. Right President
J. L. Hilkey, Secy

1st

At a meeting of the Board of Education of the Township of Barker held at the Storehouse of **R. A. McCutcheon**'s in Belington, on the **18th day of November 1870**. The following members were present Viz: **Wm. J. Right** President & **Fenelon Howes** and **W. J. Drummond** Secretary Protem.

2

Charles H. Street, this day presented to this Board a certificate from the Trustees of School district No.13 showing that he is entitled to the sum of $27.- for services as Teacher in said District commencing day of October and ending November 1870 the same is allowed & it is ordered that a draft be drawn in his favor for that amount payable out of the school fund allotted to said District.

3

Lavenia M. See this day presented to this Board a certificate from the Trustees of School District No.6 showing that she is entitled to the sum of $33 - for services as Teacher in said District for one month commencing on the day of October and ending on the day of November 1870. The same is allowed and a draft ordered to be drawn in her favor for that amount payable out of the school fund allotted to said district.

4

B. M. Woolverton this day presented to this Board a certificate from the Trustees of School District No.13 showing that he is entitled to the sum of $21.10 for the same is allowed, and it is ordered that a draft be drawn in his favor for that amount payable out of the school fund allotted to said District.

5

Ordered that **Arnold Right** be paid the sum of $100.10 out of school fund of District No.13 a draft has been drawn in his favor for that amount by order of the Board.

16   School Board Minutes

Ordered that the meeting now adjourn.
Wm J. Right   President
Wm. J. Drummond, Secretary protem

At a meeting of the Board of Education of the Township of Barker held at the storehouse of **R. A. McCutcheon**'s in Belington, on Saturday the **26th day of November 1870**. The following members were present, Viz: **Wm. J. Right**   President, **Fenelon Howes** & **Daniel Moore** and **John L. Hilkey** Secretary.

1

Joshua Proudfoot, this day has presented to this Board a certificate from the Trustees of School District No.3 showing that he is entitled to the Sum of $25.- for furnishing fewel to said District the same is allowed; and it is ordered that a draft be drawn in his favor for that amount payable out of the school fund allotted to said District.

2

Maggie E. Hilkey, this day presented to this Board a certificate from the Trustees of school District No.8 showing that she is entitled to the sum of $70.- services as teacher in said District commencing on the 31st day of October 1870 the same is allowed and it is ordered that a draft be drawn in her favor for that amount payable out of the school fund allotted to said District.

3

Bur P. Newlon this day presented to this Board a certificate from the Trustees of School District No.8 showing that he is entitled to the sum of $9.60 for furnishing 80 Bushel coal to said District the same is allowed and it si ordered that a draft be drawn in his favor for that amount payable out of the school fund allotted to said District.

4

Robt. L. Tallman, this day presented to this Board a certificate from the Trustees of School District No.1 showing that he is entitled to the sum of $100.- for 3 month services as Teacher in said District the same is allowed and it is ordered that a draft be drawn in his favor for that amount payable out of the school fund allotted to said District.

5

George Thorn, this day presented to this Board a certificate from the Trustees of School District No.1 showing that he is entitled to the sum of $5.00 for furnishing 50 bushel coal to said District the same is allowed and it is ordered that a draft be drawn in his favor for that amount payable out of the school fund allotted to said District.

6

David M. Howell, this day presented to this Board a certificate from the Trustees of School District No.12 showing that he is entitled to the sum of $20.33 for services as Teacher in said District the same is allowed and it is ordered that a draft be drawn in his favor for that amount payable out of the school fund allotted to said District.

7

M. V. Oldaker, this day presented to this Board a certificate from the Trustees of School District No.3 showing that he is entitled to the sum of $76.- for services as Teacher in said District the same is allowed, and it is ordered that a draft be drawn in his favor for that amount payable out of school fund allotted to said District.

8

Fenelon Howes, this day presented to this Board a claim for money expended in defending a suit in court with **Jacob Sipe**; **Jacob Sipe** plaintiff and the Board of Education Defendants it is allowed, and ordered that a draft be drawn to the amount of $7.05 payable out of the General School fund.

9

J. M. Baker, this day presented to this Board a certificate from the Trustees of School District No.4 showing that he is entitled to the sum of $65.- for his services as Teacher in said District the same is allowed, and it is ordered that a draft be drawn in his favor payable out of the school fund allotted to said District.

10

Ordered that **Wm. Day** be appointed Trustee in District No.1

11

Ordered that the meeting now adjourn to meet again on the 31st day of December 1870.

Fenelon Howes President protem
John L. Hilkey Secretary

18 School Board Minutes

1

J. M. Lake on the **13th day of December 1870** presented to this Board a certificate from the Trustees of School District No.14, showing that he is entitled to the sum of $30.- for services as Teacher in said District the same is allowed, and it is ordered that a draft be drawn in his favor for that amount payable out of school fund allotted to said District.

2

Lloyd Davis on the **3d day of December 1870** presented to the Board a certificate from the Trustees of School District No.14 showing that he is entitled to the sum of $5.- for furnishing coal to said District the same is allowed and it is ordered that a draft be drawn in his favor for that amount payable out of school fund allotted to said District.

3

V. F. Taylor, on the **10th day of December 1870** presented to the Board a certificate from the Trustees of School District No.2 showing that he is entitled to the sum of $33.- for one month's service as Teacher in said District commencing on the 1st day of November and ending on the 1st day of December 1870. The same is allowed and it is ordered that a draft be drawn in his favor of that amount payable out of school fund allotted to said District.

The above 3 orders were allowed by the Board of Education when not in regular meeting.

John L. Hilkey, Secretary

School Trustees - Hunters Fork District
   Lewis Price
   John Moore

Trustee Order
   Board of Education of Barker Dist please pay to the order of **H.C. Harris** nine dollars for cleaning up the Hunters Fork School house lot same to Building fund.

Lewis Price Trustee
John Moore

At a meeting of the Board of Education of the Township of Barker held at the school house in District No.8, on the **31st day of December 1870.** The following members were present, Viz: **Wm. J. Right** President, **Fenelon Howes, Daniel Moore,** and **John L. Hilkey,** Secretary.

1st

Miss **L. M. See** this day presented to this Board a certificate from the Trustees of School district No.6 showing that she is entitled to the sum of $33.- for services as Teacher is said District the same is allowed and is ordered that a draft be drawn in her favor for that amount payable out of school fund allotted to said District.

2nd

Charles M. Groves, this day presented to this Board a certificate from the Trustees of School District No.7, showing that he is entitled to the sum of $36.50 for services as Teacher in said District the same is allowed and it is ordered that a draft be drawn in his favor for that amount payable out of school fund allotted to said District.

3rd

Bur P. Newlon, this day presented to this Board a certificate from the Trustees of School District No.11, showing that he is entitled to the sum of $1.50 for furnishing Poker and Shovel to said District, the same is allowed and it is ordered that a draft be drawn in his favor for that amount payable out of school fund, allotted to said District.

4th

William F. McGee, this day presented to this Board a certificate from the Trustees of School District No.9 showing that he is entitled to the sum of $35.- for services as Teacher in said District, the same is allowed and it is ordered that a draft be drawn in his favor for that amount payable out of school fund, allotted to said District.

5

R. G. Thorn, this day presented to this Board a certificate from the Trustees of School District No.2 showing that he is entitled to the sum of $4.15 for furnishing fuel to said District, the same is allowed and it is ordered that a draft be drawn in his favor for that amount payable out of School fund allotted to said District.

6th

Israel Poling, this day presented to this Board a certificate from the Trustees of School District No.12, showing that he is entitled to the sum of $33. for services as Teacher in said District, the same is allowed, and it is ordered that a draft be drawn in his favor for that amount payable out of school fund allotted to said District.

7

A. J. Hartman, this day presented to this Board a certificate from the Trustees of School District No. 5 showing that he is entitled to the sum of $33. for services as Teacher in said District, the same is allowed and it is ordered that a draft be drawn in his favor for that amount payable out of school fund allotted to said District.

8

John L. Hilkey, this day presented to this Board a certificate from **R. A. McCutcheon** (County Superintendent) showing that he is entitled to the sum of $25. for services as Secretary for one year the same is allotted and it is ordered that a draft be drawn in his favor for that amount payable out of general School fund.

9

John L. Hilkey, this day presented to this Board a certificate from **R. A. McCutcheon**, County Superintendent, showing that he is entitled to the sum of $1.50 for one day's service for taking the Enumeration in District No.11, the same is allowed and it is ordered that a draft be drawn in his favor for that amount payable out of the School fund allotted to said District.

10

John L. Hilkey, this day presented to this Board a certificate from **R. A. McCutcheon**, County Superintendent, showing that he is entitled to the sum of $1.50 for one day's services for taking Enumeration of youth in District No.4 the same is allowed, and it is ordered that a draft be drawn in his favor for that amount payable out of school fund allotted to said District.

11

Ordered that a draft be drawn in favor of **Joseph Howes** for the sum of sixty cents to be paid out of General School fund.

Wm. J. Right (President)
John L. Hilkey

School Board Minutes 21

1

At a meeting of the Board of Education of the Township of Barker, held at the School House near Belington in District No.8; on the 7th **day of January 1871,** the following members were present. Viz: **Joseph Teter, Jun.** President. **Daniel Moore & Francis Hathaway**, and **John L. Hilkey** Secretary.

2

The Board was organized by electing **Joseph Teter** President, & **John L. Hilkey** Secretary.

3

The following persons were acknowledged to be legal Trustees by this Board - **Jesse Teter** in District No.6; **John Derrett** in District No.3 for 1 year.

4

Ordered that the Trustees having controll of School Houses in Barker Township, in each & every District shall be compelled to open the Door for public worship on the Sabbath day & for writing school and for any literary society.

5

Ordered that a settlement be made with **James W. George**, Township Treasurer.

Treasurer's indebtedness for school fund at last settlement
$1603.09
State school fund charged to Treasurer of 1870   1095.61
Levy of 1870 for School fund   425.05
Whole amount   3123.75

Cr By Drafts including all Drafts the Board issued and Delinquent list for free school $1701.89

Treasurer's indebtedness for Building fund at last settlement
$1133.98
Township levy of 1870   1064.52
     2198.40

Cr By Drafts all Board issued also Delinquent Bonds presented & Received amount $548.09
     629.70
     1177.79

School Board Minutes

On motion the Board adjourned to meet on last Saturday in January 1871 at **A. J. Wilmoth**'s Store.
        Joseph Teter President
           John L. Hilkey Secretary

1
At a meeting of the Bd. Education of Barker Township held at **A. J. Wilmoth**'s on the 4th **day of Feb. 1871** - the following members were present. Viz: **Joseph Teter Jun**. - President. **Daniel Moore** & **Francis Hathaway**, and **John L. Hilkey**, Sec.

2
This meeting were for the purpose of settleing with **James W. George** former Treasurer; settlement still unfinished & laid over, or continued for Monday the 6th day of Feb - 1871 to meet at School house No.6.

3
on Monday morning the 6th day of Feb - 1871. The Bd. Education above named met at the School House near **Jesse Teter**'s in District No.6, and reopened the settlement with **James W. George**.

4
After allowing to **James W. George** all his vouchers & offsets against Township, we find him Due to the Township of Barker in year 1870 One Thousand Seven hundred and Thirty Nine Dollars & Ninety Eight cents. See statement below.

5

Whole amount of Treasurer's indebtedness	8885.05
Whole amount of Treasurer's credits	6586.91
Commission on Township Levy at 6 percent	270.16
Commission on State funds at 1 percent	23.67
Delinquents	192.38
Tax Receipts	622.00
Cash $153.00 add 1 percent	<u>154.53</u>
	7849.65
Error of 1865 cr	9.66
Error of 1865 cr	3.38

Cr. On **Williamson**'s Bond 21.73   34.75
                                                                                     7884.42
                                                                                     1000.63

6

I. M. Lake this day presented to this Board a certificate from the Trustees of School District No.14; Showing that he is entitled to the sum of $60. - for two months services as Teacher in said district, commencing on the 5th day of Dec 1870 and ending on the 3d day of Feby. 1871 the same is allowed and it is ordered that a draft be drawn in his favor for that amount payable out of the School fund allotted to said District.

7

V. F. Taylor this day presented to this Board a certificate from the Trustees of School District No.2 showing that he is entitled to the sum of $35.- for one months services as Teacher in said district commencing on the 30th day of Nov 1870 - and ending Jan 3rd 1871 the same is allowed, and it is ordered that a draft be drawn in his favor for that amount payable out of the school fund allotted to said District.

8

Robt. L. Tallman this day presented to this Board a certificate from the Trustees of School District No.1 showing that he is entitled to the Sum of $33.33 1/3 for one months services as teacher in said District, commencing on the 29th day of November & ending on the 26th day of Dec - 1870 the same is allowed and it is ordered that a draft be drawn in his favor for that amount payable out of the school fund allotted to said Dist.

9

Harman Steerman this day presented to this Board a certificate from the Trustees of School District No. 1 showing that he is entitled to the sum of $4.75 for furnishing 50 Bushels of coal in said District the same is allowed & it is ordered that a draft be drawn in his favor for that amount payable out of the school fund allotted to said District.

10

V. F. Taylor this day presented to this Board a certificate from the Trustees of School District No.2 showing that he is entitled to the sum of $33- for one months services as Teacher in said District commencing on the 5th day of Jan - and ending on the 1st day of Feb 1871 - the same is allowed and it is ordered that a draft be drawn in his favor for that amount payable out of the school fund allotted to said District.

School Board Minutes

11

Noah I. Sipe this day presented to this Board a certificate from the Trustees of school district No.5 showing that he is entitled to the sum of $6.25 for furnishing fuel for school in said District the same is allowed and it is ordered that a draft be drawn in his favor for that amount payable out of the school fund allotted to said District.

12

Samuel Coffman this day presented to this Board a certificate from the Trustees of School District No. 11 showing that he is entitled to the sum of $12- for furnishing fuel to school taught in said District the same is allowed and it is ordered that a draft be drawn in his favor for that amount payable out of the school fund allotted to said District.

13

Margaret E. Hilkey this day presented this Board a certificate from the Trustees of School District No.8 showing that she is entitled to the sum of $30 - for one months services as Teacher in said District commencing on the 2nd day of Jan & ending on the 27th day of Jan 1871 the same is allowed and it is ordered that a draft be drawn in her favor for that amount payable out of the school fund allotted to said District.

14

R. R. Talbott this day presented to this Board a certificate from the Trustees of School District No.3 showing that he is entitled to the sum of $7 - for furnishing Top Barrel for stove belonging to said District, the same is allowed and it is ordered that a draft be drawn in his favor for that amount payable out of the Building fund allotted to said District.

15

Martin V. Oldaker, this day presented to this Board a certificate from the Trustees of School District No.3 showing that he is entitled to the sum of $76 - for services rendered as Teacher in said district, the same is allowed and it is ordered that a draft be drawn in his favor for that amount payable out of the school fund allotted to said District.

16

Lavin M. See, this day presented to this Board a certificate from the Trustees of School District No.6 showing that she is entitled to the sum of $48 - for services as Teacher in said District, the same is allowed and it is ordered that a draft be drawn in her favor for that amount payable out of the school fund allotted to said District.

School Board Minutes 25

17

J. M. Baker, this day presented to this Board a certificate from the Trustees of School District No.4 showing that he is entitled to the sum of $66 - for Two months services as Teacher in said District commencing on the 18th day of November 1870 and ending on the 26th day of January 1871, the same is allowed and it is ordered that a draft be drawn in his favor for that amount payable out of the school fund allotted to said District.

18

A. J. Hartman, this day presented to this Board a certificate from the Trustees of School District No.5 showing that he is entitled to the sum of $33- for one months services as Teacher in said District commencing on the 5th day of December 1870 and ending on the 9th day of January 1871, the same is allowed, and it is ordered that a draft be drawn in his favor for that amount payable out of the school fund allotted to said District.

19

Chas. M. Groves this day presented to this Board a certificate from the Trustees of School District No.7 showing that he is entitled to the sum of $60.75 for services as Teacher in said District, the same is allowed and it is ordered that a draft be drawn in his favor for that amount payable out of the school fund of, or allotted to said District.

20

J. W. Shomo, this day presented to this Board a certificate from the Trustees of School District No.2 showing that he is entitled to the sum of $3 - for furnishing fuel Two months for school taught in said District, the same is allowed and it is ordered that a draft be drawn in his favor for that amount payable out of the school fund allotted to said District.

21

George W. Corley, this day has presented to this Board a certificate from the Trustees of School District No.7, showing that he is entitled to the sum of $5.70 for furnishing fuel for school is said District the same is allowed and it is ordered that a draft be drawn in his favor for that amount payable out of the School fund allotted to said District.

22

Levi T. Hollen this day presented to this Board a certificate from the Trustees of School District No.14 showing that he is entitled to the sum of $2.05 for furnishing Lock to Door of said house in said District also 1 Shovel & Coal had for same the same is allowed and it is ordered that a draft be drawn in his favor for that amount payable out of the Building fund allotted to said District.

On motion the Board adjourned to meet at **A. J. Wilmoth**'s Store on Saturday 11th day of Feb 1871.

Joseph Teter President
John L. Hilkey Secretary

1

At a meeting of the Board of Education of the Township of Barker held at the Store house of **A. J. Wilmoths** on the **11th day of Feb 1871**- the following members were present. Viz: **Joseph Teter**, President, **Daniel Moore** & **Francis Hathaway** and **John L. Hilkey** Secretary.

2

Robt. L. Tallman, this day presented to this Board a certificate from the Trustees of School District No.1 showing that he is entitled to the sum of $50.- for services as teacher in said District, commencing on the 27th day of December, and ending on the 9th day of Feb 1871; the same is allowed and it is ordered that a draft be drawn in his favor for that amount payable out of the school fund allotted to said District.

3

A. J. Hartman, this day presented to this Board a certificate from the Trustees of School District No.5 showing that he is entitled to the sum of $31.35 for services as teacher in said District commencing on the 10th day of Feb 1871: the same is allowed and it is ordered that a draft be drawn in his favor for that amount payable out of the school fund, allotted to said District.

4

A. J. Wilmoth, this day presented to this Board a certificate from the Trustees of School District No. 2 showing that he is entitled to the sum of $.80 the same is allowed, and it is ordered that a draft be drawn in his favor for that amount payable out of the Building fund allotted to said District.

5

Ordered that **Joshua Proudfoot** be appointed Trustee in District No.3.

6

Ordered that **A. S. Rorhabaugh** be appointed Trustee in District No.14. The above named Trustees were qualified before secretary Bd. Ed.

7

Ordered that **James W. George** be charged with and Rec'd from District $9.05

8

Ordered that a credit be allowed to **James W. George** for the above amount $9.05 also that a credit be allowed to said **George** for cash Pd to Bd. Ed. $30.00. Also that a credit be allowed to **A. J. Wilmoth**'s note $88.88. Also that a credit be allowed to amt. Pd. by **J. M. Baker** 2.00

On motion the Board adjourned to meet on Saturday the 25th day of Feb 1871 at the School House in District No.8

Joseph Teter President

John L. Hilkey Secretary

At a meeting of the Board of Education of the Township of Barker held at School House near Belington in District No.8 on **Saturday the 25 day of Feb 1871**: the following members were present, Viz: **Joseph Teter** President, **Daniel Moore** and **Francis Hathaway**, and **John L. Hilkey**, Secy.

1

Ordained by the Bd. Ed. that School house in district No. 14 shall be opened for use of Subscription School for the term of three months for which **S. Rorhabaugh** takes charge of Key & agrees to be responsible for said house inside during school hours of said term. This order may be revoked at the pleasure of the Board.

2

Ordered that **John L. Hilkey** be appointed to receive the money on tax receipts now in his possession & that he shall post Notices at such places as may be convenient for those (knowing themselves to be indebted for said tax) stating when and where they may pay said Tax and that he shall give Notice that he will sit one day at **John M. Corley**'s to receive said tax

28 School Board Minutes

3
J. M. Baker, this day presented to this Board Two certificates from the Trustees of School District No.4 showing that he is entitled to the sum of $30.40 for 18 days services as Teacher in said District commencing on the 27th day of Jan - and ending Feb 23rd 1871 also for Poker, Shovel, Broom & Tin cup, the same is allowed and it is ordered that a draft be drawn in his favor for that amount payable out of the school fund allotted to said District.

4
Wm. F. McGee, this day presented to this Board a certificate from the Trustees of School District No.9 showing that he is entitled to the sum of $68.50 for services as Teacher in said District, the same is allowed, and it is ordered that a draft be drawn in his favor for that amount payable out of the School fund allotted to said district.

5
Miss Celia Wilson, this day presented to this Board a certificate from the Trustees of School District No.11 showing that she is entitled to the sum of $70.40 for services as Teacher in said District for Two months & twelve days (commencing on the   day of   and ending on the   day of   1871: the same is allowed and it is ordered that a draft be drawn in her favor for that amount payable out of the School fund allotted to said District.

6
John M. Ramsey, this day presented to this Board a certificate from the Trustees of School District No.10 showing that he is entitled to the sum of $3 - for furnishing fuel to said District, the same is allowed, and it is ordered that a draft be drawn in his favor for that amount payable out of the school fund allotted to said District.

7
John J. Ramsey, this day presented to this Board a certificate from the Trustees of School District No.9 showing that he is entitled to the sum of $3.50 for furnishing fuel to said District, the same is allowed and it is ordered that a draft be drawn in his favor for that amount payable out of the school fund allotted to said District.

8
Robt. L. Tallman, this day presented to this Board a certificate from the Trustees of School District No.1, showing that he is entitled to the sum of $16 2/3 - for half month services as Teacher in said District commencing on the 10th day of Feb & ending on the 23d day of Feb 1871: also for matches 20 cents & nails & crayons 30 cents, The same is allowed and it is ordered that a draft be drawn in

his favor for that amount payable out of the school fund allotted to said District.

9

Thomas W. Bowman, this day presented to this Board a certificate from the Trustees of School District No. 10 showing that he is entitled to the sum of $53 - for services as Teacher in said District, the same is allowed and it is ordered that a draft be drawn in his favor for that amount payable out of the School fund allotted to said District.

10

Lloyd Davis, this day presented to this Board a certificate from the Trustees of School District No. 14, showing that he is entitled to the sum of $2 - for furnishing fuel for use of School in said District the same is allowed and it is ordered that a draft be drawn in his favor for that amount payable out of the school fund allotted to said District.

11

Margaret E. Hilkey, presented to this Board a certificate from the Trustees of School District No. 8 showing that she is entitled to the sum of $20 - for services as Teacher in said District, commencing on the 8th day of Feb & ending on the 24th day of Feb 1871: the same is allowed and it is ordered that a draft be drawn in her favor for that amount payable out of the school fund allotted to said District.

12

Ordered that the Board adjourn to meet on the 27th day of Feb 1871 at the Greenbrier school house.

     Joseph Teter President
     John L. Hilkey Secretary

At a meeting of the Board of Education of the Township of Barker, held at the Greenbrier School house in said Township on the **27th day of Feb 1871**: the following members were present. Viz: **Joseph Teter** President, **Daniel Moore, Francis Hathaway** and **John L. Hilkey** Secretary.

1st

Allowed **Jacob Sipe** $92.16 for work done by him as per apc on the Greenbrier School house, which amount is to be a credit to **James W. George** on apc -

     Joseph Teter President
     John L. Hilkey Secretary

School Board Minutes

At a meeting of the Board of Education of the Township of Barker held at the School house near **Jesse Teter**'s District No.6 on the **1st day of March 1871**: the following members were present. Viz: **Joseph Teter** President **Daniel Moore, Francis Hathaway** and **John L. Hilkey** Secretary.

1st

Ordered that **James W. George** be credited with one Note on **Joseph Teter** bearing date March 1st 1871 and due March the 1st 1872 without interest, amount Two hundred Dollars, also one note on **Joseph Teter** hearing date March 1st 1871: and Due March the 1st 1873 without interest, for Two hundred Dollars the same to be a credit to **James W. George**, also one note on **Joseph Teter** of Two hundred Dollars bearing date March the 1st 1871: and Due march the 1st 1874 without Interest the same also to be a credit to **James W. George**.

2

Ordered that a certificate be given to **James W. George** for Six thousand three hundred and Ninety nine Dollars and Eighty seven cents amount Received by him in the year 1869: the same shall be a discharge and releace for that year for the same also a certificate for Two Thousand three hundred and Ninety Eight Dollars & Seventy Nine cents Paid by said **George** in the year 1870: Showing a balance Due from **James W. George** on Settlement One hundred & Eighty Six Dollars thirty nine cents exclusive of Interest on Six hundred Dollars.

3

Ordered that the Board adjourn to meet at the School house in District No.8 on the last Saturday in March 1871.

Joseph Teter President
John L. Hilkey Secretary

At a meeting of the Board of Education of the Township of Barker held at the school house in District No.8 on the **26th day of March 1871** the following members were present Viz: **Joseph Teter** President, **Daniel Moore, Francis Hathaway,** and **John L. Hilkey,** Secretary.

1st

Levi T. Hollen is allowed $2.00 by the Board for one day's services as arbitrator for said Bd. To settle a controversy between said Bd. & **Jacob Sipe** for a certain school house. Ordered that a draft be drawn in his favor for that amount payable out of the General school fund.

2

M. V. Oldaker, this day presented to this Board a certificate from the trustees of School District No.3 showing that he is entitled to the sum of $38. For services as teacher in said District, the same is allowed and it is ordered that a draft be drawn in his favor for that amount payable out of the school fund allotted to said District.

3

Wm. F. McGee, this day presented to this Board a certificate from the Trustees of School District No.9 showing that he is entitled to the sum of $34.50 for services as Teacher in said District, the same is allowed and it is ordered that a draft be drawn in his favor for that amount payable out of the school fund allotted to said District.

4

V. F. Taylor, this day presented to this Board a certificate from the Trustees of District No.2 showing that he is entitled to the sum of $33. for one month's services as Teacher in said District commencing on the 2nd day of February & ending March 1st 1871: the same is allowed and it is ordered that a draft be drawn in his favor for that amount payable out of the school fund allotted to said District.

5

Israel Poling, this day presented to this Board a certificate from the Trustees of District No.12 showing that he is entitled to the sum of $10.40 for services as Teacher in said District, the same is allowed and it is ordered that a draft be drawn in his favor for that amount payable out of the school fund allotted to said District.

6

Ordered that **A. V. Wilmoth** be appointed Trustee in District No.5

Ordered that the Board adjourn to meet at the School house in Dist. No.14 on the 3rd Saturday in May 1871.

    Joseph Teter Pres't
     John L. Hilkey Secty

At a meeting of the Board of Education of the Township of

School Board Minutes

Barker held at the Store House of **R. A. McCutcheon**'s in said Township on the **5th day of August 1871**: the following members were present Viz; **Joseph Teter** President, **Francis Hathaway**, and **John L. Hilkey** Secretary.

1st

Ordered by the Board that **John L. Hilkey** Deliver to **James Knotts** (Sheriff of Barbour County) the Tax receipts belonging to said Board of Education now in his hands for which said **Knotts** will receipt (for same) to said **Hilkey**.

2nd

Ordered that a Levy be laid for Building purposes 4 Mills on the Dollar's worth of property in Barker Township Real or Personal according to the Assessors report, also 3 Mills on the Dollars for Tuition funds.

3

Ordered that the Board adjourn to meet on every first Saturday in the month from hence forward.

Joseph Teter President
John L. Hilkey Secretary

At a meeting of the Board of Education of the Township of Barker held at **A. J. Wilmoth**'s Store, in said Township on the **2nd day of September 1871**: the Following members were present Viz: **Francis Hathaway** & **Daniel Moore**.

1st

Ordained that **Joseph Howes** be appointed Secretary protem. He was sworn in and took his seat with the Board to transact Business.

2

Ordered that **Fenelon Howes** be appointed to assist the Secretary **John L. Hilkey** to make settlement with the Sub districts.

3

On motion the Board adjourned to meet at **R. A. McCutcheon**'s Store on the 1st Saturday in October 1871.

Daniel Moore President
Jos. Howes, Secretary protem

School Board Minutes

According to appointment of the Board of Education of Barker Township in the County of Barbour State of West Virginia, on the **7th day of Nov. 1871**: **Maj. F. Howes** and **Jno. L. Hilkey** proceeded to make settlement to see how each district stands according to apportionment.

	Dr.		Cr.	
	$	¢	$	¢
District No.1			187	67½
District No. 2			35	72½
District No.3 in debt	48	92½		
District No.4			104	12½
District No.5			87	57½
District No.6			74	07½
District No.7			120	12½
District No.8			63	07½
District No.9			29	33½
District No.10			99	72½
District No.11			122	01½
District No.12			60	79½
District No.13			68	02½
District No. 14			83	67½

October 24, 1872 The apportionment of the School fund is as followes
One hundred and fourteen dollars to Each School District
District No. 1   114.00
District No. 2   114.00

34 School Board Minutes

District No. 3	114.00
District No. 4	114.00
District No. 5	114.00
District No. 6	114.00
District No. 7	114.00
District No. 8	114.00
District No. 9	114.00
District No. 10	114.00
District No. 11	114.00
District No. 12	114.00
District No. 13	114.00
District No. 14	114.00

At a meeting of the Board of Education of Barker Township in the County of Barbour State of West Virginia on the **7th day of Oct. 1871**. The following members were present Viz: **Jos. Teter**, President **Daniel Moore** & **John L. Hilkey** Secretary; the meeting was held at **R. A. McCutcheon**'s Store.

1st
Lloyd Davis was appointed Trustees in District No.14

2nd
R. A. McCutcheon was appointed Trustee in District No.8

3rd
I. W. Stalnaker was appointed Trustee in District No.8

4
John Hillyard was appointed Trustee in District No. 8

5th
Adam Coontz was appointed Trustee in District No. 10

6th
On motion the Board adjourned to meet on the 3d Saturday in November 1871.

    Joseph Teter, President
    John L. Hilkey, Secretary

At a meeting of the Bd. Education of Barker Township held at

School Board Minutes 35

the Storehouse of **A. J. Wilmoth**'s on Saturday the **18th day of Nov. 1871**: The following members were present Viz: **Joseph Teter Jun.** President **Francis Hathaway** & **Daniel Moore**, and **John L. Hilkey**, Secretary.

1st Appointment of Trustees

District No. 1	Harman Steerman	3 years
	George Thorn	2 years
District No.2	Haymond Coberly	3 years
District No.3	B. B. Derrett	3 years
	Matthew Edman	2 years
District No.4	Isam Yeager	3 years
District No.5	A. V. Wilmoth	3 years
	Richard Werner	2 years
District No.6	F. Howes	3 years
	John W. Harper	2 years
District No.7	Jackson Hillyard	3 years
District No. 8	R. A. McCutcheon	3 years
	Chambers Mustoe	2 years
District No.9	Laban Moore	3 years
District No.10	Solomon Wilson	3 years
	Fred Booth	2 years
District No.11	J. R. W. Smith	3 years
	Daniel Ice	2 years
District No.12	Allen Wood	3 years
District No.13	Wm. R. Moore	3 years

36 School Board Minutes

District No.14   **Lloyd Davis**   3 years
                 Hiram Rinehart   2 years

On motion the board Adjourned to meet at **R. A. McCutcheon**'s on the 2nd December 1871.
John L. Hilkey Secretary
Joseph Teter President

At a meeting of the Bd. Education of the Township of Barker held at the Storehouse of **R. A. McCutcheon**'s on Saturday the **2nd day of December 1871**: the following members were present Viz: **Joseph Teter Jun.** President, **Daniel Moore** and **John L. Hilkey** Secretary.

1st

John L. Hilkey, this day presented to this Board a certificate from **R. A. McCutcheon** County Superintendent of Free Schools, showing that he is entitled to the sum of $25.00 for services rendered as Secretary of Bd. Ed. for the year 1871: The same is allowed, and it s ordered that a Draft be drawn in his favor for that amount payable out of the General School fund of Barker Tp.

2

John L. Hilkey, this day presented to this Board a certificate from **R. A. McCutcheon** County Superintendent of Free Schools, showing that he is entitled to the sum of One Dollar for Services rendered, in taking Enumeration of Youth in District No.1 the same is allowed and it is ordered that a Draft be drawn in his favor for that amount payable out of the School fund allotted to said District.

3

John L. Hilkey, this day presented to this Board a certificate from **R. A. McCutcheon** County Superintendent of Free Schools showing that he is entitled to the sum of One Dollar for services rendered in taking Enumeration of Youth in District No.2, the same is allowed & it is ordered that a draft be drawn in his favor for that amount payable out of the School fund allotted to said district.

4

John L. Hilkey, this day presented to this Board a certificate from **R. A. McCutcheon** County Superintendent of Free Schools, showing that he is entitled to the sum of One Dollar for services rendered, in taking Enumeration of Youth in District No.7, the same is allowed & it is ordered that a Draft be drawn in his favor for that amount payable out of the School fund allotted to said District.

5

On motion the Board adjourned to meet on 1st Saturday of Jan. 1872.

Joseph Teter President
John L. Hilkey Secretary

At a meeting of the Board of Education of Barker Township County of Barbour & State od W.Va. Held at the Store house of **R. A. McCutcheon** on the 6th **day of Jan. 1872**: Members present Viz: **Joseph Teter** President, **Daniel Moore** and **John L. Hilkey**, Secretary.

1st

A. Right this day presented to this Board a certificate showing that he is entitled to the sum of $6.39 for furnishing fewel to School in District No.13, the same is allowed and it is ordered that a draft be drawn in his favor for that amount payable out of the School fund allotted to that district.

2nd

J. W. Taylor this day presented to this Board a certificate, showing that he is entitled to the sum of $90. for services rendered as Teacher in District No.5 commencing on the 16th day of Oct. and ending on the 22nd day of Dec 1871: the same is allowed, and it is ordered that a draft be drawn in his favor for that amount payable out of the School fund allotted to said district.

3d

R. A. McCutcheon, this day presented to this Board, a certificate showing that he is entitled to the sum of $5.10 for furnishing fuel & bucket to school in District No.8, the same is allowed and it is ordered that a draft be drawn in his favor for that amount, payable out of the School fund allotted to said district.

4

J. A. Dunham, this day presented to this Board a certificate from the Trustees of District No.8, showing that he is entitled to the sum of $50 - for services rendered as Teacher in said district, the same is allowed and it is ordered that a draft be drawn in his favor for that amount, payable out of the School fund allotted to said District.

5th

Joseph Howes this day made application to the Board of Education for One Dollar for one days service for Clerking for said Board. The same is allowed and it is ordered that a draft be drawn in his favor for that amount payable out of General School fund of Barker Township.

6th

Rec'd Nov. 25th 1871: of **J. L. Hilkey**; School Tax receipts on the Township of Barker amounting to Four hundred and Sixty Nine Dollars and thirty three cents ($469.33)

7th

James W. Talbott

The above is a copy, and record of a receipt give to **J. L. Hilkey**, by **Jas. W. Talbott** for Tax receipts transferred from **Jas. W. George** to Board of Education at the time said **Jas. W. George** settled with said Board of Education.

8th

Randolph Coberly Appointed Trustee in District No.12.

9th

Ordered that the Board adjourn to meet on the 1st Saturday in February 1872.

Joseph Teter President
John L. Hilkey Secretary

At a meeting of the Board of Education of the Township of Barker County of Barbour and State of West Virginia; held at the Storehouse of **R. A. McCutcheon's** on the **3d day of February 1872**: Members present were Viz: **Joseph Teter** President, **Daniel Moore** and **Francis Hathaway** and **John L. Hilkey**, Secretary.

1st

F. M. Tallman, this day presented to this Board a certificate from the Trustees of District No.5 showing that he is entitled to the Sum of $1.25 for furnishing fuel to said District the same is allowed and it is ordered that a draft be drawn in his favor for that amount payable out of the School fund allotted to said District.

2nd

Adam Coontz this day presented to this Board a certificate from the Trustees of District No.10: showing that he is entitled to the Sum of $3.50 for furnishing fuel to said District: the same is allowed and it is ordered that a draft be drawn in his favor for that amount payable out of the School fund allotted to said District.

3d

Nancy C. Sipe this day presented to this Board a certificate from the Trustees of District No.4 showing that she is entitled to the Sum of $84.00 for Teaching School in said District the same is allowed and it is ordered that a draft be drawn in her favor for that amount payable out of the School fund allotted to said District.

4th

L. D. Kerr & **Wm. L. Yeager**: This day presented to this Board a certificate from the Trustees of District No.4 Showing that they are entitled to the Sum of $5.62 for furnishing fuel for the use of School in Said District, the Same is allowed and it is ordered that a draft be drawn in their favor for that amount payable out of the School fund allotted to said District.

5th

Wm. F. McGee, this day presented to this Board a certificate from the Trustees of District No.10, Showing that he is entitled to the Sum of $87.50 for Services rendered as Teacher commencing on the 13th day of November 1871: the Same is allowed and it is ordered that a draft be drawn in his favor payable out of the School fund allotted to said District.

6th

On motion the Board adjourned to meet on the 1st Saturday of March 1872.

Joseph Teter President
John L. Hilkey Secretary

At a meeting of the Board of Education of the Township of Barker County of Barbour and State of West Virginia: held at the Storehouse of **R. A. McCutcheon** on the **2nd of March 1872**. Members present Viz: **Joseph Teter** President, and **John L. Hilkey**, Secretary.

School Board Minutes

1st

Miss **L. M. See**, this day presented to this Board a certificate from the Trustees of District No.7, showing that she is entitled to the sum of $63 - for services rendered as Teacher in said District the same is allowed and it is ordered that a draft be drawn in her favor for that amount payable out of the School fund allotted to said District.

2nd

Ordered that **Israel Poling & C. B. Carter** be and they are hereby appointed Trustees for District No.11.

Israel Poling was sworn.

At a meeting of the Board of Education of The Township of Barker in the County of Barbour and State of W.Va. held at the Storehouse of **R. A. McCutcheon** on the **31st day of August 1872** and the following Members was Presant Viz: **Daniel Moore & Francis Hathaway** and the following Business was done. **Jacob B. Godwin** was appointed Sectary of the Board and was qualified
August 31, 1872

Ordered that **Joseph Howes** be appointed Trustee in District No.10 in Room of **James England**'s Time out
August 31, 1872

Ordered that **Jethro Bennett** be appointed Trustee in District No.9 in Room of **Levi Cross** resigned

Oct 24 Ordered that **Jacob Zerkle** be appointed Trustee in District No.4 for 3 years.

Oct 24 Ordered that **John Gost** be appointed Trustee in District No.4 2 years. **Gost** was sworn.

F. Hathaway Prten

G. B. Godwin Set

At a meeting of the Board of Education of Barker Township in the County of Barbour of State of West Virginia at the house of **R. A. McCutcheon** on the **24th day of Oct 1872** and the following members were present Viz: **Daniel Moore & F. Hathaway** and the following Buisness Done the money apportioned to each district and one

hundred and fourteen dollars Due Each district.
 Ordered that District No.4 be paid $5.45 out of the General School Fund in lieu of money paid into the treasury by said trustee allowed in 1870.
 On motion the Board adjound to meet at **R. A. McCutcheon**'s on the 29 November at 12 o'clock.
Joseph Teter Jr President
G. B. Godwin Secretary

 At a meeting of the Board of Education of Barker Township in the County of Barbour & State of W. Va. At the Store house of **R. A. McCutcheon** on the **29 day of Nov 1872** & the following members was present **Joseph Teter** President, **Francis Hathaway, J. B. Godwin** & **Daniel Moore** & the following buisness done.
 November the 29 1872
 This day **Daniel Moore** Resigned as School Commissioner and **A. J. Wilmoth** was appointed and was sworn in.
1st
 This day **John W. Rhinehart** presented a certificate from the Trustees of District No.11 showing that he is Entitled to the Sum of Ten Dollars the same is allowed and it is ordered that a draft be drawn in his favor for that amount payable out of the School fund allotted to said District.
2nd
 A. J. Wilmoth this day presented a certificate from the Trustees of District No.2 showing that he is Entitled to the sum of one dollar $82 cents the same is allowed and it is ordered that a draft be drawen in his favour for that amount payable out of the School fund allotted to said District.
3d
 Fenelon Howes this day presented a certificate from the Trustees of District No.8 showing that he is Entitled to the Sum of Ten Dollars for furnishing Fuel to said District the same is allowed it is ordered that a draft be Drawn in his favor payable out of the School fund allotted to said District.
4th
 R. A. McCutcheon this day presented a certificate from the Trustees of School District No.6 Showing that he is Entitled to the Sum of one dollar $.75/100 for Stove pipe furnished to said district the same

42 School Board Minutes

is allowed it is ordered that a draft be drawn in his favour payable out of the School fund allotted to said District.

5th

A. J. Wilmoth this day presented a certificate from the Trustees of School district No.1 showing that he is Entitled to the sum of one dollar $.10/100 the same is allowed it is ordered that a draft be drawn in his favour payable out of School fund allotted to said district.

6th

C. H. Street This day presented a certificate from the Trustees from district No.7 showing that he is Entitled to the sum of Thirty Six 36.$ dollars & 50/100 the same is allowed it is ordered that a draft be drawen in his favour payable out of School fund allotted to Said district.

7th

R. A. McCutcheon made application to the Board of Education for the sum of Five dollars for Services Rendered as Secratary of Board the same is allowed and it is ordered that a draft be drawen in his favour payable out of Generats School fund.

8th

J. B. Godwin this day made application to the Board of Education for Three dollars & 16/100 for sevise rendered as Secretary of board the same is allowed it is ordered that a draft be drawen in his favour payable out of General School fund.

At a meeting of the Board of Education of Barker Township, Barbour Co. W. Va. **April 6th, 1872**, Present **Joseph Teter** Prest. **Danl Moore & Francis Hathaway**, the Following business was transacted Viz:

Order No. 273. Ordered that **Israel Poling** be paid $10.40 out of School fund District No.12.

No. 274. Ordered that **John L. Hilkey** be paid one dollar out of school fund District No.7

275. Ordered that **John L. Hilkey** be paid twenty five dollars out of Genl. School fund for services rendered as Clerk of this Board.

276. Ordered that **John L. Hilkey** be paid One dollar out of General School fund for Enumerating Distr No.1 & charged to Dist. No.1

277. Ordered that **John L. Hilkey** be paid one dollar out of Dist School fund No.2 for taking enumeration.

  Nota Bene! The above has previously been Recorded.
On motion of **Mr. Moore** Board adjourned Sine die to Meet at **R. A. McCutcheon**'s store.
    Joseph Teter President
    R. A. McCutcheon Secy

     Nov 29, 1872
 Ordered that **Oliver Zerkle** be appointed Trustee in district No.2 for 3 years.
 Ordered that **Elahue Ware** be appointed Trustee in District No.2 for 2 years.
 On motion the Board adjourn to meet at **R. A. McCutcheon**'s on the 21 day of December next.
    Joseph Teter Presidn
    J. B. Godwin Set

Orders: At a meeting of Board of Education of Barker Township **3d Saturday in May 1872**. The following orders were issued:

No.1 Ordered that **Lloyd Davis** be paid $11.00 Eleven Dollars & charged to School Dist No.14

No.2 Ordered that **J. W. Taylor** be paid $63.25 Sixty three dollars and twenty five cents & charged to school dist No.6 for teaching.

No.3 Ordered that **J. W. Taylor** be paid $75.00 Seventy five dollars out of School fund Dist No.5.

No.4 Ordered that **J. W. Taylor** be paid $15.00 Fifteen dollars out of Genl School funds & charged to dist No.5

44 School Board Minutes

No.5 Ordered that **Archibald W. Corley** be paid Seventy four dollars & sixty cents out of gen' school dist. No.1

No.6 Ordered that **Archibald W. Corley** be paid fifty dollars out of school fund of District No.1

No.7 Order Recorded on page 47

No.8 Ordered that **Jacob McLean** be paid $20.00 twenty dollars out of Dist No.14 School fund.

No.9 Ordered that **W. W. Teter** be paid $75.00 out of School fund of Dist No.14.

No.10 Ordered that **W. W. Teter** be paid $37.00 out of School fund Dist. No. 14.

No.11 Ordered that **Israel Poling** be paid $100.00 One hundred dollars & charged to School fund of Dist. No.11.

No.12 Ordered that **Danl Ice** be paid Ten dollars $10.00 out of school fund Dist No.11

No.13 Ordered that **Aaron Day** be paid Seven Dollars out of the school fund of Dist. No.1

No.14 Ordered that **John L. Hilkey** (this part is left blank)

No.15 **Israel Poling**'s order duplicate

No.16 **Israel Poling** order duplicate

No.17 Ordered that **Wm. A. Crislip** be paid $45.00 forty five dollars out of school fund of Dist No. 12.

No.18 Ordered that **Nixon Shomo** be paid $7.60 out of Dist No.7 school fund

On Motion the Board adjourned to meet the 22d June 1872.
Joseph Teter President
R. A. McCutcheon Clerk

Ordered that **A. B. Modisett** Sheriff of Barbour Co. be paid by draft on **J. W. Talbott** Treasurer of Free School money Ten dollars ($10.20) & twenty cents

in fav. of **Lewis Wilson**	$9.00
in fav. of **A. B. Modisett**	.20
in fav. of **Andrew Simons**	1.00
Total	$10.20

School Board Minutes

At a meeting of the Board of Education of Barker Township, Barbour County, W. Va. **June 22d 1872**: Members present **D. Moore** & **F. Hathaway** & **Jos. Teter** Prest. The following business was transacted Viz: Ordered that the Levy for the Scholastic Year 1872 be as follows

For building purposes 50 cents on the hundred dollars
For school purposes Tuition 25 cents on the hundred dollars.

Orders
No. 22 Ordered that **David M. Howell** be paid by draft on the Treasurer $7.48 Seven dollars & forty Eight cents for transfers from dist No.12 Meet 17th Aug. ½ p. 10 a.m.

    Joseph Teter, President
    R. A. McCutcheon, Secy

At a meeting of the Board of Education of Barker Township Barbour County W.Va. Members presant **Joseph Teter** President & **A. J. Wilmoth** & **J. B. Godwin** Sectary. Said Board met **Dec 21, 1872**. The object of said meeting was to settle with **J. W. Talbot** Sheriff of Barbour County, W. Va.

The whole settlement stands thus

Treasurer **J. W. Talbott** furnished vouchers	
To the amount of Building fund	$1062.94
Delinquent list & Releases	18.23
Treasurer's Commission	<u>24.82</u>
Treasurer's Credit	$1105.99
Treasurer is charged with building fund	<u>845.60</u>
Balance to the Treasurer credit	$260.39

The following list will show the true exhibit of the above statement of account Dec. 21st 1872 **J. W. Talbott**

		Bond Principal	in trust
No.1	**Hisam Yeager**	$ 90.00	$ 9.75
No.2	**Woods** & **Mertin**	21.34	
No.3	**Nathan Pane**	51.00	.70
No.4	**John Booth**	69.74	9.56

School Board Minutes

No.5	Hiram Yeager	90.00	11.70
No.6	Burr P. Newlon	160.06	31.12
No.7	Nathan Panes Second	41.25	7.83
No.8	Jacob Sipe	82.03	15.89
No.9	Levi Cross	96.50	8.52
No.10	A. B. Modistet	10.20	
No.11	(left blank)		
No.12	Burr P. Newlon	$160.06	$33.60

Amount of Tuition paid to each district for Tuition

District No.1

John L. Hilkey	Order No. 274	1.00
A. W. Corley	Order No. 6	56.00
A. W. Corley	Order No.5	74.60
		$125.60

District No. 2

V. F. Taylor	Order No.244	33.00
John L. Hilkey	Order No.276	1.00
V. F. Taylor	Order No.272	18.00
J. W. Shomore	Order No.254	3.00
		$55.00

District No. 3

R. B. Talbott	Order No.248	4.50
~~Nancy C. Sipe~~	~~Receipt~~	~~24.00~~
J. M. Baker	Order No.261	34.65
~~L. D. Kerr & Wm. L. Yeager~~	~~286~~	~~5.62~~
Martin V. Oldaker	Order No.249	49.95
Martin V. Oldaker	Order No.270	36.20
		$90.65

Dist 4

J. M. Baker	251	34.65
L. D. Kerr & Wm L. Yeager	286	5.63
J. M. Baker	260	30.40
Nancy C. Sipe	Receipt	24.00
		$94.67

Dist No. 5

A. J. Hartman	258	31.35
A. J. Hartman	252	11.00
H. M. Tallman	282	1.25

School Board Minutes 47

J. W. Taylor	4	15.00
		$58.60

Dist No. 6
J. W. Taylor	No.2	63.25

Dist No.7
John L. Hilkey	No. 274	1.00
M. S. See	7	63.00
C. M. Groves	253	40.75
G. W. Corley	255	3.70
Nixon Shomore	68	7.60
		$116.05

Dist No.8
J. A. Dunham	No.281	50.00
R. A. McCutcheon	279	5.10
		55.10

Dist No.9
W. F. Weese	No.261	$68.50
J. J. Ramsey	264	3.50
		72.00

Dist No.10
W. F. Reger	Order No.287	$87.50
J. M. Ramsey	Order No.263	3.00
Adam Coonts	Order No.283	3.50
		$94.00

Dist. No.11
Celia Wilson	262	$70.40
Israel Poling	16	50.00
Samuel Coffman	246	8.00
Daniel Ice	12	10.60
		$139.40

Dist No.12
Israel Poling	273	$10.40
W. A. Crislip	17	45.00
		55.40

Dist No. 13
A. Right	280	6.39
R. E. Schoonover	20	61.63
		$68.02

48 School Board Minutes

Dist No. 14

J. M. Lake	240	39.50
Lloyd Davis	1	11.00
W. W. Teter	10	37.00
Jacob McLean	8	20.00
W. W. Teter	9	<u>75.00</u>
		$182.50

The General School fund

J. L. Hilkey	No.275	25.00
Joseph Howes	284	1.00
Aaron Day	13	<u>7.00</u>
		$33.00

Delinquent list as returned by **J. W. Talbott**, Sheriff of Barbour County W.Va. is	$4.89
Released by Board Supervisors	3.11
Amount of Tuition Charged to Treasurer	634.19
Releases & Delinquent	<u>8.00</u>
	$626.19
Commission	<u>18.78</u>
	607.41
State School fund	<u>776.80</u>
Fund for Tuition	1384.21
Amount of vouchers	<u>1302.84</u>
	$81.37

Balance due Barker Township on Settlement with Treasurer

    A True Copy of **Jas. W. Talbott**'s Receipt to the Board of Education of Barker Township May 10th, 1872. Rec'd Belington, W. Va. May 10th 1872 of **R. A. McCutcheon**, Clerk of the Board of Education of Barker Township, Barbour Co., W. Va. Three several Bonds against **Joseph Teter** Viz: The first for two hundred dollars due March 1st 1872. 2nd Bond due two hundred dollars March 1st 1873.

    3rd Bond and last due March 1st 1874 ($200.00) Two hundred dollars, making a total of Six hundred dollars. To be collected and paid out as per order of Board of Education above named (Signed) **James W. Talbott**

                  Per   **A. H. Elliot**   D. S.

Oct. 4, 1872
  James W. Talbott Sheriff of Barbour County W. Va. to the Board of Education Dr. to State fund
    $1063.24/100cts $1063.24

Township Levy Year 1872
For building purposes	5 mills	$1247.94
For Tuition	2 ½ mills	$623.97

Oct 4, 1873
James W. Talbott Sheriff of Barbour County Dr. to Board Education
for State fund		$1014.83
Dist Levy at	2 ½ mills	$533.92
For Building fund	4 mills	$852.76

Oct the 16, 1874
James W. Talbott Sheriff of Barbour Dr.
To State School fund	$997.14
To Levy on land and Property (2) mills	$419.98
To Building Fund at (4) mills	$840.10

Nov the 1, 1875
James W. Talbott Sheriff of Barbour County Dr.
to State School fund	$830.63
From Levy at (2 ½) mills	$608.22
to Building Fund at (4) mills	$973.18

Oct 20, 1876
J. W. Talbott Sheriff of Barbour Co. Dr.
To State School Fund	906.83
To amount of Dist. Levy for Building	940.32
Tuition	940.32

  J. W. Fitzgerld this day presented a certificate from the Trustees of District No.7 showing that he is entitled to the sum of Eighteen dollars & 55 cts for Repairs & fewel for said Dist the same is allowed and it is ordered that a draft be drawn in his favor payable out of the School fund allotted to said District.

2nd

Albert England this day presented a certificate from the Trustees of Dist No.13 showing that he is entitled to the sum of Four dollars and 86 cts for furnishing half price to said Dist the same is allowed it is ordered that a draft be drawn in his favour payable out of the School fund allotted to said District.

3^{d}

J. A. Dunham this day presented a certificate from the Trustees of Dist No.8 showing that he is entitled to the sum of Fifty two dollars & 50/100 for services rendered as Teacher the same is allowed and it is ordered that a draft be drawn in his favour for the same payable out of school fund allotted to said District.

4th

B. Lanham this day presented a certificate from the Trustees of Dist No.5 showing that he is entitled to the sum of Thirty three dollars & 33 ½ /100 for one months teaching the same is allowed & it is ordered that a draft be drawn in his favour payable out of school fund allotted to said District.

5th

R. A. McCutcheon this day presented a certificate in behalf of **John England** from the Trustees of District No.13 for one half of fuel furnished by **John** and **Albert England** showing that he is entitled to the sum of Four dollars the same is allowed it is ordered that a draft be drawen in his favour payable out of the School fund allotted to said District.

6th

W. W. Teter this day presented a certificate from the Trustees of District No.14 showing that he is Entitled to the sum of Thirty dollars for one months Teaching the same is allowed it is ordered that a draft be drawn in his favour for the same payable out of School fund allotted to said Dist.

7th

C. H. Street this day presented a certificate from the Trustees of District No.7 showing that he is Entitled to the Sum of Thirty Six dollars and 50/100 for services rendered as Teacher the same is allowed it is ordered that a draft be drawn in his favor payable out of School fund allotted to said District on motion the Board adjourned to meet at **A. J. Wilmoths** store on the 4 Saturday in Jan. next at 10 o'clock.

Joseph Teter President

School Board Minutes 51

Jacob B. Godwin Sect

At a meeting of the Board of Education of Barker Township Barbour County W. Va. held at **A. J. Wilmoths** store on **Jan 25, 1873** The following Members presant were **Joseph Teter** President, **Francis Hathaway, A. J. Wilmoth** & **J. B. Godwin** Sect & the following Business Transacted.

1st

W. W. Teter this day presented a certificate from the Trustees of District No.14 showing he is entitled to the sum of Forty five dollars the same is allowed it is ordered that a draft be drawen in his favour payable out of the School fund allotted to said District.

2nd

R. L. Tallman this day Presented a certificate from the Trustees of District No.1 showing he is entitled to the sum of Seventy Dollars the same is allowed it is ordered that a draft be drawn in his favor payable out of the School fund allotted to said District.

3d

Elihue Ware this day presented a certificate from the Trustees of District No.1 showing he is entitled to four 35/100 Dollars for Repairs said school house the same is allowed it is ordered that a draft be drawn in his favor payable out of School fund allotted to said District.

4th

This day **Sampson S. Bonner** presented a certificate from the Trustees of District No.11 Showing he is Entitled to the sum of Six dollars 90/100 for fuel, Bucket, Dipper, Broom, and Chalk, pencils furnished to said district the same is allowed it is ordered that a draft be drawn in his favour for the same payable out of the School fund allotted to said Dist.

5th

S. C. Gainer This day presented a certificate from the Trustees of Dist No.1 showing that he is entitled to the Sum of Ten 20/100 dollars for fuel he furnished to said Dist. The same is allowed it is ordered that a draft be drawn in his favour for the same payable out of the School fund allotted to said District.

6th

A. J. Wilmoth this day presented a certificate Showing that

School Board Minutes

he is entitled to the sum of one dollar and 35/100 the same is allowed it is ordered that a draft be drawn in his favour payable out of School fund allotted to District No.5.

7th

Nancy C. Sipe this day presented a certificate from the Trustees of District No.2 showing she is entitled to The Sum of Eighty four dollars & 50/100 for services rendered as Teacher the same is allowed it is ordered that a draft be drawn in her favour payable out of the School fund allotted to said District.

8th

David M. Howel this day presented a certificate from the Trustees of Dist No.11 showing that he is Entitled to the Sum of Seventy five dollars for services as Teacher the same is allowed it is ordered that a draft be drawn payable out of School fund allotted to said District.

9th

Jacob Sipe this day presented a certificate from the Trustees of District No.5 showing he is entitled to the sum of Three & 25/100 dollars for Repairs the same is allowed it is ordered that a draft be drawn in his favour for the same payable out of School fund allotted to said District.

10th

Nimrod Champ this day presented a certificate from the Trustees of District No.2 showing he is entitled to the sum of Six dollars & 50/100 for fewel furnished the same is allowed it is ordered that a draft be drawn in his favour payable out of school fund allotted to said District.

11th

J. S. Thacker this day presented from the Trustees a certificate showing that he is entitled to the sum of $2.00 Two Dollars for repairs the same is allowed it is ordered that a draft be drawn in his favor payable out of the school fund allotted to said District No.5

Ordered that **George M. Phillips** be appointed Trustee in District No. 8 and was sworn in term 3 years.

Ordered that the District line between District No.12 and No.14 be changed so as to include **C. L. Jones** in District No. 14. On motion the Board adjourn to meet on the last Saturday in February at **A. J. Wilmoths** store at 10 o'clock.

Joseph Teter President
J. B. Godwin Sect

School Board Minutes 53

At a meeting of the Board of Education of Barker Township Barbour County W. Va. held at **Joseph Teters** on the **22 day of Feb 1873** and the following Members presant **Joseph Teter** President, **A. J. Wilmoth** and **J.B. Godwin** Sectary and the following Business Transacted Viz:

1st

J. A. Dunham this day presented a certificate from the Trustees of Dist No. 8 showing that he is entitled to the Sum of Fifty Two Dollars and 50/100 the same is allowed and it is ordered that a draft be drawn in his favour for the same payable out of School fund, allotted to said Dist.

2nd

V. Lanham this day presented a certificate from the Trustees of Dist No. 5 showing he is Entitled to the Sum of Seventeen 48/100 dollars services as teacher the same is allowed it is ordered that a draft be drawn in his favour payable out of the School fund allotted to said Dist.

3d

Nathan Rohrabaugh this day presented a certificate from the Trustees of Dist No.4 showing he is Entitled to the sum of Six dollars & 10/100 the same is allowed it is ordered that a draft be drawn in his favour payable out of school fund allotted to said Dist.

4th

G. V. Fornish this day presented a certificate from the Trustees of Dist No.4 showing he is entitled to the sum of Ninety dollars for three months Teaching the same is allowed it is ordered that a draft be drawn in his favour payable out of School fund allotted to said District.

5th

D. M. Howell this day presented a certificate from the Trustees of Dist. No. 11 showing he is Entitled to the sum of Twenty Seven dollars the same is allowed it is ordered that a draft be drawn in his favour for the same payable out of School fund allotted to said Dist.

6th

L. C. Bennett this day presented a certificate from the Trustees of Dist No.10 showing he is Entitled to the Sum of Fifty four dollars the same is allowed it is ordered that a draft be drawn in his favour for the same payable out of School fund allotted to said Dist.

7th

L. C. Bowman this day presented a certificate from the

Trustees of Dist No. 13 showing he is Entitled to the Sum of one hundred Dollars for services rendered as Teacher the same is allowed it is ordered that a draft be drawn in his favour payable out of School fund allotted to said Dist.

8th

John J. Ramsey this day presented a certificate from the Trustees of Dist No.9 showing he is entitled to the Sum of Eight dollars & 48/100 it being for fuel furnished the same is allowed it is ordered that a draft be drawn in his favour for the same payable out of School fund allotted to said District.

9

Ordered **Nimrod Champ** be paid $2.40 Two dollars & 40 our of School fund District No. 2.

10th

Wm F. McGee this day presented a certificate from the Trustees of Dist No.9 showing he is Entitled to sum of one hundred and Thirty five dollars for services as Teacher in said Dist the same is allowed it is ordered that a draft be drawn in his favour for the same payable out of School fund allotted to said District.

11th

Lewis Wilson this day presented an account to B. E. for recording deed from **Jackson Hilyard** for Two and 25/100 dollars the same is allowed it is ordered that a draft be drawn in his favour payable out of the Next General School fund.

12th

J. B. Godwin presented a claim to the Board of Ed. For Ten dollars for Services Rendered as Secretary of said Board of Education the same is allowed it is ordered that a draft be drawn in his favour for the same payable out of General School fund.

Ordered that The Board of Education Received a certain Contract with _____ **Zirkle** for a certain School house lot and Return to him his bond for the same by given Recept to be filed with the Sectary Board Education on motion the Board adjourned to meet at Bealington on the 5th day of April 1873.

March 1th 1873
1   Ordered that **A. P. Stewart** be paid Ninety five 90/100 dollars for servises Rendered as Teacher in Dist No. 12 School fund.
2   Ordered that **Allen Wood** be paid seven dollars for fuel out of Dist No.12 School fund.

March 14
3   Ordered that **W. W. Teter** be paid Forty five & 90/100 dollars for servises Rendered as teacher in Dist No. 14 out of School fund No.14
4   Ordered that **Jacob McLane** be paid Twenty dollars out of School fund Dist No. 14

April 11
5   Ordered that **C. H. Street** be paid Twenty five 55/100 dollars for servises Rendered as Teacher out of School fund Dist No. 7
6   Ordered that **F. B. Durrett** be paid Sixty Six dollars for servises Rendered as Teacher payable out of School fund Dist No.3
7   Ordered that **R. L. Tallman** be paid Sixty Six 95/100 dollars payable out of School fund Dist No.one

The above Seven orders was issued when the Board of Education was not in Regular session.

May the 31 1973
At a meeting of the Board of Education held at **A. J. Wilmoths** Store on the **31st day of May 1873**. The members presant **Joseph Teter** President, **A. J. Wilmoth, J. B. Godwin** Sect and buissness done Viz

1. **J. B. Godwin** this day presented a claim for servises Rendered as Sectarary for the sum of Eight dollars the same is allowed it is ordered that draft be drawn in his favour for the same payable out of the General School fund of Barker Township Barbour County.

2. **L. C. Bennett** this day presented a certificate from the Trustees of Dist No.10 Showing that he is Entitled to the Sum of Twenty Seven dollars for one Months Teaching the same is allowed it is ordered that a draft be drawn in his favour payable out of School fund allotted to said Dist.

3d **Isaac Coonts** this day presented a certificate from the Trustees of Dist No. 10 showing that he is Entitled to the sum of four 90/100 dollars for fuel the same is allowed it is ordered that a draft be drawen in his favour payable out of School fund allotted to said Dist.

56 School Board Minutes

On motion the Board adjourned to meet sine diu
Joseph Teter President
J. B. Godwin Sect

At a meeting of the Board of Education of Barker Township Barbour County W. Va. called at **A. J. Wilmoths** Store on the **7 of June 1873** and members present **Joseph Teter** President & **A. J. Wilmoth** on motion **G. C. Corley** was chosen Sect protem.

On motion it was ordered that **C. V. Street** be paid Sixteen dollars and 66 cts for one months teaching school in Dist No. 4 out of School fund of said Dist.

Ordered that **Nancy C. Sipe** be paid Thirty five 50 cts out of School fund of Dist No. 2

On motion the board adjourned.
Joseph Teter President
Jacob B. Godwin Sectary

At a meeting of the Board of Education of Barker District held at **R. A. McCutcheons** Store house on the **11 day of June 1873**. Members presant **Joseph Teter** President, **F. Hathaway** & **A. J. Wilmoth** on motion **F. Howes** was appointed Sect protem it was ordered that **C. V. Street** be paid Twenty one Dollars for teaching School in Dist No.4 payable out of School fund of said Dist.

Ordered that **F. M. Tallman** be paid Six dollars and 85 cts for furnishing fuel to be payable out of the School fund allotted to sub District No.5.

On motion the board Adjourned.
Joseph Teter President
J. B. Godwin Secretary

At a meeting of the Board of Education of Barker Township Barbour County West Virginia held **Aug 28th 1873** at **A. J. Wilmoths** Store for the purpose of Settlement with the Sheriff or Treasurer of Barker Township Barbour Couny and the members presant **Joseph**

School Board Minutes 57

Teter, A. J. Wilmoth and **J. B. Godwin** Sectary and not getting through with Said Settlement on Said day adjourned to **R. A. McCutcheons** Store on the 29 of Aug when Said Settlement was Completed.

Aug 29, 1873
Amount of Vouchers Received on Building Fund
Including in trust was $1371.40
B. Comm & Released $37.07 $4.25
Delinquent   7.88
Including 200 dollars on **Joseph Teter** first bond whole amount changed was   1447.94
Balance in favor of Township $76.54

Now statement of those Bonds with Principal and intrust

	Principal	Intrust
1 **John Booth** 3 Bonds of	91.25	19.92
2 **John Booth**	91.25	19.92
3 **John Booth**	91.25	19.92
Randolph Coberly	74.79	14.96
Randolph Coberly	72.50	17.89
Randolph Coberly	72.50	17.89
Nathan Pain	57.00	12.44
Levi Cross	96.50	12.55
Wm. H. Weaver	87.53	24.07
Randolph Coberly	74.79	12.04
Nisam Yeager	65.00	13.80
Levi T. Hollen	2.05	13.80

August 29, 1873   Tuition
Amount of vouchers taken up on August 28 & 29, 1873 in settlement with Treasurer by Sub Dist

District	$	cts	Comm	Received	Delinquent
1	185	93			
2	132	07	18.54	2.13	395
3	66	00			
4	200	61			
5	97	73			
6	1	75			
7	118	80			

58 School Board Minutes

8	115	00
9	143	44
10	138	90
11	158	95
12	110	38
13	108	86
14	152	90

General school fund $10.16
Making in all a total of $1741.48
Whole amount charged 1743.96
Leaving a balance due 2.48
Township Two dollars 48 cts on Tuition

Ordered that **Newton Chinworth** be paid one dollars & seventy $1.70 for Tax Erroneously Collected.

Ordered that an order be made to deliver the Sheriff a Receipt for all vouchers and other claims settled by him and his Deputy according to School law.

Joseph Teter President
J. B. Godwin Sect

At a meeting of the Board of Education of Barker District held at **R. A. McCutcheon**s store on the **13th day of Sept 1873** the members present Viz: President **Joseph Teter, Wm W. Jones, Chambers Mustoe** and **J. B. Godwin** was chosen Sect and the salaries of Teacher was agreed as follows Viz:

A Teacher having a certificate of Grade No. One shall Receive a salary of Thirty three Dollars per month and if a majority of the Subscribers agreeing may Pay him $35.00. Certificate No. 2 $28.00. No. 3 $22.00. No.4 $18.00. No. 5 $15.00.

On motion **Jackson Hilliards** was appointed Trustee in Sub district No.7 for 2 years. **Simon Swick** was appointed Trustee in Sub District No. 1 for 2 years.

It was ordered that **Joseph Howes** be appointed Trustee in Sub District No. 10 for Two years on motion the Board adjourned.

Joseph Teter President
J. B. Godwin Sect

At a meeting of the Board of Education of Barker District Barbour Co. W. Va. held at **R. A. McCutcheons** on the **2nd day of Oct. 1873**. Members presant **Joseph Teter** Pres **Wm W. Jones, Chambers Mustoe** & **J. B. Godwin** Sect and the object of the meeting was to lay a levy for the Teachers fund and Building fund which was done and it was ordered that 2 ½ mills be laid for Teachers Fund and 4 mills for Building fund. On motion the Board adjourned to meet on the 6 Oct at 8 o'clock.

        Joseph Teter President
           J. B. Godwin Sect

At a meeting of the Board of Education of Barker Dist Barbour County W. Va. at **R. A. McCutcheons** Store on the **20th of December 1873** members Presant **Joseph Teter** President, **Wm W. Jones, Chambers Mustoe** & **J. B. Godwin** Sect. The fowling Buisness Done Viz:

        1st

R. A. McCutcheon this day presented a certificate from the Trustee of Sub Dist No. 6 showing he is Entitled to The sum of one dollar & 15/10rict.0 for Furnishing Bucket & Broom the same is allowed and it is ordered that the said draft be Drawen in his favour payable out of Building fund of Barker District.

        2nd

B. P. Newlon this day presented a certificate from the Trustees of Sub Dist No. 6 showing he is Entitled to the sum of $1.25 cts for Shovel and Poker the same is allowed it is ordered that draft be drawen in his favour payable out of Building fund of Barker Dist.

        3d

R. A. McCutcheon this day presented a certificate from the Trustees of Sub District No.7 showing that he is Entitled to the sum of 45 cts the same is allowed & it is ordered a draft be drafted in his favour payable out of Building fund of Barker Dist.

        4th

C. H. Street this day presented a certificate showing that he is entitled to the sum of Thirty five dollars the same is allowed & it is ordered that a draft be drawen in his favour payable out of Teachers fund allotted to Sub Dist No. 2 Barker District.

5th

Jacob S. Thacker this day presented a certificate from the trustee of Sub district No.3 showing that he is Entitled to the sum of Eleven 90/100 dollars for fewel and Repairs the same is allowed & it is ordered that a draft be drawen in his favour Payable out of the Building fund of Barker District.

6th

David Poe this day presented a certificate from the Trustee of Sub Dist No.3 showing that he is Entitled to the Sum of Twenty Eight dollars for one months Teaching School the same is allowed & it is ordered that a draft be drawen in his favour payable out of Teachers fund allotted to same Sub District No.3.

7th

Jonathan Hathaway this day presented a certificate from the Trustee of Sub Dist No. One showing that he is Entitled to the sum of Twenty Two dollars for one months Teaching School the same is allowed & it is ordered that a draft be drawen in his favour payable out of Teachers fund allotted to said Sub District No.1

8th

A. Right this day presented a certificate from the Trustees of Sub Dist No. 13 Showing that he is Entitled to the sum of Sixteen Dollars for Furnishing fuel the same is allowed & it is ordered that a draft be drawen in his favour payable out of Building fund of Barker Dist. No.13

9th

R. L. Tallman this day presented a Certificate from the trustee of Sub District No.8 showing he is Entitled to the sum of Sixty Six dollars for Teaching School the same is allowed and it is ordered that a draft be drawen in his favour payable out of the Teachers fund allotted to said Sub District No.8

10th

R. A. McCutcheon this day presented a certificate showing that he is Entitled to the sum of one dollar for Broom, dipper & the same is allowed & it is ordered that a draft be drawen in his favour payable out of the Building fund of Barker District.

11

F. M. White this day presented a certificate from the Trustee Sub Dist No.13 showing that he is Entitled to the sum of Sixty Three cts for Broom & Shovel the same is allowed and it is ordered that a draft be drawen in his favour payable out of the Building fund Barker Dist.

12

W. W. Teter this day presented a certificate from the Trustee of Sub Dist No. 6 showing he is Entitled to the Sum of Seventy dollars the same is allowed and it is ordered that a draft be drawn in his favour payable out of the Teachers fund allotted to said Sub District No.6.

13

Abel Teter this day presented a certificate from the Trustee of Sub Dist No.6 showing that he is Entitled to the Sum of Eighteen dollars for fuel the same is allowed and it is ordered that a draft be drawn in his favour payable out of the Building fund of Barker Dist.

14

F. M. White this day presented a certificate from the Trustee of Sub Dist No.13 showing that he is Entitled to the sum of Ten Dollars for Repairs the same is allowed and it is ordered that a draft be drawn in his favour payable out of the Building fund of Barker Dist.

It was ordered that the Sheriff be Released of Ten dollars paid by **John W. Baker** to **J. W. George** on Tax for which said **Barker** has a Receipt on motion the Board adjourned to meet on the 20 day of Feb next 1874.

Joseph Teter President

J. B. Godwin   Sect Bd. Ed.

February 1874

At a meeting held at **R. A. McCutcheon**'s Store house **Feby 20th 1874**; the following business was transacted. Members present **Joseph Teter**, Pres. **Wm. M. Jones** & **Chambers Musto**.

No. 27   Ordered that **Ballard Jones** be paid Six dollars.

No. 16   Ordered that **D. M. Howell** be paid Seventy dollars $70.00 out of Teachers fund .

Order No. 28 Ordered that **Jacob A. Dunham** be paid Four Dollars $4.00 for Enumerating the Youth of Delinquent Districts.

Order No. 29 Ordered that **Wm. L. Parks** be paid $12.00

Order No. 30 That **Wm. H. Bosley** be paid 56.00

Order 31 That **James England** be paid for coal 6.00

Order 32 That **Jacob Sipe** be paid for coal 6.00

Order 33 That **Levi T. Hollen** be paid for Repairs 4.00

School Board Minutes

Order 34   That **J. B. Godwin** be paid for services 14.50
Order 20   That **F. M. White** be paid for material 1.35
Order 21   That **F. M. White** be paid for material 1.38
             Joseph Teter President
             J. B. Godwin Secretary

At a meeting of the Board of Education of Barker Dist. **Feb the 21, 1874**. The following business was transacted Viz: **Wm. M. Jones** President Protem **Chambers Mustoe** and **J. B. Godwin** Sect and Transacted the following business Viz: Orders issued.

1st

This day **F. L. Swick** presented a certificate from the Trustee of Sub Dist No. 5 in Barker District Barbour County, W. Va. showing he is Entitled to the Sum of Twenty Two dollars for one month Teaching School the same is allowed and it is ordered that a draft be drawen in his favour payable out of the Teachers fund allotted to said Sub Dist.

Ordered that **C. M. More** be paid $22.00 for one month Teaching School in sub Dist No.13 in Barker District, Barbour County, W. Va.

2nd

This day **F. P. Madden** presented a certificate from the Trustee of Sub Dist No.4 of Barker Dist. Barbour Co. W. Va. showing he is Entitled to the sum of Fifty Four dollars for 2 months teaching the same is allowed and it is ordered that a draft be drawen in his favour for the same payable out of the Teachers fund allotted to said Sub Dist.

3d

B. F. Phillips this day presented a certificate from the Trustee of Sub Dist No. 7 showing he is Entitled to the sum of Fifty Six dollars for 2 months Teaching School in said Dist the same is allowed it is ordered that a draft be drawen in his favour payable out of Teachers fund of said sub Dist. Also for 1 table $3.50 and making fires in School house $4.50 all of which a draft was drawen payable out of Building fund.

4th

W. C. Potter this day presented a certificate from the Trustee of Sub Dist No.9 showing he is Entitled to the sum of Twenty Two dollars for Teaching one month in said Sub Dist the same is allowed it is ordered that a draft be drawen in his favour payable out of the Teachers fund of said Sub Dist.

5th

David Poe this day presented a certificate from the Trustee of Sub Dist No.3 Showing that he is Entitled to the sum of Fifty Six dollars for Teaching School in said Sub Dist the same is allowed and it is ordered that a draft be drawen in his favour payable out of the Teachers fund allotted to said Sub Dist.

6th

Jonathan Hathaway this day presented a certificate from the Trustee of Sub Dist No.1 Barker District Barbour County W. Va. Showing he is Entitled to the sum of Fifty Six dollars for Teaching School 2 months in said Sub Dist the same is allowed it is ordered that a draft be drawen in his favour for the same payable out of Teachers fund allotted to said Sub District.

7th

W. W. Teter this day presented a certificate from the Trustee of Sub Dist No.6 showing he is Entitled to the Sum of Seventy dollars for Teaching School 2 months in said Sub Dist the same is allowed it is ordered that a draft be drawen in his favour for the same payble out of Teachers und allotted to said Sub Dist.

8th

R. L. Tallman this day presented a certificate from the Trustee of Sub Dist No. 8 showing he is Entitled to the Sum of Sixty Six dollars for Teaching School in said Sub Dist the same is allowed it is ordered that a draft be drawen in his favour for the same payable out of Teachers fund allotted to said Sub Dist.

9th

C. M. More presented a certificate from the Trustees of Sub Dist No.13 showing that he is Entitled to the Sum of Twenty Two Dollars for one months Teaching the same is allowed it is ordered that a draft be drawen in his favour for the same payable out of Teachers fund allotted to said Sub Dist.

10th

Ordered **C. H. Street** be paid Thirty five dollars out of Teachers fund Sub Dist No.2.
Ordered **G. W. Shomo** be paid Eight dollars & .50 Building Fund
Ordered **E. Hillyard** be paid Twelve 70/100 dollars Building fund
Ordered **J. C. Mathew** be paid Ten dollars for Fuel out of Building fund.

School Board Minutes

Ordered **M. Edmonds** be paid one 25/100 dollars out of Building fund.
Ordered **Simon Swick** be paid one 10/100 dollars out of Building fund
Ordered **F. M. White** be paid 50/100 cts out of Building Fund
Ordered **C. F. Street** be Paid Thirty Five dollars out of Teachers fund
    Sub Dist No.2
    On motion the Board adjourned to meet at Bealington on the third Friday in March 1874.

Wm. W. Jones President Protem
J. B. Godwin Sect

    At a meeting of the Board of Education of Barker District in Barbour County W. Va. held at **R. A. McCutcheons** Store **March the 20 1874**. The following members Present **Wm. M. Jones** President Protem **Chambers Mustoe** and **J. B. Godwin** Sectary and the following Business done Viz:

1

    Luther H. Kerr this day presented a certificate from the Trustee of Sub Dist No.4 showing he is Entitled to the Sum of Sixteen dollars for furnishing fuel and making fires in said Sub Dist the same is allowed it is ordered that a draft be drawn in his favour payable out of Building fund of Barker District.

2

    B. F. Phillips this day presented a certificate from the Trustees of Sub Dist No.7 showing he is Entitled to the Sum of Twenty Eight dollars for Services Rendered as Teacher the same is allowed and it is ordered that a draft be drawn in his favour payable out of Teachers fund allotted to said Sub Dist.

3d

    Jonathan Hathaway this day presented a certificate from the Trustee of Sub Dist No.1 showing that he is Entitled to Twenty Eight dollars for one month Teaching School the same is allowed and it is ordered that a draft be drawn in his favour payable out of Teachers fund allotted to said Sub Dist.

4th

    F. L. Swick this day presented a certificate from the Trustee of Sub Dist No. 5 showing that he is Entitled to Twenty Two dollars for one months Teaching the same is allowed it is ordered that a draft be drawn in his Favour payable out of the Teachers fund of said Sub District.

5th

Ordered **Ballard Jones** be paid seven 25/100 dollars for fuel & Cleaning house & building fires, Chalk, Pencils and Charge to Building fund of Barker Dist.

Ordered that **C. H. Street** be paid $9.00 out of Building fund for Building fires in Sub Dist No.2 Barker Dist.

Nathan E. and **Dyar Kelly** this day presented a certificate showing they are Entitled to the sum of Nine 50/100 dollars for fuel and Repairs to School house in Sub Dist No.11 the same is allowed it is ordered that a draft be drawn in their favour payable out of the Building fund of Barker District.

Ordered that **William Cross** be paid Twelve dollars for Boarding **W. C. Potter** a School Teacher in Sub Dist No. 9 the same is allowed it is ordered that a draft be drawn in his favour payable out of Teachers fund allotted to said Sub Dist.

William Cross this day presented a certificate from the Trustee of Sub Dist No.9 showing he is Entitled to the Sum of Ten dollars for furnishing fuel to School house in said Dist the same is allowed it is ordered that a draft be drawn in his favour payable out of the Building fund of Barker District.

Ordered **J. C. Right** be paid one dollar for Raising Chimney to School house in Sub Dist No. 13 out of Building fund Barker Dist.

Ordered **R. L. Tallman** be paid Six dollars for making fires in School house in Sub Dist No.8 out of Building fund $6.00

Ordered **David Poe** be paid Two dollars for building fires in School house in Sub Dist No.3 payable out of Building fund $2.00

Ordered **J. B. Hilliard** be paid Two dollars for Building fires in Sub Dist. No.7 out of Building fund. $2.00

Ordered **Thomas Shomo** be paid Five dollars for fuel in Sub Dist No.2 and Charge to Building fund $5.00

Ordered **A. J. Wilmoth** be paid one 15/100 dollars for Bucket, Dipper, Broom & Chalk out of Building fund $1.15.

Ordered **Wm. M. Jones** be paid Fourteen dollars out of Teachers fund Sub Dist No. 14 $14.00

Ordered **David Poe** be paid Twenty Eight for one months Teaching payable out of Teachers fund Sub Dist No. 3 $28.00

On motion the Board adjourned to meet on the last Friday in April at **R. A. McCutcheons** Store.

Wm. W. Jones President Protem
J. B. Godwin Sectary B. E.

66 School Board Minutes

At a meeting of the Board of Education held at **R. A. McCutcheons** Store house in Belington Barbour County W. Va. on the **16 day of May 1874** members Presant **Joseph Teter** President **Wm W. Jones, Chambers Mustoe** & **J. B. Godwin** Sect & the Following Buisness Done Viz:

1st

William Cross this day presented a certificate From the Trustee of Sub Dist No. 9 Showing that he is Entitled to the sum of Five Dollars for Boarding **W. C. Potter** a School Teacher in said Sub Dist the Same is allowed and it is ordered that a draft be drawn in his favour payable out of Teacher fund allotted to said Sub Dist No.9

2nd

Charles M. More this day presented a certificate from the Trustee of Sub Dist No. 13 Showing that he is Entitled to the Sum of Twenty Two Dollars for one months Teaching School the same is allowed and it is ordered That a draft be drawn in his favour for the same payable out of Teachers fund allotted to said Sub Dist.

3

F. L. Swick this day Presented a certificate From the Trustee of Sub Dist No. 5 Showing that he is Entitled to the Sum of Twenty Two Dollars for one Months Teaching School in said Sub Dist the same is allowed & it is ordered that a draft be drawn in his favour for the Same payable out of Teachers fund of said Sub Dist.

4

Ordered that **J. N. Robinson** be paid Eighty Eight dollars for Four Months Teaching School in Sub Dist No. 10 out of Teachers of said Sub Dist.

Ordered **W. W. Teter** be paid Fifty Two 50/100 dollars for Teaching in Sub Dist No. 6 and Charge to Teachers fund of Said Sub Dist.

Ordered **W. W. Teter** be paid Twelve 25/100 dollars out of Building fund.

Ordered **F. N. Robinson** be paid Nine dollars out of Building fund.

Ordered that **C. M. More** be paid Six dollars out of Building fund.

Ordered that **Nomi C. Sipe** be paid Eighty Eight Dollars out of Teachers Fund Barker Dist., Sub Dist No. 11

D. F. Elliott & Bros Presented a certificate from the Trustee of Sub Dist N0.10 Showing they are Entitled to the Sum of Ten 50/100 dollars for the lone Barrel of Stove the same is allowed it is ordered that a draft be drawn in their favour payable out of Building fund of Barker Dist.

Ordered that **Adam Coonts** be paid Six dollars for Furnishing one half of Fuel in Sub Dist No.10 out of Building fund.

Ordered **F. L. Swick** be paid Six 16/100 dollars for making Fires & the same is allowed and payable out of Building Fund.

Ordered **N. C. Sipe** be paid Eight dollars for making fires the same is allowed and payable out of Building Fund.

Ordered that **F. M. White** be paid one dollar for Bucket & Dipper for use in school house in Sub Dist No. 10 the same is allowed and payable out of Building Fund.

Ordered that **Wm. L. Parks** be paid Eight dollars for making fires in Sub Dist No. 12 the same is allowed and made payable out of Building Fund.

Ordered that **Benjamin Vickcaney** be appointed Trustee in Sub District No. 7

On motion the Board adjourned to meet at **R. A. McCutcheon**s Store on the Second Saturday in June at 10 o'clock A. M.

    Joseph Teter President
     Jacob B. Godwin Secretary

At a meeting of the Bd Education of Barker Dist Barbour Col West Va. held at **R. A. McCutcheons** Store **July the 11, 1874**. The following members Present **Joseph Teter** President, **Wm. W. Jones** & **J. B. Godwin** Secretary and the following Buisness done. Viz:

Ordered that **Isaac Price** be paid one dollar for Taking the Enumeration of Sub Dist No. 13 out of Building Fund.

Ordered **Granville Stalnaker** be paid $1.00 for Taking the Enumeration of Sub Dist No. 8 out of Building Fund.

Ordered that **Levi Cross** be paid $2.15/100 for Repairs done to School house in Sub Dist No. 9 payable out of Building Fund.

Ordered **M. Edmund** be paid Six dollars for building Fires in Sub Dist No. 3 the same is payable out of Building Fund.

Ordered **Thomas Madden** Be paid Twenty Eight dollars of Teachers fund of Sub Dist No. 5 for one months Teaching in said Sub Dist.

Simeon Phillips administrator of **Wm. C. Potter** Dec This day presented a certificate from the Trustees of Sub Dist No. 8 Showing he is Entitled to the sum of Forty dollars Subject to a credit of Twelve dollars the same is allowed it ordered that a draft be drawn in his favour Payable out of the Teachers Fund of said Sub Dist.

Simeon Phillips administrator of **Wm. C. Potter** Dec. This day presented a certificate from the Trustee of Sub Dist No. 9 showing he is Entitled to the sum of Five dollars & 75c the same is allowed and it is ordered that a draft be drawn in his favour out of the Building Fund of Barker Dist.

Ordered that **Charles N. Street** be paid Thirty dollars for one months Teaching in Sub Dist No.10 payable out of Teachers Fund Allotted to Said Sub Dist.

Ordered **C. N. Street** be paid $30.00 for one months Teaching in Sub Dist No.10 Payable out of Teachers Fund Allotted to said Sub Dist.

On motion it was ordered that **J. Shomo** was appointed Trustee in Sub Dist No. 7.

On motion the Board adjourned to meet on the 4th Saturday in August next at **R. A. McCutcheon**s Store at 10 o'clock A. M.

    Joseph Teter President
        J. B. Godwin Sectary Bd. Ed.

At a meeting of the Board of Education of Barker District Barbour W. Va. held at **R. A. McCutcheon**s store on **1st day of Sept 1874** For the purpose of settlement with Sheriff and the following members Presant **Joseph Teter** President, **Wm M. Jones, C. Mustoe** and **J. B. Godwin** Sectary and it was ordered that

    1th

J. B. Godwin be paid Four dollars for Taking the Enumeration in Delinquent Dists No. 4 & 7 out of Building Fund.

    2th

Ordered **Israel Poling** be paid one dollar out of Building fund for Taking Enumeration of Sub Dist No.11

    3

That **Joseph House** be paid one dollar out of Building Fund for Taking Enumeration Sub Dist No. 10

4

Ordered that **J. N. Ramsey** be paid one dollar out of Building fund for furnishing fuel 2 months to school house in Sub Dist No.10

5th

Ordered that **Simeon Swick** be paid one dollar out of Building fund for Taking Enumeration of Sub Dist No. 1

6th

Ordered that **M. L. Nestor** be paid Two dollars sweeping and ventilating house during Two month school in Sub Dist No. 9 be paid out of Building Fund.

7

Ordered that **A. J. Williams** be paid one dollar out of Building fund for taking the Enumeration of Sub Dist No.2

8

That **J. B. Godwin** be paid Eleven dollars out of Building Fund as part of Salary for Sectary for the School year Ending Aug 31th 1873.

9th

Thomas Madden this day presented a certificate from the Trustee of Sub Dist No. 5 showing he is Entitled to the Sum of Twenty Eight dollars for one months Teaching the same is allowed and it is ordered that a draft be drawn in his favour payable out of the Teachers fund allotted to Said Sub Dist.

10th

M. L. Nestor this day presented a certificate from the Trustee of Sub Dist No. 9 showing that he is Entitled to the sum of Fifty Six dollars For Two months Teaching the same is allowed and it is ordered that a draft be drawn in his favour payble out of Teachers fund allotted to Said Sub Dist.

11th

C. N. Street this day presented a certificate from the Trustee of Sub Dist No. 10 Showing that he is Entitled to the Sum of Eighteen dollars & 16 ½ cts for Fourteen days Teaching the same is allowed it is ordered that a draft be drawn in his Favour for the same payable out of Teachers fund allotted to said Sub District No. 10

Sept 2 Settlement made with Sheriff
Teachers Fund
Amount from State   1014.83
Amount from Levy   533.92
From other Sources 1 note of **Jos Teter**   200.00

70 School Board Minutes

From Settlement of 1872	2.48
From old Tax Receipts	469.33
From old Tax Receipts	120.73
Total Receipts	2341.29
Cr. by improperly lands	5.93
Cr. by Delinquent list	1.92
Cr. by Releases	4.02
Cr. by Old Tax Reipts Retn	101.46
Cr. by Commission of 1873	($15.66)
Commission on old Tax Collected	$22.24
Cr. by Vouchers	1786.96
Balance due Dist on Settlement	2341.29
Improperly lands	5.93
Releases	4.02
Vouchers	1786.96

Made Sept 2th 1874 for the School year Ending Aug the 31, 1873 is $554.35

Sheriff Dr.
Amount of Building Fund of Barker Dist

From Levy at 4 mills	852.76
From Settlement for 1872	76.54
Total for Building Fund	929.30
Cr. by Delinquent list Returned	3.06
Cr. by improperly lands	5.58
Cr. Releases	6.64
Cr. Commission	25.12
Cr. by Vouchers	923.20
Balance Due District	$6.10

Ordered that a levy be laid for Building Fund at 4 mills on the one Hundred dollars also 2 mills on the one hundred dollars for Teachers Fund.

Ordered that **J. B. Godwin** is Elected Sectary for the Ensuing year on motion the Board adjourned to meet on Sept the 8.

Joseph Teter President

J. B. Godwin Sect Bd Education

School Board Minutes 71

At a meeting of the Board of Education of Barker District Barbour Co. W. Va. held at **R. A. McCutcheons** Store on **Sept the 8, 1874** the following members presant **Wm. W. Jones, Chambers Mustoe** and **J. B. Godwin** Sect and **Wm. W. Jones** was made President Protem and the following Business done Viz:

Teachers Salaries was arranged and fixed at Thirty Dollars for a certificate of Grade No. One and Grade No. Two $28.00 and No. 3 $26.00 & No. 4 $20.00 and No. 5 $18.00 and Provided that a School be Run in Each Sub Dist four months and no more.

Ordered that **L. T. Holland** be paid one dollar for Taking Enumeration of Sub Dist No. 14 out of Building fund.

On motion the Board adjourned to meet on the First Saturday in Nov. next at 10 o'clock A. M.

Wm. W. Jones Pres Pro

J. B. Godwin Sect Bd. Ed.

At a meeting of the Board of Education of Barker District in the County of Barbour State of W.Va. held at **R. A. McCutcheons** Store house **Nov the 7, 1874** the members present Viz: **Joseph Teter** President **Wm W. Jones, Chambers Mustoe** and **J. B. Godwin** Sect and the following Buisness done.

1st

Thomas Madden Presented a certificate from the Trustee of Sub Dist No. 5 showing that he is Entitled to the sum of Twenty Eight dollars for one months Teaching School in said Sub Dist the same is allowed and it is ordered that a draft be drawn in his favour for the Same payable out of Teachers fund allotted to said Sub Dist.

2nd

$10.00 Ordered that **J. B. Godwin** be paid Ten dollars for making the annual Report to the County Superintendent and it was by order of Said County Superintendent payable out of Building fund of Barker Dist.

3rd

$5.35 Ordered that **Jonathan Hathaway** be paid five dollars & 35/00 for Repairs done to School house in Sub Dist No. 3 payable out fo Building fund $5.35

4th

$1.10 Ordered that **F. L. Swick** be paid one dollar and 10 cts for Broom, Chalk & the same is allowed and made payable out of Building

72 School Board Minutes

fund.

5th

Ordered **Thomas Madden** be paid Fifty cents for dipper to use in School Room it is allowed & payable out of Building fund.

Ordered that **Dr. Wm. E. Byrd** be appointed Trustee in Sub Dist No. 8 in Room of **Joseph House** Resigned

On motion the Board adjourned to meet at **R. A. McCutcheon**s Store on the Second Saturday in December next at 10 o'clock A.M.

Joseph Teter President
J. B. Godwin Sect

At a meeting of the Board of Education of Barker District Barbour County W. Va. held at **R. A. McCutcheon**s Store house on the **12 day of December 1874** the members present was **Joseph Teter** President and **J. B. Godwin** Sect and the following Business done Viz.:

1st

John M. Godwin this day presented a certificate from the Trustee of Sub Dist (No.11) showing that he is Entitled to the Sum of (28) Twenty Eight Dollars for one months Teaching School in said Sub Dist the same is allowed and it is ordered that a draft be drawn in his favour the same payable out of the Dist fund allotted to said Sub Dist.

2

F. B. Durrett this day presented a certificate from the Trustee of Sub Dist (No.14) showing that he is Entitled to the sum Thirty Dollars for one months Teaching School in said Sub Dist the same is allowed and it is ordered that a draft be Drawen in his favour payable out of the Teachers fund allotted to said Sub Dist.

3d

F. L. Swick this day presented a certificate from the Trustee of Sub Dist (No.1) showing that he is Entitled to the sum of (28) Twenty Eight dollars for one months Teaching School in said Sub Dist the same is allowed and it is ordered that a draft be Drawen in his favour payable out of the Teachers fund of Said District.

School Board Minutes 73

4th

Jonathan Hathaway this day presented a certificate from the Trustee of Sub Dist (No.3) showing that he is Entitled to the Sum of Thirty Dollars (30) for one months Teaching School in said Sub Dist the same is allowed and it is ordered that a draft be drawn in his favour payable out of the Teachers fund of said Dist.

5th

Ordered that **F. M. White** be paid one dollar & seventy cts ($1.70) out of Building for 1. Bucket, 1. Broom, 1 Dipper, 1. Box Chalk .75; .35; .50; .10.

6th

Ordered that **F. L. Swick** be paid Two Dollars (2.00) for making fires one month in School house in Sub Dist No.1 payable out of Building fund.

7th

Ordered that **R. A. McCutcheon** be paid Three 90/100 dollars ($3.90) for bill of Goods for use in School Room in Sub dist (No.13) payable out of Building fund Barker Dist.

8th

Ordered that **Able Teter** be paid Eight dollars ($8.00) for one hundred bushels coal furnished to School house in Sub Dist (No.8) payable out of Building fund of Barker Dist.

9

Ordered that **Edward S. Talbott** be paid Twelve dollars Twenty five cents ($12.75) for one hundred Bushels coal furnished to school house in Sub Dist (No.3) payable out of Building fund of Barker Dist.

10th

Ordered that **Jonathan Hathaway** be paid (2.00) Two dollars for making fires in school room in Sub Dist (No.3) for one month payable out of Building fund of Barker Dist.

11

Ordered that **Joseph C. Yeager** be paid Ten dollars & seventy five ($10.75) for furnishing one hundred bushels of Coal to school house in Sub Dist (No.5) payable out of Building fund of Barker Dist.

On motion of **George Digman** it was ordered that he be Transferred from Sub Dist (No.14) to sub (Dist No. 13) for Two years.

On motion the Board adjourned to meet at **R. A. McCutcheon**s Store house on the 2nd Saturday of February 1875 at 10 o'clock W. Va.

School Board Minutes

Joseph Teter President
J. B. Godwin Sectary

Bealington Feb the 13, 1875
At a meeting of the Board of Education of Barker District Barbour County W. Va. held at **R. A. McCutcheons** Store **13 Feb 1875** members presant Viz: **Joseph Teter**, President **Wm. W. Jones, Chambers Mustoe** and **J. B. Godwin** Sect and the following Buisiness done.

1st

J. A. Dunham this day Presented a certificate from the trustee of Sub Dist No. 8 showing that he is Entitled to the sum of Thirty dollars for one month Teacher School in said Sub Dist the same is allowed and it is ordered that a draft be drawen in his favour for the same payable out of Teachers fund allotted to said Sub Dist.

2

Thomas Madden this day Presented a certificate from the Trustee of Sub Dist No. 6 showing he is Entitled to the sum of Thirty dollars ($30) for one months Teaching School in said Sub Dist the same is allowed and it is ordered that a draft be drawen in his favour for the same payable out of Teachers fund of said Sub Dist.

3d

C. H. Street this day presented a certificate from the Trustee of Sub Dist (No.10) Showing that he is Entitled to the sum of Thirty dollars (30) for one month Teaching is said Dist the same is allowed and it is ordered that a draft be drawen in his favour payable out of Teachers Fund of said Dist.

Caroline V. Street this day Presented a certificate from the Trustee of Sub Dist (No.7) showing she is to be Entitled to the sum of Twenty Eight (28) dollars for one months Teaching school in said Sub Dist the same is allowed and it is ordered that a draft be drawen in her favour payable out of Teachers fund of said Sub Dist.

Jonathan Hathaway this day Presented a certificate from the Trustee of Sub Dist (No.3) Showing he is Entitled to the Sum of Sixty (60) dollars for two months Teaching School in said Sub Dist the same is allowed and it is ordered that a draft be drawen in his favour payable out of Teachers fund allotted to said Sub Dist.

W. A. Gaunt this day Presented a certificate from the Trustee of Sub Dist (No.10) showing he is Entitled to the sum of Fifty Two (52.00) dollars for two months Teaching School in Said Sub Dist the same is allowed and it is ordered that a draft be drawn in his favour payable out of Teachers fund allotted to said Sub Dist.

This should have been recorded in Nov. 1874 Oversight of Sec. **J. B. Godwin. C. H. Street** this day Presented a certificate showing that he is entitled to the sum of Thirty (30) dollars for one months Teaching School in said Sub Dist the same is allowed and it is ordered that a draft be drawn in his favour payable out of Teachers fund for Said Sub Dist.

F. B. Durrett this day Presented a certificate from the Trustee of Sub Dist (No.14) Showing that he is Entitled to the sum of Thirty (30) dollars for one month Teaching school in said Sub Dist and the same is allowed and it is ordered that a draft be drawn in his favour payable out of The Teachers fund of Said Sub Dist.

J. M. Godwin this day Presented a certificate from the trustee of Sub Dist (no.11) Showing he is Entitled to the Sum of Twenty Eight (28) dollars for one month Teaching school in said Sub Dist and the same is allowed and it is ordered that a draft be drawn in his favour payable out of the Teachers fund of Said Dist.

A. D. Corder this day Presented a certificate from the Trustee of Sub Dist No. 12 showing that he is Entitled to the sum of Twenty Eight (28) dollars the same is allowed and it is ordered that a draft be drawn in his favour payable out of the Teachers fund allotted to said Dist.

R. L. Tallman this day Presented Two Certificates from the Trustee of Sub Dist (No.4) Showing he is Entitled to the sum of Sixty (60) dollars for Two months Teaching School in Said Sub Dist the same is allowed and it is ordered that a draft be drawn in his favour for the same payable out of Teachers fund allotted to said Dist.

F. B. Durrett this day Presented to the Board a certificate from the Trustee of Sub Dist (No.14) showing he is Entitled to the Sum of Thirty (30) dollars for one month Teaching in said Sub Dist the same is allowed and it is ordered that a draft be drawn in his favour of the same payable out of Teachers fund allotted to Said Sub Dist.

F. L. Swick This day Presented a certificate from the Trustee of Sub Dist (No.1) Showing that he is Entitled to the Sum of Twenty Eight (28) dollars for one months Teaching in Said Sub Dist the same is allowed and it is ordered that a draft be drawn in his favour for the same payable out of Teachers fund allotted to said Dist.

W. A. Street this day Presented a certificate from the Trustee of Sub Dist (No.9) showing he is Entitled to the Sum of Twenty Eight (28) dollars for one month Teaching school in said Sub Dist the same is allowed and it is ordered that a draft be drawen in his favour payable out of Teachers fund of said Dist.

  C. H. Street this day Presented a certificate from the Trustee of Sub Dist (No.13) showing he is Entitled to the sum of Thirty (30) dollars for one month Teaching School in said Dist the same is allowed and it is ordered that a draft be drawen in his favour payable out of the Teachers fund of said Dist.

  W. A. Street this day Presented a certificate from the Trustee of Sub Dist (No.9) showing that he is Entitled to the Sum of Twenty Eight (28) dollars for one month Teaching School in said Sub Dist the same is allowed and it is ordered that a draft be drawen in his favour for the same Payable out of the Teachers fund allotted to said Dist .

  Ordered $4.00. Ordered that **Jonathan Hathaway** be paid for (4) dollars for making Fires for (2) months in school house in sub Dist (No.3) out of Building fund.

  Ordered Feb 13, 1875 $6.68 also $3.50 Ordered that **Daniel Ice** be paid Six 68/100 dollars for furnishing Coal to School house in sub Dist (No.11) also three 50/100 dollars for Repairs to said house in Sub Dist (No.11) all the above is allowed and ordered paid out of Building fund of Barker Dist.

  Ordered $0.50 that **R. A. McCutcheon** be paid fifty cts for 1 shovel and Poker the same is allowed payable out of Building fund Barker Dist.

  Ordered $4.00 **C. H. Street** be paid Four (4) dollars for making fires in school house in sub Dist (No.13) the same is made payable out of Building fund.

  Ordered $1.00 **W. L. Parks** one dollar for Taking the Enumeration of Sub Dist for year Ending Aug 30 1874 the same is allowed and ordered paid out of Building fund Barker Dist.

  Ordered $12.25 That **George N. Shomo** be paid Twelve Dollars and Twenty five cents ($12.25) for furnishing fuel for School house in Sub Dist No.7 payable out of Building fund Barker District.

  Ordered That **Joseph P. Gross** be paid Four 55/100 Dollars for furnishing One Hundred Bushels of Coal for School house in Sub Dist (No.9) payable out of Building fund Barker Dist.

  Ordered $4.00 That **Solomon Coffman** be paid Four (4.00) Dollars for repairing School house in Sub Dist. (No.7) payable out of Building fund of Barker Dist.

  Ordered $0.30 That **F. M. White** be paid Thirty cts. (0.30) payable out of Building fund of Barker Dist.

Ordered That **J. B. Godwin** be paid Two (2.00) Dollars for Stationaries furnished to the Board of Education, payable out of Building fund of Barker Dist.

This should be recorded (2.00) Nov 1874. Ordered That **C. H. Streets** be paid Two ($2.00) Dollars for making fires in School house in Sub Dist No.7 payable out of Building fund of Barker District.

Ordered $14.30 That **Wm. B. Jones** be paid Fourteen 30/100 Dollars for furnishing fuel for School house Sub Dist No.14 payable out of Building fund of Barker District.

Ordered $12.00 That **Benjamin Parks** be paid Twelve Dollars for furnishing One Hundred & Thirty bushels of coal for the School House Sub Dist. No.12 payable out of Building fund of Barker District.

Ordered $12.00 That **James England** be paid Twelve Dollars for furnishing fuel to School house in Sub Dist (No.14) payable out of Building fund of Barker District.

Ordered $10.00 That **F. M. Howes** be paid Ten Dollars for furnishing one Hundred Bushels of coal for Sub Dist (No.6) payable out of Building fund of Barker Dist.

Ordered $6.85 That **A. Right** be paid Six 85/100 Dollars for furnishing fuel to School house in Sub Dist payable out of Building fund of Barker Dist.

Resolved by the Board of Education of Barker District Barbour County West Virginia that they will build one coal House for Each School House is each Sub district in Barker district and that they will on the 3rd day of April next Sell to the lowest responsible Bidder The construction of said coal houses reserving to themselves the right to accept Either of the bidders or to reject all of them.

Said coal houses to be built as follows Six by Eight feet Square and six feet high to the Eaves of the roof to be Sloped both ways. The sills to be Six by Eight inches square. The corner posts to be four by six inches square with the necessary studding between the corner posts to be weather boarded on the outside with six inch poplar plank and to be lined on the inside with inch plank with convenient door for pulling in coal and putting it out, and closing the same. Sills to be of oak and all the lumber to be good & free from cracks & wind shakes. Houses to be completed the 1st August 1875. Payments for said houses as follows: Viz; Ordered on the Treasurer of Barbour County given when houses are built & rec't by the Bd of Education, One half to be paid out of the June Levy of 1875 and one half out of the Levy of the Year 1876, with interest at Six per cent from date of orders. Said work to be done in a good workman like manner. Each contractor will be required to file with the clerk before proceeding to work a bond for the faithful performance of his duty with approved security. Said houses each to have a floor of inch oak plank with two Slecpers.

      Joseph Teter President
      J. B. Godwin Sectary

  At a meeting of the Board of Education of Barker Dist. Barbour County W. Va. held at **R. A. McCutcheons** Store house on the **third day of April 1875** and the following members Presant Viz: **Joseph Teter** President, **Wm W. Jones, Chambers Mustoe** & **J. B. Godwin** Secty and the following Buisiness was Transacted.

  N. C. Sipe Presented a certificate from the Trustee of Sub Dist (no.2) Showing that She is Entitled to the sum of Seventy Eight dollars it being for Teaching three months School the same is allowed and it is ordered that a draft be drawen in her favour for the same payable out of Teachers fund of said Sub Dist.

  A. T. Corder this day presented a certificate from the trustee of Sub Dist (No. 12) showing that he is Entitled to the Sum of Eighty Four dollars for three months Teaching school in said Sub Dist the same is allowed and it is ordered that a draft be drawen in his favour payable out of the Teachers fund of said Sub Dist.

  W. A. Gaunt this day presented a certificate from the Trustee of Sub Dist (No.10) Showing he is Entitled to the sum of Twenty Six Dollars for one months Teaching in said Sub Dist the same is allowed and it is ordered that a draft be drawen in his favour for the same payable out of Teachers fund allotted to said Sub Dist.

  W. A. Street This day presented a certificate showing he is Entitled to the Sum of Twenty Eight dollars for one months Teaching in Sub Dist (No.9) the same is allowed and it is ordered that a draft be drawen in his favour for the same payable out of the Teachers fund of said Sub Dist.

  F. B. Durrett this day presented a certificate from the trustee of Sub Dit (No.14) Showing that he is Entitled to the sum of Thirty dollars for one months Teaching School in Sub Dist the same is allowed and it is ordered that a draft be drawen in favour for the same payable out of Teachers fund allotted to said Sub Dist.

  J. A. Dunham this day presented a certificate from the

Trustee Sub Dist (No.5) to the Board of Education showing that he is Entitled to the sum of Thirty dollars for one months Teaching School in said Sub Dist the same is allowed and it is ordered that a draft be drawn in his favour for the same payable out of Teachers fund allotted to said Sub Dist.

 J. A. Godwin this day presented to the Board a certificate from the Trustee of Sub Dist (No.11) Showing that he is Entitled to the Sum of Twenty Eight dollars for one months Teaching School in said Sub Dist the same is allowed and it is ordered that a draft be drawn in his favour for the same payable out of Teachers Fund allotted to said Sub Dist.

 F. L. Swick this day presented a certificate to the Board from the Trustee of Sub Dist (No.1) Showing that he is Entitled to the Sum of Twenty Eight dollars for one months Teaching School in said Sub Dist the same is allowed and it is ordered that a draft be drawn in his favour for the same payable out of Teachers fund allotted to said Sub Dist.

 Jonathan Hathaway this day presented a certificate from the Trustee of Sub Dist (No.3) Showing that he is Entitled to the sum of Thirty Dollars for one months Teaching School in Said Sub Dist the same is allowed and it is ordered that a draft be drawn in his favour payable out of Teachers fund allotted to said Sub Dist.

 Ira L. Evrit this day presented to the Board a certificate From the Trustee of Sub Dist (No.5) showing that he is Entitled to the sum of Twenty Six dollars for one months Teaching School in said Sub Dist the same is allowed and it is ordered that a draft be drawn in his favour payable out of Teachers fund allotted to said Sub Dist.

 Ordered **Solomon Ganer** be paid Ten & 50 for fuel furnished to Sub Dist (No.1) Payable Building fund.

 N. C. Sipe this day presented to the Board a certificate from the Trustee of Sub Dist (No.2) showing that she is Entitled to the sum of Seventy Eight dollars for three months School in said Sub Dist the same is allowed and it is ordered that a draft be drawn in her favour payable out of Teachers fund allotted to said Sub District.

 Ordered that **I. L. Evrit** be paid nine dollars on Sub Dist of Building fund for making fires $8.50, 1 Broom 30 cts, Poker 25 cts $9.05

 Ordered that **C. E. Shomo** be paid Six dollars out of Building fund for making Fires in School Room in Sub Dist (No.7)

 Ordered **F. M. Tallman** be paid Two dollars and 40c for Repairs to School house in Sub Dist (No.5) payable out of Building

School Board Minutes

Fund.

Ordered **Thomas Madden** be paid Two dollars for making fires one in Sub Dist (No.6) and (50) cts for Repairing Stove & 75 cts for 5 paines window glass all payable out of Building fund.

Ordered **R. L. Tallman** be paid Sixty five cents for one lock for School house in Sub Dist (No.4) out of Building fund.

Ordered that **James Knotts** be paid Two dollars for joints of Stove pipe and 1 Broom for School house in Sub Dist (No.12) payable out of Building fund of Barker Dist.

Ordered that **R. A. McCutcheon** be paid one dollar for 2 joints stove pipe for School house in Sub Dist (No.6) out of Building fund.

Ordered that **C. H. Street** be paid Two dollars for making fires in Sub Dist (No.13) payable out of Building fund.

Ordered **W. A. Gaunt** be paid Eight dollars for making fires for four months in Sub Dist (No.10) out of Building fund.

Ordered that **A. T. Corder** be paid Eight dollars out of Building for making fires in School house in Sub Dist No.12

Ordered **F. L. Swick** be paid Six dollars out of Building fund for making fires in School house in Sub Dist (No.1)

On motion of **Joshue Proudfoot** an Order that be made to open the School houses for the Grange to meet in and that they be Responsible for damage done by them if any.

Ordered that **Jonathan Hathaway** be paid fifty cents for Chalk furnished to school house in Sub Dist (No.13) payable out of Building fund also Two dollars for making fires one month is said Sub Dist.

Ordered that **John Chinworth** be paid out of Building fund one dollar and Seventy five cents for repairs done to school house in Sub Dist (No.12)

Ordered That **Thomas Champ** be paid Ten 50/100 dollars out of Building fund for Furnishing 105 Bushels Coal for School house in Sub Dist (No.2)

Ordered that **N. C. Sipe** be paid Eight dollars out of Building fund for making fires four months in Sub Dist (No.2)

Ordered that **Christian Ghost** be paid Six dollars out of Building fund for making fires in School house in Sbu Dist (No.4)

Ordered that **J. S. Skidmore** be paid Two 30/100 dollars out of Building fund for Repairs to School house in Sub Dist No.12

Ordered that **W. A. Street** be paid Six dollars out of Building fund for making fires in School house in Sub Dist No.9

Ordered **J. M. Godwin** be paid out of Building fund Eight 80/100 dollars for making fires & necessaries Furnished to School house in Sub Dist (No.11)

Ordered that **F. B. Durrett** be paid Eight dollars out of Building fund for making fires in School house in Sub Dist No.14

Ordered that **L. N. Kerr** be paid Twelve dollars out of Building fund for furnishing fuel for School house in Sub Dist No.4

On motion the Board adjourned to meet on the last Saturday in April at **R. A. McCutcheon**s store at Ten O'clock A. M.

Joseph Teter President
J. B. Godwin Sectary

At a meeting of the Board of Education of Barker Dist Barbour County W. Va. held at **R. A. McCutcheon**s Store this **7 day of June 1875** and the following members Preseant **Joseph Teter** President, **Wm. W. Jones** & **J. B. Godwin** Sectary and the following Buisness done.

J. A. Dunham presented a certificate from the Trustee of Sub Dist (No.8) Showing that he is Entitled to the Sum of Thirty Dollars for one month Teaching School in said Sub Dist the same is allowed and it is ordered that a draft be drawn in his favour for the same payable out of the Teachers fund of Barker Dist allotted to said Sub Dist.

Ordered that **R. D. Kerr** be paid Twelve 54/100 dollars out of Teachers fund for Tax Erroneous collected by **James W. George** and the same is Refunded.

Ordered that **J. A. Dunham** be paid Eight dollars for Building Fires payable out of Building fund of Barker Dist.

Ordered that **W. J. Hollen** be paid Eight dollars for Coal house and Two dollars for putting glass in windows payable out of Building fund of Barker Dist.

Ordered that **J. L. Evrit** be paid Seventy Eight dollars $78.00 for Teaching School in Sub District (No.5) for Three months the same is allowed payable out of the Teachers fund allotted Said Sub Dist.

Ordered that **C. V. Street** be paid Twenty Eight dollars $28.00 for Teaching School in Sub Dist (No.7) one month the same is allowed payable out of Teachers Fund of said Sub Dist.

Ordered that **W. A. Gaunt** be paid Twenty Six dollars $26.00 out of Teachers Fund for one month Teaching in Sub Dist (No.10) the same is allowed payable out of Teachers fund allotted to said Sub Dist.

Ordered that **J. M. Godwin** be paid Twenty Eight dollars $28.00 for Teaching School in Sub Dist (No.11) the same is allotted and payable out of Teachers fund allotted to Sub Dist (No.11)

Ordered that **F. L. Swick** be paid Twenty Eight dollars for one months teaching school in Sub Dist (No.1) the same is allowed and payable out of Teachers Fund Allotted to said Sub Dist.

Ordered that **C. V. Street** be paid Twenty Eight dollars $28.00 for one month Teaching School in Sub Dist (No.7) the same is allowed and payable out of Teachers fund allotted to said Dist.

Ordered that **Thomas Madden** be paid Thirty dollars $30.00 for Teaching School in Sub Dist (No.6) one month the same is Allowed and payable out of Teachers fund allotted to said Dist.

Ordered that **C. F. Street** be paid Thirty dollars $30.00 for one month Teaching School in Sub Dist (No.13) the same is Allowed payable out of Teachers fund allotted to Said Dist.

The last seven orders Should have been Entered in the proseedings of the Board at their meeting in April the 3d third but was omitted by an over sight of the Secatary.

On motion the Board adjourned sign die
Joseph Teter President
J. B. Godwin Sectary

At a call meeting of the Board of Education held at **R. A. McCutcheon**s Store on **26th of June** the following members present: **Joseph Teter** President, **W. W. Jones** & **C. Mustoe, R. A. McCutcheon** Sect. Pro Tem. The following business was transacted Viz:

Order 100 426.00 Ordered that **R. L. Tallman** be paid Twenty Six Dollars out of Teachers fund of Barker Dist.

Order 102 ($9.00) Ordered that **Isaac Price** be paid Nine Dollars for Bording **W. A. Street** out of Teachers fund of Barker Dist Sub District No. 13.

Order 101 ($19.00) Ordered that **W. A. Street** be paid Nineteen Dollars out of Teachers fund of Barker Dist.

Order 103 $2.00 Ordered that **W. A. Street** be paid Two Dollars out of Building fund for making fires at School house No.13 Barker Dist.

School Board Minutes 83

Order 104 $28.00 Ordered that **W. A. Street** be paid Twenty Eight Dollars for one months Teaching School Payable out of Teachers fund: Board of Education acting as Trustee for Sub Dist No.9 of Barker Dist.

Order 105 $2.00 Ordered that **W. A. Street** be paid Two Dollars for building fires in Schoolhouse in Sub Dist No.9, out of Building fund of Barker Dist.

Order 106 $30.00 Ordered that **Thomas Madden** be paid Thirty Dollars out of Teachers fund of Barker District.

Order 107 $30.00 Ordered that **Thomas Madden** be paid Thirty Dollars for Teaching one month School in Sub District No.6 in Barker Dist.

On motion the Board adjourned Sign Die
Joseph Teter President
J. B. Godwin Secretary

At a meeting held at **R. A. McCutcheon**s Store on the **23rd of Aug 1875** for the purpose of counting the votes of Barker Dist.; the following members present **Joseph Teter**, President, **Wm W. Jones & Chambers Mustoe** & **J. B. Godwin** Secretary. Upon counting the votes it was found that **W. W. Corder** received 53 votes for County Superintendent and that **Pansy Marteny** received 227 votes.

That **Joseph Teter** Received a majority for President of Board of education & that **Wm. W. Jones** Received 166 for Commissioner & that **R. A. McCutcheon** Received 154 votes, **Wm. A. Street** Received 143 votes, & **M. Edmonds** Received 56 votes.

Ordered that **Thomas Madden** be paid one Dollar for making fires for a month payable out of Building fund of Barker Dist.

Ordered that **Israel Poling** be paid one Dollar for taking the enumeration of sub Dist No.11 and charge to Building fund of Barker Dist.

Ordered that **J. B. Godwin** be paid Ten Dollars for taking the enumeration of Sub Distr. Nos. 2, 4, 5, 7, 8 and 14 Payable out of Building fund of Barker Dist.

On Motion the Board adjourned to meet on the 27th of Aug. at **R. A. McCutcheon**s store at 10 o'clock A. M.

It is ordered that **Joseph Teter** be declared elected as

84 School Board Minutes

President of the Board of Education of Barker Dist, Barbour Co., W. Va. for the term ending September 1877, And further for the same term of office **Wm. W. Jones & R. A. McCutcheon** were elected as School Commissioners for the same District & County.

Joseph Teter President

J. B. Godwin Sect

At a meeting of the Board of Education of Barker Dist, Barbour Co. W. Va. held at **R. A. McCutcheons** Store on the **28th Aug. 1875**. The following members present **Joseph Teter, Jr., Wm. M. Jones, C. Mustoe** and **J. B. Godwin** Secretary. The object of the meeting was to settle with the Treasurer. Settlement made with the following results Viz.

Total Teachers fund	1971.50
From State	997.17
From District Levy	419.98
From Settlement of 1874	554.35
Credit by Releases	2.17
Credit by Delinquent list	6.75
Credit by Commission	12.33
Credit by Amount of Vouchers	1600.54
Credit by List of Old Tax Receipts returned	25.40
Credit by Ten Dollars refunded to **John M. Baker**	10.00
Credit by Twelve Dol. and fifty four cts. refunded to **R. D. Kerr** for use of **E. Halls** Heir	12.54
Balance due Barker Dist on Settlement Three hundred Dollars & Eleven cts	$300.11

Amount for Building Fund		$840.10
Balance on Settlement of 1873 was		6.10
	Total	$846.20

Amount Commission	$24.68
Releases	4.34
Delinquent	2.64

Amount of Building Bonds	Principal	Interest
One in favor of **Nathan Panin**	57.00	19.28
One in favor of **Jacob Sipe**	82.03	2.40
One in favor of **William H. Weaver**	87.53	34.57
One in favor of **Daniel E. Willmoth**	88.79	35.07
	$315.35	121.32
Total Amount of Bonds		$436.67
Balance Due Barker Dist.		13.40

On Motion Board adjourned Sine Die
Joseph Teter President
J. B. Godwin Sec. B. Ed.

At a meeting of the Board of Education of Barker Dist., held at R. A. McCutcheons Store on the **14th** day of Sept. 1875: The following members present **W. W. Jones** President Protem, **R. A. McCutcheon** & **J. M. Godwin** Secretary Protem; The following business was done. Ordered that **J. M. Godwin** be appointed Secretary Protem. Ordered that the Levy be laid as follows: For Building 40 cts on the $100. valuation and that 25% for Teachers fund.

Ordered that we set the salary of Teachers as follows No. 1 = $30.00, No.2 = 28.00, No.3 = 24.00, No.4 = 20.00, No. 5 = 18.00 (Valentine District)

On motion of **Levi Cross, W. M. Biby** & others it was ordered that a new District be made including the following persons and with the following boundries Viz: Commencing on Laurel Hill at **Henry Barte's**, thence West so as to include said **Bartes** thence running with the range of hills between the heads of Hunters Fork, Sugar Creek, and Wolf Run to the Morgantown Pike: thence South with said Pike so as to include **John** and **Robert Dunhams**, thence South so as to include **Booths**; Thence North with the County line to the Beginning & That the new Dist. Be called Valentine and it is further ordered that they have a School if they can procure a suitable House and that the Board be under no liability. It was further ordered that **Wm. M. Biby** be appointed Trustee is Sub Dist No. 15 Barker Dist.

Ordered that **J. B. Godwin** be appointed Secretary of the Board of Education of Barker Dist for Two Years for 1875-1876.

Order No. 1 Ordered that **Isaac Price** be paid one Dollar for taking Enumeration in Sub Dist No. 11.

86   School Board Minutes

Order No. 2 Ordered that **Levi Cross** be paid Two Dollars for taking Enumeration in Sub Dist No. 9 for Two years 1874 and 5.
Wm W. Jones, P. T.
J. M. Godwin, Sect. Protem

At a meeting of the Board of Education of Barker Dist. Barbour County W. Va. at **R. A. McCutcheons** Store house on the **27 day of Nov 1875** the Following officers Present **Joseph Teter** President **Wm W. Jones** and **R. A. McCutcheon & J. B. Godwin** Sect and the following Buisness done.

Ordered $1.43 That **F. M. White** be paid one dollar and Forty Three cts Payable out of Building fund Barker District.

Ordered $12.50 That **Harmen Steerman** be paid Twelve 50/100 dollars out of Building Fund Barker Dist.

Ordered $3.00 That **J. Y. Booth** be paid three dollars for Fewel to sub Dist (No.2) Payable out of Building Fund Barker District Barbour County.

Ordered $1.25 That **John Right** be paid one 25/100 dollars for Broom, Bucket, dipper for School house in Sub Dist No. 13 payable out of Building Barker Dist.

Ordered $1.00 That **Simen Swick** be paid one dollar for Taking the Enumeration of Youths in Sub Dist (No.1) payable out of Building fund of Barker District.

Ordered $9.35 That **A. Right** be paid Nine 35/100 dollars for Coal and Glass Furnished to School house in Sub Dist No. 13 payable out of Building fund of Barker Dist.

Ordered $3.45 That **J. D. Chineworth** be paid three 45/100 dollars for Repairs to School house in Sub Dist (No.2) payable out of the Building fund.

Ordered $14.50 That **Andes Mclane** be paid Fourteen 50/100 dollars for Delivery one hundred and 25 bushels of coal to School house in Sub Dist No. 12 payable out of Building fund.

Ordered $1.00 That **F. M. White** be paid one dollar for Broom and Bucket and 4 lbs nares payable out of Building fund of Barker Dist.

Ordered that **A. J. Williams** be Transferred from Sub Dist (No.2) to Sub District (No.1) said Transfer to be Permanent and lasting as long as the Rocks and Hills may stand.

C. H. Street Presented a certificate from the Trustee of Sub Dist (No.10) Showing that he is Entitled to the Sum of Thirty dollars for one months Teaching School in said Sub Dist the Same is allowed and it is ordered that a draft be Drawn in his favour payable out of Teachers fund Sub Dist.

On motion the Board adjourned to meet on the 25 day of December 1875.

Wm W. Jones President P. T.
Jacob B. Godwin Sectary

At a meeting of the Board of Education held at **R. A. McCutcheon**s Store house on the **25th day of December 1875** the following members present **Joseph Teter** President, **Wm. W. Jones, R. A. McCutcheon** and **J. B. Godwin** Sectary and the following buisiness Done Viz.

1st

C. V. Street this day presented a certificate from the Trustee of Sub Dist (No.4) Showing that she is Entitled to the sum of Twenty Eight dollars for one month teaching school in said Sub Dist the same is allowed and it is ordered that a draft be drawn in her favour payable out of Teachers fund allotted to said Sub Dist.

2nd

F. B. Durrett this day presented a certificate from the Trustee of Sub Dist (No.14) Showing that he is Entitled to the Sum of Thirty dollars for one month Teaching school in same and ordered that a draft be drawn in his favour payable out of Teachers fund of said Sub Dist.

3d

W. W. Teter this day presented a certificate from the Trustee of Sub Dist (No.6) showing that he is Entitled to the sum of Thirty dollars for one month Teaching School in said Dist the same is allowed and it is ordered that a draft be drawn in his favour payable out of Teachers fund of said Dist.

4th

J. M. Godwin this day presented a certificate from the Trustee of Sub Dist (No.13) Showing that he is Entitled to the sum of Twenty Eight dollars for Teaching school in said Dist for one month the

88   School Board Minutes

same is allowed and it is ordered that a draft be drawn in his favour for the same payable out of Teachers fund of said Sub Dist No.13.

5th

R. M. Baker this day presented a certificate from the Trustee of Sub Dist (No.12) Showing that he is Entitled to the sum of Twenty Eight dollars for one month Teaching school in said Dist the same is allowed and it is ordered that a draft be drawn in his favour payable out of Teachers fund of said Dist.

6th

Thomas Madden this day presented a certificate from the Trustee of Sub Dist (No.1) Showing that he is Entitled to the sum of Thirty dollars for one month Teaching School in said Dist for one month the same is allowed and it is ordered that a draft be drawn in his favour payable out of Teachers fund allotted to said Dist.

7th

W. A. Street this day presented a certificate from the Trustee of Sub Dist (No.5) Showing that he is Entitled to the sum of Thirty dollars for one months Teaching in said Dist the same is allowed and it is ordered that a draft be drawn in his favour payable out of Teachers fund allotted to said Sub Dist

8th

W. A. Gaunt this day presented a certificate from The Trustee of Sub Dist (No.7) Showing that he is Entitled to the Sum of Twenty Eight dollars for one months Teaching School in Said Dist the same is allowed and it is ordered that a draft be drawn in his favour payable out of Teachers fund allotted to said Sub Dist.

9th

C. N. Street this day presented a certificate from the Trustee of Sub Dist (No.10) showing that he is Entitled to the sum of Thirty dollars for one months Teaching School in same the same is allowed and it is ordered that a draft be drawn in his favour for the same payable out of the Teachers fund allotted to the said Sub Dist.

Ordered that **Abel Teter** be paid Eleven dollars for fuel furnished (1.10 Bushels) to school house in Sub Dist (No.6)

Ordered Payable out of Building fund Barker Dist that **J. M. Good** be paid one dollar and fifty cts for Repairs to School house in Sub Dist No.6 payable out of Building fund of Barker District.

Ordered that **F. M. White** be paid 80 cts for coal for School Room in Sub Dist (No.10) payable out of Building fund Barker Dist.

Ordered That **J. M. Godwin** be paid four dollars out of Building fund for making fire in school room in Sub Dist No. 13.

Ordered that **A. S. Rhorabaugh** be paid Nine 75/100 dollars for furnishing Coal to School house in Sub Dist (No.14) payable out of Building fund Barker District.

Ordered that **J. N. Bonner** be paid Eleven dollars for Repairs done to School house (No.11) and Seven dollars for fuel furnished at School house (No.11) payable out of Building fund Barker Dist.

Ordered that **C. H. Street** be paid Six dollars four of which is for making fires in Sub Dist (No.10) and Two was assigned to him by **W. A. Street** and for making fires in Sub Dist No. 5 all payable out of Building fund Barker Dist.

Ordered that **J. M. Ramsey** be paid Ten dollars for Coal furnished to School house (No.10) payable out of Building Br. D.

Ordered that **Able Teter** be paid Ten dollars for Coal furnished to Sub Dist (No.8) payable out of Building fund Barker District.

Ordered that **F. L. Swick** be paid 50 cts for Broom to be used in School Room payable out of Building fund of Barker District.

Ordered that **F. M. White** be paid one 05/100 dollars for one rod and Shovel to use in school room (No.5) Sub Dist payable out of Building fund Barker District.

C. H. Teter this day presented a certificate from the Trustee of Sub Dist (No.3) showing that he is Entitled to the sum of Thirty dollars for one month Teaching in Sub Dist (No.3) the same is allowed and it is ordered that a draft be drawn in his favour payable out of Teachers fund allotted to said Dist.

On motion there was five Coal houses Taken up and Bonds issued one in Sub District No.4 and one in No.5 and one in No.11 and one No.12, one in No.13 and

On Motion **L. T. Hollen** was appointed Trustee in Sub Dist (No.14).

On Motion the Board adjourned to meet on the last Saturday of Jan 1876 at 9 o'clock at **R. A. McCutcheons**.
    Joseph Teter President
      J. B. Godwin Secretary Bd. Ed.

At a meeting of the Board of Education held at **R. A. McCutcheon**s Store house on the **Eighth day of January 1876** and the members present was **Joseph Teter** President, **Wm. W. Jones, R. A. McCutcheon** and **J. B. Godwin** Sectary and the following buisiness Done Viz.

1st

W. S. Shurtleff this day presented a certificate from the Trustee of Sub Dist (No.9) Showing that he is Entitled to the sum of Sixty dollars for two months Teaching school in said Dist it is ordered that a draft be drawn in his favour for the same payable out of Teachers fund allotted to said Dist No.9.

2nd

C. F. Teter this day presented a certificate from the Trustee of Sub Dist (No.3) showing that he is Entitled to the sum of Thirty dollars for one month Teaching The same is allowed and it is ordered that a draft be drawn in his favour payable out of Teachers fund allotted to said Sub Dist No.3

3d

F. B. Durrett this day presented a certificate from the Trustee of Sub District (No.14) Showing that he is Entitled to the sum of Thirty dollars for one month Teaching School in Said Sub District the same is allowed and it is ordered that a draft be drawn in his favour for the same payable out of the Teachers fund allotted to said Dist.

4th

W. A. Gaunt this day presented a certificate from the Trustee of Sub Dist (No.7) showing that he is Entitled to the Sum of Twenty Eight dollars for one month Teaching School in said Dist the Same is allowed and it is ordered that a draft be drawn in his favour for the same payable out of Teachers fund allotted to said Dist (no.7)

W. A. Street this day presented a certificate from the Trustee of Sub Dist (No.5) Showing that he is Entitled to the sum of Thirty dollars for Teaching or Trying to Teach School in said Dist the same is allowed and it is ordered that a draft be drawn in his favour payable out of Teachers fund allotted to said Dist.

6th

C. H. Street this day presented a certificate from the Trustee of Sub Dist (No.10) that he is Entitled to the sum of Thirty dollars for one month Teaching or Trying to imitate those that do Teach School in said Dist the same is allowed and it is ordered that a draft be drawn in his favour payable out of Teachers fund allowed to said Dist (No.10)

Ordered that **S. Thacker** be paid 50 cts for mending damper of stove payable out of Building fund Barker Dist.

Ordered **W. S. Shurtliff** be paid four dollars for making fires in School room paid out of Building fund.

Ordered that **W. A. Gaunt** be paid four dollars for making fires in school room in Dist (No.7) paid out of Building fund.

Ordered **F. M. White** be paid one 50/100 dollars for (3) joint stove pipe for use in school house in Sub Dist (No.9) paid out of Building fund.

Ordered that **F. M. White** be paid Twenty dollars for Stove $20.00, one Coal hod .80, fire shovel .25, one wood bucket .25, one cup .10, one broom .45, one joint 1 inch stove pipe .50, one hood 1.35, bottom joint 1.00, 2 joints Eathern pipe at 85c 1.70, 80 lbs freight at 1.44 cts 1.00, Commission .25 Making a total of $27.65 All of which is payable out of Building fund.

Ordered that **Thomas Bartlett** be and hereby is permanently Transferred from Sub Dist (No.2) to Sub Dist (No.6)

Ordered that **James Booth** be and hereby is Permanently Transferred from Sub District (No.2) to Sub District (No.1)

On motion of **W. W. Jones, Daniel Ice**s Coal houses was both Taken up and a draft issued for Fifteen 75/100 & also one bond on the District of Barker for Fifteen 75/100 dollars also one Coal house for **J. B. Godwin** that he built in Sub Dist (No.13) and bonds issued and also 2 Coal houses that **Jacob Sipe** built one is Sub Dist (No.5) and one is Sub Dist (No.4) for which bonds was issued.

On motion the Board adjourned to meet at **A. J. Wilmoth**s old Store house on the 18 day of Jan 1876 at 9 o'clock A.M.

Joseph Teter President
J. B. Godwin Sect Bd. Ed.

At a meeting of the Board of Education of Barker District, Barbour County W. Va. held at **R. A. McCutcheon**s Store house on the **29 day of January 1876** the following members present **Joseph Teter** President, **W. W. Jones, R. A. McCutcheon** and **J. B. Godwin** Sectary and the following buisiness Done Viz.

W. W. Teter this day presented a certificate from the Trustee fo Sub Dist (No.6) Showing that he is Entitled to the sum of Thirty dollars for one month Teaching school in said Dist the same is allowed and it is ordered that a draft be drawn in his favour for the same payable out of Teachers fund of said Dist.

C. V. Street this day presented a certificate from the Trustee of Sub Dist (No.4) showing that she is Entitled to the sum of Twenty Eight dollars for Teaching School in said Dist the same is allowed and it is ordered that a draft be drawn in her favour for the same payable out of Teachers fund of said Dist.

Jacob A. Dunham this day presented a certificate from the Trustee of Sub District (No.15) Showing that he is Entitled to the sum of Thirty dollars for one month Teaching School in said Dist the same is allowed and it is ordered that a draft be drawn in his favour for the same payable out of the Teachers fund of said Dist.

Thomas Madden this day presented a certificate from the Trustee of Sub Dist (No.1) showing that he is Entitled to the sum of Thirty dollars for one month Teaching School in said Dist the Same is allowed and it is ordered that a draft be drawn in his favour for the same payable out of Teachers fund of Said Dist.

W. A. Street this day presented a certificate from the Trustee of Sub Dist (No.5) Showing that he is Entitled to the sum of Thirty dollars for one month teaching School in Sub Dist (No.5) the same is allowed and it is ordered that a draft be drawn in his favour payable out of Teachers fund of said Dist.

Ordered that **Cornelius Corley** be paid Thirteen 50/100 for furnishing fuel to school house in Sub Dist (No.7) payable out of Building fund of Barker Dist Barbour County W. Va.

Ordered that **W. A. Street** be paid Four dollars for making in School Room in Sub Dist (No.5) and charge to Building fund.

Ordered that **C. H. Street** be paid Two Dollars for making fires in School Room in Sub District (No.10) Charge to Building fund.

Ordered that **Patrick Tahney** be paid Three dollars for Building a Stove Chimney in School House in Sub District (No.6) and Charge to Building Fund of Barker District.

On motion the Board adjourned to meet at **A. J. Wilmoths** old Store house on the 12th day of Feb 1876.

Joseph Teter President
J. B. Godwin Sect Bd. Ed.

At a meeting of the Board of Education of Barker Dist Barbour County W. Va. held at **R. A. McCutcheons** Store house on the **26 day of Feb 1876** the Following members presant **Joseph Teter**

President, **W. W. Jones, R. A. McCutcheon** and **J. B. Godwin** Sectary and the following buisiness Done Viz.

1st

J. M. Godwin this day presented a certificate from the Trustee of Sub Dist (No.13) Showing that he is Entitled to the sum of Fifty Six dollars for two months Teaching school in said Sub Dist the same is allowed and it is ordered that a draft be drawen in his favour for the same payable out of Teachers fund of said Dist.

2nd

W. A. Street this day presented an order from the Trustee of Sub Dist No.5 showing that he is entitled to the sum of Thirty dollars for one months teaching in said Dist., The same is allowed and it is ordered that a draft be drawen in his favour payable out of Teachers fund allotted to said District.

W. A. Gant this day presented an order from the Trustee of Sub District No.7 entitling him to the sum of Twenty Eight dollars for one months teaching school in said dist and it is ordered that a draft be drawen in his favour for the same payable out of the Teachers fund of said Dist.

W. W. Teter this day presented a certificate showing that he is Entitled to the sum of Thirty dollars for one month Teaching School in Sub Dist (No.6) the same is allowed and it is ordered that a draft be drawen in his favour for the same payable out of Teachers fund of said Sub Dist.

J. A. Dunham this day presented a certificate from the Trustee of Sub Dist (No.15) showing that he is Entitled to the sum of Thirty dollars the same is allowed and it is ordered that a draft be drawen in his favour payable out of Teachers fund of said Dist.

W. S. Shurtleff this day presented a certificate from the Trustee of Sub Dist (No.9) Showing that he is Entitled the Sum of Thirty dollars for one months Teaching School in said Dist the same is allowed and it is ordered that a draft be drawen in his favour payable out of Teachers fund of said Dist.

C. F. Teter this day presented a certificate from the Trustee of Sub Dist No. 3 Showing that he is Entitled to the Sum of Thirty Dollars for one months Teaching School in Said Dist the same is allowed and it is ordered that a draft be drawen in his favour Payable out of Teachers fund of said Dist.

John M. Godwin this day presented from Trustee of Sub Dist No.10 an order showing that he is entitled to the sum of Twenty Dollars for one month teaching the same is allowed and it is ordered that a

94 School Board Minutes

draft be drawn in his favor for the same payable of the teachers fund of said dist.

C. V. Street this day presented a certificate from the Trustee of Sub Dist No.4 showing that she is entitled to Twenty Eight Dollars for one months teaching school in said Dist; the same is allowed and it is ordered that a draft be drawn in her favor for the same payable out of the teacher fund of said District.

B. F. Phillips this day presented an order from the trustee of Sub Dist No.8 showing that he is entitled to Fifty-six Dollars & also another of Twenty Eight dollars for teaching three months school in said Dist the same is allowed and it is ordered that an order be drawn in his favor for the same payable out of the Teachers fund of said District.

J. H. Robinson this day presented an order from the Trustee of Sub Dist No.11 showing that he is entitled to Forty Eight dollars for two months in said dist; the same is allowed and it is ordered that a draft be drawn in his favor payable out of the teachers fund of said Dist; Also for four dollars & forty cts ($4.40) for making fire and broom furnished payable out of the Building fund of said district.

W. S. Shurtleff this day presented a certificate from the Trustee of Sub Dist (No.9) showing that he is Entitled to the sum of Thirty dollars for one months Teaching School in said Dist the same is allowed and it is ordered that a draft be Drawen in his favour payable out of Teachers fund of Barker District.

Thomas Madden this day presented a certificate from the Trustee of Sub Dist (No.1) showing he is Entitled to the sum of Sixty dollars the same is allowed and it is ordered that a draft be drawn in his favour for the same payable out of Teachers fund of said Dist.

Building fund

Ordered that **F. M. White** be paid Ten dollars and twenty three cts

121 lbs. Stove casting at 6 cts	$7.26
Rail Road Freight	.60
Storage	.25
Wagon Freight	.90
	$9.00
1 Bucket	.25
1 dipper	.08
1 Coal Hod	.90
Total amount	$10.23

Ordered $8.93 that **Thomas Madden** be paid out of Building fund Eight dollars & ninety three cts. for making fires & c.

School Board Minutes 95

Ordered 8.00 & 1.00 that **V. F. Teter** be paid out of Building fund of Barker Dist. Nine dollars for making fires, Glass, dipper & furnished by him.

Ordered 2.00 that **V. H. Street** be paid Two Dollars for making fires out of Building fund of Barker Dist. Barbour County.

Ordered that **F. B. Durrett** be paid Eight dollars for building fires &c payable out of Building fund of Barker Dist.

Ordered that **J. M. Godwin** be paid Four Dollars for making fires &c payable out of Building fund of Barker Dist.

Ordered that **Wm. Cade** be paid Eleven dollars & ninety five cts for furnishing coal; payable out of Building fund of Barker District.

Ordered that **W. S. Shurtleff** be paid Four dollars for making fires; payable out of Building fund of Barker Dist.

Ordered that **Joshua Proudfoot** be paid Twelve dollars for furnishing coal Payable out of Building fund of Barker Dist.

Belington W. Va. Feb. 26th 1876

At a meeting of the Board of education of Barker Dist at Belington, Barbour Co. W. Va. The Board of Education resolved to hire a teacher for Dist No. 2.

On motion the Board adjourned to meet on the last Saturday in March, 1876 at **R. A. McCutcheons** Store at 10 o'clock A. M.

Joseph Teter

J. B. Godwin Sect Bd. Ed.

At a meeting of the Board of Education of Barker District Barbour County W. Va. held at **R. A. McCutcheons** Store on the **25th day of March 1876** the following members presant **Joseph Teter** President, **W. W. Jones, R. A. McCutcheon** and **J. B. Godwin** Sect and the following Buisiness Done

1st

W. A. Gaunt this day presented a certificate from the Trustee of Sub Dist (No.7) Showing that he is Entitled to the sum of Twenty Eight dollars for one months Teaching in said Sub Dist the same is allowed and it is ordered that a draft be drawen in his favour payable out of Teachers fund of said Sub Dist.

J. A. Dunham this day presented a certificate from the Trustee of Sub Dist (No.15) showing that he is Entitled to the sum of Thirty dollars for one months Teaching in said Dist the same is allowed and it is ordered that a draft be Drawen in his favour payable out of Teachers fund of said Dist.

B. F. Phillips this day presented a certificate from the Trustee of Sub District (No.8) Showing that he is Entitled to the sum of Twenty Eight dollars for one month Teaching School in said Dist the same is allowed and it is ordered that a draft be drawn in his favour for the same payable out of the Teachers fund of said Dist.

C. H. Street caried off a certificate that should have been Recalled in the Feb meeting but sent it back sometime ago and it shows he is Entitled to and got an order for Thirty dollars payable out of Teachers Fund allotted to Sub Dist (No.11) of Barker District.

F. B. Durrett this day presented a certificate from the Trustee of Sub Dist (No14) showing that he is Entitled to the Sum of Sixty dollars for Teaching two months in said Dist. The Same is allowed and it is ordered that a draft be drawn in his favour payable out of Teachers fund of said Dist.

Ordered that **B. F. Phillips** be paid Eight dollars for making fires 4 months in school house in Sub Dist No.8.

Ordered that **R. M. Baker** be paid Eight dollars for making fires in School Room in Sub Dist (No.12) the same is made payable out of Building fund.

Ordered that **Thomas Moran** be paid Twelve dollars for furnishing fuel to School house in Sub Dist (No.9) payable out of Building fund.

Ordered that **Hezakiat Corley** be paid four dollars for making fires in School house in Sub Dist (No.7) payable out of Building fund.

Ordered that **W. W. Teter** be paid Eight dollars for making fires and &c payable out of Building fund of Barker Dist.

Ordered that **F. M. White** be paid Two 85/100 dollars for Broom & 4 Joints 7in Stove pipe School Dist (No.7) payable out of Building fund.

Ordered that **Lewis Zirkle** be paid Twenty Seven 52/100 dollars for Coal and other necesaries furnished to school house in sub Dist No.4

Ordered that **Solomon C. Ganers** Coal houses be Received which was done and bonds is used for the same one built in Sub Dist (No.1) one in (No.2) and one in (No.3)

Ordered that **C. F. Teters** Coal house be Rec and Bonds

issued.
Ordered **Jacob Sipe** be paid for one Coal house which he built in Sub Dist (No.7) was taken and Bonds issued.
On motion adjourned to meet on the last Saturday of April next at **R. A. McCutcheon**s Store at Belington at 1 o'clock.
   Joseph Teter
     J. B. Godwin Sect Bd. Ed.

At a meeting of the Board of Education of Barker District Barbour County W. Va. held at **R. A. McCutcheon**s Store on the **29 day of April 1876** members presant **Joseph Teter** President, **W. W. Jones, R. A. McCutcheon** and **J. B. Godwin** Sect the following Buisiness Done
 R. M. Baker this day presented a certificate from the Trustee of Sub Dist (No.12) Showing that he is Entitled to the sum of Eighty Four Dollars For Four months Teaching School in said Dist the same is allowed and it is ordered that a draft be drawn in his favour for the same payable out of Teachers fund of said Dist.
 J. A. Dunham this day presented a certificate from the Trustee of Sub Dist (No.15) showing that he is Entitled to the sum of Thirty dollars for one months Teaching in said Dist the same is allowed and it is ordered that a draft be Drawn in his favour payable out of Teachers fund of said Dist.
 J. H. Robinson this day presented a certificate from the Trustee of Sub District (No.11) Showing that he is Entitled to the sum of Twenty Four dollars for one month Teaching School in said Dist The same is allowed and it is ordered that a draft be drawn in his favour for the same payable out of Teachers fund allotted to said Sub Dist and one other for the same amount and same service as teacher of Sub Dist (No.11).
 W. W. Teter this day presented a certificate from the Trustee of Sub Dist (No.6) showing that he is Entitled to the Sum of Thirty Dollars for one months Teaching in said Sub Dist the same is allowed and it is ordered that a draft be drawn in his favour payable out of Teachers fund allotted to said Sub Dist. from the Trustee of Sub Dist (No.6)
 Able Teter this day presented a certificate from the Trustee

of Sub Dist (No.6) showing that he is Entitled to the Sum of Two dollars for Coal furnished to School house in Sub Dist (No.6) ordered paid out of Building fund of Barker Dist.

J. B. Godwin this day presented a claim for Stationerys furnished to the Board for $2.50 Two 50/100 dollars ordered paid out of Building fund.

J. A. Dunham this day presented a certificate from the Trustee of Sub Dist (No.15) showing that he is Entitled to the sum of Eight dollars for making fires 4 months ordered paid out of Building fund.

C. V. Street this day Presented a certificate from the Trustee of Sub Dist (No.4) Showing that she is Entitled to the sum of Eight dollars for one months Teaching in said Sub Dist the same is allowed and it is ordered that a draft be Drawen in her favour payable out of Teachers fund of said Sub Dist.

On motion the Board adjourned to meet on the last Saturday of May next at one o'clock P.M. at **R. A. McCutcheon**s store.

Joseph Teter President
J. B. Godwin Sect Bd. Ed.

At a meeting of the Board of Education held at **R. A. McCutcheon**s on the **24th day of June 1876** and the members Presant **W. W. Jones, R. A. McCutcheon** and **J. B. Godwin** Sect the following Buisiness Done Viz

1st

Ordered that **A. V. Wilmoth** be paid Ten dollars out of the Building fund for Furnishing coal to school house in Sub Dist (No.5) ordered paid out of Building fund.

Ordered that **J. M. Ramsey** be paid one dollar for Taking the Enumeration of Sub Dist No.10 out of Building fund.

Ordered that **J. M. Cauley** be paid one dollar for taking the enumeration of Sub Dist (No.7) out of Building fund.

Ordered that **Wm. L. Parks** be paid one dollar out of Building fund for Taking the Enumeration of Sub Dist No.12 for the year 1875.

Ordered that **W. M. Biby** be paid one dollar out of Building fund for Taking the Enumeration of Sub Dist No.15.

Ordered that **A. V. Wilmoth** be paid one dollar out of Building fund for Taking the Enumeration of Sub Dist No. 5 for the year 1874.
On motion the Board adjourned to meet at **R. A. McCutcheon**s Store on the last Saturday of July next at one oclock P.M.
    Wm. W. Jones P T
     J. B. Godwin Sect Bd. Edn

At a meeting of the Board of Education at **R. A. McCutcheon**s on the **29 day of July 1876** the following members Present **Joseph Teter** President **W. W. Jones, R. A. McCutcheon** and **J. B. Godwin** Sect and the following Buisiness Done Viz
      1st
  F. S. Swick this day presented a certificate from the Trustee of Sub Dist (No.2) Showing that he is Entitled to the sum of Forty Dollars for Teaching School in said Dist the same is allowed and it is ordered that a draft be Drawn in his favour for the Same payable out of the Teachers fund allotted said Sub Dist.
  Ordered that **Wm. Cross** be paid one dollar out of Building fund for Taking the Enumeration of Sub Dist No.9 ordered Paid.
  Ordered That **Solomon Wilson** be paid Two dollars out of Building fund for Taking the Enumeration of Sub Dist (No.10) for the years 1874 & 75.
  Ordered That **J. A. Wagoner** be paid one dollar out of the Building fund for Taking the Enumeration of Sub Dist No.12 for 1876.
  On motion the Board adjourned to meet at **R. A. McCutcheon**s Store on the last Saturday of August next at 1 o'clock P.M.
    Joseph Teter President
     J. B. Godwin Sect Bd. Ed.

At a meeting of the Board of Education of Barker Dist. Barbour County W. Va. held **Aug the 25 1876** at **R. A. McCutcheon**s Store house for the purpose of settling with the Treasurer of Barbour County

School Board Minutes

and the following members present **Wm. W. Jones, R. A. McCutcheon** and **J. B. Godwin** settlement made with the following Results Viz.

Balance from settlement of 1875	$300.11
From State	830.72
From Levy	608.22
From Delinquent Land Sold	3.53
Total Teachers fund	$1742.58
Released for 1876	$5.39
Delinquent Returned for 1876	4.58
Commission on $608.	17.95
Amount of Vouchers Rec	$1634.00
Amount Due District	$80.66
Amount of Building Fund of Barker District	
Amount from Settlement of 1875	$13.40
From levy	$973.18
Amount of Vouchers Rec	$526.10
Amount of Releases & Delinquent list	$15.14
Commission	$28.74

One Bond in favor of **Randolph Coberly** for $74.79 with interest 28.42

Two Bonds in favor of **Daniel C. Wilmoth** for $88.77 Each interest 40.31 Each

One Bond in favor of **Nathan Pain** for $21.25 Interest 9.56

Balance due Dist $68.28

On motion the Board adjourned to meet on the first Monday in Sept 1876.

At a meeting of the Board of Education of Barker Dist. Barbour County W. Va. held **Sept 7, 1876** at **R. A. McCutcheons** Store the following members present **Joseph Teter** President **J. B. Godwin** the following business was done.

The balance of Teachers for the ensuing yr was fixed as follows:

No. 1 Certificate	32.00
No. 2 Certificate	30.00
No. 3 Certificate	23.00
No. 4 Certificate	15.00
No. 5 Certificate	12.00

and that persons holding professional Certificates Board of Examiners and Co. Supt. Be classed in with No. One.

Ordered that the No. of months to be taught shall be 4, in the present S. Y.

On motion of **R. A. McCutcheon** it was ordered that trustees let contracts for coal not to exceed 10 cts per and said coal to weigh eighty lb to the bushel.

Ordered that there shall be no teacher out of surplus in the treasury after the School term of 4 mos: shall have clo. The Levy for Teachers fund was laid at 4 mills on the Dollar and Building fund 4 mills on the one dollar.

Ordered that **F. L. Swick** be paid twenty (20) Dollars for one months teaching School in Sub Dist No.2 and was drawn in his favor.

It was Ordered that **J. B. Godwin** be paid fourteen (14) Dollars for taking enumeration of Youths and a draft was drawn in his favor on Sheriff (Youths of Barker Dist.)

Ordered that **C. V. Street** be paid Eight (8) dollars for Teaching in Sub Dist. No.4 and a draft was drawn in her favor.

Ordered that **F. L. Swick** be paid five (5) Dollars for making fires and sweeping School house in Sub Dist No.2 and a draft was drawn in his favor payable out of Building fund.

Ordered that **F. L. Swick** be paid Twenty (20) dollars for Teaching one months school in Sub Dist No.2 and a draft was drawn in his favor.

Ordered that **R. G. Thorn** be paid one (1) dollar for taking enumeration of Youths in Sub Dist No.2 a draft drawn in his favor.

On motion Board adjourned to meet on the last Saturday October 1876.

Wm. W. Jones President
    Jacob B. Godwin Sec .Bd. Ed. B. D.

At a called meeting of the Board of Education of Barker Dist. held at **R. A. McCutcheon**s Store on the **7 day of Nov 1876** members present **Joseph Teter, W. W. Jones, R. A. McCutcheon** and **J. B. Godwin** and the following Buisness done.

Ordered that **Albert Rhorabaugh** be paid Twelve Dollars for Furnishing 125 bushels of Coal to School house in Sub Dist (No.12) payable out of Building fund of Barker Dist.

Ordered that **Albert Rhorabough** be paid fifteen 50cts Dollars for Repairing School house in Sub Dist (No.12) payable out of Building fund of Barker District.

Ordered that **R. A. McCutcheon** be paid one dollar 68 c out of building fund of Barker Dist.

Ordered that **R. M. Godwin** and **Solomon Yock** be and is hereby Transfered from Sub Dist (No.13) to Sub Dist (No.10) for one year.

On motion the Board adjourned to meet on the second Saturday of Dec next at one o'clock.
      Joseph Teter
       J. B. Godwin Sectary Bd. Ed.

Dist of Barker **Dec 9th, 1876**

At a meeting of the Board of Education of Barker Dist. Barbour Co. W. Va. held at **R. A. McCutcheon**s Store; the following members present **Joseph Teter,** President **W. W. Jones, R. A. McCutcheon** The following Business was done.

Ordered that **W. S. Shurtleff** be paid Thirty two (32) dollars for one months teaching School in Sub Dist No.10 payable out of Teachers fund of Barker Dist and a Draft was drawn in his favor.

Ordered that **B. F. Phillips** be paid Thirty (30) dollars for teaching one month in Sub Dist No.14 Barker Dist payable out of Teachers fund and a draft was drawn in his favor.

Ordered that **C. V. Street** be paid Thirty 30 Dollars for teaching in Sub Dist No.9 payable out of Teachers fund of Barker District and draft drawn.

Ordered that **A. H. Teter** be paid Thirty two (32) Dollars for Teaching School in Sub Dist No.12 payable out of Teachers fund of Barker Dist of Barbour Co. and a draft was drawn in his favour.

Ordered that **F. B. Durrett** be paid Thirty two (32) dollars for

Teaching School in Sub Dist No.1 payable out of Teaching fund of Barker Dist and a draft was drawn in his favor.

Ordered that **James H. Thomas** use of **R. A. McCutcheon** fifty cent also one for Thirty cents for No.10 payable out of Building fund of Barker Dist.

Ordered that **R. A. McCutcheon** be paid one 35/100 Dollars for Dist No.2 payable out of Building fund Barker Dist.

Ordered that **R. A. McCutcheon** be paid fifty cents payable out of Building fund.

Ordered that **E. P. Cross** be paid Two dollars for making fires payable out of Building fund.

Ordered that **W. M. Poe** be paid Ten dollars for furnishing fuel in Sub Dist No.11 payable out of Building fund.

Ordered that **James Coffman** be paid Thirty dollars for teaching in Sub Dist No.13 payable out of Teachers fund also an order for Two dollars for making fires payable out of Building fund.

Ordered that **E. Buckey** be paid Eight 20/100 dollars payable out of Building fund.

Ordered that **J. B. Godwin** be paid Ten dollars for annual report of Board; payable out of Building fund of Barker District, Barbour Co. W. Va.

Ordered that **J. M. Good** be paid one 75/100 Dollar for repairs payable out of Building fund.

Ordered that **Abel Teter** be paid Two 40/100 Dollars for fuel furnished in Sub Dist No. 6 payable out of Building fund.

Ordered that **B. B. Durrett** be paid Nine 85/100 Dollars for fuel furnished in No. 3 and other stationary payable out of Building fund.

Ordered that **Wm J. Right** for use of **L. C. Elliot** Eight 75/100 Dollars for furnishing fuel in Sub Dist No.15 payable out of Building fund.

Ordered that **R. A. McCutcheon** be paid Twenty five cts. payable out of Building fund.

Ordered that **Granvill Stalknaker** be paid One Dollar for taking enumeration in Sub Dist No.8 payable out of Building fund.

Ordered that **W. A. Street** be paid Thirty two dollars for one months teaching in Sub Dist No.5 payable out of Teachers fund.

Ordered that **W. A. Street** be paid two dollars for making fires in Sub Dist No. 5 payable out of Building fund.

On motion the Board adjourned to meet the 2d Saturday in

School Board Minutes

January 1877.
Joseph Teter President
J. B. Godwin Sec'y Bd. Ed.

At a meeting of the Board of Education of Barker Dist. Barbour held at **R. A. McCutcheon**s Store on the **13 day of Jan. 1877** The members present **Joseph Teter,** President **W. W. Jones, R. A. McCutcheon** and **J. B. Godwin** Sect and the following Buisiness done Viz

1st

B. F. Phillips this day Presented to the Board a certificate from the Trustee of Sub Dist (No.14) showing that he is entitled to the sum of Thirty Dollars for one months Teaching the same is allowed and it is ordered that a draft be drawn in his favour for the same payable out of Teachers fund of Barker Dist.

Ordered that **W. S. Moore** be paid Five dollars for Repairs to school house in Sub Dist No.9 allowed.

Ordered that **S. T. Hollen** be paid Nine dollars and 35/100 payable out of Building fund and Allowed.

Ordered that **Susan Street** be paid Eight dollars for imitation of those that teaches school in Barker Dist as the said **Susan Street** claims to be Entitled to the sum of Eight dollars the same is allowed and payable out of any money in the hands of the Sheriff of Barbour County belonging to the Teachers fund of Barker Dist. Sub Dist No.13.

Ordered that **W. A. Street** be allowed for one month Teaching Thirty Two Dollars payable out of Teachers Fund of Barker Dist Barbour County.

Ordered that **James Coffman** be paid Thirty dollars for one months Teaching in Sub Dist (No.13) payable out of Teachers Fund of Barker Dist.

Ordered that **Laben Moore** be paid Thirty Two $32.75/100 dollars for Repairs and lumber the same is allowed payable out of Building fund of Barker Dist.

Ordered that **E. P. Cross** be paid Two dollars for making fires in school house in Sub Dist (No.9) payable out of the Building fund.

Ordered that **R. A. McCutcheon** be paid 40 cts for one Broom payable out of Building fund.

School Board Minutes

Ordered that **J. M. Ramsey** be paid Seven 90/100 dollars for Furnishing Coal to school house in Sub Dist (No.13) the same payable out of Building fund.

C. F. Teter this day presented a certificate from the Trustee of Sub Dist (No.12) showing him to be Entitled to the sum of Thirty Two Dollars it is allowed and it is ordered that a draft be drawn in his favour payable Teachers fund.

Ordered **Wm. Bolton** be paid $8.31 Eight 31/100 dollars for fuel Furnished to School house in Sub Dist (No.14) payable out of Building fund.

Ordered that **Marion Right** for use of **R. A. McCutcheon** be paid Two dollars for Building fires in school house in Sub Dist (No.15) the same is allowed.

Ordered that **C. V. Street** this day be allowed Thirty dollars for one month Teaching School in Sub Dist (No.9) the same is made payable out of Teachers fund.

Ordered that **W. S. Shurtleff** this day be allowed Thirty Two Dollars for one month Teaching School in Sub Dist (No.10) the same is allowed and made payable out of Teachers fund.

Ordered that **W. A. Gaunt** be paid Thirty dollars for one month Teaching School in Sub Dist (No.7) the same is allowed and made payable out of Teachers fund of Barker District.

S. R. Phillips this day presented a certificate showing that She is Entitled to the sum of Thirty Dollars for one months Teaching School in Sub Dist (No.11) the same is allowed and made payable out of Teachers fund of Barker Dist.

Ordered that **R. L. Tallman** be paid Thirty Two dollars for one month Teaching school in Sub Dist (No.4) the same is allowed and made payable out of the Teachers fund of Barker Dist.

Ordered that Miss **Nora Moore** be paid Thirty Two dollars for one months Teaching School in Sub Dist (No.2) the same is allowed and made payable out of the Teachers Fund of Barker Dist.

Ordered that **J. A. Dunham** be paid Thirty Two dollars for one months Teaching in Sub Dist (No.15) the same is allowed and made payable out of the Teachers fund of Barker Dist.

Ordered that **Thomas Madden** be paid Thirty Two dollars for one month Teaching School in Sub Dist (No.6) the same is allowed and made payable out of the Teachers fund of Barker Dist in Barbour County W. Va.

On motion the Board adjourned to meet on the second Saturday of Feb. Next at 1 o'clock P.M.

School Board Minutes

Joseph Teter President
J. B. Godwin Sectary B. E.

At a Special meeting of the Board of Education held on the **20 day of Jan 1877** at **R. A. McCutcheon**s Store members present **Joseph Teter,** President **W. W. Jones, R. A. McCutcheon** and **J. B. Godwin** Sect the following Buisiness Done Viz
1st
Ordered that the clerk be authorized to Receive from the hands of the Sheriff of Barbour County one note against **Joseph Teter** calling for Two Hundred dollars and the Sheriff is by this order Released from any obligation to the Board of Education on account of said note.

Ordered that **R. A. McCutcheon** be paid Seven 55/100 dollars payable at Building fund of Barker Dist.

Ordered that **R. A. McCutcheon** be paid 70c out of Building fund of Barker Dist.

Joseph Teter President
J. B. Godwin Sect B. Ed.

At a meeting of the Board of Education in Barker District in the County of Barbour and state of W. Va. held on the **Tenth (10th) day of February 1877** at **R. A. McCutcheon**s Store house and the members present **Joseph Teter** (Pres), **W. W. Jones, R. A. McCutcheon** and **J. B. Godwin** Sect and following Buisiness was Transacted Viz.

F. B. Durrett this day presented a certificate from the Trustee of Sub Dist (No.1) Showing that he is Entitled to the sum of Thirty Two Dollars for one months Teaching in said Sub Dist the same is allowed and it is ordered that a draft be drawn in his favour for the same payable out of the School fund of said Dist.

S. R. Phillips this day presented to this Board a certificate from the Trustee of Sub Dist (No.11) showing that she is Entitled to the sum of Thirty dollars for one months Teaching in said Sub Dist the same is allowed and it is ordered that a draft be Drawen in Her favour for the same payable out of Teachers fund of said Barker Dist.

J. A. Dunham This day presented a certificate from The Trustee of Sub District (No.15) Showing that he is Entitled to the sum of Thirty Two dollars for one months Teaching School in said Sub Dist the same is allowed and it is ordered that a draft be drawn in his favour for the same payable out of Teachers fund allotted to said Sub Dist

C. F. Teter this day presented to the Board a certificate from the Trustee of Sub Dist (No 12) showing that he is Entitled to the Sum of (32.00) Thirty Two dollars for one months Teaching in said Sub Dist the same is allowed and it is ordered that a draft be drawn in his favour for the same payable out of Teachers fund allotted to said Sub Dist.

Miss **C. V. Street** This day presented a certificate to the Board Showing that she is Entitled to the sum of (30.00)Thirty Dollars for one months Teaching in Sub Dist (No.9) the same is allowed and it is ordered that a draft be Drawen in her favour for the same payable out of the Teachers fund of said Dist.

Jonathan Hathaway this day presented a certificate to the Board from the Trustee of Sub Dist (No.3) showing that he is Entitled to the sum of Sixty Four Dollars for Two months Teaching school in said Dist the same is allowed and it is ordered that a draft be drawn in his favour for the same payable out of Teachers fund of said Dist.

W. W. Teter this day presented a certificate to the Board from The Trustee of Sub District (No.8) showing that he is Entitled to the sum of Sixty Four Dollars for Two months Teaching School in Barker Dist the same is allowed and it is ordered that a Draft be Drawen in his favour for the same payable out of Teachers fund of Said Dist.

James Coffman this day presented a certificate from the Trustee of Sub Dist (No 13) Showing that he is Entitled to the Sum of Thirty Dollars for one months Teaching School in said Sub Dist the same is allowed and it is ordered that a draft be drawn in his favour for the same payable out of Teachers fund allotted to said Dist.

Miss **Nora Moore** this day presented a certificate from the Trustee of Sub Dist (No.2) Showing that she is entitled to thirty two Dollars and the same was allowed and ordered that a draft be drawn in her favor payable out of Teachers fund of said Dist.

W. A. Gaunt this day presented a certificate from the Trustee of Sub Dist (No.7) showing that he is entitled to Thirty dollars for one months teaching; the same was allowed and ordered that a draft be drawn in his favor for the same payable out of Teachers fund of said district.

W. A. Street this day presented a certificate from The Trustee of Sub District (No.5) showing that he is entitled to Thirty Two dollars for one months teaching the same is allowed and ordered that a draft be drawn in his favor payable out of Teachers fund of said dist.

W. S. Shurtleff this day presented from the trustee of Sub Dist (No 10) showing that he is entitled to Thirty two dollars; the same is allowed and it is ordered that a draft be drawn in his favor payable out of Teachers fund allotted to said District.

Thomas Madden this day presented a certificate from the Trustee showing that he is entitled to Thirty two dollars for one months teaching in sub dist (No.6) the same was allowed & it is ordered that a draft be drawn in his favor payable out of the Teachers fund of said Dist.

W. A. Gaunt this day presented a certificate from trustee of sub dist (No.7) showing that he is entitled to the sum of Thirty dollars; the same is allowed and it is ordered that a draft be drawn in his favor payable out of Teachers fund of said District.

B. F. Phillips this day presented a certificate from The Trustee of Sub District No.14 showing that he is entitled to the sum of Thirty dollars the same was allowed and it was ordered that a draft be Drawn in his favor payable out of Teachers fund of said District.

F. B. Durrett this day presented a certificate from the Trustee of Sub Dist No 1 showing that he is entitled to Thirty Two Dollars; the same is allowed and it is ordered that a draft be drawn in his favor for the same payable out of Teachers fund of said District.

Ordered that **J. W. Skidmore** be paid Three 10/100 Dollars out of Building fund for repairs on school house in Sub Dist No.2 of Barker District.

Ordered that **J. Y. Booth** be paid Ten dollars out of Building fund for fuel for Barker Dist; Sub Dist No. One.

Ordered that **W. A. Street** be paid Four 30/100 Dollars for making fires &c out of Sub Dist No.5 out of Building fund.

Ordered that **J. S. Ramsey** be paid 75/100 Dollars for removing one dead horse from lot in Sub Dist No.10 out of Building fund.

Ordered that **G. M. Shomo** be paid four 86/100 Dollars for repairs to school house in sub district No. 7 out of Building fund.

Ordered that **E. P. Cross** be paid Two Dollars out of Building fund for making fires in Sub Dist No.9

School Board Minutes

Ordered that **R. A. McCutcheon** be paid 25/100 Dollars out of Building fund for poker for School house in Sub Dist No.10

Ordered that **B. B. Durrett** be paid One Dollar out of Building fund for repairing chimney in Sub Dist No.3

Ordered that **W. W. Teter** be paid one 45/100 Dollar out of Building fund for Stove pipe, diper, &c.

Ordered that **Abel Teter** be paid Eleven 50/100 Dollars out of Building fund for furnishing fuel in Sub District No.8

Ordered that **A. V. Wilmoth** be paid Nine 50/100 Dollars out of Building fund for fuel furnished Sub Dist No.5

Ordered that **Hubert Shomo** be paid four Dollars out of Building fund for making fires in sub Dist No.2

Ordered that **R. M. Right** for use of **R. A. McCutcheon** be paid two Dollars out of Building fund for fire making in Sub Dist No. 15

Ordered that **Wm. England** be paid Two 50/100 Dollars out of Building fund for fuel furnished Sub Dist No.10

Both included in one order

Ordered that **James England** be paid Two 50/100 Dollars out of Building fund for fuel furnished Sub District No. 10

Ordered that **Solomon Coffman** be paid Eleven 20/100 Dollars out of Building fund for fuel furnished in Sub Dist No.7

Ordered that **R. A. McCutcheon** be paid 55/100 Dollars out of Building fund for Bucket &c furnished Sub Dist No.6

Ordered that **W. S. Shurtleff** be paid Eight Dollars out of Building fund for making fires in Sub Dist No.10

At a meeting of the Board of Education of Barker District at **R. A. McCutcheon**'s Store **Feb 10, 1877**; It is ordered that the Treasurer of Barker District, Barbour Co. W. Va. pay no money to **W. J. Schoonover, Daniel C. Wilmoth** nor to **Lorenzo Denton** or their assignees, until an action now pending in the Circuit Court of Barbour Co on the same claim is decided.

Ordered By the Board of Education that the usual fee be paid **Wm T. Ice** for defense of the suit brought by **Isaac W. Wilmoth** vs Board of Ed. of Barker Dist. and the Secretary of our Board is hereby ordered to issue a note of Thirty Dollars to **Wm. T. Ice**.

On motion the Board adjourned to meet at Belington on the 10 of March 1877.
    Joseph Teter President
    J. B. Godwin Sect B. E.

  At a meeting of the Bd of Ed of Barker Dist Barbour Co. W. Va., held **March 10, 1877** The following members present President **Joseph Teter,** Commissioners **W. W. Jones & R. A. McCutcheon;** The following Business done Viz.

  Miss **Nora Ware** this day presented a certificate from the Trustee of Sub Dist No.2 Showing that she is entitled to Thirty Two Dol; the same is allowed and it was ordered that a draft be drawn in her favor for the same payable out of Teachers fund.

  W. S. Shurtleff this day presented a certificate from the Trustee of Sub Dist No.11 showing that he is entitled to $26.00 Twenty Six Dollars that same was allowed and it is ordered that a draft be drawn in his favor for the same payable out of Teachers fund.

  Thomas Madden this day presented a certificate from Trustee of Sub District No.6 showing that he is Entitled to Thirty Two dollars for one months Teaching School in said Sub Dist the same is allowed and it is ordered that a draft be drawen in his favour for the same payable out of Teachers fund.

  B. F. Phillips this day presented a certificate from the Trustee of Sub Dist No 14 showing that he was entitled Twenty Four Dol; the same is allowed and it is ordered that a draft be drawn in his favour for the same payable out of Teachers fund.

  Ordered that **B. F. Phillips** be paid Seven 75/100 Dollars out of Building fund for making fires in Sub Dist No. 14.

  C. V. Street this day presented a certificate from the Trustee of Sub Dist No.9 showing that she is Entitled to Twenty four Dollars; the same is allowed and it is ordered that a draft be drawn in her favor for the same payable out of Teachers fund.

  J. A. Dunham this day presented a certificate from Trustee for Sub District No.15, showing that he is Entitled to Thirty Two Dollars; the same is allowed and it is ordered that a draft be drawn in his favor for the same payable out of the Teachers fund.

  S. R. Phillips this day presented a certificate from Trustee in

School Board Minutes 111

Sub Dist No 11 showing that she is entitled to Thirty Dollars; the same was allowed and it is ordered that a draft be drawn in her favor for the same payable out of the Teachers fund.

W. W. Teter this day presented a certificate from Trustee in Sub Dist No.8 showing that he is entitled to Thirty two Dollars; the same was allowed and it was ordered that a draft be drawn in his favor payable out of Teachers fund.

W. A. Street this day presented a certificate from Trustee of Sub Dist No.5 showing that he is entitled to Twenty Six Dollars; the same was allowed and it was ordered that a draft be drawn in his favor for the same payable out of Teachers fund.

Ordered that **W. A. Street** be paid Two Dollars out of Building fund for making fires in Sub Dist No. 5

Ordered that **Randolph Coberly** be paid Seven 60/100 Dollars out of Building fund for Building fires in Sub Dist No. 12

James Coffman this day presented a certificate for 19 days from Trustee in Sub Dist No.13 showing that he is entitled to Twenty four Dollars; the same is allowed, and it was ordered that a draft be drawn in his favor for the same payable out of the Teachers fund.

Ordered that **James Coffman** be paid Six Dollars out of Building fund for making fires &c.

Ordered that **Thos. Moran** be paid Eight 40/100 Dollars out of Building fund for furnishing fuel.

Ordered that **S. R. Phillips** be paid seven 50/100 Dollars out of Building fund for making fires &c.

Ordered that **Lewis Zirkle** be paid ten 60/100 Dollars out of Building fund for furnishing fuel in Sub Dist No.4

Ordered that **R. A. McCutcheon** be paid Nine 50/100 Dollars out of Building fund for lower band of Stove, Sub Dist No.9

Ordered that **Thomas Madden** be paid seven 80/100 Dollars out of Building fund for making fires &c.

Ordered that **E. P. Cross** be paid one 85/100 Dollars out of Building fund for making fire &c.

Ordered that **R. G. Thorn** be paid 90/100 Dollars out of Building fund for wood, Stove pipe, &c.

Ordered that **Jonathan Hathaway** be paid Eight 30/100 Dollars out of Building fund for making fire, Broom, &c.

Ordered that **Hubert Shomo** be paid Three 63/100 Dollars out of Building fund for making fires, &c.

Ordered that **W. A. Gaunt** be paid Seven 80/100 Dollars out of Building fund for making fires, &c.

Ordered that **F. B. Durrett** be paid Eight Dollars out of Building fund for making fires, &c.

W. W. Teter this day presented a certificate from Trustee of Sub Dist No.8 Showing that he is entitled to Twenty one 85/100 Dollars; the same was allowed and it was ordered that a draft be drawn in his favor for the same payable out of Teachers fund.

Ordered that **W. W. Teter** be paid Seven 42/100 out of Building fund for making fires &c.

Ordered that **J. A. Dunham** be paid four dollars out of Building fund for making fires &c.

Ordered that **R. L. Tallman** be paid one 65/100 Dollars out of Building fund for repairs, stationery, &c.

Ordered that **R. L. Tallman** be paid Seven 63/100 Dollars out of Building fund for making fires &c.

Ordered that **Wm. J. Right** be paid 70/100 Dollars out of Building fund for fuel.

Thomas Madden this day presented a certificate from Trustee of Sub Dist No.6 showing that he is entitled to Twenty Six Dollars; the same is allowed and it was ordered that a draft be drawn in his favor for the same payable out of the Teachers fund.

Miss **Nora Moore** this day presented a certificate from Trustee of Sub District No.2 showing that she is entitled to Twenty Six Dollars; the same was allowed and it was ordered that a draft be drawn in her favor for the same payable out of Teachers fund.

F. B. Durrett this day presented a certificate from Trustee of Sub Dist No 1 showing that he is entitled Twenty Six Dollars; the same was allowed and a draft was drawn in his favor for the same payable out of Teachers fund.

C. F. Teter this day presented a certificate from Trustee of Sub Dist No.12 showing that he is entitled to Twenty Six Dollars; the same was allowed and it was ordered that a draft be drawn in his favor for the same payable out of the Teachers fund.

R. L. Tallman this day presented a certificate from Trustee of Sub District No.4, showing that he was entitled to Sixty four dollars; the same was allowed and it was ordered that a draft be drawn in his favor for the same payable out of the Teachers fund.

Jonathan Hathaway this day presented a certificate from Trustee of Sub Dist No 3 showing that he is entitled to the sum of Thirty Two Dollars; the same is allowed and it is ordered that a draft be drawn in his favor payable out of Teachers fund.

R. L. Tallman this day presented a certificate from Trustee in Sub Dist No.4 showing that he is entitled to Twenty Six Dollars; the same is allowed and it is ordered that a draft be drawn in his favor payable out of Teachers fund.

J. A. Dunham this day presented a certificate from Trustee of Sub Dist No.15 showing that he is entitled to Twenty Six Dollars; the same is allowed and it is ordered that a draft be drawn in his favor for the same payable out of teachers fund.

S. R. Phillips this day presented a certificate from Trustee in Sub Dist No.11 showing that he is entitled to Twenty four Dollars; The same is allowed, and it was ordered that a draft be drawn in his favor for the same payable out of the Teachers fund.

W. A. Gaunt this day presented a certificate from Trustee of Sub Dist No.7 showing that he is entitled to Twenty Four Dollars; the same is allowed and it is ordered that a draft be drawn in his favor for the same payable out of Teachers fund.

Jonathan Hathaway this day presented a certificate from Trustee in Sub Dist No.3 showing that he is entitled to Twenty Six Dollars; The same is allowed, and it was ordered that a draft be drawn in his favor for the same payable out of Teachers fund.

On motion the Board adjourned to meet at Belington on the first Sat. in April 1877.

Joseph Teter President
J. B. Godwin Sect. B. Ed.

At a meeting of the Board of Education of Barker Dist., Barbour Co. W. Va., held at **R. A. McCutcheons August 23, 1877,** The following members present; President **Joseph Teter,** and **R. A. McCutcheon.** The object of the meeting being settlement with the Sheriff and the result is as follows:

State school fund	$906.89
From District Levy	940.32
From Settlement of 1876	80.66
From other sources	<u>1.25</u>
	1929.12

114 School Board Minutes

Releases	Cr. 2.68
Releases	Cr. 3.02
Delinquent list	Cr. 10.78
Commission	27.72
Amount of Vouchers	$1928.05
Balance due District	$1.07

1876 Amount of Building fund

Balance from last year	$68.28
From District Levy	940.32
	1008.60
Releases	2.68
Releases	3.02
Delinquent list	10.78
Commission	$27.71
Amount of Vouchers and old Tax receipts	$1003.51
Balance due District	$5.09

A list of Tax receipts received from the Sheriff **J. W. Talbott** and credited to him

Year
1870 One receipt for $21.00 vs. **Berlin & Huffman**
1870 One receipt for   6.30 vs. **F. Berlin**
1869 One receipt for   6.75 vs same
1869 One receipt for   22.50 vs **Berlin & Huffman**
1873 Part of one receipt 19.50 out of $40.50 **Berlin & Huffman.** Total amount due 76.05 to **J. W. Talbott**.

Ordered that **J. B. Godwin** be paid Nine Dollars out of Building fund for part of salary as Secretary and also Two 50/100 for stationeries furnished the Board.

Ordered that **Joseph Teter** be paid Eight Dollars for taking enumeration of 4 Sub Districts in Barker District, out of Building fund.

Ordered that **J. B. Godwin** be paid Twelve Dollars for taking enumeration of six Sub Districts in Barker District payable out of Building fund.

On motion the Board adjourned sine die.

Joseph Teter President
J. B. Godwin Sect B. E.

At a meeting of the Board of Education held at **Dr. Harvyes** office **Sept the 6 1877** for the purpose of organization and they organized by the Election of **J. B. Godwin** as Sectary and the following members Present **Joseph Teter** President **Phillip Ramsey & Henry Barte** and the following Buisiness done.

The Regulation of Teachers Salaries To Wit
A Teacher with a Certificate of Grade No. 1 to Receive $29.00
No. 2 to Receive   25.00   No. 3 to Receive   18.00
No. 4 to Receive   14.00   No. 5 to Receive   10.00

Next in order was to appoint Three Trustees in Each Sub Dist.

Sub Dist No.1	Simon Swick	3 years
	Iasiah Wilson	2 years
	Wm. Steerman	1 year
Sub Dist No.2	J. B. Teter	3 years
	Henry Keiser	2 years
	Elihue Ware	1 year
Sub Dist No.3	Francis Hathaway	3 years
	Joshua Proudfoot	2 years
	M. Edmonds	1 year
Sub Dist No.4	Alpheus Wilson	3 years
	Melvile O Bryan	2 years
	L. D. Kerr	1 year
Sub Dist No.5	A. V. Wilmoth	3 years
	R. L. Tallman	2 years
	R. T. George	1 year
Sub Dist No.6	Jesse Teter	3 years
	A. B. Wilmoth	2 years
	Jas Simpson	1 year
Sub Dist No.7	Milton Hart	3 years
	Joseph Elbon	2 years
	N.P. Recter	1 year
Sub Dist No.8	F. T. Elliott	3 years
	R. A. McCutcheon	2 years

116 School Board Minutes

	G. Stalnaker	1 year
Sub Dist No.9	Simpson George	3 years
	Hamilton Funk	2 years
	Wm Cross	1 year
Sub Dist No.10	Adam Coonts	3 years
	J. N. Ramsey	2 years
	Solomon Wilson	1 year
Sub Dist No.11	C. B. Carter	3 years
	Israel Poling	2 years
	S. B. Poe	1 year
Sub Dist No.12	Lewis Corley	3 years
	Joshua Bartlett	2 years
	Thomas Holbert	1 year
Sub Dist No.13	Alpheus Moore	3 years
	J. C. Right	2 years
	Albert Price	1 year
Sub Dist No.14	Jacob Mclain	3 years
	Himan Rinehart	2 years
	Henry Ridgway	1 sworn in
Sub Dist No.15	W. J. Right	3 years
	Laben Moore	2 years
	John Cade	1 year

Ordered that **W. M. Bibey** be paid one Dollar for taking the enumeration of Sub Dist No.15 out of Building fund of Barker Dist Barbour Co.

Ordered that **John Right** be paid one dollar for the same.

On motion the Board adjourned to meet on the 15th of Sept at Belington at one o'clock.

Joseph Teter President
J. B. Godwin Sect B. E.

School Board Minutes 117

At a meeting of the Board of Education of Barker Dist Barbour County W.Va. held on the **15th day of Sept 1877** at Belington the Following Members Present **Phillip Ramsey, Henry Barte & J. B. Godwin** Sect and the following Buisiness Done Viz.

1st

It is ordered that the Sheriff of Barbour Collect 35 cts on each one hundred Dollars of Taxable Property of Barker Dist for Teachers fund and also 25 cents on the one Hundred dollars for the Building fund.

2nd

Ordered that the Schools be kept in operation for four months in Each Sub District.

3d

Ordered by the Board that the fuel furnished is not to Exceed Ten Dollars in any Sub Dist at the School house therein & the same be let to the lowest bidder said fuel to be advertised at some publick place in the Sub Dist.

4th

Ordered that **J. M. Ramsey** be paid one dollar for Taking the Enumeration in Sub Dist for the year 1877.

On motion **Wm. R. Moore** was appointed Trustee in Sub Dist No.10 in Room of **Adam Coonts.**

On motion the Board adjourned to meet on the 13 day of Nov. next at 1 o'clock P.M.

Henry Barte President Protem
J. B. Godwin Sect Bd. Ed.

At a meeting of the Board of Education of Barker Dist Barbour County W.Va. on the **3d day of Nov 1877** the Following Members Present **Joseph Teter** President, **Phillip Ramsey, Henry Barte & J. B. Godwin** Sect.

1st

Ordered that **E. Buckey** be paid one 55/100 dollars for Door lock, Broom, Putty, Glass, Nails &c Payable out of Building fund of Barker Dist.

2d

Ordered that **Daniel Sipe** be paid one dollar for Repairs Done to School House in Sub Dist No.5 payable out of Building fund of

118   School Board Minutes

Barker Dist.

3d

Ordered that **Able Teter** be paid Ten dollars for fuel furnished in Sub Dist (No.6) Payable out of Building fund of Barker Dist.

4th

Ordered that **J. B. Godwin** be paid Ten dollars for Making the annual Report of the Board of Education of Barker Dist payable out of Building fund &c

On motion of the President it was ordered that **Alexander Talbott** be appointed Trustee in Sub Dist No.5 in Room of **A. V. Wilmoth**.

On motion to adjourn to meet on the 3 Saturday of November at 10 o'clock A.M.

Joseph Teter President
J. B. Godwin Sect

At a meeting of the Bd of Ed of Barker Dist Barbour Co. W. Va. Met at Belington on the **15th day of Dec, 1877** the following members present **Joseph Teter, Phillip Ramsey, Henry Barte & J. B. Godwin** Sect and the Following Business done Viz.

1st

W.S. Shurtleff this day presented to the Board showing that he is entitled to the sum of Twenty Nine Dollars for one months Teaching School in Sub Dist No.10 the same is allowed and it is ordered that a draft be drawn in his favour for the same payable out of Teachers fund of Barker Dist Barbour Co. W.Va.

John F. Hunt presented to the Board a certificate from the Trustee of Sub Dist No.12 showing that he is entitled to the sum of Eighteen dollars for one month Teaching School in said Dist the same is allowed and it is ordered that a draft be drawn in his favor for the same payable out of Teachers fund of Barker Dist, Barbour Co. W. Va.

C. F. Teter this day presented a certificate to the Board showing that he is Entitled to the sum of Twenty Nine Dollars for one month Teaching in Sub Dist (No.2) the Same is allowed and it is ordered that a draft be Drawen in his favour payable out of Teachers fund of Barker Dist, Barbour Co. W. Va. also Four Dollars for Sweeping and making fires for Two months payable out of Building fund of Barker Dist.

M. E. Harris this day presented a certificate to the Board from the Trustees of Sub Dist (No 9) showing that she is Entitled to the sum of Twenty-Nine dollars for one month Teaching in said Sub Dist; the same is allowed and it is ordered that a draft be drawn in her favour for the same payable out of Teachers fund.

J. A. Hillyard this day presented to the Board a certificate from the Trustees of Sub Dist (No.7) showing that he is Entitled to the sum of Twenty Five Dollars for one months Teaching School in said Sub Dist the same is allowed and it is ordered that a draft be Drawen in his favour for the same payable out of Teachers fund.

Thomas Madden this day presented to the Board a certificate from the Trustees of Sub District (No.4) showing that he is Entitled to the sum of Twenty Nine dollars for one months Teaching School in said Sub Dist the same is allowed and it is ordered that a draft be drawn in his favor for the same payable out of the Teachers fund of Barker Dist.

C. F. Teter this day presented to the Board a certificate from the Trustees of Sub Dist (No 2) showing that she is Entitled to the sum of Twenty Nine dollars for one months Teaching in said Sub Dist the same is allowed and it is ordered that a draft be drawn in her favour for the same payable out of Teachers fund of Barker Dist, Barbour Co. W. Va.

A. B. Moore this day presented to the Board a certificate from the Trustees of Sub Dist (No.15) showing that he is Entitled to the sum of Twenty Nine dollars for one months Teaching in said Dist the same was allowed and it was ordered that a draft be drawn in his favor payable out of Teachers fund of Barker Dist, Barbour Co. W. Va.

Ordered 6.62 That **William Corley** be paid Six 62/100 dollars for 115 bushels Coal Furnished to School house in Sub Dist No.7 payable out of Building Fund of Barker Dist Barbour Co. W. Va.

Ordered $15.43 That **E. Buckey** be paid out of building fund 15 43/100 dollars for Top and middle Barrel of Stove & 3 Joints Stove pipe (No.6)

Ordered .40c That **E. Buckey** be paid out of Building for 1 Broom & one Cap 40 cts (No.10)

Ordered $4.00 that **Lloyd Davis** be paid Four Dollars for one hundred bushels Coal payable out of Building fund Barker Dist.

Ordered $9.50 That **Randolph Coberly** be paid 9 50/100

dollars out of Building fund for Fuel Furnished Sub Dist No.12

Ordered $2.60 That **Thomas Madden** be paid 2 60/100 dollars for making fires & sweeping, 1 Tin Bucket & 1 cup payable out of Building fund.

Ordered $2.00 That **J. M. Godwin** be paid Two Dollars for sweeping & making fires.

Ordered $1.40 **Henry Warner** be paid (one) 1 40/100 dollar for Repairing &c No. 5 payable out of Building fund.

Ordered $1.50 That **Alpheus Moore** be paid one 50/100 dollar out of Building fund for Repairs to School (No.13)

Ordered $4.30 That **B. S. Jones** be paid Four 30/100 dollars for 100 bushel Coal furnished to School house Sub Dist No.11 payable out of Building fund Barker Dist, Barbour Co., W. Va.

Ordered $4.00 That **L. E. Right** be paid Four dollars for coal Furnished to School house in Sub Dist No.15 payable out of Building fund.

Ordered $5.75 That **L. D. Kerr** be paid Five 75/100 dollars for Repairs to School house in Sub Dist (No.4) payable out of Building fund, B. Dist. and Ordered Eight dollars for Furnishing fuel to School house in Sub Dist (No.4)

Ordered $8.50 That **Joshua Proudfoot** Eight 50/100 dollars for Furnishing fuel in Sub Dist (No.3) payable out of Building fund Barker Dist.

Ordered That **Wm. England Jr.** be paid Six 75/100 dollars for furnishing fuel to School house in Sub Dist (No.10) payable out of Building, Barker Dist, Barbour Co., W. Va.

Ordered 41.38 that **E. Buckey** be paid one 28/100 dollar for Broom .30, 1 Tin Bucket .65, 1 cup .08, 1 shovel .25 payable out of Building fund Sub Dist No. 13

Ordered $13.70 That **E. Buckey** be paid Thirteen 70/100 dollars out of Building fund for the following articles Viz. 1 coal hod .75, 1 Bucket .75, 1 poker .20, 14 1/4 lb Stove pipe at 12 ½ per lb 1.68, 1 Broom .25, also 2 Part of Stove 8.00, Freight 2.00, Total $13.70 for use in School house in Sub Dist No.13

Ordered $5.20 That **Francis Hathaway** be paid five 20/100 dollars out of Building fund for Repairs done to school house in Sub Dist No.3

Ordered $1.57 That **R. A. McCutcheon** be paid one 57/100 dollars out of Building fund for 1# 8 D nails .50, 1 coal hod .75, 1 Broom .35c, & 5 lits Glass. No. 13

Resolved by the Board that after the Trustees of Sub Dist

No.11 did dismiss **J. M. Godwin**, a Teacher from his School for the lack of having Thirty five per cent of the Enumeration of said Sub Dist and upon the petition of **Israel Poling** and **C. B. Carter** two of the Trustees of said school the Board agrees to Reinstate said Teacher and to continue all the Schools unless Charges are perfered in writing and proven Regardless of the per cent Required notwithstanding.

Upon an application of **S. B. Poe** it was ordered that **Richard M. Bolton** be transferred from Barker to Glade Dist for this school year & also **Thomas McLane**.

Ordered That **F. House** be Transferred from Sub Dist No. 6 to No.8

Ordered that **Robert Johnson** be Transferred from No. 1 to No. 2 and also to include **Samuel Rucker** in Sub Dist No.2

Ordered that **W. T. Ice** be paid Thirty 90/100 dollars out of Building fund as fee in a suit in behalf of the Board of Education.

On motion the Board adjourned to meet at Belington on the 26 day of Jan 1878 at 10 o'clock A.M.
   Joseph Teter President
    J. B. Godwin Sect B. E.

At a meeting of the Board of Education held at Belington **Jan the 26th, 1878** the members Present **Joseph Teter,** President **Phillip Ramsey, Henry Barte** & **J. B. Godwin** Sect and the following Business done Viz.

    1st

Miss **M. V. Teter** this day presented to the Board from the Trustees of Sub Dist (No.6) showing that she is entitled to the sum of Twenty Nine Dollars for one months Teaching School in said Dist. The same is allowed and it is ordered that a draft be drawn in her favour for the same payable out of Teachers fund of Barker Dist Barbour Co. W.Va.

    2nd

R. S. Tallman this day a certificate to the Board from the Trustees of Sub Dist (No.5) showing that he is entitled to the sum of Twenty Nine dollars for one month Teaching in said Dist the same is allowed and it is ordered that a draft be drawn in his favor for the same payable out of Teachers fund of Barker Dist.

School Board Minutes

3d

J. M. Godwin this day presented a certificate to the Board from the Trustees of Sub Dist (No.11) Showing that he is Entitled to the sum of Twenty Five dollars for one month Teaching School in said Sub Dist the Same is allowed and it is ordered that a draft be Drawen in his favour payable out of Teachers fund of Barker Dist.

4th

J. F. Right this day presented a certificate to the Board from the Trustees of Sub Dist (No 13) showing that he is Entitled to the sum of Twenty Five Dollars for one month Teaching School in said Sub Dist the same is allowed and it is ordered that a draft be drawen in his favour for the same payable out of Teachers fund of Barker Dist.

5th

F. B. Durrett this day presented a certificate to the Board a certificate showing that he is Entitled to the sum of Fifty Eight dollars for Two months Teaching School in Sub Dist (No.14) the same is allowed and it is ordered that a draft be drawen in his favour for the same payable out of Teachers fund of Barker District, Barbour Co. W. Va.

A. J. Hathaway this day presented to the Board a certificate from the Trustees of Sub District (No.3) showing that he is Entitled to the sum of Thirty Six dollars for two months Teaching School in said Dist the same is allowed and it is ordered that a draft be drawn in his favor for the same payable out of the Teachers fund of Barker Dist.

A. B. Moore this day presented a certificate to the Board showing that he is Entitled to the sum of Twenty Nine dollars for one months Teaching School in Sub Dist (No.15) the same is allowed and it is ordered that a draft be drawn in his favour for the same payable out of Teachers fund of Barker Dist.

J. F. Right This day presented a certificate from the Trustees of Sub Dist (No.13) showing that he is Entitled to the sum of Twenty Five dollars the same is allowed and it was ordered that a draft be drawen in his favour payable out of Teachers fund of Barker Dist.

M. E. Harris this day presented a certificate from the Trustees of Sub Dist (No.9) to the Board showing that she is Entitled to the sum of Twenty Nine dollars for one months Teaching School in said Sub Dist the same is allowed and it is ordered that a draft be drawen in her favour for the same payable out of Teachers fund of Barker District.

R. L. Tallman this day presented a certificate from the Trustees of Sub District (No.5) to the Board showing that he is Entitled to the sum of Twenty Nine dollars for one months Teaching School in

School Board Minutes 123

said Dist the same is allowed and it is ordered that a draft be drawn in his favor for the same payable out of the Teachers fund of Barker Dist.

J. A. Hillyard this day presented a certificate to the Board from the Trustees of Sub Dist (No.7) showing that he is Entitled to the sum of Twenty Five dollars for one months Teaching in said Sub Dist the same is allowed and it is ordered that a draft be drawn in his favour for the same payable out of Teachers fund of Barker Dist, Barbour Co. W. Va.

W. S. Shurtleff this day presented a certificate from the Trustees of Sub Dist (No.10) showing that he is Entitled to the sum of Twenty Nine dollars for one months Teaching School in said Dist the same is allowed and it was ordered that a draft be drawen in his favour payable out of Teachers fund of Barker Dist, Barbour Co., W. Va.

Garison Stalnaker this day presented a certificate to the Board from the Trustees of Sub Dist (No.8) showing that he is Entitled to the sum of Fifty Eight dollars for Two months Teaching School in said Dist the same is allowed and it is ordered that a draft be drawn in his favour for the same payable out of Teachers fund of Barker District.

J. H. Hunt this day presented a certificate from the Trustees to the Board showing that he is Entitled to the sum of Eighteen dollars for one month Teaching school in said Dist the same is allowed and it is ordered that a draft be drawen in his favour payable out of Teachers fund of Barker Dist.

Ordered 2.00 **S. B. Poe** be paid Two dollars Repairing Stove &c in School house in Sub Dist (No.11) payable out of Building fund Barker Dist.

Jonathan Hathaway this day presented to the Board a certificate from the Trustees of Sub Dist (No.1) showing that he is Entitled to the sum of Fifty Eight Dollars for two months Teaching School in Said Dist the same is allowed and it was ordered that a draft be drawen in his favour payable out of Teachers fund of Barker Dist, Barbour Co., W. Va.

Ordered .33 that **E. Buckey** be paid .33 cts out of Building fund for 1 Shovel & 10x12 glass.

Ordered $1.70 That **R. A. McCutcheon** be paid one 70/100 dollars out of building fund for 1leden Bucket .75, 1 dipper .15, 1 Joint Stove pipe .50, 1 Broom .30

Ordered $8.60 that **R. A. McCutcheon** be paid Eight 60/100 dollars out of Building fund for the following 2 lb (No.2) 143 lbs. Total $8.60

Ordered 4.00 **E. P. Cross** be paid four Dollars out of Building fund for making fires in School house Sub Dist (No.9)

Ordered $5.00 that **Wm England Jr.** be paid out of Building fund for fuel furnished to School house in Sub Dist (No.13) to the amount of Five dollars.

Ordered $4.00 15/100 that **A. F. Right** be paid Four dollars out of Building fund for making Fires for Two months in Sub Dist No.13

Ordered $2.00 that **Thomas Madden** be paid Two dollars for making fires one month payable out of Building fund in Sub Dist No. 4

Ordered $18.00 that **Amos Mathew** be paid out of Building fund for the Following items Viz. for Fuel (No.11) $3.90, for Repairing School house in Sub Dist (No.11) $7.00, for Repairing Roof $4.10, for windows $3.00

Ordered $10.00 that **J. Y. Booth** be paid Ten dollars for 83 Bushels Coal Furnished to School house in Sub Dist (No.2) out of Building fund.

Ordered $2.00 that **J. M. Godwin** be paid Two dollars out of Building fund for sweeping and making fires in Sub Dist (No.11)

Ordered $1.00 that **J. M. Steerman** be paid one dollar out of Building fund for Taking the Enumeration of Sub Dist (No.1) in 1877.

Ordered that $1.60 **Cicero Phillips** be paid one 60/100 dollars for Repairs done to school house in Sub Dist (No.8) pable out of Building fund.

Ordered $6.50 that **William Steerman** be paid Six 50/100 for something the order does not say for what payable out of Building fund. I suppose it is for Coal.

Ordered $6.00 that **John Waggle** be paid Six dollars out of Building fund of Barker Dist for one hundred Bushels of Coal Sub Dist (No.5)

Ordered $4.00 that **W. S. Shurtleff** be paid four dollars for sweeping and making fires payable out of Building fund Br. Dist.

On motion of the President the Board adjourned to meet at Belington on the 23 day of March 1878 at 10 o'clock A. M.

Joseph Teter President
J. B. Godwin Bd. Ed.

At a meeting of the Board of Education of Barker Dist. held at Belington, Barbour Co, W. Va. **March 2, 1878** the members Present

J. Teter, President Phillip Ramsey, & Henry Barte & J. B. Godwin Sect and the following Business done Viz.

Ordered that **C. F. Teter** be paid fifty Eight Dollars for two months School in Sub Dist (No.2) and Charge to Teachers fund and also four Dollars for making fires Charge to Building fund & also one 25 cts for Coal Bucket, Shovel .467 Charged to Building fund.

Ordered that **J. F. Right** be paid Fifty Dollars for two months Teaching School in Sub Dist (No.13) Charged to Teachers Fund also four dollars for building fires Two months and Charge to Building fund Barker Dist.

Ordered that **M. V. Teter** be paid Thirty four Dollars for Two months Teaching School in Sub Dist (No.6) and Charge to Teachers fund.

Ordered that **M. V. Teter** be paid Twenty Nine Dollars for one month Teaching School in Sub Dist (No.6) and Charge to Teachers fund and also **J. M. Teter** be paid Eight dollars out of Building fund for building fires and sweeping &c.

Ordered that **Thomas Madden** be paid four dollars for making fires and sweeping and Charge to Building fund.

Ordered that **W. S. Shurtleff** be paid four dollars for Sweeping and making fires & charge to Building fund.

Ordered that **Jonathan Hathaway** be paid fifty Eight dollars for Two months teaching School in Sub Dist (No.1) and Charge to Teachers fund.

Ordered that **M. E. Harris** be paid Fifty Eight dollars for Two months Teaching school in Sub Dist (No.9) and Charge to Teachers fund.

Ordered that **J. A. Hillyard** be paid Eight dollars for sweeping and making fires & Charge to Building fund.

Ordered that **Thomas Moran** be paid Seven & 44 cts for fuel furnished Sub Dist (No.9) and Charge to Building fund.

Ordered that **G. J. Stalnaker** be paid Eight dollars for making fires & sweeping & charge to Building fund.

Ordered that Miss **M. V. Teter** to be paid Twenty four dollars for Teaching School in Sub Dist (No.6)

Ordered that **F. B. Durrett** be paid Forty Nine & 30 cts for Teaching School in Sub Dist (No.14) and Charge to Teachers fund.

Ordered that **W. S. Shurtleff** be paid Twenty Nine dollars for one month Teaching School in Sub Dist (No.10) & Charge to Teachers fund.

School Board Minutes

Ordered that **Jonathan Hathaway** be paid Eight dollars for making fires & sweeping and Charge to Building fund.

Ordered that **G. J. Stalnaker** be paid Fifty Eight dollars for Two months Teaching school in Sub Dist (No.8) and Charge to Teachers fund.

Ordered that **A. J. Hathaway** be paid Thirty Six dollars for Two months Teaching School in sub Dist (No.3) & charge to Teachers fund.

Ordered that **R. L. Tallman** be paid Twenty Nine dollars for one month Teaching School in Sub Dist (No.5) and Charge to Teachers fund.

Ordered that **A. J. Hathaway** be paid Eight dollars & 25 cts for making fires & Bucket and Charge to Building fund.

Ordered that **J. A. Hillyard** be paid Fifty dollars for two months Teaching School in Sub Dist (No.7) and Charge to Teachers fund.

Ordered that **J. M. Godwin** be paid Twenty five dollars for one months Teaching School in Sub Dist (No.11) and Charge to Teachers fund.

Ordered that **E. P. Cross** be paid four Dollars for making fires in School house in Sub Dist (No.9) and Charge to Building fund.

Ordered that **R. L. Tallman** be paid Twenty Nine dollars for one month Teaching School in Sub Dist (No.5) and charge to Teachers fund also Eight dollars for making fires and 15 cts for one Broom and Charge to Building fund.

Ordered that **Thomas Madden** be paid Fifty Eight dollars for Two months Teaching school in Sub Dist (No.4) and Charge to Teachers fund.

Ordered that **J. M. Godwin** be paid Twenty five dollars for one month Teaching School in Sub Dist (No.11) and charge to Teachers fund of Barker Dist. This order should have been entered in the December meeting.

Ordered that **W. S. Shurtleff** be paid Twenty Nine dollars for one months Teaching school in Sub Dist (No.10) and Charge to Teachers fund of Barker Dist.

Ordered that **A. B. Moore** be paid Twenty Nine dollars for one month Teaching School in Sub Dist (No.15) and Charge to Teachers fund.

Ordered that **A. B. Moore** be paid Eight dollars for making fires &c and Charge to Building fund and also Twenty Nine dollars for one month Teaching in Sub Dist (No.15) & charge to Teachers fund.

Ordered that **F. B. Bennett** be paid Eight dollars for Building fires in School house in Sub Dist (No.14) and Charge to Building fund.

Ordered that **J. M. Godwin** be paid four dollars for making fires in School house in Sub Dist (No.11) and Charge to Building fund and also Twenty one dollars & 61 cts for one month Teaching School in Sub Dist (No.11) and Charge to Teachers fund.

Ordered that **J. F. Hunt** be paid Thirty Six dollars for Two months Teaching School in Sub Dist (No.12) and Charge to Teachers fund and also Eight dollars for making fires & Charge to Building fund.

Ordered that **Jacob Sipe** be paid Eleven dollars for one Coal house built at Sub Dist (No.8) & Charge to Building fund.

On motion the Board adjourned.
Joseph Teter President
J. B. Godwin Sectary Bd. Ed.

At a meeting of the Board of Education of Barker Dist Barbour Co. W. Va. met at Belington **Aug the 31, 1878** the following members present **Phillip Ramsey, Henry Barte & J. B. Godwin** Sect and the following Buisiness Done Viz.

1st Ordered that **J. B. Godwin** be paid 2 50/100 dollars for Furnishing the Board with Stationarys for the school year Ending Aug 31, 1878 and Charge to Building fund.

Ordered that **Israel Poling** use of **W. G. Godwin** be paid one dollars for Taking the Enumeration of Sub Dist (No.11) and Charge to Building fund of Barker Dist, Barbour Co.

Ordered that **Albert Talier** be paid one dollars for Taking the Enumeration of Sub Dist (No.13) and Charge to Building fund.

Ordered that **Wm. Cross** be paid one dollar for Taking the Enumeration of Sub Dist (No.9) and Charge to Building fund, B. Dist.

Ordered that **W. J. Right** be paid one dollar for Taking the Enumeration of Sub Dist (No.15)Charge to Building fund.

Ordered that **H. P. Rector** be paid one dollar for Taking the Enumeration of Sub Dist (No.7) and Charge to Building fund.

Ordered that **W. R. Moore** be paid one dollar for Taking the Enumeration of Sub Dist (No.10) and Charge to Building fund.

Ordered that **R. A. McCutcheon** be paid one dollar for Taking

the Enumeration of Sub Dist (No.8) and Charge to Building fund.
On motion the Board adjourned to meet on the 7 day of Sept at Two O'clock P.M.
Joseph Teter President
J. B. Godwin Sect Bd. Ed.

At a meeting of the Board of Education of Barker District held at the Odd Fellows Hall in Belington on the **7 day of Sept 1878**, the following members present **Joseph Teter, P. Ramsey, Henry Barte & J. B. Godwin** Sectary Bd Ed the following Business Done Viz. the appointment of Trustees was first in order in Sub Districts No.1, 2, 3, 4, 5, & 6 were all reappointed and sub Dist No.7 (Blank) **Simonds** was appointed in Room of **Joseph Elbon** Removed & **J. M. Cauley** in Room of **H. P Recter** in (No.8), **G. Stalknaker** reappointed (No.9) **Wm. Cross** reappointed in Sub Dist (No.10) **Solomon Wilson** reappointed in (No.11), **Daniel Ice** in Room of **S. B. Poe** (No.12) **Randolph Coberly** in Room of **Thomas Holbert**(No.13) **J. B. Godwin** in Room of **Albert Price** No.14, **Henry Ridgeway** reappointed in (No.15), **John Cade** was reappointed.

Next in order was the Regulating the Teachers Salaries as followes for a
Grade No. one Shall Receive $24.00
For a Grade No. Two the sum of $21.00
For a Grade No. Three the sum of $18.00
For a Grade No. Four the sum of $13.00
For a Grade No. Five the sum of $9.00

Ordered that the Teachers have the Privalige of making fires in the School house in which they Teach.

Ordered that The Trustees shall sell out the fuel to the lowest bidder by Given at least Two weeks notice at three of the most Public places in the Dist.

Ordered that These be kept Four months School in Each Sub Dist in Barker District.

Ordered that Teachers holding State and normal certificates and members of Board of Examiners County Supt Free Schools be classes with Grade No. One.

On motion of **P. Ramsey** the Board adjourned to meet on the

14th day of Sept at 2 o'clock P.M.
Joseph Teter President
J. B. Godwin Sect Bd. Ed.

At a meeting of the Board of Education of Barker Dist held **Sept 14, 1878** at Belington the object of which was to settle with the Sheriff of Barbour Co, W. Va. Members present **Joseph Teter**, President & **Henry Bartee, J. B. Godwin** Sect. The following claims were presented and the Sheriff credited with the same

No.		$
61	A. B. Moore	29.00
106	R. L. Tallman	29.00
52	Garrison Stalnaker	58.00
43	G B. Durrett	58.00
46	M. E. Harris	29.00
38	Isaac F. Right	25.00
18	C. F. Teter	29.00
34	A. B. Moore	29.00
19	C. F. Teter	29.00
39	M. V. Teter	29.00
29	Thomas Maddin	29.00
7	J. M. Godwin	25.00
17	W. S. Shurtleff	29.00
40	R. T. Tallman	29.00
21	M. E. Harris	29.00
42	Thomas Maddin	29.00
36	John F. Hunt	18.00
60	Isaac F. Right	25.00
65	John F. Hunt	18.00
100	C. F. Teter	29.00
96	M. E. Harris	58.00
77	G. J. Stalnaker	58.00
84	I. F. Right	46.61
66	J. A. Hillard	25.00
50	W. S. Shurtleff	29.00
78	A. J. Hathaway	36.00

School Board Minutes

82	J. F. Hunt	36.00
72	R. L. Tallman	29.00
76	John A. Heilliard	50.00
31	John A. Heilliard	25.00
78	Thomas Maddin	58.00
73	M. V. Teter & R. G. George	24.00
54	A. J. Hathaway	26.00
75	F. B. Durrett	49.30
45	R. L. Tallman use of E. Buckey	29.00
44	John N. Godwin	25.00
71	John M. Godwin	25.00
103	M. V. Teter	29.00
137	C. V. Street	8.00
72	R. L. Tallman	29.00
92	W. S. Shurtleff	29.00
83	John M. Godwin	21.61
70	W. S. Shurtleff	29.00

Amount of Delinquent List	$13.48
Commission on $840.99	$25.22
	38.70
Amount of Vouchers Received	$1377.52
Balance Due Dist	1416.22
Amount charged to Sheriff for the School year 1877	
To order on **J. W. Talbott**	1.07
To State school fund	888.67
To Dist Levy	854.22
Total Amount	1743.96
Balance Due District	$366.50

No. of Orders		Amount
35	Francis Hathaway	5.20
81	Thomas Madden	4.00
57	W. S. Shurtleff	4.00
47	John Waggle in sted of J. Right	6.00
11	Thomas Proudfoot	8.50

77	J. F. Hunt	8.00
6	Daniel Sipe	1.00
5	Able Teter	10.00
67	William Steerman	6.50
93	W. S. Shurtleff	4.00
104	G. M. Teter	8.00
94	E. P. Cross	4.00
37	William England	6.75
81	Jonathan Hathaway	8.00
85	J. F. Right	4.00
30	William Corley	6.62
135	F. S. Swick	5.00
00	J. B. Godwin	7.87
	Intrust on same to May 27, 1878	1.18 ½
66	Cicero Phillips	1.06
63	E. Buckey	1.70
64	E. Buckey	0.33
64	Jacob Sipe	20.00
	Intrust on same to May 2, 1878	3.00
90	J. A. Hillyard	8.00
	Daniel Ice	15.75
	Intrust on same May 25, 1875	3.00
	Jacob Sipe	24.00
	Intrust on same Jan 25, 1878	
22	Slage Davis	5.00
27	E. Buckey	1.28
32	R. A. McCutcheon	0.40
26	R. A. McCutcheon	1.57
28	E. Buckey	13.70
33	E. Buckey	15.43
4	J. B. Godwin	10.00
59	I. F. Right	4.00
49	J. M. Godwin	10.00
	Should be 2.00	
14	J. M. Godwin	2.00
3	J. M. Godwin	1.00
2	John Right	1.00
12	William T. Ice	13.90
13	Thomas Madden	2.60

132 School Board Minutes

15	Randolph Coberly	9.50
24	L. D. Kerr	13.75
16	B. L. Jones	4.30
20	C. F. Teter	4.00
7	E. Buckey	1.55
10	L. E. Right	10.00
25	Alpheus Moore	1.50
53	Amos Matthew	18.00
68	William England	5.00
48	J. Y. Booth	10.00
1	W. M. Bible	1.00
57	E. P. Cross	4.00
23	Henry Werner	1.40
97	Thomas Madden	7.44
107	R. L. Tallman	8.15
55	R. A. McCutcheon	8.60
69	S. B. Poe	2.00
86	J. M. Godwin	4.00
58	J. M. Steerman	1.00
113	J. B. Godwin	4.00

Amount of Delinquent list	$7.70
Commission $480.51	$13.41
Amount of Vouchers Rec'd	$438.93

Jacob Hudkins Sheriff of Barbour County to Board of Education from Dist Levy $488.26
On acct of Building fund
Balance due Dist $28.87
Add Eight Dollars to the above as Error 8.00
36.87

On motion of the President there was a levy laid for the Teachers fund of 2 mills on one hundred of Taxable Property and also it was ordered that there be 2 ½ mills Collected on each one hundred dollars valuation of Both Real and Personal property of Barker Dist for Building fund. On motion of the President the Board adjourned to meet on the Second Saturday of Dec next at 10 o'clock A.M. at Belington.

Joseph Teter President
J. B. Godwin Sect

Office of the County Supt.
Sept 25, 1878
    I hereby certify that I have examined the Sec's Books and found them correct as far as I am able to determine.
    Perry Marteney, Co. Supt.

    At a meeting of the Board of Education of Barker Dist, Barbour County, W. Va. held at Belington **Dec the 14th 1878** the following Members present **Phillip Ramsey, Henry Barte** and **Joseph Teter** leaving in about the middle of the session and the following Buisiness Transacted, Viz.

1st

    W. S. Shurtleff this day presented to the Board a certificate from the Trustees of Sub Dist (No.10) showing that he is Entitled to the sum of Twenty Four dollars for one months Teaching in said Sub Dist the same is allowed and it is ordered that a draft be drawn in his favour payable out of Teachers fund of Barker Dist.

2nd

    L. C. Bennett this day presented a certificate showing that he is Entitled to the sum of Eighteen dollars for one months Teaching in Sub Dist (No.15) the same is allowed and it is ordered that a draft be drawn in his favour payable out of Teachers fund of Barker Dist.

    A. F. Right this day presented a certificate from the Trustees of Sub Dist (No.13) showing that he is entitled to the sum of Eighteen dollars for one months Teaching in said Sub Dist the same is allowed and it is ordered that a draft be Drawen in his favour payable out of Teachers fund of Barker Dist.

    G. J. Stalnaker this day presented a certificate from the Trustees of Sub Dist (No.7) showing that he is Entitled to the sum of Twenty One dollars for one month Teaching in said Sub Dist the same is allowed and it is ordered that a draft be Drawen in his favour payable out of Teachers fund of Barker Dist.

    J. M. Godwin this day presented a certificate from the Trustees of Sub Dist (No.1) showing that he is Entitled to the sum of Eighteen dollars for one month Teaching in said Sub Dist the same is allowed and it is ordered that a draft be drawn in his favour payable out of Teachers fund of Barker Dist

    G. W. Baughman This day Presented a certificate from the

Trustees of Sub Dist (No.11) showing that he is Entitled to the sum of Twenty one dollars for one month Teaching in said Sub Dist the same is allowed and it is ordered that a draft be drawen in his favour payable out of Teachers fund of Barker Dist.

Ordered that **G. N. Shomo** be paid Eight 06/100 dollars for fuel furnished to Sub Dist (No.7) Payable out of Building fund.

Ordered that **R. A. McCutcheon** be paid one 60/100 dollars for one Broom, 1 lock & 1 cup the same is allowed payable out of Building fund (No.9)

Ordered that **Able Teter** be paid five 50/100 dollars for repairs to School house in Sub Dist (No.6) and also $12 50/100 for fuel furnished in Sub Dist (No.6) all payable out of Building fund B. Dist.

Ordered that **B. S. Jones** be paid four 75/100 dollars for fuel furnished to Sub Dist (No.14) payable out of Building fund of Barker Dist.

Ordered that **Joseph Teter** be paid Ten Dollars for taking the Enumeration of various Sub Dists by order of Co. Supt payable out of Building fund.

Ordered that **Jacob Mclane** be paid Two 13/100 Dollars for Broom, 1 dipper 18x10 Glass, 13 ½ lbs stove pipe at 12 ½ cts p. pound payable out of Building fund.

Ordered that **A. R. Right** be paid Twelve Dollars for Coal and Repairs done to School house in Sub Dist (No.15) payable out of Building fund.

Ordered that **Laben Moore** be paid Twenty four 80/100 dollars for Repairing School house in Sub Dist (No.9) payable out of Building fund.

Ordered that **John Right** be paid Seventeen dollars for Repairs done to School house in Sub Dist (No.13) payable out of Building Fund.

Ordered that **Charles Ridgway** be paid Six 90/100 dollars for fuel furnished to School house in Sub Dist (No.12) payable out of Building fund.

Ordered that **G. W. Baughman** be paid Two dollars for making fires and sweeping school house payable out of Building fund.

Ordered that **J. R. Carter** be paid Two dollars for hauling Stone from **J. I. Meoss** store and one dollars for Glass and puty the same is payable out of Building fund total of $3.00 (No.14)

Ordered that **Jossiah Wilson** be paid Two dollars for Repairs done to School house in Sub Dist (No.1) payable out of Building fund.

Ordered that **Lewis Wilson** be paid Six 75/100 dollars for Recording three Deeds for the Board of Education for the Board of Education to be paid out of Building fund.

Ordered by the Board of Education of Barker District that the Trustees of Sub Dist (No.12) of Barker District, Barbour County Transfer the following named persons Viz. **Bell Shockey, Rebecca Shockey, John W. Shockey, Harriet Shockey, Martin B. Daugherty, Malisa A. Daugherty, Elijah G. Poling, Sarah M. Shockey, William E. Shockey** to Sub District (No.6) in Phillippi District, Barbour County, W. Va.

Ordered that the same Trustees do Transfer the Children of **B. W. Fisher** to the Jerusalem School in Phillippi Dist, Same Co.

Ordered that the Trustees of Sub Dist (No.10) of Barker Dist are hereby ordered to Transfer the following named persons to Sub Dist (No.3) in Glade Dist. Viz. **Delilah Hill, Jacob Hill, Olive Hill**, all in the county Barbour and State of West Virginia.

Ordered by the Board of Education of Barker District Barbour County that a Coal house be built in Sub Dist (No.15) of said District to be built according to the plan upon which the other Coal houses was built and that said house be sold out today to the lowest Responsible bidder by said bidder Given bonds and Security said house to be Completed in forty five days from this date December the 14, 1878. Ordered that said Contract was awarded to **J. B. Godwin** at Nine Dollars.

On motion it was ordered that the Board do adjourn to meet Jan 25, 1879 at 1 o'clock P.M.
   Joseph Teter President
   J. B. Godwin Sect B. E.

At a meeting of the Board of Education of Barker District, Barbour County, W. Va. held at Belington on the **25 day of Jan 1879** the members present **Joseph Teter**, President, **Henry Barte, Phillip Ramsey** and **J. B. Godwin**, Sect and the following Buisiness Done Viz.

F. B. Durrett this day presented a certificate from the Trustees of Sub Dist (No.14) Showing that he is Entitled to the Sum of Twenty one dollars for one months Teaching in said Sub Dist the same

136   School Board Minutes

is allowed and it is ordered that a draft be drawn in his favour payable out of Teachers fund of Barker Dist.

I. F. Right this day presented a certificate from the Trustees of Sub Dist (No.13) Showing that he is Entitled to the Sum of Eighteen dollars for one months Teaching in said Sub Dist the same is allowed and it is ordered that a draft be drawn in his favour payable out of Teachers fund of Barker Dist.

R. E. Kerr this day presented a certificate from the Trustees of Sub Dist (No.9) Showing that he is Entitled to the Sum of Eighteen dollars for one months Teaching in said Sub Dist the same is allowed and it is ordered that a draft be drawn in his favour payable out of Teachers fund of Barker Dist.

Ordered that **R. S. Tallman** be paid Twenty four Dollars for one month Teaching payable out of Teachers fund (No.2)

Ordered that **Hannah Obrien** be paid out of Teachers fund Eighteen dollars for one months Teaching in Sub Dist (No.4)

Ordered that **Martin Madden** be paid Eighteen dollars for one month Teaching in Sub Dist (No.5) payable out of Teachers fund of Barker Dist.

Ordered that **R. L. Tallman** be paid Twenty Four Dollars for one month Teaching School in Sub Dist (No.2) payable out of Teachers fund.

Miss Alice Wilmoth this day presented to the Board a certificate from the Trustees of Sub Dist (No.12) Showing that she is Entitled to the sum of Thirty Six dollars for two months Teaching in said Sub Dist the same is allowed and it is ordered that a draft be drawn in her favour payable out of Teachers fund of Barker Dist.

L. C. Bennett this day presented a certificate from the Trustees of Sub Dist (No15) Showing that he is Entitled to the Sum of Eighteen dollars for one months Teaching in said Sub Dist the same is allowed and it is ordered that a draft be drawn in his favour payable out of Teachers fund.

G. J. Stalnaker this day presented a certificate from the Trustees of Sub Dist (No.7) Showing that he is Entitled to the Sum of Twenty one dollars for one months Teaching in said Sub Dist the same is allowed and it is ordered that a draft be drawn in his favour payable out of Teachers fund.

W. S. Shurtleff this day presented a certificate from the Trustees of Sub Dist (No.10) Showing that he is Entitled to the Sum of Twenty four dollars the same is allowed and it is ordered that a draft be drawn in his favour payable out of Teachers fund.

School Board Minutes   137

J. M. Godwin this day presented to the Board a certificate showing that he is Entitled to the Sum of Eighteen dollars for one months Teaching in Sub Dist (No.1) the same is allowed and it is ordered that a draft be drawen in his favour payable out of Teachers fund.

Miss Hannah OBrien this day presented a certificate Showing that she is Entitled to the Sum of Eighteen dollars for one months Teaching in Sub Dist (No.4) the same is allowed and it is ordered that a draft be drawen in her favour payable out of Teachers fund of Barker Dist.

Ordered that D. G. McCauley be paid Nine dollars for furnishing Ninety Bushels Coal to Sub Dist (No.3) payable out of Building fund

Ordered that R. A. McCutcheon be paid for one coal hod 65 cts and two lits of Glass .16 Total 0.81 payable out of Building fund.

Ordered that Daniel OBrien be paid Six Dollars for Repairs to School house in Sub Dist (No.6) payable out of Building fund.

Ordered that J. M. Godwin be paid $4.00 for sweeping and making fires in Sub Dist (No.1) payable out of Building fund of Barker District.

Ordered that Wm. Steerman be paid five dollars for coal furnished to school house in Sub Dist (No.1) payable out of Building fund.

Ordered that Josiah Wilson be paid one dollar & 48 cts for Stove pipe & Repairing Chimney in Sub Dist (No.1) payable out of Building fund.

Ordered that T. B. Teter be paid Twelve 27/100 dollars for fuel $11.50 & Repairs 77c to school house in Sub Dist (No.2) and charge to Building fund.

Ordered that W. S. Shurtleff be paid Four dollars for sweeping and making fires in school house in Sub Dist (No.10) and charge to Building fund.

Ordered that I. F. Right be paid Four dollars for making fires and for sweeping in school house in Sub Dist (No.13) & charge to Building fund

Ordered that R. A. McCutcheon be paid one dollar for broom &c and charge to Building fund.

Ordered that F. C. Shockey be paid Two 50/100 dollars for making 2 new seats & Repairing one 1 joint stove pipe, 1 window Glass and charge to Building fund.

138   School Board Minutes

Ordered that **C. F. Teter** be paid Forty Eight dollars for Two months Teaching in Sub Dist (No.6) and charge to Teachers fund and also four dollars for making fires $4.00 in Sub Dist (No.6) and charge to Building fund.

Ordered that **F. B. Durrett** be paid Twenty one dollars for Teaching school in Sub Dist (No.14) payable out of Teachers fund of Barker Dist.

Ordered that **F. B. Durrett** be paid Four dollars for sweeping and making fires in Sub Dist (No.14) and charge to Building fund.

Ordered that **R. A. McCutcheon** be paid Sixty .60cts for one Broom, 1 shovel & one cup used in School house in Sub Dist (No.15) and charge to Building fund.

Ordered that **G. J. Stalnaker** be paid Four dollars for sweeping and making fires in School house in Sub Dist (No.7) & charge to Building fund.

On motion the Board adjourned to meet on the Fourth Saturday of Feb 1879 at Belington at one O'clock P.M.
  Joseph Teter President
   J. B. Godwin Sect B. E.

At a meeting of the Board of Education of Barker District, Barbour County, W. Va. on the **fourth Saturday of Feb 1879** held at **R. A. McCutcheon**'s Store the following members Present **Joseph Teter**, President, **Phillip Ramsey, Henry Barte,** & **J. B. Godwin**, Sect B. E. and the following Buisiness Done Viz.

This day **W. S. Shurtleff** presented a certificate from the Trustees of Sub Dist (No.10) Showing that he is Entitled to the Sum of Twenty four dollars for one months Teaching in said Sub Dist the same is allowed and it is ordered that a draft be drawen in his favour payable out of Teachers fund of Barker Dist., Barbour Co. W. Va.

J. F. Right this day presented a certificate from the Trustees of Sub Dist (No.13) Showing that he is Entitled to the Sum of Eighteen dollars for one month Teaching in said Sub Dist the same is allowed and it is ordered that a draft be drawen in his favour payable out of Teachers fund of Barker Dist. and also Two dollars for sweeping and making fires.   **R. L. Tallman** this day presented a certificate from the Trustees of Sub Dist (No.2) Showing that he is Entitled to the Sum of Twenty four dollars for one months Teaching in said Sub Dist the same is allowed and it is ordered that a draft be drawn in his favour payable out of Teachers fund.

Miss **S. R. Phillips** this day presented a certificate from the Trustees of Sub Dist (No.8) Showing she was Entitled to the Sum of Eighty four for 4 months Teaching in said Sub Dist the same is allowed and it is ordered that a draft be drawn in her favour payable out of Teachers fund of Barker Dist.

Jonathan Hathaway This day presented a certificate from the Trustees of Sub Dist (No.3) Showing he is Entitled to the Sum of Sixty three dollars for Three months Teaching in said Sub Dist the same is allowed and it is ordered that a draft be Drawn in his favour payable out of Teachers fund of Barker Dist.

L. C. Bennett this day presented a certificate from the Trustees of Sub Dist (No.15) showing that he is Entitled to the Sum of Eighteen dollars for one months teaching in said Dist the same is allowed and it is ordered that a draft be drawn in his favour payable out of Teachers fund of Barker Dist.

R. E. Kerr this day presented a certificate from the Trustees of Sub Dist (No.8) Showing that he is Entitled to the Sum of Eighteen dollars for one months Teaching in said Dist the same is allowed and it is ordered that a draft be drawn in his favour payable out of Teachers fund of Barker Dist.

J. F. Right this day presented a certificate from the Trustees of Sub Dist (No.13) Showing that he is Entitled to the Sum of Eighteen dollars for one month Teaching in said Sub Dist the same is allowed and it is ordered that a draft be drawn in his favour payable out of Teachers fund of Barker Dist. and also Two dollars for sweeping and making fires.

Martin Madden this day presented a certificate from the Trustees of Sub Dist (No.5) Showing that he is Entitled to the Sum of Eighteen dollars for one months Teaching in said Dist the same is allowed and it is ordered that a draft be drawn in his favour payable out of Teachers fund of Barker Dist.

G. W. Baughman this day presented a certificate from the Trustees of Sub Dist (No.11) Showing that he is Entitled to the Sum of Twenty one dollars for one month Teaching in said Sub Dist the same is allowed and it is ordered that a draft be drawn in his favour payable out of Teachers fund of Barker Dist. and also Two dollars for sweeping and making fires out of Building fund.

Ordered that **G . W. Baughman** be paid Twenty one dollars out of Teaching fund for one months Teaching and be ordered that he be Paid Two dollars for sweeping and making fires payable out of Building fund.

Ordered that **L. W. Corley** be paid Ninety cts for 1 Broom, 1 coal Bucket .70 the same is allowed and made payable out of Building fund.

Ordered that **W. M. Poe** be paid Three dollars and 95 cents for Fuel furnished to Sub Dist (No.11) payable out of Building fund.

Ordered that **R. A. McCutcheon** be paid Twenty five cents for one shovel for (No.9) payable out of Building fund.

Ordered that **W. A. Shurtleff** be paid Four dollars for sweeping and making fires in School room (No.11) payable out of Building fund.

Ordered that **Abraham George** be paid Five 50/100 dollars for Repairs to School house in Sub Dist (No.4) payable out of Building fund.

Ordered that **John Gest** be paid Seven 75/100 dollars for fuel furnished to School house in Sub Dist (No.4) payable out of Building fund.

Ordered that **Ballard Jones** be paid One 42/100 dollars for fuel furnished for School house in Sub Dist (No.14) payable out of Building fund.

Ordered that **William England** be paid Seven dollars for furnishing Coal to School house in Sub Dist (No.10) payable out of Building fund.

Ordered that **Monroe Phillips** be paid Eight dollars for making fires and sweeping School Room (No.8) payable out of Building fund.

Ordered that **Francis Hathaway** be paid One 15/100 dollars for Shovel, Bucket, Broom in school house in Sub Dist (No.3) payable out of Building fund.

On motion the Board Received the Coal house in Sub Dist No.15 built by **G. B. Godwin** and issued bonds on the Builidng fund and on motion the board adjourned to meet at **R. A. McCutcheon**s Store on the Fourth Saturday of March 1879 at 1 oclock PM.

        Joseph Teter President
        J. B. Godwin Sect

School Board Minutes 141

At a meeting of the Board of Education of Barker District, Barbour County, W. Va. met at **R. A. McCutcheons** Store on the **Fourth Saturday in March 1879** members Present **Joseph Teter**, President, **Henry Bartee, Phillip Ramsey** & **J. B. Godwin**, Sect Bd. Ed. and the following buisiness done Viz

Miss **Alice Wilmoth** this day presented to the Board a certificate from the Trustees of Sub Dist (No.12) Showing that she is Entitled to the Sum of Thirty dollars for Two months Teaching School in said Sub Dist (No.12) the same is allowed and it is ordered that a draft be drawn in her favour for the same payable out of Teachers fund of Barker District.

J. M. Godwin This day presented to the Board a certificate from the Trustees of Sub Dist (No.1) Showing that he is Entitled to the Sum of Thirty Six dollars for Two months Teaching in said Sub Dist the same is allowed and it is ordered that a draft be drawn in his favour for the same payable out of Teachers fund and also Four dollars for sweeping and making fires for 2 months payable out of Building fund. This order is cut to $31.14 for non attendance to the institute.

W. S. Shurtleff This day presented a certificate to the Board from the Trustees of Sub Dist (No.10) Showing that he is Entitled to the Sum of Twenty Four dollars for one month Teaching in said Sub Dist the same is allowed and it is ordered that a draft be drawn in her favour for the same payable out of Teachers fund.

Ordered that **Hannah OBrien** be paid Eighteen dollars for one month Teaching in Sub Dist (No.4) payable out of Teachers fund.

Ordered that **Jonathan Hathaway** be paid Twenty one dollars for one month Teaching in Sub Dist (No.3)

Ordered that **G. W. Baughman** be paid Twenty one dollars out of Teachers fund for one month Teaching in Sub Dist (No.11) and also four dollars for making fires and sweeping.

Ordered that **R. L. Tallman** be paid Twenty four Dollars out of Teachers fund for one month Teaching in Sub Dist (No.2) also Eight dollars for sweeping and making fires out of Building fund.

L. C. Bennett this day presented a certificate to the board from the Trustees of Sub Dist (No.15) Showing that he is Entitled to the Sum of Eighteen dollars for one month Teaching School in said Dist the same is allowed and it is ordered that a draft be drawn in his favour for the same payable out of Teachers fund and also Eight dollars for making fires and sweeping payable out of Building fund of Barker District.

Ordered that **E. P. Talbott** be paid Eight 50/100 dollars for fuel furnished to school house in Sub Dist (No.5) 1 Joint pipe .50, 1 Broom .30 Total $9.30 payable out of Building fund.

Ordered that **G. H. Throop** be paid use of **R. A. McCutcheon** five dollars for Repairs to School house in Sub Dist (No.8) payable out of Building fund.

Ordered that **R. E. Kerr** be paid Eighteen dollars for one month Teaching in Sub Dist (No.9) the same is allowed and made payable out of Teachers fund of Barker Dist.

Ordered that **James Coberly** be paid Eight dollars for making fires four months payable out of Building fund.

Ordered that **Simon Hoover** be paid 25 cents Repairing windows on School house in Sub Dist No. 4 payable out of Building fund.

Ordered that **D. P. Teter** be paid Four Dollars for making Fires in School house in Sub Dist (No.6) payable out of Building fund.

Ordered that **Hannah OBrien** be paid Four Dollars making fires and sweeping 2 months in School house (No.4) payable out of Building fund.

Ordered that **Martin Madden** be paid Eight dollars for sweeping and making fires in School house in Sub Dist (No.5) payable out of Building fund.

Ordered that **Solomon Harris** be paid Eight dollars for Chimney $1.25 and making butts and putting them on window shutters Total $9.25 payable out of Building fund.

Ordered that **Hannah OBrien** be paid Two Dollars for sweeping and making fires for one month in School room (No.10) payable out of Building fund.

This day **G. J. Stalnaker** presented a certificate from the Trustees of Sub Dist (No.7) Showing that he is Entitled To the Sum of Forty Two dollars the same is allowed and it is ordered that a draft be drawn in his favour payable out of Teachers fund of Barker Dist. and also Four dollars for sweeping and making fires Two months payable out of Building fund.

Ordered that **F. B. Durrett** be paid Four dollars for making fires and sweeping Two months in School Room in Sub Dist (No.14) payable Building fund.

Ordered that **E. T. Bennett** be paid Five 50/100 dollars for fuel furnished to Sub Dist (No.9) payable out of Building fund.

Ordered that **R. E. Kerr** be paid Four dollars for making fires and sweeping Two months in School Room in Sub Dist (No.9) payable out of Building fund.

Ordered that **R. E. Kerr** be paid Eighteen dollars for one month Teaching School in Sub Dist (No.9) payable out of Teachers fund.

Ordered that **Jonathan Hathaway** be paid Eight dollars for making fires and sweeping in School Room in Sub Dist (No.3) payable out of Building fund of Barker Dist.

On motion the Board adjourned without day

Joseph Teter President
J. B. Godwin Secty

At a special meeting of the Board called **May the 10th 1879** at **R. A. McCutcheons** Store at Belington for the purpose of Transacting Buisiness and members present **Joseph Teter**, President, **Henry Bartee**, & **J. B. Godwin**, Sect Bd. Ed. and the following buisiness done Viz.

1st

It was ordered that the Trustees of Each Sub Dist Extend their Schools long Enough to Expend the Sum of Twenty Five Dollars Each.

Ordered that **Eugene Swick** be paid Two dollars for Twenty Bushel of Coal furnished to School house in Sub Dist (No.1) payable out of Building fund of Barker Dist Barbour County W. Va.

March 28, 1879 this ordered should have been recorded in the March Meeting of the Board but was an oversight of the Sectary.

Martin Madden presented a certificate from the Trustees of Sub Dist (No.5) Showing that he is Entitled to the sum of Thirty Six dollars for Two months Teaching School in said Sub Dist the same is allowed and it is ordered that a draft be Drawen in his favour for the same payable out of Teachers fund of Barker Dist Barbour County W. Va.

C. F. Teter this day presented by Miss **M. V. Teter** a certificate Showing that he is Entitled to the sum of 48. Forty Eight dollars for Two months Teaching School in said Sub Dist (No.6) the same is allowed and it is ordered that a draft be drawen in his favour for the same payable out of Teachers fund.

Ordered that **R. A. McCutcheon** be paid for one Stove bottom & Grate 2.70$, Storage 25 cts, Total Two 95/100 dollars the same is allowed and payable out of Building fund.

May 2th

Miss **Hannah OBrien** this day presented to the Board a certificate from the Trustees of Sub Dist (No.4) Showing that she is Entitled to the sum of Eighteen dollars for one month Teaching School in said Dist the same is allowed and it is ordered that a draft be Drawn in her favour for the same payable out of Teachers fund of B. Dist and also Two dollars for Sweeping and making fires for one month and also one broom 30 ¢ & one joint Stove pipe 50 ¢ $2.80.

On motion the board adjourned to meet at Belington on the fourth Saturday of June next at 2 o'clock PM

Joseph Teter President
J. B. Godwin Sect Bd. Ed.

At a meeting of the Board of Education held at Belington on the **28th day of June, 1879**. Members present **Joseph Teter**, President, **Henry Bartee**, & **J. B. Godwin**, and the following buisiness done Viz

Miss **S. R. Phillips** presented a certificate from the Trustees of Sub Dist (No.8) showing that she is Entitled To the Sum of Twenty five dollars the same is allowed and it is ordered that a draft be drawn in her favour payable out of Teachers fund of Barker Dist.
June 28, 1879

G. W. Baughman this day presented a certificate from the Trustees of Sub Dist (No.11) Showing that he is Entitled To the Sum of Twenty five dollars for Teaching school in said Dist the same is allowed and it is ordered that a draft be drawn in his favour payable out of Teachers fund.
June 25, 1879

I. F. Right This day presented a certificate Showing that he is Entitled To the Sum of Twenty five dollars For Teaching School in Sub Dist (No.13) the same is allowed and it is ordered that a draft be drawn in his favour for the same payable out of The Teachers fund of Barker Dist. and also Four dollars for sweeping and making fires Two months payable out of Building fund of Barker Dist of Barbour County W. Va.
June 27, 1879

Jonathan Hathaway this day presented to the Board a

certificate Showing from the Trustees of Sub Dist (No.7) Showing he is Entitled To the Sum of Twenty five dollars for Teaching school in Sub Dist (No.3) the same is allowed and it is ordered that a draft be drawn in his favour payable out of Teachers fund.

June 28, 1879

L. C. Bennett this day presented a certificate from the Trustees of Sub Dist (No.15) Showing that he is Entitled To the Sum of Twenty five dollars the same is allowed and it is ordered that a draft be drawn in his favour payable out of Teachers fund.

F. B. Durrett this day presented a certificate from the Trustees of Sub Dist (No.14) Showing that he is Entitled To the Sum of Thirty Six 30/100 dollars for Two months Teaching in Said Dist the same is allowed and it is ordered that a draft be drawn in his favour payable out of Teachers fund.

Ordered that **C. N. Street** be paid Twenty five dollars for Teaching one month in Sub Dist (No.12) payable out of Teachers fund.

Ordered that **J. M. Godwin** be paid Twenty five dollars for one month Teaching in Sub Dist (No.14) Payable out of Teachers Fund.

On motion Board adjourned to on the 20 day of July at 1 o'clock PM.

Belington.   **Joseph Teter** President
                         J. B. Godwin Sect

At a meeting of the Board of Education held at Belington Barbour Co. W. Va. on the **26th day of July, 1879** the members present **Joseph Teter**, President, **Henry Bartee, Phillip Ramsey** & **J. B. Godwin**, Sect B. Ed. and the following Buisiness done Viz

1st

Miss **M. V. Teter** this day presented to the Board a Certificate from the Trustees of Sub Dist (No.1) Showing she is Entitled To the Sum of Twenty five dollars the same is allowed and it is ordered that a draft be drawn in her favour payable out of Teachers fund of Barker Dist.

C. F. Teter this day presented a certificate from the Trustees of Sub Dist (No.6) showing that he is Entitled To the Sum of Twenty five dollars the same is allowed and it is ordered that a draft be drawn in his favour payable out of Teachers fund.

L. C. Bennett this day presented a certificate from the

Trustees of Sub Dist (No.9) Showing that he is Entitled To the Sum of Twenty five dollars for Teaching School in said Dist the same is allowed and it is ordered that a draft be drawn in his favour payable out of Teachers fund.

Ordered that **Hamilton Fink** be allowed one dollar for Taking the Enumeration of Sub Dist (No.9) payable out Building fund.

On motion the Board adjourned to meet at **Jacob B. Godwin**s Aug the 3d 1879

    Joseph Teter President
    J. B. Godwin Sect

At a meeting of the Board to be held at **J. B. Godwin** on the **third day of August 1879 Joseph Teter** came and adjourned without day

    Joseph Teter President
    J. B. Godwin Sect

At a Special meeting of the Board of Education met at Belington on the **second Tuesday of August 1879** the members present **Henry Bartee, Phillip Ramsey** & **J. B. Godwin**, Sect and adjourned without finishing the Buisiness that was before the Board and do meet again on the Twenty third to conclude the Buisiness Before the Board.

Ordered that **W. S. Shurtleff** be paid Twenty Five dollars for Teaching one month in Sub Dist (No.10) Payable out of Teachers fund.

Ordered that **J. A. Hillyard** be paid Twenty Five dollars for Teaching one month in Sub Dist (No.7) Payable out of Teachers fund.

    Henry Barte Pt
    J. B. Godwin Sect

At a meeting of the Board of Education of Barker Dist. Barbour

School Board Minutes 147

Co. W. Va. met at Belington on the **23 day of August, 1879** the following members Present **Joseph Teter**, President, **Henry Barte & J. B. Godwin**, Sect the object of the meeting was to settle with the Sheriff of Barbour County and settlement made with the following results

Amount of State School fund	$1061.90
Amount from Dist levy	485.20
Amount from last settlement	366.50
Total Teachers fund	1913.60
Commission on $485.20	14.35
	1439.35
Due Dist	$474.25
Delinquent list	7.75

And the following is the vouchers Received of the Sheriff
Amount of vouchers Rec on Teachers fund   1439.35

No.		$ Cts
116	G. W. Baughman	25.00
108	Hannah O'Brien	15.57
107	C. F. Teter	24.00
106	Alice Willmoth	18.00
104	G. J. Stalnaker	42.00
102	R. E. Kerr	18.00
97	R. L. Tallman	24.73
101	Martin Madden	4.86
96	Martin Madden	8.00
94	R. E. Kerr	18.00
95	Martin Madden	22.33
89	L. C. Bennett	18.00
62	Jonathan Hathaway	58.00
93	Philippi District	13.00
82	F. B. Durrett	36.30
	G. W. Baughman	21.00
79	J. Hathaway	63.00
83	J. Hathaway	21.00
73	W. S. Shurtleff	24.00
78	Hannah O'Brien	18.00
3	S. R. Phillips	84.00
72	I. F. Right	31.00

148 School Board Minutes

	Geo. W. Baughman	42.00	
72	L. C. Bennett	18.00	
57	Martin Madden	18.00	
50	I. F. Right	18.00	
35	G. J. Stalnaker	21.00	
47	F. B. Durrett	21.00	
42	L. C. Bennett	18.00	
34	Alice Willmoth	36.00	
33	J. M. Godwin	18.00	
52	R. E. Kerr	18.00	
4	Martin Madden	18.00	
9	Hannah O'Brien	18.00	
2	G. W. Baughman	21.00	
23	F. B. Durrett	21.00	
7	J. M. Godwin	18.00	
8	I. F. Right	18.00	
5	L. C. Bennett	18.00	
6	W. S. Shurtleff	24.00	
15	G. J. Stalnaker	21.00	
95	C. F. Teter	29.00	
102	M. V. Teter	34.00	
98	F. B. Durrett	10.84	
88	A. B. Moore	56.69	
79	J. Hathaway	58.00	
133	M. V. Teter	25.00	
125	C. F. Teter	25.00	
131	C. F. Teter	25.00	
124	M. V. Teter	25.00	
123	C. H. Street	25.00	
83	J. M. Godwin	31.14	
69	R. E. Kerr	18.00	
31	W. S. Shurtleff	24.00	
77	R. L. Tallman	24.00	

Balance Due Barker District on settlement $474.25
Made Aug 23 day of 1879
Amount of vouchers Received was $1439.35

Amt. of Building fund
Acct Due from last settlement   76.33

School Board Minutes 149

From Dist Levy			606.50
By Delinquent Lists		$6.19	
By Commissioners		$18.18	
		24.37	682.83

No.		
118	Eugene Swick	2.00
88	L. C. Bennett	8.00
120	W. J. Right	1.00
121	J. B. Godwin	2.50
133	Joseph Teter	8.00
134	C. F. Teter	9.00
17	G. W. Baughman	2.00
11	A. R. Right	12.00
99	Martin Madden	8.00
59	R. T. George	1.00
110	Albert Price	1.00
91	F. B. Durrett	8.00
39	Wm Steerman	5.00
12	Laben Moore	24.20
20	G. N. Shomo	8.06
37	James Browning	4.80
111	E. T. Bennett	5.50
84	J. M. Godwin	4.00
45	J. B. Godwin	9.00
14	Charles Ridgway	6.90
16	A. Moore	6.00
38	G. T. Stalnaker	4.00
10	Lewis Wilson	6.75
89	A. B. Moore	8.00
100	E. P. Talbott	9.30
75	J. F. Right	4.00
80	A. J. Hathaway	8.25
85	James Coberly	8.00
115	W. R. Moore	1.00
1	J. B. Godwin	10.00
95	G. T. Stalnaker	8.00
109	J. Poling use of W. G. Godwin	1.00
116	R. A. McCutcheon	1.00
112	W. J. Right	1.00

150 School Board Minutes

3	J. B. Godwin	15.00
105	Thomas Madden	4.00
111	William Cross	1.00
66	John Gost	7.75
71	Solomon Harris	9.25
40	J. B. Teter	12.27
46	Thomas Holbert	1.00
87	B. F. Teter	4.00
	G. W. Baughman	6.00
74	W. S. Shurtleff	4.00
44	F. C. Shockey	2.50
36	L. G. McCauley	4.50
21	Josiah Wilson	2.00
101	E. F. Teter	5.25
13	B. Jones	4.75
61	B. Jones	1.42
26	Joseph Teter	10.00
62	B. P. Newlon	7.25
24	Abel Teter	9.00
63	W. M. Poe	3.85
48	F. B. Durrett	4.00
19	Abel Teter	18.00
25	John Right	17.00
22	R. A. McCutcheon	1.60
18	J. R. Carter	3.00
43	R. A. McCutcheon	1.41
27	J. Meshane	2.43
67	R. A. McCutcheon	.25
30	W. S. Shurtleff	4.00
114	H. P. Rector	1.00
29	Josiah Wilson	1.45
51	J. F. Right	4.00
98	R. L. Tallman	8.00
60	Abram George	5.50
32	J. M. Godwin	4.00
68	R. E. Kerr	4.00
56	Simon Hoover	.25
92	Francis Hathaway	1.15
81	Jonathan Hathaway	8.00

103	R. E. Kerr	4.00
113	G. H. Taook use of R. A. McCutcheon	5.00
91	Hannah OBrien	6.00
105	G. J. Stalnaker	4.00
64	William England	7.00
90	F. B. Durrett	4.00
135	Simon Swick	1.00

Amount of vouchers received   475.50
Balance Due Dist $207.33

J. B. Godwin Sect B. E.

Meadowville, W. Va.
August 29th 1879
    This certifies that I have examined the books of **Jacob B. Godwin**, Secty Bd. Ed. of Barker district and find them correct, so far as I am able to determine. The Secty has also made his annual report as required by law and the Board will please allow him $10.00 as per law.

Perry Marteney Co. Supt.

    At a meeting of the Board of Education of Barker Dist Barbour County W. Va. at Belington this **6th Sept 1879** consisting of **W. S. Shurtleff**, President, and commissioners **J. H. Durrett, M. Howes, Henry Bartee** and **C. Phillips**. After duly organizing and appointing **F. B. Durrett**, Secretary the following business was transacted.
    The following named persons were appointed Trustee of his Dist, Sub District No.1 **J. M. Steerman**, No.2 **Henry Keyser**, No.3 **J. D. Thacker**, No. 4 **Patrick McGinnis**, No. 5 **James Rinehart**, No. 6 **J. M. Hathaway**, No. 7 **Tery Simons**, No. 8 **T. T. Elliott**, No.9 **S. S. Cross**, No.10 **W. R. Moore**, No.11 **James Poling**, No.12 **James Tompson**, No. 13 **Noah Kettle**, No. 14 **Henry Ridgway**, No. 15 **W. J. Right**. Ordered by the Board of Education That Teachers holding No. One certificate shall receive not exceeding 22 Dollars, No. 2 21

Dollars, No. Three 12 Dols.

Ordered that there shall be four months School in each sub District, Further that the School shall commence on the first Monday in November.

It was further agreed that the following named Teachers Shall teach the schools in Barker District, Viz. Sub District No. 1 **M. OBrien**, No. 2 **A. J. Hathaway**, No. 3 **Jonathan Hathaway**, No. 4 **R. E. Kerr**, No.5 **R. L. Tallman**, No. 6 **Nannie Sipe**, No. 7 **L. C. Bennett**, No. 8 **R. J. Dunham**, No.9 **J. S. Poling**, No.10 **James Coffman**, No.11 **J. F. Right**, No. 12 **S. T. Hartman**, No. 13 Vacant, No. 14 **J. M. Godwin**, No. 15 **S. R. Phillips**.

Ordered that the school levy be 15 cents on one hundred Dols for School purposes, For Building fund 20 cts on 100 Dols of Taxable property. Teachers salary No.1 22 Dollars, No. 2 21 Dollars, No. 3 12 Dols.

Ordered that the Trustees of each Sub District Sell the coal, after giving at least 10 days notice, by posting a notice in three different places, to the least bidder, And the contract shall be for coal enough to last the whole term of four months.

On motion of commissioner **Bartee** the Board adjourned to meet at **R. A. McCutcheons** Store on the first Saturday in October 1879 at one o'clock P.M.

W. S. Shurtleff, President
F. B. Durrett, Sec. Bd. Ed.

Office of Board of Education of Barker School District, in the County of Barbour, State of West Virginia. At a meeting of the Board held on the **4th day of October 1879.** Present **W. S. Shurtleff**, President, and **J. H. Durrett, M. Howes, H. Bartee** and **C. Phillips**, Commissioners.

Ordered That **W. W. Jones** be appointed trustee of Sub Dist No. 14.

Ordered That **A. W. Stalnaker** teach the School in Sub Dist No. 13.

Ordered That **C. B. Carter** be paid 1.00 Dol. for taking numeration in Sub Dist No. 11.

Ordered That **J. B. Godwin** be paid 10.00 Dols. for making annual report.

Ordered That **R. J. Dunham** be permitted to commence teaching school in Sub Dist No. 8 on the first Monday in October.

Ordered That **R. A. McCutcheon** be paid 1.50/100 Dol. having a certificate from trustee of Sub Dist No. 10 for Lock, Broom, Dipper Etc.

Ordered That **R. L. Tallman** be paid $25.00 for teaching school in Sub Dist No. 5 having a certificate from Trustees.

On motion of **M. Howes** the Board adjourned to meet on the first Saturday in December 1879 at **R. A. McCutcheons** Store.

W. S. Shurtleff President
J. B. Durrett Secretary

Office of Board of Education of Barker School District, in the County of Barbour, State of West Virginia. At a meeting of the Board held on the 6th **Dec 1879.** Present **W. S. Shurtleff**, President, and **J. H. Durrett, M. Howes, H. Bartee** and **C. Phillips,** Commissioners. There being a vacancy in Trustee in Sub District No. 7 and 8 it was Ordered that **J. R. Hillyard** be appointed Trustee in Sub Dist No. 7 and **R. A. McCutcheon** in Sub Dist No. 8. The following list of claims were presented and allowed and Drafts given as follows, School Fund. For Teaching **J. M. Godwin**, Twenty one Dollars, **R. L. Tallman** Twenty Two Dollars payable out of School Fund. Miss **H. C. Sipe** Twenty Two Dollars, **R. J. Dunham** Twenty Two Dollars, **Jonathan Hathaway** Twenty Two Dollars, **S. P. Hartman** Twenty Two Dollars, **J. S. Poling** Twenty one Dollars, **L. C. Bennett** Twenty one Dollars, **A. W. Stalnaker** Twenty one Dollars, **James Coffman** Twenty one Dollars. Payable out of Building Fund **J. R. W. Smith** Nine Dols for furnishing fuel Sub Dist No. 12 Twelve. **J. B. Godwin** Eleven Dols. 27 cts witness fee. Suit between Board and **McCauley. Jesse Teter** Nine Dols 15 cts for fuel Sub Dist No. Six. **Luther Kerr** Eight Dols 20 cts fuel and Repairs Sub Dist No.4. **Ballard Jones** Eight Dols 12 cts for fuel Sub Dist No. 14.

R. T. George Eight 50/100 Dollars for fuel Sub Dist No. Five

J. M. Godwin Two Dols for building fires in School room Sub Dist No. 14.

154 School Board Minutes

Emmett R. Kerr Two Dols for building fires in School room Sub Dist No. 4.

William England Seventy five cents for repairs Sub Dist No. 10.

R. J. Dunham Two Dollars for building fires in School room Sub Dist No. 8.

William Day Six 25/100 Dollars for fuel to Sub Dist No. 1 (one).

R. A. McCutcheon several Drafts No. 24, 25 and 26 amounting to Two 61/100 Dols for furnishing dippers, brooms &c to Trustees for use in School room.

Marcus Moore Seven 55/100 Dollars for furnishing coal Sub Dist No. 15.

J. R. Hillyard Seven 50/100 Dollars for furnishing coal Sub Dist No. 7.

L. C. Bennett Two Dols for building fires in School room Sub Dist No. 7.

Laban Moore Two 25/100 Dols for making door to School house Sub Dist No. 9.

R. A. McCutcheon 35/100 for lock to door Sub Dist No. 9.

J. M. Ramsey Nine 75/100 Dols for coal Sub Dist No. 13.

J. M. Ramsey Four 90/100 Dols for furnishing coal to Sub Dist No. 10.

J. M. Corley One Dol for taking Enumeration in Sub Dist No. 7 A.D. 1878

Albert England Ten Dols for furnishing fuel Sub Dist No. 8.

Albert Price Twelve Dollars for repairing School House Sub Dist No. 13.

A. W. Stalnaker Two Dollars for building fires in School room Sub Dist No. 13.

James Coffman Two Dollars for building fires in School room Sub Dist No. 10.

Ordered that the President and Secretary of this Board be and are hereby authorized to sign orders on the sheriff in vacating said Board.

On motion of commissioner **Howes** the Board adjourned to meet at **R. A. McCutcheon**s Store on the first Saturday in February 18 at one oclock P.M.

W. S. Shurtleff President
F. B. Durrett Sec. Bd. Ed.

At a meeting of the Board of Education of Barker District Barbour County West Virginia, at Belington on the **7th day of February 1880**, members present, **W. S. Shurtleff**, President **F. M. Howes, J. H. Durrett** and **Henry Bartee**, commissioners.

1st **James Tompson** Trustee of Sub District No. 12 presented to the Board a claim in favor of **B. F. Shaffer** for 26 26/100 Dollars for repairs to School House in said Sub District. The Board after considering the claim, and being petitioned not to allow said claim by the Tax Payers of Said Sub District No.12 decided it incorrect but passed an order in favor of **B. F. Shaffer** amount $16.00 Which said **Tompson** refused to accept.

An order on the school fund in favor of **R. E. Kerr** a Teacher, for Twenty Two Dollars ($22) also an order in favor of **M. N. OBrien** a teacher for Forty Two Dollars ($42). Also an order in favor of **James Coffman** a teacher for Twenty One Dollars ($21) also an order in favor of Miss **S. R. Phillips** a teacher for Forty Four Dollars $44. also an order in favor of **John M. Godwin** a teacher for Twenty one Dols $21, an order in favor of **Isaac F. Right**, a Teacher for Forty Two Dollars ($42.) also an order in favor of **James S. Poling**, a teacher, for Twenty one Dollars ($21) also an order in favor of **L. C. Bennett**, a teacher, for Forty Two Dollars ($42) also an order in favor of **R. J. Dunham**, a teacher, for Forty Four Dollars ($44) also an order in favor of **A. W. Stalnaker**, a teacher, for Forty Two Dollars, ($42). All payable out of the Teachers Fund.

Also an order on the Building fund in favor of **A. W. Stalnaker** for building fires for school room Sub Dist No. 13 for Four Dollars.

Ordered that **S. T. Hartman** be paid Forty Four Dollars out of the School Fund

Ordered that **R. J. Dunham** be paid Four Dols. from the Building Fund.

Ordered that **John T. Moss** be paid Two 60/100 Dollars from the Building fund.

Ordered that **Nathan Kelley** be paid Six 50/100 from the Building fund.

Ordered that **R. E. Kerr** be paid Forty Four Dollars out of the School Fund.

Ordered that **R. E. Kerr** be paid Four Dollars from the Building fund.

Ordered that **Jonathan Hathaway** be paid Forty Four Dollars out of the School Fund

156 School Board Minutes

Ordered that **James Coffman** be paid Twenty one Dols. from the Building fund.

Ordered that **James Coffman** be paid Four Dols from the Building fund.

Ordered that **L. C. Bennett** be paid Four Dollars from the Building fund.

Ordered that **R. A. McCutcheon** be paid Four Dols from the Building fund.

Ordered that **R. A. McCutcheon** be paid Thirty five cents from the building fund.

Ordered that **J. D. Thacker** be paid One 85/100 Dols from the Building fund.

Ordered that **A. J. Hathaway** be paid Forty Two Dols from the School Fund.

Ordered that **John C. Right** be paid One Dol. from the Building fund.

Ordered that **R. L. Tallman** be paid Twenty Two Dols. out of the School Fund.

On motion of the president the Board adjourned, to meet at **R. A. McCutcheon**s Store on the first Saturday in April 1880, at One oclock P.M.

W. S. Shurtleff
F. B. Durrett Secretary

At a meeting of the Board of Education of Barker District Barbour County West Virginia, this **3d day April 1880**, at Belington in said Co. Members present were **W. S. Shurtleff**, Pres **Henry Bartee, John H. Durrett** and **F. M. Howes**, commissioners. The Secretary of this Board made a report this day of the several orders drawn by him and the president, on the Sheriff on account of the Teachers fund and the Building fund respectively since the last meeting of the Board, which is as follows.

An order on the School fund in favor of **John M. Godwin** a teacher for Twenty one Dollars $21. Also an order on The School fund in favor of **S. P. Hartman** a teacher for Twenty Two Dollars 422. Also an order on Building fund in favor of **S. P. Hartman** for Eight Dollars $8. Also an order on the School fund in favor of **R. J. Dunham** a teacher for Twenty Two Ds $22. Also an order on the Building fund in favor of **R. A. Dunham** for Two Dollars $2. Also an order on the School fund in favor of Miss **S. R. Phillips** for Forty Four Dols $44. Also an order in favor of **S. R. Phillips** for Eight Dollars $8. on the Building fund. Also an order on the School fund in favor of **John M. Godwin** a teacher for Twenty one Dols $21. Also an order on the School fund in favor of **Jas. S. Poling** for Forty Two Dollars $42. Also an order on the Building fund in favor of **Jas. S. Poling** for Eight Dols $8. Also an order on the School fund in favor of **A. W. Stalnaker** a teacher for Twenty One Dols $21. Also an order on the Building fund in favor of **A. W. Stalnaker** for Two Dols. $2. Also an order on the School fund in favor of **Nancy C. Sipe** a teacher for Sixty Six Dols $66. Also an order on the Building fund in favor of **Nancy C. Sipe** for Eight Dols $8. Also an order on the Building fund in favor of **John M. Godwin** for Six Dols $6. Also an order on the School fund in favor of **S. C. Bennett** a teacher for Twenty one Dols. for Two Dols $2. Also an order on the School fund in favor of **J. F. Right** a teacher for Forty Two Dollars $42. Also an order in favor of **J. F. Right** for Eight Dols. on the Building fund. Also an order on the School fund in favor of **R. E. Kerr** a teacher for twenty two Dollars $22. Also an order on the Building fund in favor of **R. E.Kerr** for two Dols. 42.

Ordered that **R. A. McCutcheon** be paid 95 cents from the Building fund Sub Dist No. 8

Ordered that **R. A. McCutcheon** be paid One Dollar and 99 cts from the Building fund Sub Dist No. 2

Ordered that **John J. Ramsey** be paid Five Dols.and 94 cts from the Building fund Sub Dist No. 9

Ordered that **A. J. Hathaway** be paid Forty two Dols out of the School fund.

Ordered that **A. J. Hathaway** be paid Eight Dols out of the Building fund.

Ordered that **Jacob Sipe** be paid one Dol. and 25 cts out of the Building fund Sub Dist No. 5

Ordered that **D. G. McCauley** be paid Four Dollars and 50 cts out of the Building fund Sub Dist No. 3

Ordered that **M. N. OBrien** be paid Forty Two Dollars School fund.

Ordered that **M. N. OBrien** be paid Four Dols. out of Building fund.

Ordered that **Jonathan Hathaway** be paid Twenty Two

158 School Board Minutes

Dollars School fund.
Ordered that **Jonathan Hathaway** be paid Eight Dols. from the Building fund.
Ordered that **R. L. Tallman** be paid Forty four Dollars School fund.
Ordered that **R. L. Tallman** be paid Eight Dols and 35 cents out of Building fund.
Ordered that **Jacob Hudkins** Sheriff of Barbour County be and is hereby commanded to pay off an execution in his hands against this Board, in favor of **E. J. McCauley** for 15 Dollars and forty cents and charge to Building fund of Barker Dist.
Ordered that **R. A. McCutcheon** be paid eighty cents from Building fund Sub Dist No. 113
Ordered that **B. F. Shaffer** be paid Eighteen Dollars from Building fund of Sub Dist No. 12 for Repairs.
On motion of **F. M. Howes** the board adjourned without appointing a day for the next meeting.
        W. S. Shurtleff President
           F. B. Durrett Sec. Bd. Ed.

At a Special meeting of the Board of Education of Barker District Barbour Co. West Va. On the **12th day of June 1880**.. Members present were **W. Scott Shurtleff**, Pres. and **F. M. Howes, Henry Bartee,** and **John H. Durrett** commissioners.
It was ordered that Philippi District be paid Seventeen 95/100 Dollars from the School fund of Barker District for teaching transferred pupils from Sub Dist No. 12 .
Ordered that **John M. Godwin** be paid Two Dollars for taking Enumeration of youths in Sub Dist No. 10 payable out of Building fund, the above claim being certified by County Superintendent.
Ordered that **James Coffman** to School teacher be paid Twenty one Dollars from School fund for services rendered as Teacher in Sub Dist No. 10.
Ordered that the Board do now adjourn to meet at **R. A. McCutcheon**s store on the 19th day of June 1880 at two oclock P.M.
        W. S. Shurtleff President
           F. B. Durrett Sec Bd. Ed.

School Board Minutes 159

At a meeting of the Board of Education of Barker District Barbour County West Virginia, this **21st day of August 1880**. Members present were **W. S. Shurtleff**, Pres **Henry Bartee, John H. Durrett** and **F. M. Howes**, commissioners.

The object of the meeting being to settle with **Jacob Hudkins** Sheriff of Barbour County W. Va. which result is as follows.

School fund
Sheriff of Barbour Co.   Dr.

Balance Due on Settlement from settlement last year	$474.25
From District levy	$365.88
From State School fund	$896.52
Total	$1736.65

Sheriff of Barbour credited by the following No. and amount of vouchers

No. 28	R. S. Tallman	24.00
No. 41	Same	24.00
No. 55	C. F. Teter	48.00
No. 54	Hannah OBrien	18.00
No. 58	W. S. Shurtleff	24.00
No. 106	C. F. Teter	24.00
No. 110	Alice Wilmoth	18.00
No. 115	Sallie R. Phillips	25.00
No. 119	L. C. Bennett	25.00
No. 122	J. A. Hillyard	25.00
No. 126	L. C. Bennett	25.00
No. 128	J. F. Right	25.00
No. 129	W. S. Shurtleff	25.00
No. 2	R. S. Tallman	25.00
No. 6	J. M. Godwin	21.00
No. 7	R. S. Tallman	22.00
No. 8	N. C. Sipe	22.00
No. 18	R. J. Dunham	22.00
No. 22	S. P. Hartman	22.00
No. 23	J. S. Poling	21.00
No. 28	L. C. Bennett	21.00
No. 38	A. W. Stalnaker	21.00
No. 40	Jas. Coffman	21.00
No. 42	R. E. Kerr	22.00

160 School Board Minutes

No. 43	M. N. OBrien	42.00
No. 44	Jas. Coffman	21.00
No. 45	Sallie R. Phillips	44.00
No. 47	J. F. Right	42.00
No. 48	J. S. Poling	21.00
No. 49	L. C. Bennett	42.00
No. 50	R. J. Dunham	44.00
No. 51	A. W. Stalnaker	42.00
No. 53	S. P. Hartman	44.00
No. 57	R. E. Kerr	44.00
No. 60	Jas. Coffman	21.00
No. 69	R. S. Tallman	22.00
No. 71	S. P. Hartman	22.00
No. 84	A. W. Stalnaker	21.00
No. 90	R. E. Kerr	22.00
No.107	Philippi District	17.95
No. 88	I. F. Right	42.00
No. 86	L. C. Bennett	21.00
No. 98	M. N. OBrien	42.00
By Delinquent list		5.08
By Commission		10.82
By Discrepancy		.10
Total Credit		$1202.95
Sheriff of Barbour Co. Js.		1736.65
Same Cr		1202.95
Balance Due Barker Dist		$533.70

on Settlement made this 21st Aug 1880
Amount of unsettled orders given by Board 474 Dols.
Amt unexpended by Bd. Ed. $59.70

Building Fund

Balance Due from Settlement of last year	$207.33
Balance Due District - levy	487.82
Discrepancy	2.45
Total to Credit of District	697.60

Sheriff of Barbour Co. credited by the following No and amount of vouchers
To Due bills   E. J. McCauley case   21.50

No. 53	Danl. OBrien	6.00
No. 56	C. F. Teter	4.00
No. 65	Monroe Phillips	8.00
No. 76	L. W. Corley	0.95
No. 109	Miss Hannah OBrien	2.80
No. 112	R. A. McCutcheon	9.75
No. 127	Hamilton Fink	1.00
No. 132	J. B. Godwin	3.00
No. 136	Same	15.00
No. 3	C. B. Carter	1.00
No. 4	J. Morgan Ramsey	1.00
No. 5	R. A. McCutcheon	1.50
No. 6	Jacob B. Godwin	10.00
No. 9	John R. W. Smith	9.00
No. 10	Jacob B. Godwin	11.27
No. 11	Jesse Teter	9.15
No. 12	Luther Kerr	8.20
No. 13	Ballard Jones	8.12
No. 14	R. Taylor George	8.50
No. 15	John M. Godwin	2.00
No. 16	R. E. Kerr	2.00
No. 17	William England	0.75
No. 19	R. Jona Dunham	2.00
No. 21	William Day	6.25
No. 24	R. A. McCutcheon	0.50
No. 25	Same	1.36
No. 26	Same	0.75
No. 27	Marquis Moore	7.55
No. 29	J. B. Hillyard	7.50
No. 30	Luther C. Bennett	2.00
No. 31	Laban Moore	2.25
No. 32	R. A. McCutcheon	0.35
No. 33	J. M. Ramsey	9.75
No. 34	Same	4.90
No. 35	J. M. Corley	1.00
No. 36	Albert England	10.00
No. 37	Albert Price	12.00
No. 39	A. W. Stalnaker	2.00
No. 41	Jas. Coffman	2.00

162 School Board Minutes

No. 52	A. W. Stalnaker	4.00
No. 54	R. J. Dunham	4.00
No. 55	John T. Moss	2.50
No. 56	Nathan Kelley	6.50
No. 58	R. E. Kerr	4.00
No. 61	Jas. Coffman	4.00
No. 62	L. C. Bennett	4.00
No. 63	B. F. Shaffer	18.00
No. 64	R. A. McCutcheon	4.00
No. 65	Same	.35
No. 66	J. D. Thacker	1.85
No. 68	J. C. Right	1.00
No. 72	S. P. Hartman	8.00
No. 74	R. J. Dunham	2.00
No. 75	R. A. McCutcheon	0.95
No. 77	S. R. Phillips	8.00
No. 79	A. W. Stalnaker	2.00
No. 87	L. C. Bennett	2.00
No. 91	R. E. Kerr	2.00
No. 92	R. A. McCutcheon	1.99
No. 93	J. J. Ramsey	5.94
No. 95	A. J. Hathaway	8.00
No. 96	Jacob Sipe	1.25
No. 97	David G. McCauley	4.50
No. 99	M. N. OBrien	4.00
No. 103	R. S. Tallman	8.35
No. 105	J. M. Godwin	2.00
	Albert Reger and Son	23.65
No. 89	J. F. Right	8.00
By Commission		14.43
By Delinquent list		6.81
Amount of vouchers &c received		$384.72
Leaving a balance Due Barker Dist		312.88

W. S. Shurtleff President
F. B. Durrett Sec.

Meadowville, Barbour Co. W. Va.
Sept. 4th 1880

This is to certify that I have examined the books of **F. B. Durrett** and find them correct also I have examined the annual report and find it correct the Board of Education will allow him an order for $10.00 for the same as required by law.

A. B. Moore Co.Supt.

At a meeting of the Board of Education of Barker District Barbour County West Virginia, this **6th September 1880**. Members present were **W. S. Shurtleff**, Pres **H. Bartee, J. H. Durrett** and **F. M. Howes**, and **Cicero Phillips** commissioners.

Ordered that there be Four months School in each Sub District of Barker Dist.

Ordered that the School Levy be Twenty cents on each $100. valuation which val. is $245. 683.16 amount levied $491.36 for schools.

Ordered that the levy for building purposes be ten cents for each $100. valuation which amounts to $245.68 to amount levied $736.04 for both funds.

Ordered that the teachers salary be and is hereby fixed as follows. For teachers holding No.1 certificate 24 Dollars, No. 2, 21 Dollars. No. 3 12 Dollars.

Ordered that the schools commence on the first Monday in November 1880.

There being a vacancy in Trustee in Sub District No. 1 caused by the resignation of **J. B. Steerman** it is ordered that **Simon Swick** be and is hereby appointed to fill said vacancy, also in Sub Dist No. 6 there being a vacancy caused by the resignation of **J. M. Hathaway** it is ordered that **Jesse Teter** be and is hereby appointed to fill said vacancy.

Ordered the following named teachers be employed to teach the free schools in Barker District. Sub District

No. 1   **Jonathan Hathaway** (grade of certificate No. one)
No. 2   **Andrew J. Hathaway** (Grade of certificate No.one)
No. 3   Miss **Nova Moore** (Grade of certificate No. one)

164 School Board Minutes

No. 4 **R. E. Kerr** (Grade of certificate No. one)
No. 5 **Miss N. C. Sipe** (Grade of certificate No. Two)
No. 6 **Mrs. M. V. Teter** (Grade of certificate No. One)
No. 7 **Monroe Phillips** (Grade of certificate No. Two)
No. 8 **Mrs. M. E. Harris** (Grade of certificate No. one)
No. 9 **G. W. Shaffer** (Grade of certificate No. Two)
No. 10 **Jas. Coffman** (Grade of certificate No. One)
No. 11 **Miss S. R. Phillips** (Grade of certificate No. One)
No. 12 **J. A. Hillyard** (Grade of certificate No. Two)
No. 13 **G. M. Right** (Grade of certificate No. 2)
No. 14 **W. W. Right** (Grade of certificate No. 2)
No. 15 **R. J. Dunham** (Grade of certificate No. one)

Ordered that **F. B. Durrett** be paid Twenty Five Dollars from the Building fun for services rendered as Secretary and for making annual report to **A. B. Moore** County Supt.

Ordered that the Board do now adjourn to meet on the last Sat. in (25) September 1880 at one oclock P.M.

W. S. Shurtleff President
F. B. Durrett Sec. Bd. Ed.

Belington, Barbour Co. West Virginia

At a meeting of the Board of Education, this **25 Sept. 1880**. Members present were **W. S. Shurtleff**, Pres **H. Bartee, F. M. Howes**, and **C. Phillips** commissioners. It was ordered that **Cornelius Corley** be and is hereby employed to repair the School house in Sub District No. 7 for the sum of $45.

On motion the Board adjourned to meet on the last Sat. (30) in October 1880 at one oclock P.M.

W. S. Shurtleff President
F. B. Durrett Sec. Bd. Ed.

At a meeting of the Board of Education of Barker District Barbour Co West Virginia at Belington on the **20th October 1880**. Members present were **W. S. Shurtleff**, Pres **H. Bartee, J. H.**

Durrett and **Cicero Phillips**, com. It appearing to the Board that there is a vacancy in Trustee in Sub Dist No. 12 caused by the resignation of **Jas. Tompson** it is ordered that **John Findley** be and is hereby appointed to fill said vacancy.

Ordered that **Cornelius Corley** be paid Forty Five Dollars for repairs done to School house in Sub Dist No. 7 from the Building Fund

Ordered that **Geo. E. Sipe** be paid Four Dols and 25 cents from the Building Fund.

Ordered that **E. T. Kade** be paid Seven Dols .25 cts from the Building Fund

Ordered that **F. D. Valentine** be paid Two hundred and Twenty Five Dollars from the Building Fund, For one School house and lot, in Sub Dist No. 15, **Valentine** having made a deed to the Board of Education for the School house and lot above mentioned.

On motion the Board adjourned to meet at Belington on the first Sat. in December 1880 at one oclock P.M.

W. S. Shurtleff President
F. B. Durrett Sec.

Belington

At a meeting of the Board of Education of Barker District Barbour Co West Va. on the **4th day of Dec. 1880**. Members present were **W. S. Shurtleff**, Pres **H. Bartee, J. H. Durrett, F. M. Howes** and **Cicero Phillips**, commissioners.

Ordered that **James Coffman** be paid (24) Twenty Four Dollars from the School Fund.

Ordered that **R. E. Kerr** be paid (24) Twenty Four Dollars from the School Fund.

Ordered that Miss **Nora Moore** be paid Twenty Four (24) Dollars from the School Fund.

Ordered that Miss **Sallie R. Phillips** be paid Twenty Four Dollars from the School Fund.

Ordered that **Monroe Phillips** be paid Twenty Two Dollars from the School Fund.

Ordered that **J. R. Cross** be paid Two Dollars Seventy five from the Building Fund.

Ordered that **B. S. Jones** be paid Eight 10/100 Dollars from the Building Fund.

166 School Board Minutes

Ordered that **Harmon Werner** be paid Eight Dollars from the Building Fund.

Ordered that **J. R. Hillyard** be paid Six 50/100 Dollars from the Building Fund.

Ordered that **E. M. Moore** be paid Five 75/100 Dollars from the Building Fund.

Ordered that **J. Y. Booth** be paid Seven 45/100 Dollars from the Building Fund.

Ordered that Miss **N. C. Sipe** be paid Twenty one Dollars from the School Fund.

Ordered that **John W. Ward** be paid Eighty Five cents from the Building Fund.

Ordered that **Isiah Moore** be paid One 10/100 Dollars from the Building Fund.

Ordered that **John Findley** be paid One 50/100 Dollars from the Building Fund.

Ordered that **Jas Poling** be paid Seventy Five cents from the Building Fund.

Ordered that **Alexander Talbott** be paid Eight Dollars from the Building Fund.

Ordered that **Geo. E. Talbott** be paid Six 40/100 Dollars from the Building Fund.

Ordered that **W. W. Right** be paid Twenty One Dollars from the School Fund.

Ordered that **Geo. M. Right** be paid Twenty One Dollars from the School Fund.

Ordered that Mrs. **M. E. Harris** be paid Twenty Four Dollars from the School Fund.

Ordered that **R. J. Dunham** be paid Twenty Four Dollars from the School Fund.

Ordered that **L. H. Kerr** be paid Nine Dollars from the Building Fund.

Ordered that **Abel Teter** be paid Five 50/100 Dollars from the Building Fund.

Ordered that **John Arbogast** be paid Five Dollars from the Building Fund.

Ordered that **E. G. Hoffman** be paid One 90/100 Dollars from the Building Fund.

On motion of **F. M. Howes** the Board adjourned to meet on the first Saturday in January 1881 at **R. A. McCutcheons** Store at one

oclock P.M.
W. S. Shurtleff President
F. B. Durrett Sec.

At a meeting of the Board of Education of Barker District Barbour Co. West Va. on the **1st day of Jan. 1881** Members present were **W. S. Shurtleff**, Pres **Henry Bartee, J. H. Durrett** and **Cicero Phillips**, commissioners.

Ordered that the President and Secretary of this Board be and are hereby authorized to Sign orders on the School fund in vacation of Said Board.

Ordered that **Geo. W. Shaffer** be paid Forty Two (42) Dols. from the School Fund.

Ordered that Miss **M. V. Teter** be paid Twenty Four (24) Dols. from the School Fund.

Ordered that Miss **Nora Moore** be paid Twenty Four (24) Dols. from the School Fund.

Ordered that **Monroe Phillips** be paid Twenty (20) Dollars from the School Fund.

Ordered that **Dan'l Day** be paid Nine 75/100 Dols. from the Building Fund.

Ordered that **William Day** be paid Two 10/100 Dollars from the Building Fund.

Ordered that **Josiah Wilson** be paid One Dol. from the Building Fund.

Ordered that **R. A. McCutcheon** be paid Fifteen 30/100 Dollars from the Building Fund.

On motion of **H. Bartee** the Board adjourned to meet on the first Saturday in February 1881 at Belington one oclock P.M.
W. S. Shurtleff President
F. B. Durrett Sec.

At a meeting of the Board of Education of Barker School District Barbour Co. West Virginia at Belington on the **5th day of**

School Board Minutes

February 1881. Members present were **W. S. Shurtleff**, Pres **H. Bartee, J. H. Durrett**, commissioners, it was

Ordered that **Jas. Coffman** be paid Twenty Four Dollars from the School Fund.

Ordered that **R. E. Kerr** be paid Twenty Four Dollars from the School Fund.

Ordered that Miss **M. V. Teter** be paid Forty Eight Dollars from the School Fund.

Ordered that **Jas. Coffman** be paid Twenty Four Dollars from the School Fund.

Ordered that **Jas. Ramsey** be paid Four 95/100 Dollars from the Building Fund.

Ordered that **William Cross** be paid Seven Dollars from the Building Fund.

Ordered that **R. E. Kerr** be paid Twenty Four Dollars from the School Fund.

Ordered that **E. Buckey** be paid Two 75/100 Dollars from the Building Fund.

Ordered that **J. A. Hillyard** be paid Forty Two Dollars from the School Fund.

Ordered that **R. E. Kerr** be paid Six Dollars from the Building Fund.

Ordered that **M. E. Harris** be paid Twenty Four Dollars from the School Fund.

On motion the Board adjourned to meet March 12th 1881 at **R. A. McCutcheon**s Store at one oclock P.M.

W. S. Shurtleff President
F. B. Durrett Secretary

At a meeting of the Board of Education of Barker District Barbour Co. West Virginia on the **12th day of March 1881** at Belington in said county and state. Members of the Board present were **W. S. Shurtleff**, Pres **Henry Bartee**, and **J. H. Durrett**, commissioners the following list of orders were passed.

Ordered that **R. J. Dunham** be paid Forty Eight (48) Dollars from the School fund.

Ordered that Miss **Nora Moore** be paid Twenty Four Dollars

School Board Minutes

from the School fund.

Ordered that **Jonathan Hathaway** be paid Ninety Six Dollars from the School fund.

Ordered that **Jonathan Hathaway** be paid Eight Dollars from the Building fund.

Ordered that **A. J. Hathaway** be paid Ninety Six Dollars from the School fund.

Ordered that **A. J. Hathaway** be paid Eight Dollars from the Building fund.

Ordered that Miss **Nora Moore** be paid Twenty Four Dollars from the School fund.

Ordered that **J. H. Durrett** be paid Eight Dollars from the Building fund for building Fires Dist No.3

Ordered that **R. E. Kerr** be paid Twenty Four Dollars from the School fund.

Ordered that **R. E. Kerr** be paid One Dollar from the Building fund.

Ordered that Miss **N. C. Sipe** be paid Sixty Three Dollars from the School fund.

Ordered that Miss **N. C. Sipe** be paid Eight Dollars from the Building fund.

Ordered that Miss. **M. V. Teter** be paid Twenty Four Dols. from the School fund.

Ordered that Miss **M. V. Teter** be paid Eight Dollars from the Building fund.

Ordered that **Monroe Phillips** be paid Forty Two Dollars from the School fund.

Ordered that **Monroe Phillips** be paid Eight Dollars from the Building fund.

Ordered that **Geo. W. Shaffer** be paid Forty Two Dollars from the School fund.

Ordered that **Geo. W. Shaffer** be paid Eight Dollars from the Building fund.

Ordered that Miss **S. R. Phillips** be paid Seventy Two Dollars from the School fund.

Ordered that Miss **S. R. Phillips** be paid Eight Dollars from the Building fund.

Ordered that **Jas. Coffman** be paid Twenty Four Dollars from the School fund.

Ordered that **Jas. Coffman** be paid Eight Dollars from the

170 School Board Minutes

Building fund.

Ordered that **Geo. W. Right** be paid Sixty three Dollars from the School fund.

Ordered that **Geo. W. Right** be paid Eight Dollars from the Building fund.

Ordered that **J. A. Hillyard** be paid Forty Two Dollars from the School fund.

Ordered that **J. A. Hillyard** be paid Eight Dollars from the Building fund.

Ordered that **W. W. Right** be paid Sixty three Dollars from the School fund.

Ordered that **W. W. Right** be paid Eight Dollars from the Building fund.

Ordered that **J. D. Thacker** be paid Thirty cents from the Building fund.

Ordered that **R. Jona. Dunham** be paid Six Dollars from the Building fund.

Ordered that **W. S. Davis** be paid Seven Dols and 20 cts from the Building fund.

Ordered that **Levi Fitzwater** be paid Four Dols and 25 cents from the Building fund.

Ordered that **E. O. Baker** be paid Two Dollars from the Building fund.

Ordered that **R. J. Dunham** be paid Twenty Four Dollars from the School fund.

Ordered that **Randolph Coberly** be paid Ten Dollars from the Building fund.

Ordered that **S. E. Shires** be paid Two Dollars from the Building fund.

Ordered that Philippi District be paid Twenty one Dollars 70 cents from School fund.

Ordered that Miss **M. E. Harris** be paid Forty Eight Dollars from School fund.

Ordered that Miss **M. E. Harris** be paid Eight Dollars from Building fund.

On motion the Board adjourned. Sine Die.

W. S. Shurtleff President

F. B. Durrett Secretary

Meadowville Barbour Co. W. Va.
July 14, 1881

This is to certify that I have examined the book of **B. F. Durrett** and find it correct. The Board of Education will allow him an order for his services as Sec'tary for Barker district to the amt. of $15.00 and I have examined his report and find it correct, except the settlement which is not yet made. The Board will allow him $10.00 for the same.

A. B. Moore

At a meeting of the Board of Education of Barker District Barbour Co. West Virginia at Belington on the **4th day of July 1881** Consisting of **W. S. Shurtleff**, President and **Solomon Coffman** and **William M. Bibey** commissioners after duly organizing and appointing **John Right** Secretary the following business was transacted as follows.

Renumbering the Sub Dist of Barker District

No. 1	Beaver Creek
No. 2	Belington
No. 3	Independence
No. 4	Huntersfork
No. 5	Sugar Creek
No. 6	Wolf Run
No. 7	Ten Mile
No. 8	Mouse Run
No. 9	Bills Creek

Also the Following named persons were appointed Trustee of his Sub Dist as Follows to serve one, Two and three years.

Sub Dist		Years
No. 1	**Jackson Hillyard**	1
	D. J. Shomo	2
	B. P. Newlon	3
No. 2	**R. A. McCutcheon**	1
	J. J. Newlon	2
	D. S. Talbott	3
No. 3	**Laben Moore**	1
	John Dunham	2

School Board Minutes

	W. J. Right	3
No. 4	Simpson Cross	1
	J. W. Holler	2
	William Cross	3
No. 5	J. M. Ramsey	1
	W. R. Moore	2
	F. M. Howes	3
No. 6	J. C. Right	1
	Alpheus Moore	2
	Albert Price	3
No. 7	Lewis Jones	1
	Jacob McLane	2
	F. B. Durrett	3
No. 8	John Finley	1
	Randolph Conberley	2
	John Wagner	3
No. 9	Israel Poling	1
	C. B. Carter	2
	James Poling	3

It is so ordered there will be 4 month of School Taught also ordered there be Nine Teachers Employed and Salary of Grade of Certificate per month as Follows

No. 1 Certificate   Twenty Four Dollars
No. 2 Certificate   Twenty Two Dollars
No. 3 Certificate   Fifteen Dollars

The Board also Leevyed for School Purposes 25 cents on the one hundred Valuation and Leveyed for Building purposes 40 cents on the one hundred Valuation.

It is so ordered by the board that the schools Commence on the First Monday in November 1881. On motion the board adjourned to meet on the third Saturday of July 1881 to settle with the Sheriff at **R. A. McCutcheons** store.

                W. S. Shurtleff President
                  John Right Secretary

At a meeting of the Board of Education of Barker District Barbour Co. West Virginia this **16th day of July 1881.** Members present **William Bibey** Pres Protem and **Solomon Coffman** Commissioner the object of the Meeting to settle with the Sheriff **Jacob Hudkins** which result is as Followes.

School Fund

Jacob Hudkins Sheriff   Dr.
Balance Due on Settlement From Settlement of last year $172.07
From District Leevey   392.30
From State School Fund   402.46
Total $964.53

Sheriff of Barbour Credited by the Following No. and amount of vouchers

No.	Name	Amount
117	J. M. Godwin	25.00
46	J. M. Godwin	21.00
59	Jonathan Hathaway	44.00
70	J. M. Godwin	21.00
73	R. J. Dunham	22.00
76	Miss S. R. Phillips	44.00
78	J. M. Godwin	21.00
82	James W. Poling	42.00
102	R. L. Tallman	44.00
	James Coffman	21.00
7	James Coffman	24.00
8	R. E. Kerr	24.00
9	Miss Nora Moore	24.00
11	Monroe Phillips	22.00
18	Miss N. C. Sipe	21.00
25	W. W. Right	21.00
26	G. M. Right	21.00
27	Miss M. E. Harris	24.00
28	R. J. Dunham	24.00
33	G. W. Shaffer	42.00
34	Miss M. V. Teter	24.00
35	Miss Nora Moore	24.00
66	Monroe Phillips	20.00
41	James Coffman	24.00
42	R. E. Kerr	24.00
43	Miss M. V. Teter	48.00
44	James Coffman	24.00

174 School Board Minutes

47	R. E. Kerr	24.00
49	J. A. Hillyard	42.00
51	M. E. Harris	24.00
53	Miss Nora Moore	24.00
56	A. J. Hathaway	96.00
131	C. V. Street	08.00
58	Miss Nora Moore	24.00
60	R. E. Kerr	24.00
62	Miss N. C. Sipe	63.00
64	M. V. Teter	24.00
66	Monroe Phillips	42.00
68	George W. Shaffer	42.00
70	Miss S. R. Phillips	72.00
72	James Coffman	24.00
74	George M. Right	63.00
76	J. A. Hillyard	42.00
88	Philippi District	21.70
10	S. R. Phillips	24.00
20	Jonathan Hathaway	22.00
114	Jonathan Hathaway	25.00
67	A. J. Hathaway	42.00
94	A. J. Hathaway	42.00
100	Jonathan Hathaway	22.00
52	R. J. Dunham	48.00
54	Jonathan Hathaway	96.00
85	R. J. Dunham	24.00
By improperly amt. on		00.00
Assessors Books		00.31
By amt. Delinquent list		03.67
Sheriff Com.		14.62
Total Credit		$1763.30

Building Fund
Balance on Settlement made July 16th 1881   9 cents
District Levey $624.63
Sheriff of Barbour County Credited by the Following No. and amt of Vouchers

No.	Name	Amt
55	Jonathan Hathaway	8.00
101	Jonathan Hathaway	8.00

86	Randolph Coberly	10.00
85	J. M. Godwin	6.00
83	Levi Fitzwater	4.25
81	J. D. Thacker	0.30
80	R. J. Dunham	6.00
79	W. W. Right	63.00
78	W. W. Right	8.00
77	J. A. Hillyard	8.00
75	G. M. Right	8.00
73	James Coffman	8.00
71	Miss S. R. Phillips	8.00
69	G. W. Shaffer	8.00
67	Monroe Phillips	8.00
65	Miss M. V. Teter	8.00
63	Miss N. C. Sipe	8.00
59	J. H. Durrett	8.00
57	A. J. Hathaway	8.00
48	E. Buckey	2.25
46	Wm Cross	7.00
45	James Ramsey	4.95
40	R. A. McCutcheon	15.80
39	Joseph Wilson	1.00
38	Daniel Day	2.10
37	William Day	9.95
32	E. G. Huffman	1.90
31	John Arbogast	5.00
30	Able Teter	5.50
29	G. W. Kerr	9.00
24	George E. Talbott	8.00
23	A. C. Talbott	8.00
21	John Finley	1.50
20	Isaiah Moore	1.10
19	J. W. Ward	0.85
17	J. G. Booth	7.45
16	E. M. Moore	5.75
15	J. B. Hillyard	6.50
14	Harmon Warner	8.00
13	B. S. Jones	8.10
6	F. D. Valentine	225.00

School Board Minutes

5	E. T. Cade		7.25
4	S. S. Boner		9.00
3	George E. Sipe		4.25
2	E. Corley		45.00
1	F. B. Durrett		25.00
104	R. A. McCutcheon		0.80
83	James W. Poling		8.00
81	Miss N. E. Sipe		8.00
	W. J. Right	Fee bill	0.65
	W. J. Right	Do	1.00
	E. McColley	Do	1.00

Amt. Improperly on the Assessors Books   0.16
Amt. Delinquent list   1.86
Sheriff Com   7.31
Total Credit   658.48

    Ordered that **F. B. Durrett** be Paid Twenty Five Dollars out of Building Fund.
    On motion the Board Adjourned to meet on Saturday October the 29th 1881 at 9 A.M.
          W. S. Shurtleff President
          John Right Secty

    At a Call Meeting of the Board of Education of Barker District held on **August 13th 1881.** Members Present **W. S. Shurtleff,** President, **Wm M. Bibey** and **Solomon Coffman** Commissioners the Following Business was Transacted appointing **D. J. Shomo** Trustee instead of **Perry Simon** in Sub District No. 1 also ordered that **F. B. Durrett** be paid Five Dollars out of building Fund for Services in Taking Numeration by order of County Superintendent.
          W. S. Shurtleff President
          John Right Secy

No. 32   Sub Dist No. 6   **G. M. Right**   Grade of Certificate One
No.___   Sub Dist No. 1   **W. W. Right**   Grade of Certificate One

School Board Minutes 177

No. 13	Sub Dist No. 9 **Alice Wilmoth** Grade of Certificate One
No. 34	Sub Dist No. 7 **B. B. Roahrbough** Grade of Certificate Two
No. 22	Sub Dist No. 4 **J. S. Poling** Grade of Certificate Two
No. 35	Sub Dist No. 6 Miss **S. R. Phillips** Grade of Certificate One
No. 91	Sub Dist No. 8 **J. H. Robinson** Grade of Certificate Three
No. 40	Sub Dist No. 3 **J. A. Dunham** Grade of Certificate One
No. 2	**B. F. Burdett** Grade of Certificate One

    At a Call Meeting of the Board of Education of Barker District Barbour County W. Va. Held at Belington on the **8th day of October 1881.** Members Present **W. S. Shurtleff,** President, **Solomon Coffman,** Commissioner the Following Business was Transacted appointing **Wm S. Parks** Trustee in Sub Dist No. 8 instead of **Randolph Coberly** also **Newton Chenoweth** instead of **John Finley** in same Dist. No. 8 and also **C. Corley** as Trustee in Room of **B. P. Newlon** Moved away in Sub Dis. No. 1 also ordered that **J. T. Moss** be Paid Two Dollars out of building Fund.
                W. S. Shurtleff President
                John Right Secty

    At a Meeting of the Board of Education of Barker District Barbour County W. Va. Held on **Saturday October 29, 1881. W. S. Shurtleff,** President and **Solomon Coffman & Wm M. Bibey** Commissioners the Following Business was Transacted. On motion to adjourn To meet on the Second Saturday 10th of December 1881 at 1 oclock P.M.
                W. S. Shurtleff President
                John Right Secty

178 School Board Minutes

At a Meeting of the Board of Education of Barker District Barbour County W. Va. held at Belington on **Saturday Dec 10th, 1881. Wm M. Bibey** President Protem and **Solomon Coffman** Commissioners the Following Business was Transacted Viz.

Ordered that **J. D. Jones** be paid Six Dollars & 75 cts of Building Fund.

Ordered that **F. Howes** be paid Six Dollars out of Building Fund.

Ordered that **R. M. Bennett** be paid Six Dollars & 75 of Building Fund.

Ordered that **J. W. Ward** be paid Ninety cents out of Building Fund.

Ordered that **W. J. Hillyard** be paid Five Dollars & 75 cts out of Building Fund.

Ordered that **S. R. Phillips** be paid Twenty Four Dollars of School Fund.

Ordered that **W. W. Right** be paid Twenty Four Dollars out of School Fund.

Ordered that **Right & Shurtleff** be paid Two Dollars & 45 cts of Building Fund.

Ordered that **G. M. Right** be paid Twenty Four Dollars out of Building Fund.

Ordered that **Albert Price** be paid Seven Dollars out of Building Fund.

Ordered that **J. C. Right & Albert Price** be paid Ten Dollars out of Building Fund.

On motion the Board adjourned to Meet at Belington on the Second Saturday of January the 14th 1882 at 1 oclock P.M.

    W. S. Shurtleff President
      John Right Scty

At a Meeting of the Board of Education of Barker District Barbour County West Virginia held on the **14th day of January 1882**. **W. S. Shurtleff,** President and **Solomon Coffman** Commissioners The Following Business was Transacted Viz.

The Board appointed **A. J. Row, J. W. Corley** and **John**

Corley as Trustees in Sub District No. 1 in Room of **J. J. Shomo** and **Jackson Hillyard** Resined & **C. Corley** Moved out of District.

Ordered That **A. M. Wilmoth** be paid Forty Eight Dollars out of School Fund.

Ordered That **B. B. Rhorabough** be paid Forty Four Dollars out of School Fund.

Ordered That **B. B. Rhorabough** be paid Four Dollars & Fifteen cts out of Building Fund.

Ordered That **G. M. Right** be paid Twenty Four Dollars out of School Fund.

Ordered That **J. S. Poling** be paid Twenty Two Dollars out of School Fund.

Ordered That **W. S. Parks** be paid Eight Dollars & Ninelty cts out of Building Fund.

Ordered That **J. S. Poling** be paid Twenty Two Dollars out of School Fund.

Ordered That **William Cross** be paid Eight Dollars out of Building Fund.

Ordered That **Daniel Ice** be paid Twenty Seven Dollars & 50 out of Building Fund.

Ordered That **Jackson Hillyard** be paid Eight Dollars out of Building Fund.

Ordered That **R. A. McCutcheon** be paid 75 cts out of Building Fund.

Ordered That **W. W. Right** be paid Twenty Four Dollars out of School Fund.

Ordered That **John Right** be paid Seven Dollars & 50 cts out of Building Fund.

On Motion the Board adjourned To Meet at Belington on Saturday the 21st 1882.

W. S. Shurtleff President
John Right Scty

At a Meeting of the Board of Education held on the **21st day of January, 1882**. **W. S. Shurtleff**, President, **William M. Biby** and **Solomon Coffman** Commissioners the Following Business was

School Board Minutes

Transacted (Viz) appointing the Following Named persons as Trustees in Sub Dist No.1 **B. P. Newlon** in Room of **A. J. Row** and **H. P. Rector** in Room of **G. W. Corley**. Charges against **W. W. Right** a School Teacher in Sub Dist No. 1 Filed by **Jackson Hillyard** and **D. J. Shomo** Rejected on the grounds that they not being Legal the Said **Jackson Hillyard** and **D. J. Shomo** not being any more Trustees.

Ordered that **Right** and **Shurtleff** be paid Two Dollars & 70 cts of Building Fund

Ordered that **J. A. Dunham** be paid Twenty Four Dollars out of School Fund.

Ordered that **J. A. Dunham** be paid Two Dollars out of Building Fund

Ordered that **S. R. Phillips** be paid Twenty Four Dollars out of School Fund.

On motion the Board adjourned to Meet on Saturday February the 18th 1882 at 1 oclock P.M. at Belington.

W. S. Shurtleff President
John Right Scty

At a Meeting of the Board of Education of Barker District Barbour County West Virginia held on **Saturday February the 18th 1882. W. M. Biby** President Protem and **Solomon Coffman** Commissioners The Following Business was Transacted (Viz)

Ordered that **J. H. Robinson** be paid Forty Five Dollars out of School Fund on motion the Board adjourned to Meet on Saturday March the 25th 1882 at 1 oclock P.M. at Belington.

W. S. Shurtleff President
John Right Secty

At a Meeting of the Board of Education of Barker District Barbour County West Virginia held on **March 25th, 1882** at Belington.
W. S. Shurtleff President, **Solomon Coffman** and **W. M. Biby** Commissioners all of whom being present the Following Business was Transacted (Viz)

Ordered that **G. M. Right** be paid Forty three Dollars & 65 cts out of School Fund.

Ordered that **G. M. Right** be paid Seven Dollars & 65 cts out of Building Fund.

Ordered that **J. A. Dunham** be paid Sixty Seven Dollars & 64 cts out of School Fund.

Ordered that **J. A. Dunham** be paid Five Dollars & 65 cts out of Building Fund.

Ordered that **R. A. McCutcheon** be paid One Dollar & 7cts out of Building Fund.

Ordered that **A.. M. Wilmoth** be paid Forty Eight Dollars out of School Fund.

Ordered that **A. M. Wilmoth** be paid Eight Dollars out of Building Fund.

Ordered that **Levi Fitzwater** be paid Four Dollars & 95 cts out of Building Fund.

Ordered that **J. H. Robinson** be paid Seven Dollars & 65 cts out of Building Fund.

Ordered that **S. R. Phillips** be paid Forty three Dollars & 70 cts out of School Fund.

Ordered that **S. R. Phillips** be paid Eight Dollars out of Building Fund.

Ordered that **B. F. Burdett** be paid Ninety One Dollars & 70 cts out of School Fund.

Ordered that **B. F. Burdett** be paid Eight Dollars out of Building Fund.

Ordered that **J. S. Poling** be paid Forty Dollars out of School Fund.

Ordered that **J. S. Poling** be paid Seven Dollars & 65 cts out of Building Fund.

Ordered that **E. G. Hoffman** be paid One Dollar & 85 cts out of Building Fund.

Ordered that **James Coberly** be paid One Dollar & 25 cts out of Building Fund.

Ordered that **B. B. Rhorabough** be paid Forty Dollars out of School Fund.

Ordered that **B. B. Rhorabough** be paid Three Dollars & 65 cts out of Building Fund.

Ordered that **E. G. Hoffman** be paid One Dollar & 82 cts out of Building Fund.

School Board Minutes

Ordered that **Right & Shurtleff** be paid Seventeen Dollars out of Building Fund.

Ordered that **Solomon Coffman** be paid Six Dollars & 65 cts out of Building Fund.

Ordered that **W. M. Bibey** be paid Six Dollars out of Building Fund.

Ordered that **W. S. Shurtleff** be paid Six Dollars out of Building Fund.

Ordered that **John Right** be paid Seven dollars & 50 cts out of Building Fund.

On motion the Board adjourned Sine Die.

W. S. Shurtleff President
John Right Secty

At a Meeting of the Board of Education of Barker District Barbour County West Virginia this **15th day of June, 1882**. Members Present **W. S. Shurtleff,** President, **W. M. Biby** and **Solomon Coffman** Commissioners the object of this Meeting is to Settle with **J. C. Heatherley** Sheriff of Barbour County which Result is as Follows

School Fund

J. C. Heatherley Sheriff Dr. to Barker District on School Fund on Settlement made June 15th 1882.

Bal. Due on Settlement	$25.42
Total Credits	$768.70

Building Fund

Balance Due on Settlement June 15th 1882	$272.02
Total Credits	$304.35
Delinquent	2.51
Commission	11.69
Amt. of Executions & Fee bills	58.96
	377.51

On motion of **W. S. Shurtleff** it was ordered that **T. T. Elliott, J. B. Godwin** and **J. F. Robinson** be and is hereby appointed a committee to Meet the Board of Education of Valley District at their place of Meeting on the 3rd day of July 1882 for the purpose of ascertaining what proportion of the original debt of Barker and Valley

District they are willing to pay and report to the Board of Education of Barker District as soon there after as possible also ordered that the Board of Education of Glade District be notified of $16.66 2/3 that is due Barker District for Four months beginning Nov. 7, 1881 and Ending March 7th 1882.

Salary of Teacher	$84.00
Fueal	8.00
Making Fires	8.00
	100.00

Average attendance 30 pupils Making 3.33 2/3 per pupil.
    On Motion the Board adjourned to Meet on the First Monday in July 1882 at 9 A. M.

                  W. S. Shurtleff President
                  John Right Secty

    At a Meeting of the Board of Education of Barker District Barbour County West Virginia Members Present **W. S. Shurtleff,** President, **W. M. Biby** and **Solomon Coffman** Commissioners the Following Business was Transacted (Viz) appointing of Trustees.

Sub Dist No.		Years
1	H. P. Rector	3
	B. P. Newlen	2
	John Corley	1
2	R. A. McCutcheon	3
	D. S. Talbott	2
	J. J. Newlen	1
3	Laben Moore	3
	W. J. Right	2
	John Dunham	1
4	Simpson Cross	3
	Wm. Cross	2
	J. W. Holler	1

School Board Minutes

5	Albert England	3
	F. M. Howes	2
	W. R. Moore	1
6	J. C. Right	3
	A. Price	2
	Alpheus Moore	1
7	L. T. Hollen	3
	F. B. Durrett	2
	Jacob McClain	1
8	W. S. Parks	3
	Sanford Poling	2
	Randolph Coberly	1
9	Dyer Kelley	3
	Jas. Poling	2
	C. B. Carter	1

Also the Salery of Teachers
No. 1   Certificate   25.00 Dollars
No. 2   Certificate   22.00 Dollars
No. 3   Certificate   18.00 Dollars

Also ordered that Schools begin on the 1st Monday in November 1882.

Also Leveyed for School purposes 20 cents on the one hundred Valuation Making $318.00
State School Fund   612.72
                                               930.72

Levey on the Buildihg Fund
50 cents as a Special levey Making $795.00
And 15 cents for fewel &c Making   238.50
                                               1033.50

Ordered that the Trustees do advertise in three Public Places and then Sell out the Coal to Run a 4 month School to the lowest Responsable Bidder on Motion the Board adjourned.

W. S. Shurtleff President
John Right Scty

October 10th 1882
No. 52   Sub Dist No. 7 **Ida M. Teter** Grade of Certificate Two
No. 59   Sub Dist No. 5 **S. R. Phillips** Grade of Certificate One
No. 67   Sub Dist No. 6 **Geor. M. Right** Grade of Certificate One
No. 61   Sub Dist No. 3 **Florence Wilmoth** Grade of Certificate Two
No. 62   Sub Dist No. 8 **Jas Coberly** Grade of Certificate Three
No. 60   Sub Dist No. 9 **Alice Wilmoth** Grade of Certificate One
No. 43   Sub Dist No. 4 **James Coffman** Grade of Certificate One
No. 81   Sub Dist No. 1 **Samuel Moran** Grade of Certificate Three
No. 97   Sub Dist No. 2 **J. A. Dunham** Grade of Certificate One

At a Meeting of the Board of Education of Barker District Barbour County W.Va. held **Dec 9th 1882**. Members Present **W. S. Shurtleff,** President, **W. M. Biby** and **Solomon Coffman** Commissioners the Following Business was Transacted (Viz)

Ordered that **W. M. T. Bolton** be paid Six Dollars out of Building Fund.

Ordered that **Wm. Cross** be paid Ten Dollars out of Building Fund.

Ordered that **A. R. Right** be paid Four Dollars & 85 cts of Building Fund.

Ordered that **Jas. Coberly** be paid Eighteen of School Fund.

Ordered that **Alpheus Moore** be paid Nine & 50 cts of Building Fund.

Ordered that **John Right** be paid Ten Dollars out of Building Fund.

Ordered that **Seymour Phares** be paid 75 cts out of Building Fund.

Ordered that **Ballard S. Jones** be paid Eight &40 cts of Building Fund.

Ordered that **Jas Coberly** be paid Two Dollars out of Building Fund.

Ordered that **Right & Shurtleff** be paid Three Dollars & 70 cts out of Building Fund.

On motion the Board adjourned to Meet on the 2 Saturday in January the 20th 1883 at 1 oclock P.M.

School Board Minutes

W. S. Shurtleff President
John Right Secty

At a Meeting of the Board of Education of Barker District Barbour County W.Va. Held at Belington on the **20 day of January 1883.** Members Present **W. M. Biby** President Protem and **Solomon Coffman** Commissioner the Following Business was Transacted (Viz) Ordered That **W. J. Right Jr** be paid Four Dollars out Building Fund.
Ordered That **A. J. Row** be paid Sixty Five cts out Building Fund.
Ordered That **G. M. Right** be paid Fifty Dollars out School Fund.
Ordered That **G. M. Right** be paid Four Dollars out Building Fund.
Ordered That **John Booth** be paid One Dollar & 86 cts out Building Fund.
Ordered That **E. T. Cade** be paid Four Dollars & 89 cts out Building Fund.
Ordered That Miss **F. C. Wilmoth** be paid Twenty Two Dollars out School Fund.
Ordered That **J. A. Dunham** be paid Fifty Dollars out School Fund.
Ordered That **R. A. MCutcheon** be paid 67 cents out Building Fund.
On Motion the Board adjourned to Meet on the 5th Saturday in March the 31st at 1 oclock P.M.

W. S. Shurtleff President
John Right Secty

Know Business Transacted on the 31st day of March on the account of not being a quorum of the Members

W. S. Shurtleff President
John Right Scty

At a Meeting of the Board of Education of Barker District Barbour County W.Va. held at Belington on the **14th day of April**

1883. Members Present **W. S. Shurtleff,** President **W. M. Bibey** & **Solomon Coffman** Commissioners the Following Business was Transacted (Viz)

Appointing **G. M. Right** Secretary in Room of **John Right** Resigned.

Ordered that **Jas Coffman** be paid Twenty Five Dollars of School Fund.

Ordered that **Alice Wilmoth** be paid Fifty Dollars of School Fund.

Ordered that **Florence Wilmoth** be paid Twenty Two Dollars of School Fund.

Ordered that **Samuel Moran** be paid Eighteen Dollars of School Fund.

Ordered that **James Coffman** be paid Fifty Dollars of School Fund.

Ordered that **James Coffman** be paid Twenty Five Dollars of School Fund.

Ordered that Miss **Ida M. Teter** be paid Eighty Eight Dollars of School Fund.

Ordered that **Samuel Moran** be paid Thirty Six Dollars of School Fund.

Ordered that **Jas Coffman** be paid Twenty Five Dollars of School Fund.

Ordered that **Jas Coberly** be paid Fifty Four Dollars of School Fund.

Ordered that **S. R. Phillips** be paid One Hundred Dollars of School Fund.

Ordered that **J. A. Dunham** be paid Fifty Dollars of School Fund.

Ordered that **F. C. Wilmoth** be paid Sixty Six Dollars of School Fund.

Ordered that **Samuel Moran** be paid Eighteen Dollars of School Fund.

Ordered that **John M. Cauley** be paid Three Dollars & 30 cts of Building Fund.

Ordered that **A. D. Row** be paid Thirty cents of Building Fund.

Ordered that **G. M. Right** be paid Four Dollars out of Building Fund.

Ordered that **R. A. McCutcheon** be paid Two Dollars out of Building Fund.

School Board Minutes

Ordered that **L. T. Hollen** be paid Nine Dollars & 14 cts out of Building Fund.

Ordered that **F. C. Wilmoth** be paid Eight Dollars out of Building Fund.

Ordered that **A. M. Wilmoth** be paid Eight Dollars of Building Fund.

Ordered that **James Coffman** be paid Eight Dollars of Building Fund.

Ordered that **J. W. Bartlett** be paid Eight Dollars & 75 cts of Building Fund.

Ordered that **James Coberly** be paid Six Dollars out of Building Fund.

Ordered that **J. T. Moss** be paid Two Dollars & 94 cts of Building Fund.

Ordered that **Martin Hillyard** be paid Eight Dollars of Building Fund.

Ordered that **John Right** be paid Fifteen Dollars of Building Fund.

Ordered that **Right & Shurtleff** be paid Nine Dollars 33 cts of Building Fund.

Ordered that **Samuel Moran** be paid Eight Dollars & 40 cts of Building Fund.

Ordered that **S. B. Poe** be paid Nine Dollars & 90 cts of Building Fund.

Ordered that **S. R. Phillips** be paid Eight Dollars out of Building Fund.

Ordered that **Hanning Mclane** be paid Four Dollars of Building Fund.

Ordered that **E. G. Huffman** be paid One Dollar & ten cts of Building Fund.

Ordered that **W. S. Shurtleff** be paid One Dollar out of Building Fund.

Ordered that **J. C. Heatherly** be paid Twenty Dollars out of Building Fund.

Ordered that Philippi District be paid Sixteen Dollars & 98 cts of School Fund.

On Motion the Board adjourned Sine Die only to Settle with the Sheriff when He notifyes the Board

W. S. Shurtleff President
John Right Scty

At a Meeting of the Board of Education of Barker Dist Barbour Co West Virginia this **28th day of June 1883**. Members Present **W. S. Shurtleff,** President **W. M. Bibey** & **Solomon Coffman** Commissioners the object of the meeting being to settle with **J. E. Heatherly** Sheriff of Barbour Co. the reulst being as follows.

School Fund Balance Due District on Settlement $101.99

Building Fund Balance Due District on Settlement $1015.91
    W. S. Shurtleff President
     G. M. Right Sect

At a meeting of the Board of Education of Barker Dist Barbour Co. W.Va. this **2nd day of July 1883** members present **Levi Cross** President **Henry Barte, Randolph Coberly** and proceeded to Elect a Sectary and **J. B. Godwin** was chosen for Two years. Next in order was the appointment of Trustees and the following names was Presented Viz.

Sub Dist No.		Years
1	J. M. Corley	3
2	J. J. Newlon	3
3	John Booth	3
4	James Coonts	3
5	Phillip Ramsey	3
5	Solomon Wilson	2
5	James England	1
6	Alpheus Moore	3
6	John Prise	1
7	Henry Ridgway	3
8	S. W. Corley	3
8	B. Holbert	2
8	J. A. Wagner	1
9	J. H. Robinson	3
9	Abraham Poling	1

Ordered that the schools be kept open for instruction four

School Board Minutes

months commencing on the first Monday in Nov next and the number of Teachers to be Employed is nine.

Next in order was Teachers Salaries

A Certificate No.1 $25.00
A Certificate No.2   22.00
A Certificate No.3   18.00

Also it was ordered that a levy be laid for Teachers fund and that 15 cts was laid on the $100 dollars and for Building fund at 40 cts was laid on the $100 dollars the amount of Personal & Real Property as Returned by the Assessor is as followes

Personal Property	49265.00
Real Estate	130707.75
Total	$179972.75

And it is ordered that the Trustees advertise and sell the fuel to the lowest Bidder for a four months School

Ordered that the Trustees of the Several Sub Dist do not go to any extra Expense in Repairing School houses for this year at least.

Ordered that the Treasurer be charged as followes

From State School fund	$566.10/100 dollars
From Dist Levy	$269.95
Total School fund	$836.05

For Building fund from levy at 40c $710.85c

On motion the Board do now adjourn to meet on the 16 day of Oct next at the Belington School house at 1 oclock P.M.

            Levi Cross Pres
                G. B. Godwin Sectary B. E.

At a meeting of the board of Education held at **Right and Shurtleffs** Store on the **5th of Sept 1883** the members present **Levi Cross** President **Henry Bartee,** and the following buisiness done.

On motion of the President it was ordered that a note against **Joseph Teter** be placed in the hands of the proper officer for collection.

And it was ordered that **Levi Cross** be and is hereby authorized to institute suit or do any other thing nessary to do to collect from Valley Dist the answer due from said Valley District to Barker on a debt Existing at the time of Division of said Barker District.

School Board Minutes 191

And When as **Jacob Hudkins** late Sheriff of Barbour County on the 16th day of July 1881 made his annual settlement with the Board of Education of Barker District in said County and at said settlement was found indebted to the board on act of Teachers fund $172.07 and on account of Building fund .09c it is ordered that said **Jacob Hudkins** do pay to **James E. Heatherly** Sheriff of said County the said amount to be by him account for as he is Required by law to account for the same as other school money and it is further ordered that an order be drawn by the board on said **Hudkins** in favor of said **Heatherly** for the said sum of $172.07c Tuition fund and also an order for the said sum of 09 cents Building fund by order of the Board of Education this 5th day of September 1883.

On motion the board adjourned to meet on the 16 day of Oct next at 1 oclock P.M.
    Levi Cross Pres
    J. B. Godwin Sectary B. E.

At a meeting of the Board of Education of Barker Dist Barbour Co. W. Va. at **J. W. Waid**s Store on the **16 day of Oct 1883**. Members present **Levi Cross** President **Henry Barte,** Comm. and the following buisiness done.

1st On motion **J. C. Finley** was appointed a trustee of Sub Dist (No.8) for 3 years and also **Ira Finley** for 2 years on motion of **Henry Barte**.

It is ordered that the President and Sectary of this Board be authorized to sign in vacation all proper orders for the payment of money out of Teachers fund or Building fund and that they do Report the amount so drawn on each fund to the next meeting of this Board.

On motion of **H. Barte** it was ordered that **J. N. Ganer** be appointed Trustee in Sub Dist (No.7)

On motion the Board do now adjourn to meet at **T. N. Hudkins** Store at a call of the President.
    Levi Cross President
    J. B. Godwin Sect B. E.

School Board Minutes

At a meeting of the Board of Education of Barker Dist Barbour County W. Va. met at Belington **Dec 11th 1883** the following members presant **Levi Cross** President **Henry Barte, R. A. McCutcheon** and **J. B. Godwin** Sect and the following Buisiness done.

At a meeting of the Board of Education of Barker District held at Belington West Virginia **Dec 11th 1883**, It was ordered by the said Board of Education that **Levi Cross** our president be & hereby is authorized to employ counsel to prosecute any & all suits vs. the Board of Education of Valley District or its Board of Education for tis equitable share of the whole debt resting vs. Barker District at the tie Valley District was cut off.

Given under our hand
Henry Barte

Ordered that **F. E. Heatherly** Sheriff of Barbour County be charged with Two hundred & nine dollars and Forty one cents (209.41) as evidenced by his Receipt Executed by **Hezekiah J. Thompson** his deputy dated November the 14th 1883 and also **J. E. Heatherly** Recpt of same date for same amount. Ordered that **Jacob Hudkins** late Sheriff of Barbour County or his sureties be credited with ($172.07) on Teachers fund and 09 cts on Building fund Paid by his securities and Itemised as follows.

Order No. 89   48.00
Order No. 80   66.00
Order No. 61   1.00
Order No. 84   2.00
Order No. 87   2.00
Order No. 22   .75
Order No. 50   6.00
Total Sum   125.75
Also in cash   46.41
                 $172.16

The orders above Rec on this day filed with our Secretary Dec 11th 1883.

Ordered that **Daniel Ice** be paid Ten dollars for Furnishing fuel to Sub Dist (No.8) out of Building fund.

Ordered That **Alpheus Moore** be paid Ten dollars for fuel to Sub Dist (No.7) charge to Building fund.

Ordered that **William Cross** be paid Seven dollars 90 cts for fuel furnished to Sub Dist (No.4) and charge to Building fund.

Ordered that **Right & Shurtleff** be paid Thirteen dollars and 68 cents as per four orders all issued in one draft and on one (No.3) for 9 03/100, 1 on (No.6) $3.65c, 1 on (No.1) for 65 cts & one on (No.2) for 35 and charge to Building fund.

Ordered that **James Coberly** be paid Eighteen dollars out of Teachers fund for one month Teaching at (No.9)

Ordered that **A. G. Bartlett** be paid $22.00 out of Teachers fund for one months Teaching in Sub Dist (No.7)

Ordered that **G. M. Right** be paid Twenty five dollars for one months Teaching School in Sub Dist (No.2) payable out of Teachers fund of Barker Dist Barbour County W. Va.

Belington W. Va **Dec the 11th 1883**
The Board of Education of Barker Disrict

The Board of Education of Valley District Greeting All of Barbour County W. Va. Gentlemen after mature consideration we deem it best to refer the settlement of Existing accounts between our Respective Boards of Education to a competent committee of Three men to adjust and settle and their action to be conclusive and Each Board to pay half the Expenses of Such Settlement we solisit cooperation Given under our hands &c.

On motion the Board adjourn to meet on the 2nd Saturday of Jan 1884.
    Levi Cross
      J. B. Godwin Sect B. E.

At a meeting of the Board held at **T. Hawkins** Store on the **12th day of Jan 1884** the following Members Present **Levi Cross** President **Henry Barte & R. A. McCutcheon**. The following bisiness was Transacted Viz.

Ordered that **T. T. Elliott** was appointed a Trustee of Sub Dist (No.2) to fill the vacancy cause by **Martin Hillyard** failing to act.

Ordered that **A. Right** be paid one Dollar & 30 cts action vs. **F. B. Durrett** at.al Trustee of Ten Mile School House payable out of

Building fund B. Dr.

Ordered that **Jethro Bennett** be paid one dollar & Twenty cents his cost in afore said Action.

Ordered that **S. Ramsey** be paid Seventy Five cents as witness fee in a fore said action out of Building fund.

Ordered that **James Coberly** be paid Eighteen dollars for one months Teaching School in Sub Dist (No.9) payable out of Teachers fund of Barker District.

Ordered that **A. G. Bartlett** be paid Twenty two dollars for one month Teaching in Sub Dist (No.7) payable out of Teachers fund of Barker Dist Barbour Co. W. Va.

Ordered that **B. P. Newlon** be paid 6.00$ Six also 25c for a poker payable out of Building fund.

The Sectary of this Board Made Report this day Jan the 12th 1884 of the several orders Drawen by him and the President on the Sheriff on act of the Teachers fund and Building fund Respectfully since the last meeting of this Board which is as followes.

An order on the Teachers fund in favour of **W. W. Right** A Teacher for Twenty Five dollars also an order in favour of **James Coffman** a Teacher for Twenty five Dollars also an order in favour of Miss **Anna OBrien** a Teacher for Twenty Two dollars also an order on the Building in favour of **A. R. Right** for Six dollars for fuel to Sub Dist (No.3)

Also an order in favour of **M. E. Harris** a Teacher for Twenty Five dollars also an order in favour of **C. M. Murphy** a Teacher for Twenty Two dollars.

Ordered that **E. G. Huffman** be paid out of Building fund for the following articles Viz. 1 Bucket Tin 45c, 1 Tin cup .05c, 1 Broom etc, 1# puttty 10c.

On motion the Board adjourned to meet at **T. N. Hawkins** Store on the 2nd Saturday of Feb 1884 at 10 A.M.

    Levi Cross President
    J. B. Godwin Sectary

At a meeting of the Board of Education of Barker District Barbour Co. W. Va. held at **Hawkins** Store on the **ninth day of Feb 1884** members present **H. Barte , R. A. McCutcheon**. And the following Buisiness was Transacted Viz.

The Sect of this Board made Report this day of the Several orders issued by him and the President on the Sheriff on act of the Teachers fund and Building fund Respectfully Since the last meeting of this Board which is an followes an order on Teachers fund in favour of **James Coffman** A teacher for Twenty Five dollars also an order on the Teachers fund in favour of **M. E. Harris** A Teacher for Twenty Five dollars.

Ordered that **E. G. Huffman** be paid Three dollars & 1cts for 1 Dipper .10, 1 Tin Bucket .45, 1 Broom .25, Stove pipe 16c & charge for putting up pipe .79 Glass and Tacks .13, 1 Shovel .25, Total $3.01 Payable out of Building fund of Barker District.

Ordered That **S. R. Kelley** be paid Ten dollars for fuel furnished to School house in Sub Dist No.6 payable out of Building fund.

Ordered That **W. S. Pharis** Five 95/100 dollars for 100 hundred Bushels Coal Three dollars for Repairs to School house in Sub Dist (No.2) payable out of Building fund.

Ordered That **J. J. Newlon** be paid Fifty cts for School.

Ordered That **James Coffman** be paid Twenty Five dollars for one months Teaching in Sub Dist (No.6) payable out of Teachers fund.

Ordered That **A. G. Bartlett** be paid Twenty Two dollars out of Teachers fund for one month Teaching in Sub Dist (No.7)

Ordered That **R. B. Durrett** be paid Ten dollars out of Building fund for one lot of land where School house (No.7) now Stands and deed made and acknowledge for same.

On motion The Board adjourned to meet on the 3d Saturday of March at 10 Oclock A.M.
    Levi Cross President
    J. B. Godwin Sectary B. E. B.

At a meeting of the Board of Education Barker Dist, Barbour Co. W. Va. at Belington on the **15th day of March 1884**. Members present **Levi Cross** President, **H. Barte & R. A. McCutcheon**. And the following Buisiness Done Viz.

Ordered that **W. W. Right** be paid Twenty five dollars for one months Teaching School in Sub Dist (No.6) payable out of Teachers fund of Barker Dist.

Ordered that **G. M. Right** be paid Seventy Five Dollars for three months Teaching in Sub Dist (No.2) of Barker Dist payable out of Teachers fund of said Dist.

Ordered that Miss **M. E. Harris** be paid Fifty Dollars for Two months Teaching in Sub Dist (No.4) of Barker Dist payable out of Teachers fund of said Dist.

Ordered that **J. A. Dunham** be paid one hundred Dollars for 4 months Teaching in Sub Dist (No32) of Barker Dist payable out of Teachers fund of said Dist.

Ordered that **A. G. Bartlett** be paid Twenty Two Dollars for 1 month out of Barker Dist Teachers fund for one month Teaching in Sub Dist (No.7) of Barker Dist payable out of Teachers fund of said Dist.

Ordered that **J. T. Meoss** be paid Seven & Twenty Six cts (7.26) for Glass, nails, Stove Barrel, Broom, Coal hod &c payable out of Building fund of Barker District also an order of 1883 Signed by Randolph Coberley Trustee for one Dollar & 92 cts (1.92) for Bucket, Cup, Broom, Shovel, Glass & latch payable out Building fund of Barker Dist.

Ordered that **W. R. Coonts** be paid (6.75) for furnishing Fuel to Sub Dist (No.5) payable out Building fund of Barker Dist.

Ordered that **James Coffman** be paid Eight Dollars & 80 cts for Sweeping and making fires payable out of Building fund of Barker District.

Ordered that **James Coberly** be paid Eight Dollars & 80 (8.80) for sweeping and making fires payable out of Building fund of Barker District.

Ordered that **T. H. Hawkins** be paid .30 Thirty cts for 1 Broom payable out of Building fund of Barker District.

Ordered that **A. G. Bartlett** be paid Eight dollars for sweeping and making fires payable out of Building fund of Barker District.

Ordered that **F. C. Shockey** be paid Thirteen dollars & 30 cts for Repairs done to School house in Sub Dist (No.8) payable out of Building fund of Barker District Barbour County W. Va.

Ordered that **Josiah Poling** be paid Four dollars 45 cts (4.45) for fuel furnished to School house in Sub Dist (No.9) payable out of Building fund of Barker District.

Ordered that **J. A. Dunham** be paid Eight dollars for sweeping & making fires payable out of Building fund of Barker Dist.

Ordered that **W. W. Right** be paid Eight dollars for sweeping & making fires in Sub Dist (No.6) payable out Building fund of Barker District.

Ordered that **G. M. Right** be paid Eight dollars for sweeping & making fires in School house in Sub Dist (No.2) payable out of the Building fund of Barker District.

On motion the Board adjourned to meet at a call of the President.

Levi Cross President
J. B. Godwin Sect B. E.

At a meeting of the Board of Education Barker Dist, Barbour Co. W. Va. held at Belington on the **20th June 1884** for the purpose of settling with the Sheriff of Barbour Co. and the following members present **Levi Cross** Pres, **Henry Barte & R. A. McCutcheon**. with the following Results.

Teachers Fund

Amount of State School fund	$566.10
From last settlement	101.99
From levy	269.95
Total	$938.04

Amount of vouchers Received on Teachers fund

No. 1	A. G. Bartlett	22.00
No. 2	James Coberley	18.00
No. 3	G. M. Right	25.00
No. 4	W. W. Right	25.00
No. 5	James Coffman	25.00
No. 6	Anna Obrien	22.00
No. 7	M. E. Harris	25.00
No. 8	C. M. Murphy	22.00
No. 9	James Coberley	18.00
No. 10	A. G. Bartlett	22.00
No. 11	James Coffman	25.00
No. 12	M. E. Harris	25.00
No. 13	James Coffman	25.00

198 School Board Minutes

No. 14	A. G. Bartlett	22.00
No. 15	C. M. Murphy	22.00
No. 16	W. W. Right	50.00
No. 17	Anna Obrien	44.00
No. 18	James Coberley	36.00
No. 19	C. M. Murphy	14.00
No. 20	James Coffman	25.00
No. 21	W. W. Right	25.00
No. 22	G. M. Right	75.00
No. 23	M. E. Harris	50.00
No. 24	J. A. Dunham	100.00
No. 25	A. G. Bartlett	22.00
No. 35	Samuel Moran (18)	18.00
Amount of vouchers Received		$818.79
Balance Due Barker District		$119.34

Amount of Building fund of Barker District
From settlement of last year	1015.99
From levy of District	710.85
From Receipt of **J. E. Heatherley** Sheriff	54.03
From Receipt of **J. E. Heatherley** Sheriff	<u>209.41</u>
	1990.28
Delinquent list $9.50	
Commission $35.47	<u>44.97</u>
Amount of vouchers Received on Building fund	$1945.31

No. 1	Alpheus Moore	10.00
No. 2	William Cross	7.90
No. 3	Daniel Ice	10.00
No. 4	Right & Shurtleff	13.68
No. 5	W. H. Helpeinstein	2.90
No. 6	A. R. Right	6.00
No. 7	E. G. Huffman	2.30
No. 8	B. P. Newlon	6.25
No. 9	Samuel Ramsey	10.75
No. 10	A. Right	1.30
No. 11	Jethro Bennett not settled	1.20
No. 12	J. J. Newlon	0.50
No. 13	W. S. Pharis	8.45
No. 14	E. G. Huffman	3.01
No. 15	S. R. Kelley	10.00

No. 16	John Booth 1883	1.86
No. 36	J. W. Corley	3.30
No. 1	G. M. Right	10.00
No. 16	F. B. Durrett	10.00
No. 17	Josiah Poling	4.45
No. 18	James Coberley	8.80
No. 19	J. T. Meoss not settled	1.92
No. 20	J. T. Meoss not settled	7.26
No. 21	F. C. Shockey	13.30
No. 22	G. W. Holbert	8.80
No. 23	W. R. Coonts	6.75
No. 24	James Coffman	8.80
No. 25	T. N. Hawkins	00.30
No. 26	A. G. Bartlett	8.00
No. 27	S. A. Shanaberger	8.80
No. 28	W. W. Right	8.00
No. 29	J. A. Dunham	8.00
No. 30	G. M. Right	8.00
No. 31	Levi Cross	8.40
No. 32	J. B. Godwin	.75
No. 25	Levi Cross pron County Sup	6.00
No. 26	Henry Barte	6.00
No. 24	R. A. McCutcheon	4.50
No. 5	R. Coberley	
	Used J. B. Godwin	1.50
Total amt		272.32

By Sending orders on **Samuel Woods**
Wm. T. Ice &c judgment vs. Barker Dist
J. E. Heatherly Dr.
To whole amt of Building Fund of Barker Dist $1826.60
June 20th, 1884 $1990.28 - $1826.60 = $163.63
Leaving bal due on settlement of one hundred and sixty three and sixty-eight cents to the B. E.
  On motion the Board adjourned to meet on the first Monday in July next.
     Levi Cross President
       J. B. Godwin Sect

School Board Minutes

July 9, 1884

This is to certify that I have this day examined the books of **J. B. Godwin,** Sect Board of Education of Barker Dist and find them correct. I have also examined his annual report and accepted the same. The B. of Ed. will please allow him ten dollars for making said annual report.

      E. D. Gall Co. Supt.

At a meeting of the Board of Education Barker Dist, Barbour Co. W. Va. at Belington met at **R. A. McCutcheons** house in Belington on the **12th day of July 1884.** members present **Levi Cross** President, **Henry Bartee & R. A. McCutcheon** and the following bisiness done Viz.

On motion of **H. Bartee** that there be nine Teachers Employed four months Each.

On motion of **R. A. McCutcheon** that salaries by as followes per month in this District be for a certificate No. one do Receive Twenty five dollars per month, a No. 2, to Rec $22.00 per month, a (No.3) To Receive $18.00 per month.

On Motion it was ordered that a levy be laid on the taxable property of Barker Dist for Teachers fund of Twenty cts on the one hundred dollars whole amount of Real & personal property 188.820.40 Amount of levy $377.64 Also 40 cts on the $100 for Building fund Amount of Property $188.820.46 amount of levy $755.28

Next in order was the appointment of Trustees

Sub Dist		Years
No. 1	**Jackson Row**	3
No. 2	**Dr. Tobbott** re appointed	3
No. 3	**F. D. Valentine**	3
No. 4	**Simpson Cross**	3
No. 5	**S. D. Coonts**	3
No. 6	**Isaac N. Poling**	3
No. 7	**J. D. Ball**	3
No. 8	**George Currents**	3
No. 9	**Abraham Poling** Re appointed	3

Ordered that the Schools commence on the first Monday of

November next.

On motion of **H. Barte** that the secretary of this board do Receive $15.00 for servises as Sect B. E. B. D.

Ordered that **L. T. Hollen** be paid 70 cts for Glass in School house No. 7

Ordered that **J. B. Godwin** be paid $10.00 for making the annual Report of Barker Dist payable out of building fund.

Ordered that **C. M. Murphy** be Paid five 80/100 dollars for making fires & sweeping in school house in Sub Dist No.1 payable out of Building fund.

Also Six dollars to **Levi Cross** for attending to suit payable out of Building fund.

The Board do now adjourn to meet at Belington on the 28th day of July 1884.

      Levi Cross President
      J. B. Godwin Sect B. E.

At a meeting of the Board of Education Barker Dist, Barbour Co. W. Va. at Belington held on the **28th day of July 1884** at **T. N. Hawkins** Store. Members presant **Levi Cross** President, **R. A. McCutcheon & Henry Barte** the following Buisiness Done Viz.

On motion of **R. A. McCutcheon** that the board of Education do buy of **Thomas Kane** and Co. one hundred and sixty victor Seats to be used in 8 School houses in Barker Dist

It was also ordered that the Sheriff be charged as followes

State School fund for 1884	$446.61
From District Levy	377.64
From Board of Examiners	1.13
From a mistake in last years amount by Co. Sup.	5.35
Total	$830.73

Also ordered that the Sheriff be charged
On account of Building fund as followes
From Dist Levy $755.28

Ordered That **T. T. Elliott** be paid 1.60/100 dollars out Building fund.

Ordered that **J. B. Godwin** be paid four 60/100 dollars as witness fees payable out of Building fund.

    Ordered that **Levi Cross** be paid five 10/100 dollars as witness out Building fund.

    On motion the board do not adjourn to meet at a Call of the Sect.

                  Levi Cross President
                  J. B. Godwin Sect

    At a call meeting of the Board of Education of Barker Dist Barbour Co. W.Va. at **T. H. Hawkins** Store on the **28 day of August 1884** members presant **Levi Cross** President **R. A. McCutcheon & H. Bartee** and the following Buisiness done. Viz.

    1. **C. B. Carter** was appointed a Trustee in Sub Dist No. 9 in Room of **James Poling** time out for 3 years.

    2nd That **W. G. Godwin** be appointed a Trustee in room of **J. C. Right** time out in Sub Dist (No.6) for 3 years.

    On motion of **R. A. McCutcheon** this day made an order for one hundred and sixty victor seats & desks and their voting for the motion was **R. A. McCutcheon** and **Henry Barte** and **Levi Cross** voted in the negative.

    On motion the Board adjourned to meet on the 27 day of Sept at 9 oclock A.M.

                  Levi Cross President
                  J. B. Godwin Sect B. E.

    At a meeting of the Board of Education Barker Dist, Barbour Co. W. Va. at Belington held on the **28th day of September 1884** members present **Levi Cross** President, **R. A. McCutcheon** and the following Buisiness Done Viz.

    1st On order Rec from Glade Dist for Transferred puples to the amount of Twelve Dollars and Sixty cents and also an order issued to Glade Dist for puples Transfered from Barker Dist to Glade Dist amounting to Twenty Three dollars and Twelve cents and charge to

Teachers fund of Barker Dist.
   On motion the Board adjourned.
      Levi Cross President
         J. B. Godwin Sect B. E.

   At a meeting of the Board of Education of Barker District at Belington on the **Eighth day of Nov 1884** members present **T. T. Elliot,** President **Henry Barte & R. A. McCutcheon** the following Buisiness done. Viz.
   First the appointment of Trustees. **Milton Hart** was appointed a Trustee in Sub Dist No.1 For 3 years & **H. C. Rosenberger** was appointed a Trustee in Sub Dist (No.2) (for the unexpired term of **T. T. Elliot** resigned) Co. Supt. It was also Resolved that the President and Sectary be authorised to issue order on the Teachers fund in vacation of the Board.
   Ordered that an order be issued for **Thomas Kane** & Co. for Eighty Two 70/100 dollars for Victor seats for school house (No.2) payable out of Building fund.
   Ordered that **T. H. Hawkins** be paid Ten 44/100 dollars for Repairs in Stove &c payable out of Building fund of Barker Dist.
   On motion the Board adjourned to meet on the 13 day of Dec 1884 at 1 oclock, P.M.
   Ordered that the Sheriff be charged with Thirteen 20/100 dollars on building fund.
      T. T. Elliott President
         J. B. Godwin Sect. B. E.

   At a meeting of the Board of Education of Barker District Barbour Co. W.Va. held at Belington on the **13th day of Dec 1884** Members Present **T. T. Elliot** President **H. Barte & R. A. McCutcheon** and the following Buisiness done. Viz.
   The Sectary of the Board made Report of the Several orders

issued by him and the president on the Teachers fund and Building fund Respectfully an order in favour of **J. M. Cade** use of **J. B. Godwin** for Seven 50/100 dollars for hauling Victor seats from Webster to Sub Dist (No.2) payable out of building fund of Barker District. Also an order on the Teachers fund in favour of Miss **Flora Dadisman** a Teacher for Twenty Five $25.00 dollars also an order in favour of Miss **Alice Harris** a Teacher for Twenty Five dollars also an order in favour of **J. W. Ramsey** a Teacher for Twenty Five dollars and also an order in favour of Miss **Florence E. Wilmoth** a teacher for Twenty Five dollars also an order in favour of Miss **Effie C. Matlick** a Teacher for Twenty Five dollars.

 Ordered that **Alpheus Moore** be paid Eighteen 87/100 dollars Nine 81/100 dollars for fuel and Repairs to Sub Dist (No.9) and Nine 06/100 for Coal and Glass Furnished to School house (No.6) payable out of Building fund.

 Ordered That **J. J. Newlon** be paid Three 60/100 dollars for Storage on School desks .55, putting down desks 2.50, putting in Glass .25, One bucket and 1 cup .30, Payable out of Building fund .60 3.60

 Ordered that **J. W. Ward** be paid for one broom .25, for 3 window lights .25, for one joint stove pipe .25, payable out of Building fund .75

 Ordered that **W. S. Phares** be paid Six dollars & 25 cts for one hundred bushels Coal furnished to School house in Sub Dist (No.2) payable out of Building fund.

 Ordered that **W. S. Shurtleff** be paid .70 for 1 coal hod, 1 Broom .35, 5 10x12 Glass .50, 1 bucket .25, one fire Shovel .25, one cup .05, 1 poker .20, 3 Joints stove pipe making a total of $3.05 payable out of building fund.

 Ordered That **B. P. Newlon** be paid Six dollars for one hundred bushels coal furnished to Sub Dist (No.1) payable out of Building fund.

 On motion it was ordered that the Trustees of Sub Dist (No.3) be allowed to set out a privy for use of said School house according to Specifications furnished.

 On motion it was ordered that **J. J. Newlon** be authorised to furnish Chalk to Each Sub District to the amount of 30 cts Each and also a thermometer for Each School house in Barker District and that when Schools close for the Trustees to Remove the same to a place of Safety and Replace them at the commencement of the next School.

On motion the Board adjourned to meet at Belington on the 2nd Saturday of Jan. 1885 at 1 Oclock P.M.
   T. T. Elliott President
   J. B. Godwin Sectary

  At a meeting of the board of Education of Barker District Barbour Co. W. Va. held at Belington **Jan 10th 1885**. Members presant **T. T. Elliott** President, **Henry Barte** and **R. A. McCutcheon** and the following buisiness done Viz.
  First The Sect of this Board made Report of the Several orders drawen by him and the president on the sheriff on account of the Teachers fund and Building fund Respectfully since the last meeting of the Board which is as followes.
  An order on the Teachers fund in favour **C. M. Blake** a Teacher for Twenty Two Dollars also an order in favour **James Coffman** a Teacher for Twenty Five Dollars. Also an order in favour of Miss **Alice Harris** a Teacher for Twenty Five $. Also an order in favour of **J. W. Ramsey** a Teacher for Twenty Five Dollars.
  Ordered That **J. N. Poling** be paid Four dollars for making black board in School house in Sub District (No.6) payable out of Building fund of Barker Dist.
  Ordered That **E. T. Cade** use of **T. N. Hawkins** be paid Five 50/100 dollars for sealing and black board in School house in Sub Dist (No.3) the same is allowed and payable out of Building fund of Barker Dist.
  On motion the board do now adjourn to meet on the Second Saturday of March next at one Oclock P.M.
   T. T. Elliott President
   J. B. Godwin Sectary

  At a meeting of the board of Education of Barker District Barbour Co. W. Va. held at Belington **March the 21st 1885**. Members present **T. T. Elliott** President, **Henry Barte** and **R. A. McCutcheon** and the following buisiness done Viz.

The Sect of this board made Report this day of the several orders drawen by him and the President on the Sheriff on act of the Teachers fund and Building fund Respectively since the last meeting of the board which is as followes.

On order in favour **C. M. Blake** a Teacher for $22.00 also an order in favour of **James Coffman** a Teacher for 25.00 Dollars also an order in favour of **J. A. Dunham** a Teacher for Fifty dollars also an order in favour of Miss **Flora Dadisman** a teacher for 25.00 dollars also an order in favour of **J. A. Dunham** for $4.00 on the Building fund for sweeping and making fires also an order in favour of **G. T. Howell** for nine 25/100 dollars on building fund for fuel Furnished to Sub Dist (No.8)

Also an order in favour of Miss **Alice Harris** a Teacher for $25.00 dollars also an order in favour of **J. W. Ramsey** a Teacher for $25.00 dollars also an order in favour of Miss **Flora Dadisman** a Teacher for $50.00 dollars also an order in favour of **James Coffman** a Teacher for Twenty five dollars also an order in favour of **J. W. Ramsey** a Teacher for Twenty five dollars.

Order **W. M. Biby** be paid $6. 62/100 dollars for Repairs to School house (No.8) and Three 2/100 dollars for half interest in building privy and 10c for bolts to stove payable out of building fund of Barker Dist.

Also **E. T. Cade** use of **C. F. Teter** Trustee of **T. H. Hawkins** three 3. 37/100 dollars half interest in building privy also **S. H. McLane** be paid Eight dollars for sweeping and making fires in School house (No.7) also that Miss **Alice Harris** be paid Eight 15/100 dollars for sweeping & making fires one chalk in Sub Dist (No.6)

Ordered that **J. J. Newlon** be paid 30c chalk furnished to Sub Dist (No.2)

Ordered that **Effie C. Matlick** be paid Eight Dollars for sweeping & making fires in Sub Dist (No.2)

Ordered that **Florence C. Wilmoth** be paid Eight dollars for sweeping and making fires in School house (No.1)

Ordered that **J. W. Ramsey** be paid Eight dollars for sweeping & making fires in School house (No.5)

Ordered that **James Coffman** be paid Eight 30/100 dollars for sweeping and making fires & chalk in School house (No.9)

Ordered that **C. M. Blake** be paid Eight dollars for sweeping & making fires & stove barel 4.10 Chalk .15, 1 Broom .25, 1 cup .05, use in School house in (No.9) all $12.55 dollars.

Ordered that **John Booth** be paid one 57/100 dollars for plank furnished to Sub Dist (No.3)

Ordered that **J. R. Valentine** Six 25/100 for furnishing fuel to Sub Dist (No.3) payable out of Building fund of Barker District.

Ordered that **Laben Cross** be paid $5.89/100 dollars for furnishing fuel to School house in Sub Dist (No.4) payable out of Building fund.

Ordered that **William England** seven 90/100 dollars for Coal Furnished to School house in Sub Dist (No.7) also Three 80/100 dollars for Repairing Coal house Total $11.70

Ordered that **J. A. Dunham** be paid Four Dollars for Sweeping & making fires in School house (No.3)

Ordered that **Alice M. Wilmoth** be paid Eight dollars for sweeping & making fires in school house in Sub Dist (No.4)

Ordered that **E. G. Huffman** be paid for the following act one box chalk .20, 1 fire shovel .25, one coal hod 70c, 4 window glass .32 one Broom .25 Total $1.72

This day **Alice M. Wilmoth** presented a certificate from the Trustees of Sub Dist (No.4) showing that she was Entitled to the Sum of one hundred Dollars for four months Teaching in Said Sub Dist the same is allowed and payable out of Teachers fund.

Also **J. A. Dunham** this day Presented a certificate from the Trustees of Sub Dist (No.3) showing that he is Entitled to the Sum of Fifty dollars for two months Teaching in Said Sub Dist the same is allowed and payable out of Teachers fund.

Also Miss **E. C. Matlick** presented a certificate from the Trustees of Sub Dist (No.2) showing that she is Entitled to the Sum of Seventy five Dollars payable out of Teachers fund.

C. M. Blake this day presented a certificate from the Trustees of Mouse Run showing that he is Entitled to the Sum of Forty four Dollars the same is allowed and a draft was Drawen in his favour for the same payable out of Teachers fund.

Miss **Alice Harris** this day presented a certificate from the Trustees of Sub Dist (No.6) showing that she was Entitled to the Sum of Twenty five Dollars for Two months Teaching the same is allowed and payable out of Teachers fund of Barker Dist.

F. C. Wilmoth presented a certificate from the Trustees of Sub Dist (No.1) showing that she was Entitled to the Sum of Fifty the same is allowed and payable out of Teachers fund of Barker Dist.

James Coffman this day presented to the board showing that he was Entitled to the Sum of Twenty five Dollars for one months Teaching in Said Sub Dist (No.9) the same is allowed and payable out of Teachers fund of Barker Dist.

Ordered that the Trustees of Sub Dist (No.2) be allowed to Repair the school house in said Sub Dist and also to fence the same

On motion the Board Adjourned to meet and Examine the Situation and decided to let it Remain for the being.

The Board will meet to settle with the Sheriff on the 26 day of June 1885 at Belington at 9 oclock A.M.

T. T. Elliott President
J. B. Godwin Sect B. E.

At a meeting of the Board of Education of Barker District held at Belington on the **26 day of June 1885.** Members present **T. T. Elliott** President **Henry Barte, R. A. McCutcheon**. The object of the meeting was to settle with the Sheriff Settlement was made with the following results.

James E. Heatherly	Dr.	Teachers fund
To balance due from last settlement		$119.34
Tot State School fund		446.61
To District Levy		377.64
To Board of Examiners		1.13
To Error last year		5.35
Total		950.07
Delinquent list		5.70
		945.34
Commission		18.59

List of orders received

1	**Anna Obrien**	22.00
2	Glade District	23.12
3	**Alice Harris**	25.00
4	**J. M. Ramsey**	25.00
5	**Flora Dadisman**	25.00
6	**E. C. Matlick**	25.00

7	F. C. Wilmoth	25.00
8	C. M. Blake	22.00
9	James Coffman	25.00
10	Alice Harris	25.00
11	J. W. Ramsey	25.00
12	James Coffman	25.00
13	C. W. Blake	22.00
14	J. A. Dunham	50.00
15	Flora Dadisman	25.00
16	Alice Harris	25.00
17	J. W. Ramsey	25.00
18	Flora Dadisman	50.00
19	James Coffman	25.00
20	J. W. Ramsey	25.00
21	A. M. Wilmoth	100.00
22	F. C. Willmoth	25.00
24	F. C. Willmoth	50.00
24	C. M. Blake	22.00
25	E. C. Mattic	75.00
26	J. A. Dunham	50.00
27	Alice Harris	25.00
28	James Coffman	25.00

Amount of vouchers Rec	957.11
Also Two Drafts from Philippi Dist	42.40
Whole amount of vouchers	999.81
Amount charged to sheriff	$950.07
Due Sheriff **J. E. Heatherly**	49.74
To order	49.74

J. E. Heatherly Sheriff of Barbour County Dr.

To Barker Dist on act of Building Fund	
To Barker Due from settlement of last year	$163.68
To District Levy	755.28
From other Sources	14.60
Total	$933.16
To Delinquent list	$11.99
To Comission	$37.10

School Board Minutes

No.		
1	J. B. Godwin	10.00
2	L. T. Hollen	.70
3	C. M. Murphy	5.80
4	Levi Cross	6.00
5	T. T. Elliott	1.60
6	J. B. Godwin	4.60
7	Levi Cross	5.10
8	T. H. Hawkins	10.14
9	Thomas Kane & Co.	82.70
10	J. M. Cade use J. B. Godwin	7.50
11	B. P. Newlon	6.00
12	W. S. Pharis	6.25
13	J. Ward	00.75
14	J. J. Newlon	3.60
15	W. S. Shurtleff	3.05
16	Alpheus Moore	18.87
17	J. N. Poling	4.00
18	E. T. Cade use J. H. Hawkins	5.50
19	J. A. Dunham	4.00
20	G. T. Howell	9.25
21	A. M. Wilmoth	8.80
22	James Coffman	8.30
23	C. M. Blake	12.55
24	J. W. Ramsey	8.00
25	E. G. Huffman	1.72
26	William England	11.70
27	S. H. Mclane	8.00
28	Alice Harris	8.15
29	Laben Cross	5.85
30	F. C. Wilmoth	8.80
31	E. C. Matlick	8.80
32	John Booth	1.57
33	J. R. Valentine	6.25
34	Wm. M. Biby	9.62
35	E. T. Cade use C. F. Teter	3.37
36	J. A. Dunham	4.00
37	J. J. Newlon	.30
38	J. W. Ward	.25

20	J. T. Moss	7.26
11	Jethro Bennett	1.20
19	J. T. Moss	1.92
3	Levi Cross	6.00
1	J. B. Godwin	15.00
13	R. A. McCutcheon	6.00
11	T. T. Elliott	6.00
12	Henry Barte	6.00
39	W. R. Coonts	5.00

To Balance on the **Wilmoth** Judgment	101.43
Fee bill of Sheriff	.75
Fee bill of **Elliott**	1.25
Fee bill of **J. D. Johnson**	1.30
The amount of vouchers Received	$946.43
Amount Brought over of Building fund	$946.93
Amount of vouchers Rec of Sheriff	946.93

Ordered that **J. E. Heatherly** be paid Fourteen 77/100 dollars and charge to Building fund of Barker Dist. The **J. E. Heatherly** be paid Forty Nine 74/100 dollars and charge To Teachers fund of Barker District Barbour County.

That **W. R. Coonts** be paid five dollars for fuel furnished to Sub Dist (No.5) payable out of Building fund of Barker Dist.

On motion the Board do now adjourn to meet at Belington on the Sixth day of July at 7 Oclock A. M.

J. B. Godwin Sect B. E.

I have worked for two days trying to understand the last settlement with the Sheriff. The sheriff promised to bring in his books showing that the settlement is correct but has failed to do so. I have to assume that it is correct as your Sect. can give me no information concerning it. The book is in such a shape that it is impossible to make it balance with the settlement.

E. D. Gall Co. Supt.

212 School Board Minutes

July 6, 1885
  Ordered that the Board adjourn till Saturday 25 of July 1885 at 8 oclock A. M. to consider settlement between Barker district and sheriff and also to consider the different Branches teachers shall teach.
     Geo. McCutcheon Sect.
     T. T. Elliott Pres

August 1st 1885
  At a meeting of the Board of Education held on the **1st day of August 1885** at Belington P.O. present Dr. **D. S. Talbott** and **H. Barte** the following business Transacted.
  On motion it is ordered that the President **T. T. Elliott** procure the lot that the Mouse Run School house stands on by leasing it for 5 years if possible.
  On motion it is ordered that the president of the Board **T. T. Elliott** be and is authorized by the Board to make contracts for delivering seats at the School Houses.
  On motion it is ordered that the Trustees be and are required by the Board to be at as small Expense as possible during the present School year in the way of procuring Fuel and all other Expenses.
  Ordered that meetings Shall not be held in School Houses without consent of the Board.
  On motion the Board adjourned till The 1st Saturday in November 1885.
     Geo. M. McCutcheon Sect
     T. T. Elliott Pres

6th July 1885
  At a meeting of the Board held on the **6th day of July 1885** present **T. T. Elliott** president and **H. Barte** and Dr. **D. S. Talbot** members of Board.
  On motion of **D. S. Talbot** it is ordered that **Geo**

McCutcheon be and is hereby appointed secretary of this Board.

On motion it is ordered that the following Named persons be appointed Trustees in following named sub districts for a time of 3 years.

Dist No.	Names of Trustees appointed
1	**John Cauley**
2	**H. C. Rosenburger** and **R. A. McCutcheon** to fill unexpired term of Dr. **D. S. Talbott**
3	**Jethro Bennett**
4	**Lewis Price**
5	**Solomon Wilson**
6	**Alpheus Moore**
7	**Jacob Mclean**
8	**Lewis W. Corley**
9	**Wm. R. Moore**

Ordered that school shall be taught 4 months in the year in Each sub district

Teachers Salaries
No. 1   Twenty Eight dollars
No. 2   Twenty two dollars
No. 3   Eighteen dollars

1885 Contracts between Teachers and Trustees
No. 1 **James Coffman** Grade of Certificate 1, Sub District No. 4
No. 2 **Lucy Rohr** Grade one, Sub Dist No. 2
No. 3 **W. W. Right** Grade one, Sub Dist No. 6
No. 4 **Florence C. Wilmoth** Grade 1 Sub Dist No. 9
No. 5 **Alice Wilmoth** Grade 1, Sub Dist No. 5
No. 6 **Anna O Brien** Grade 1, Sub Dist No. 8
No. 7 **Sallie R. Phillips** Grade 1, Sub Dist No. 1
No. 8 **W. B. Baker** Grade 1
No. 9 **A. L. Taylor** Grade 2, Sub Dist No. 2

Amount of personal property levied on 6/748.00 Real Estate levied on 130.627.95

We hereby levy on above amounts. 43 cts on Each 100.00 for Teachers Fund. Also 40 cts on Each 100.00 for Building Fund. Secretarys Salary 15.00

214 School Board Minutes

The Board will not pay over Eight dollars for Building Fires, Cleaning Houses &c.

Order given on sheriff to **J. B. Godwin** for one dollar & twenty five cts for Stationery for use of the Board the Board requires Trustees to use all Economy possible in procuring Fuel for school Houses.

Statement of the debt of School house No. 10. Two bonds issued and made payable to **Daniel C. Wilmoth** and **Lorenzo Denton** the first bond for $625.00 The second bond for $475.00 Total $1100.00 June 20, 1884 1st payment was made. Interest for 14 years, 5 mos & 25 days 956.08. Principal & interest $2056.08 Deduct first payment 1554.28 Interest on same for 1 year & 6 days 30.60 Prin & interest   532.40 2d payment was $420.13 And also 101.43 Leaving bal due on judgement   10.84

At a call meeting of the Board **Oct 12, 1885** present **T. T. Elliott** & Dr. **D. S. Talbott** for the purpose of giving orders on Sheriff to **A. H. Andrews** & Co. for two Hundred and thirty Eight dollars & 6 cents for School Disks delivered at Philippi also an order to **W. D. H. Jarvin** agt. of G.& G. R. R. for Freight on School Desks of twenty three dollars & 23 cents on motion the Board adjourned till 1st Saturday in Nov. 1885.

Geo. McCutcheon Sect
T. T. Elliott Pres

1885
Nov 7th Belington, W. Va.

Persuant to an adjourned meeting, the Board of Education of Barker District met today. Present, **T. T. Elliott**, President, Dr. **D. S. Talbott** and **Henry Barte** Comms: and transacted the following business Viz.

1. Ordered that **Glascock** & **Lovett** be paid Ninety five (95) cents out of building fund.
2. Ordered that **R. A. McCutcheon** be paid for services rendered in obtaining a Lease from **Allen Wood** & furnishing 1 Grate   3.50

3. Ordered that **L. H. Campbell** be paid for painting Belington School house 2 coats & the seats &c   33.00
4. Ordered that **John L. Price** be paid for repairing Mouse Run school house   8.00
5. Ordered that **John M. Cade** be paid for hauling School desks & delivering same   33.00
6. Ordered that **T. T. Elliott** be paid for cash he paid Rail Road Apt on school desks   3.20
7. Ordered that **W. S. Shurtleff** be paid for school supplies as per his acct filed 1.75
All of the above orders are charged to the Building fund.
8. Ordered that **John L. Price** be & he is hereby appointed trustee for sub district No. 8. He qualified.
9. Ordered that **Jackson Hillyard** be & he is hereby appointed Trustee of Sub Dist No.1
10. Ordered that the Trustees be instructed to see that care is properly taken of all school property and that the Teacher is held responsible for damages done.
11. On motion the Board adjourned to meet the first Saturday in January 1886 at G & L's Store at 1 oclock P.M.
12. Ordered that Trustees incur no expenses without consent of Board of Ed.

     R. A. McCutcheon Sec Protem
      T. T. Elliott Pres

1886 Belington **Jan 2**
  At a meeting of the Board of Education of Barker district at **Glascock** & **Lovett**s Store present **T. T. Elliott** president & **H. Barte** commis. The following business Transacted
  Ordered that **J. S. Hollen** be paid three dollars & 50 cents for Black board made and put up by him at School house No. 7
  Ordered that **Glascock** & **Lovet** be paid sixty cents for mdse for School House No. 2
  Ordered that **C. F. Teter** be paid thirty five dollars & no cents for Fee Bill of **Jas Halls** held by him against Barker district.
  Ordered that **B. P. Newlon** be paid Four dollars for Building Fires at School House No. 2

Ordered that **Wm. R. Moore** be paid one dollar & Eighty five cents for Fastening seats, Furnishing glass, broom & coal School No. 9

Ordered that **A. Right** & Son be paid one dollar & fifteen cents 1.15 it being for mdse Furnished School No. 6

Ordered that **A. Moore, N. Poling & W. G. Godwin** be paid One dollar For Fastening down desks at School House No.6

Ordered that **Jacob Mclean** be paid One dollars for Fastening down seats at School House No.7

Ordered that **Sol Wilson** be paid One dollar & Fifty cents for putting down seats & furnishing lock &c

Ordered that **A. Phillips** be paid three dollars for repairing School House No. 4

Ordered that **J. M. Poling** be paid two dollars for Black board furnished sub district No.4

Ordered that **J. A. Dunham** be paid twenty Eight dollars for teaching One month in Sub Dist No. 3

On motion the Board Adjourned to meet 2d Saturday in March 1886.

T. T. Elliott Pres
Geo Mc Cutcheon Sect

March 13, 1886
Office of the Board of Education of Barker Dist Barbour County

At a meeting of the Board held on **13th day of March 1886** present **T. T. Elliott** Pres & **H. Barte** Member of Board. The following business Transacted

Order No. 23. Ordered that **J. W. Poling** be paid nine dollars & 50 cts for building privies Dist No.9

Order No. 24. Ordered that **Isaac Price** be paid seven dollars & 83 cts for furnishing fuel

Order No. 25. Ordered that **James Coffman** be paid One dollar & 50 cts for putting down benches and Blk Board

Order No. 26. Ordered that **W. C. Moore** be paid Six dollars for coal furnished dist No. 6

Order No. 27. Ordered that **Joshua Bartlett** be paid Eight dollars and seventy five cents for furnishing fuel to dist No.8

Order No. 28. Ordered that **J. N. Bibey** be paid six dollars and seventy five cents for furnishing fuel to School House No.3

Order No. 29. Ordered that **W. B. Baker** be paid Eight dollars for building fires & sweeping house dist No.7

Order No. 30. Ordered that **L. H. Ray** be paid one dollar & 20 cts for 12# of Stove pipe furnished Mouse Run School

Order No. 31. Ordered that **C. T. Fisher** be paid fifty cents for Lock furnished Mouse Run School house

Order No. 32. Ordered that **G. W. Valentine** be paid Eight dollars for making fires Sub dist No.3

Order No. 33. Ordered that **W. S. Shurtleff** be paid three dollars & sixty one cents for Lock, mdse, chalk l cflth furnished School Houses No. 1 -7 & cfh

Order No. 34. Ordered that **R. A. McCutcheon** be paid two dollars& 35 cts for freight & hauling Casting

Order No. 35. Ordered that **W. W. Right** be paid Eight dollars for building fires Sub dist No.6

Order No. 36. Ordered that **W. F. Newlon** be paid seven dollars & Fifty cents for furnishing Coal dist No.1

Order No. 37. Ordered that **B. P. Newlon** be paid Six dollars & ninety nine cents for furnishing Coal to Belington School House

Order No. 38. Ordered that **Josh Bartlett** be paid 75 cts

Order No. 39. Ordered that **Wm England** be paid Ten dollars for furnishing fuel for School in Sub Dist No.7

Order No. 40. Ordered that **Wm England** be paid 8.40 Eight dollars & 40 cts for fuel furnished School house No.9

Order No. 41. Ordered that **S. R. Phillips** be paid Eight dollars for building fires Sub dist No.7

Order No. 42. Ordered that **J. W. Bartlett** be paid Eight dollars for building fires in Sub dist No.8

On motion it is ordered that the Board of Education give the Trustees Liberty to open the School Houses for all Orthodox denominations to hold religious worship for Sunday Preaching, Sunday Schools, Literary Schs but not for protracted meeting by the Trustees assuming the Houses properly taken care of for the period of seven months from this data March 1886 at that time to be closed against religious worship.

Ordered that the Board of Education meet Mar 20, 1886 for the purpose of hearing complaints against and Defence of **Geo W. Currance** a Trustee of Dist No. 8

School Board Minutes

Ordered that the Board Adjourn till Saturday Mar 20, 1886
Geo McCutcheon Sect

At a meeting of the Board of Education of Barker Dist Barbour Co. W. Va. held at the Store of **Glascock** & **Lovett Mar 20, 1886** present **T. T. Elliott** president & **H. Barte** Commis. The following business Transacted.

Ordered that **G. J. Stalnaker** be paid 4.00 for building Fires Sub dist No.2

Ordered that **J. T. Moss** be paid 1.60 for mdse furnished Mouse Run School House.

Ordered that **F. C. Wilmoth** be paid 8.00 for building Fires in Sub dist No.9

Ordered that **A. M. Wilmoth** be paid 8.00 for building Fired in Sub dist No. 5

Ordered that **James Coffman** be paid 8.00 for building Fires in sub dist No. 4

Ordered that the Board adjourn till meeting called by Sheriff
Geo McCutcheon Sect

June 17

At a meeting of the Board of Education **June 17, 1886** present **T. T. Elliott** president & Dr. **D. S. Talbot, H. Barte** Commissioners the following business transacted

Ordered that **J. W. Talbott** be paid & D. M. & M. Co. be paid Eight dollars for Black board furnished School House No. 9

Ordered that **Joseph Teter** be paid three dollars witness fee in Suit between Valley & Barker dists

Ordered that **J. V. Johnson** be paid for use of **J. A. Williamson** three dollars and Eighty cents.

School Board Minutes 219

At a meeting of the Board of Education of Barker District, Barbour County West Virginina held at **Glascock** and **Lovett**s store in Belington W. Va **June 1886**. The following officers present **T. T. Elliott** president & the object of the meeting being to settle with the Sheriff. Settlement was made with following results
J. W. Robinson S. B. C. to Barker District

To District Levy	$827.21
To State School fund	292.16
	1119.37

List of Orders received Teachers Fund

No.	Teachers Orders	$ ¢
1	W. B. Baker	28.00
2	W. W. Right	28.00
3	Annie OBrien	28.00
4	James Coffman	28.00
5	Lucy Rohr	28.00
6	Flora C. Wilmoth	28.00
7	Sallie R. Phillips	28.00
8	Lucy Rohr	28.00
9	J. A. Dunham	28.00
10	W. W. Baker	28.00
11	W. W. Right	28.00
12	James Coffman	28.00
13	J. A. Dunham	28.00
14	Sallie R. Phillips	28.00
15	Flora C. Wilmoth	28.00
16	Alice Wilmoth	28.00
17	Alice Wilmoth	28.00
18	A. L. Taylor	22.00
19	W. B. Baker	28.00
20	James Coffman	28.00
21	Anna Obrien	28.00
22	Anna Obrien	28.00
23	W. B. Baker	28.00
24	W. W. Right	28.00
25	W. W. Right	28.00
26	Sallie R. Phillips	28.00
27	Sallie R. Phillips	28.00

220 School Board Minutes

28	A. L. Taylor	22.00	
29	J. A. Dunham	28.00	
30	J. A. Dunham	28.00	
31	Flora Wilmoth	28.00	
32	Flora Wilmoth	28.00	
33	Alice M. Wilmoth	28.00	
34	Alice M. Wilmoth	28.00	
35	James Coffman	28.00	
36	Anna Obrien	<u>28.00</u>	
		274.00	
To amt brot up			722.11
Total			$996.11
Release			.43
Delinquent			4.72
Commission			41.25
29	**James E. Heatherly**	49.74	
10	**Alice Harris**	25.00	
Order from Philippi dist on Barker			<u>21.70</u>
			1138.81
Amt due Sheriff on Settlement			19.47
			1138.84

J. W. Robinson S. B. C. to Barker District
To District Levy $772.08

List of Orders on Building Fund

No.		$ ¢
1	J. B. Godwin	1.25
2	J. B. Godwin	10.00
3	A. H. Andrews & Co.	238.66
4	W. D. F. Jarvin	23.23
5	L. H. Campbell	33.00
6	Glascock & Lovett	.95
7	R. A. McCutcheon	3.50
8	W. S. Shurtliff	1.75
9	Jno M. Cade	8.00
10	Jno. M. Cade	33.00
11	T. T. Elliott	3.20
12	J. S. Hollan	3.50
13	Glascock & Lovett	.60
14	C. F. Teter	35.00

School Board Minutes

15	B. J. Newlon	4.00
16	W. R. Moon	1.85
17	A. Right & Sons	1.15
18	A. Moore, I.N. Poling, W. G. Godwin	1.00
19	Jacob Mc Lane	1.00
20	Solomon Wilson	1.50
21	A. Phillips	3.00
22	I. N. Poling	2.00
23	J. W. Poling	9.50
24	Isaac C. Price	7.83
25	James Coffman	1.50
26	W. C. Moon	6.00
27	Joshua Bartlett	8.75
28	J. N. Biby	6.75
29	W. B. Baker	8.00
30	H. L. Roy	1.20
31	C. T. Fisher not paid	.50

This order was issued but not laturn up by Sheriff, not settled in this Settlement

32	G. W. Valentine	8.00
33	W. S. Shurtliff	3.61
34	R. A. McCutcheon	2.35
35	W. W. Right	8.00
36	W. F. Newlon	7.50
37	B. P. Newlon	6.99
38	Joshua Bartlett	.15
39	Wm. England	10.00
40	Wm. England	8.40
41	Sallie R. Phillips	8.00
42	Joshua Bartlett	8.00
43	G. J. Stalnaker	4.00
44	Jno T. Moss	1.60
45	F. C. Wilmoth	8.00
46	A. M. Wilmoth	8.00
47	James Coffman	8.00
48	Solomon Wilson	8.00
49	Cicero Phillips	8.65
Total		$578.57

222 School Board Minutes

J. B. Godwin	15.00	
J. E. Heatherly	14.77	
J. J. Newlon	.30	
Total		608.64
Release		.49
Delinquent		4.39

Commission	38.36
Henry Barte	6.00
J. V. Johnson use of J. A. W.	3.80
T. T. Elliott	6.00
Dr. **D.S. Talbot**	6.00
Less order No. 31 See note	.50
Bal due district on Settlement	<u>98.90</u>
	772.08

The Board Adjourned to meet the 5th day of July 1886 to lay levy & c at 8 oclock AM
     Geo McCutcheon Sect

  Statement of Settlement between **J. W. Robinson** Sheriff of Barbour County and Board of Education of Barker District Barbour County for the year Ending June 30th 1886. Settlement was made 17th day of June 1886.

1886 **J. W. Robinson** Sheriff in account with Barker Dist
June 17 by amount due Sheriff on teachers Fund Cr. $19.47
June 17 to amount due dist on Building Fund $98.90
    Geo P. McCutcheon Sect

Amount of State School Fund for the year commencing July 1st, 1886 and ending June 30th 1887 is $732.24 Amount assessed in Barker dist 53771.00 personal property. Amount assessed in Barker dist 130627.95 Real Estate.

School Board Minutes 223

At a meeting of the Board of Education held at **Glascock & Lovetts** Store on the 5th **day of July 1886** present **T. T. Elliott** president, Dr. **D. S. Talbott** & **H. Barte** members the following business Transacted.

Order of 4 months Schools commencing 1st November 1886 amount Levied on 53.771 personal property. Orders that 20 cts be Levied on the $100.00 for Teachers fund. Ordered that 20 cts be levied on the 100 for Building fund.

Teachers Salaries
No. 1 Certificate   28.00 Twenty -Eight dollars
No. 2 Certificate   22.00 Twenty two dollars
No. 3 Certificate   18.00 Eighteen

1886 Contracts between Teachers & Trustees
Sept 24   **W. B. Baker** Ten Mile, Grade 1, District No. 7
Oct 23   **S. J. McLane**, Grade 2, District No. 8
Nov 3   **Allie J. Smith** Grade 2, District No. 4
Nov 3   **W. C. Moore** Grade 3, District No. 6
Nov 3   **J. W. Ramsey** Grade 1
Nov 3   **A. L. Taylor** Grade 1, District No. 2
Nov 3   **J. A. Dunham** Grade 1, District No. 3
Nov 1   **Flora C. Wilmoth** Grade 1, District No. 9
Nov 3   **Dinah Wood** Grade 3, District No.1

Trustees appointed for 3 years
Dist No. 1   **B. P. Newlon**
Dist No. 2   **J. J. Newlon**
Dist No. 3   **William Bibey**
Dist No. 4   **William Cross**
Dist No. 5   **Samuel D. Coonts**
Dist No. 6   **Isaac Poling**
Dist No. 7   **A. Rhorabough**
Dist No. 8   **Columbus Findley**
Dist No. 9   **C. B. Carter**

On motion the Board Adjourned to meet first Saturday in Nov. at 1 oclock

T. T. Elliott Pres
Geo McCutcheon

School Board Minutes

Philippi **July 10th 1886**
    This is to certify that I have examined the Annual Report of **Geo M. McCutcheon** Sec B. of E. of Barker District and find it to be correct in the main Board of Education will please give him an order on the Sheriff of Barbour Co. for ten dollars as required by law.
        W. D. Zinn Co. Supt.

    At a meeting of the Board of Education held on the **2d day of Oct 1886** at the Store of **L. B. Lovett** & Bros the following business Transacted.
    Ordered that **A. H. Andrews** & Co. of N. Y. be paid by an order drawn on the Sheriff of Barbour County $215.43, $23.23 deducted as freight from $238.66 their statement.
    On motion the Board adjourned to meet Second Saturday in November.
        Geo McCutcheon Sect. B. E.
        T. T. Elliott Pres

    At a meeting of the Board of Education held on **13 day of November 1886** at the Store of **L. B. Lovett** & Bros the following business transacted
    Ordered that **Wm. England** be paid by order on Sheriff Seven dollars and Eighteen cents for furnishing Coal to School House No. 4
    Ordered that **W. S. Shurtleff** be paid two dollars for mdse furnished School House No. 3
    Ordered that **Laben Moore** be paid thirty Six dollars and twenty five cents for Repairing School House No. 3
    Ordered that **A. Right** & Sons be paid five dollars and 13 cts for mdse furnished School House No. 4
    Ordered that **M. Peck** be paid Fourteen dollars & 63 cents for service as Commissioner in law suit between Valley & Barker dists.
    Ordered that **Salathiel Cross** be paid forty two dollars and

ninety five cents $42.95 for Repairing School House No. 4
On motion the Board adjourned to meet the Second Saturday in January 1887.
    Geo McCutcheon Sect Board of Education
    T. T. Elliott Pres

On motion of Board **Martin Hillyard** was appointed trustee in Sub dist No. 2 to fill vacancy of **J. J. Newlon**
On motion **Nixon Shomo** was appointed Trustee in Sub dist No. 1 Hillyard School to fill vacancy of **B. P. Newlon**
Board adjourned to meet 2nd Saturday in January 1887.

P.S. **Hayes Corley** was also appointed trustee in district No. 1 to fill vacancy of **John McCauley** or for 2 years.

Held on the 8th **of January 1887** At a meeting of the Board of Education of Barker district present **T. T. Elliott** president, **H. Barte & D. S. Talbott** Commis. The following business was transacted.
On motion it is ordered that **S. E. Ice** pay fifty cents per month for the privilege of going to School in sub district No.9
Ordered that **John Right** & son be paid three dollars & 70 cts for making recitation desks for Belington School House.
Ordered that **Frank Thompson** be paid Sixty five cents for making Shovel for School House No. 9
Ordered that **Daniel Ice** be paid Fifty seven dollars & 65 cts for repairing school House No. 9
Ordered that **C. B. Carter** be paid one dollar & 68 cts for stove pipe, grate & crayon for School House No. 9
Ordered that **S. E. Yoke** be paid thirty four dollars & 50 cts for Repairing School House No.9
Ordered **A. J. Poling** be paid Eleven dollars & 30 cts for building privies & covering Coal House in sub dist No. 6

Ordered that **A. F. Rhorabough** be paid 1.50 One dollar & .50 for repairs on School House No.7

Ordered that **L. B. Lovett** & Bros be paid One dollar & Fifty five cents for mdse sub dist No. 2

Ordered that **Wm. E. Byrd** be paid Seven dollars for priveys built by him in sub dist No. 2

Ordered that **Martin Hillyard** be paid thirteen dollars & 35 cts for building priveys in sub dist No.2

Ordered that **M. Hillyard** be paid Six dollars for Coal furnished Sub Dist No. 2

On motion it is ordered that the 3d Saturday in January be set as time of trial of **Abraham Poling** trustee in sub dist No.9

On motion it is ordered that the board of Education submit at the next meeting whether Barker district Shall have a graded School or not

Ordered that the Board Adjourn to meet the 3d Saturday in January at 1 oclock

   Geo McCutcheon Sect
    T. T. Elliott Pres

At a meeting of the Board of Education held on **15th day of January 1887** at the Store of **L. B. Lovett** & Bro present **T. T. Elliott** president, **H. Barte & D. S. Talbott** Commissioners the following business was transacted.

Ordered that **W. S. Shurtliff** be paid One dollar & 32 cts.

On motion it is ordered that the charges against **Abraham Poling** a trustee of sub dist No.9 is not Sufficient for discontinuing him

On motion the Board Adjourned to meet 2d Saturday in February 1887.

   Geo McCutcheon Sect
    T. T. Elliott Pres

At a meeting of the Board of Education held on **12th day of**

School Board Minutes 227

February 1887 at **L. B. Lovett** & Bro Store present **T. T. Elliott** president, **H. Barte & D. S. Talbott** Commissioners the following business was transacted.

On motion it is ordered that **C. B. Carter & Abraham Poling** be & are dismissed from Trusteeship in Sub dist No.9 this being day of trial and they are not present.

Ordered that **James Poling** be appointed Trustee in Sub dist No.9 to fill Vacancy of **Abraham Poling**

Ordered that **Daniel Ice** be appointed trustee in Sub dist No. 9 to fill vacancy of **C. B. Carter**.

On motion it is ordered that **Daniel Ice** paid one dollar & 25 cts for Lumber & work done in sub dist No.9

Ordered that **David Canfield** be paid Six dollars for furnishing Coal for Stringtown School.

Ordered that **John M. Cade** be paid one dollar for repairing stove in Sub dist No.3

Ordered that **J.J. Newlon** be paid seventy five cts for repairing Stringtown Schools Stove

Ordered that **J. M. Ramsey** be paid seven dollars & sixty cents for Coal furnished sub dist No.5

Ordered that **J. B. Godwin** be paid forty cents for repairs on stove

Ordered that **W. S. Shurtliff** be paid forty cents for stove damper

Ordered that **A. Right** be paid fifteen dollars & 30 cts for mdse furnished Sub dist No. 5

On motion it is ordered that the Board adjourn to meet the 3d Saturday in March 1887.

Geo McCutcheon Sect
T. T. Elliott Pres

At a meeting of the Board of Education held at **L. B. Lovett & Bro Store** on the **29th day of March 1887** present **T. T. Elliott** president, **H. Barte & D. S. Talbott** Commissioners the following business was transacted.

Ordered that **S. H. Mclean** be paid Eight dollars and 20 cts

School Board Minutes

for building fires & 1 box chalk

Ordered that **Joshua Bartlett** be paid nine dollars & 90 cts for Coal furnished Mouse Run School

Ordered that **W. B. Baker** be paid Eight dollars for building fires in sub dist No.7

Ordered that **Jackson Hillyard** be paid five dollars & 65/100 for Coal & 1 days work in sub dist No.1

Ordered that **Isaac Coonts** be paid two dollars & 35/100 cts for Repairs In School House No.5

Ordered that **Chas Shomo** be paid four dollars & 73 cts for making fires in sub dist No.1

Ordered that **Barton Cross** be paid Eight dollars for building fires in sub dist No.4

Ordered that **W. C. Moore** be paid Eight dollars & 20 cts for making fires & 1 box chalk in sub dist No.6

Ordered that **W. S. Shurtliff** be paid fifty cents for mdse furnished School House No.3

Ordered that **John W. Ramsey** be paid Eight dollars for making fires in sub dist No.5

Ordered that **A. Right** & Son be paid Seven dollars & 30 cts for Coal & mdse furnished School House 4

Ordered that **W. R. Moore** be paid 45 cts for broom & crayon furnished School House No.9

Ordered that **Frederick Moore** be paid Nine dollars & 94 cts for Coal furnished sub dist No.6

Ordered that **C. O. Baker** be paid 50 cts for Mdse furnished sub dist No.1

Ordered that **J. A. Dunham** be paid Eight dollars for making fires in sub dist No.3

Ordered that the Board Adjourn to meet the 1st Saturday in April 1887.

     Geo McCutcheon Sect
     T. T. Elliott Pres

At a meeting of the Board of Education held on **2 day of April 1887** at the Store of **L. B. Lovett** & Bro the following business Transacted, present **T. T. Elliott** president, Dr. **D. S. Talbott** Commis

Ordered that **H. L. Ray** be paid seventy cents for 1 bucket & 1 Dipper Sub Dist No.8

Ordered that **L. B. Lovett** & Bros be paid sixty cents out of building fund.

Ordered that **Flora C. Wilmoth** be paid Eight dollars for building fires in Sub Dist

Ordered that the Board adjourn until Settlement with Sheriff members called together by President

Geo McCutcheon Sect
T. T. Elliott Pres

At a meeting of the Board of Education of Barker District of Barbour County West Virginia held at Belington at **L. B. Lovett** & Bros Store **June 1887** the following officers present **T. T. Elliott** president, **H. Barty** and **D. S. Talbott** Commissioners . The object of this meeting being to settle with Sheriff settlement - made with the following result.

To State School fund		732.24
Amt recd from **Daniel Ice**		1.00
To District Levey		368.80
		1102.04

No.		$ ¢
1	W. B. Baker	28.00
2	S. H. Mclane	22.00
3	A. L. Taylor	28.00
4	J. W. Ramsey	28.00
5	Abie J. Smith	22.00
6	J. A. Dunham	28.00
7	W. B. Baker	28.00
8	W. C. Moore	18.00
9	W. C. Moore	18.00
10	Flora C. Wilmoth	28.00
11	S. H. Mclane	22.00

230 School Board Minutes

12	Abie J. Smith	22.00
13	J. W. Ramsey	28.00
14	V. L. Taylor	28.00
15	Flora C. Wilmoth	28.00
16	W. B. Baker	28.00
17	W. C. Moore	18.00
18	S. H. Mclane	22.00
19	Abie J. Smith	22.00
20	A. P. Taylor	28.00
21	J. W. Ramsey	56.00
22	W. B. Baker	28.00
23	Flora C. Wilmoth	28.00
24	Abie J. Smith	22.00
25	W. C. Moore	18.00
26	S. H. Mclane	22.00
27	J. A. Dunham	84.00
28	Dinah Wood	72.00
29	A. L. Taylor	28.00
30	Flora Wilmoth	28.00
		880.00

Amt due on last years settlement 19.47
Delinquent 1.40
Commission 18.48
919.34
Balance due dist. 1102.04

J. W. Robinson S. B. C. Barker Dist Dr.
To Dist Levey 737.60
Bal due district on last years settlement 98.90
Money collected on lands sold .14
Sheriff claims 14 cts instead of 2.34 in this settlement in clk of court

No.		$ ¢
	Geo T. McCutcheon	15.00
1	Geo T. McCutcheon	10.00
2	A. H. Andrews	215.43
3	Wm. England	7.18
4	W. S. Shurtleff	2.00
5	Laben Moore	36.25

6	A. Right	5.13
7	M. Patton for J. A. Williamson	14.63
8	Salathiel Cross for A. Right	42.95
9	John Right and Son	3.70
10	Frank Thompson	.65
11	Daniel Ice	57.65
12	C. B. Carter	1.68
13	S. E. Yoke	34.50
14	A. J. Poling	11.30
15	A. H. Rorabugh	1.00
16	J. B. Lovett and Bro.	1.55
17	Wm. E. Byrd	7.00
18	Martin Hillyard	13.35
19	M. Hillyard	6.00
20	W. S. Shurtliff	1.32
21	Daniel Ice	1.25
22	David Canfield	6.00
23	John Cade	1.00
24	J. J. Newlon	.75
25	J. M. Ramsey	7.60
26	J. B. Godwin	.40
27	W. S. Shurtliff	.40
28	A. Right & Son	15.30
29	S. H. Mc Lane	8.20
30	Joshaway Bartlet	9.90
31	W. B. Baker	8.00
32	Jackson Hillyard	5.65
33	Isaac Kunst	2.35
34	Chas Showmore	4.75
35	Barton Cross	8.00
36	W. C. Moore	8.20
37	W. S. Shurtliff	.50
38	J. W. Ramsey	8.00
39	A. Right & Son	7.30
40	W. R. Moore	.45
41	Fred Moore	9.94
42	E. O. Baker	.50
43	J. A. Dunham	8.00
44	A. L. Taylor	8.00

232 School Board Minutes

45	**H. L. Ray**	.70
46	**L. B. Lovett** and Bro	.60
47	**Flora Wilmoth**	8.00
48	**S. E. Yoak**	5.73

Delinquent   2.81
Amt paid Commissioner   6.00
C. F. Fisher   .50
Order **J. E. Heatherly**   133.43
Commission   36.83
Joseph Teter   3.00
P.M.& M. Company   8.00
The **J. E. Heatherly** interest on order
Fee bills against Board

| 49 | **Geo P. McCutcheon** | <u>2.75</u> |
| | | 836.64 |

June 21 1887
Statement of Settlement between **J. A. Williamson** D. C. for **J. W. Robinson** Sheriff of Barbour County and Barker district

Teachers fund
Amt due dist on settlement 182.69
Amt to lay levys on for 1887
Total value of real Estate   131793.00
Total value of Personal Property 64904.00

    T. T. Elliott Pres
     Geo P. McCutcheon Sect

Amount of State School fund $807.74

  At a meeting of the Board of Education held on the **21st day of July 1887**present **W. S. Phares** president, **John Ward & D. S. Talbott** Comm the following business was transacted

Ordered that **Geo McCutcheon** be & is appointed Sect.
Ordered that 4 months school shall be taught in every dist.
Ordered that 9 Teachers shall be employed in Barker.
Ordered that Teachers Salaries shall be as follows
No. Ones be paid $28.00 per month
No. Twos be paid $22.00 per month
No. Threes be paid $18.00 per month
    On motion it is ordered that the Board adjourn to meet the 16 day of July 1887.
Geo McCutcheon Sect

    At a meeting of the board of Education held on **16th day of July 1887** present **W. S. Phares** president, **John Ward & D. S. Talbott** Commissioners the following business was transacted.
    On motion it is ordered that 5 cts be levied on the $100.00 for teachers fund.
    Ordered that 35 cts be levied on 100.00 for Building
Trustees appointed for 3 years

Dist
1   **M. Hart**
2   **Cicero Phillips** for 2 years and **Daniel Day** for 3 years
3   **Henry Barte** for 3 years & **George Booth** for 2 years
4   **John Moore** be appointed for 3 years
5   **Samuel D. Coonts** be appointed for 3 years
6   **Isaac Price** Senior be appointed for 3 years
7   **John D. Ball** be appointed for 3 years
8   **Daniel Chenoweth** be appointed for 3 years
9   **James Poling** be appointed for 3 years
    On motion it is ordered that the Board adjourn
Geo McCutcheon Sect

1887 Contracts between Teachers & Trustees
Aug   **James Coffman** Grade 1, District No. 4
Aug 10   **Minnie Rogers** Grade 2, District No. 2

School Board Minutes

July 30	**Samuel H. Mclean** Grade 1, District No. 8
Aug 13	**H. J. Price** Grade 1, District No. 5
Aug 26	**Cora Dunham** Grade 1, District No. 3
Aug 15	**W. S. Hayes** Grade 1, District No. 1
Aug 15	**Maggie Obrien** Grade 1, District No. 9
Aug 15	**Hattie Jenkins** Grade 1, District No.7
Aug 15	**O. H. Shanabarger** Grade 2, District No. 6

At a meeting of the Board of Education held on the **19th day of November 1887** at **John Ward**s Store present **W. S. Phares** president and **John Ward & D. S. Talbott** Commissioners the following business transacted

On motion it is ordered that **Daniel Chenoweth** be paid One dollar & 25 cts for Mdse furnished Sub dist

On motion it is ordered that **Alph Moore** be paid Nine dollars 9.00 for Coal furnished sub dist No.6

Ordered that **W. S. Shurtliff** be paid nine dollars 80cts for mdse furnished sub dists No. 2 & 4.

Ordered that **R. M. Godwin** be paid forty four $44.00 for Ceiling School House No.6

Ordered that **Guy V. Ward** be paid one dollar for mdse & hauling & putting up stove in sub dist No. 2

Ordered that **W. S. Phares** be paid five dollars 75/100 for Coal furnished sub dist No. 2

Ordered that **M. V. L. Corrick** be paid three dollars & 25 cts for putting up Chimney in sub dist No. 2

Ordered that **Daniel Day** be paid 1.25 one dollar & 25cts for working on Chimney sub dist No. 2

Ordered that **L. N. Viquesney** be paid Eighty nine dollars & eighty nine cents 89.89 for Roofing Ceiling & painting School House No.1

On motion the Board adjourned to meet the 3d Saturday in January 1888.

Geo P. McCutcheon Secty

At a meeting of the Board of Education held on the **21st day of January 1888** at **John Ward**s Store the following members present **W. S. Phares** president Dr. **D. S. Talbott & John Ward** Commissioners the following business transacted

On motion it is ordered that **Alpheus Moore** be paid Eight dollars and fifty cents for Coal & repairs sub dist No.6

Ordered that **L. B. Lovett** & Bro be paid four dollars & 05 cts for mdse furnished sub dists No.3 & 7

Ordered that **William England** be paid seven dollars for fuel furnished sub dist No. 7

Ordered that **Jackson Hillyard** be paid four dollars & 25 cts for Coal furnished sub dist No.1

On motion the Board adjourned to meet on the 1st Saturday in April at 1 oclock at **John Ward**s store.

Geo P. McCutcheon Sect

At a call meeting of the Board of Education held on the **23rd day of January** at **John Ward**s Store present **W. S. Phares** president & **John Ward** Commissioner the following business transacted

Ordered that **S. L. Howell** be paid Eight dollars & 70 cts for Coal & Repairs School House in sub dist No.8

On motion the Board adjourned to meet the 1st Saturday in April at 1 oclock at **John Ward**s Store.

Geo P. McCutcheon Sect

At a call meeting of the B. E. of Barker District Barbour County West Va. held on the **1st day of February 1888** at **John Ward**s Store the following members present **W. S. Phares** president **John Ward** & Dr. **D. S. Talbott** Commissioners the following business transacted

On motion it is ordered that **Hattie Jenkins** teacher of

School Board Minutes

school Sub dist No. 7 having been discharged by the trustees, Continue her School.
  Ordered that the Board adjourn to meet the 1st Saturday in April at 1 oclock
    Geo McCutcheon Sect

  At a call meeting of the Board of Education held on the **21st day of February 1888** at **John Ward**s Store the following members present **W. S. Phares** president **John Ward** & Dr. **D. S. Talbott** Commissioners the following business transacted
  T. T. Elliott withdrew his charges against Miss **Rogers** teacher at Belington School.
  Board adjourned to meet Feb 11 at 2 oclock at **John Ward**s Store.
    Geo McCutcheon Sect

  At a call meeting of the Board of Education held on the **11th day of Feb 1888** at **John Ward**s Store the following members present **W. S. Phares** president **John Ward** & Dr. **D. S. Talbott** the following business transacted
  Ordered that **S. R. Moore** be paid Six dollars & 64 for furnishing fuel for Sub dist No. 4
  Ordered that **Cicero Phillips** be continued as trustee in Sub dist No.2
  Board adjourned to meet 1st Saturday in April at 1 oclock at **John Ward**s Store
    Geo McCutcheon Sect

At a meeting of the Board of Education held on the **7th day of April 1888** at **John Ward**s Store. **W. S. Phares** president Dr. **D. S. Talbott & John Ward** Commissioners the following business transacted

On motion it is ordered that the following trustees orders should be paid **Cora Dunham** Eight dollars for making fires sub dist No.3.

W. S. Shurtliff two dollars for 8 Joints 7in Stove pipe Sub dist No.7

S. H. Mclean Eight dollars for making fires sub dist Mouse Run School. **A. Right** & Sons 2.80 for Mdse furnished Sub dist 5 & 6. **James Coffman** Eight dollars for making fires Sub dist No.4. **Ulysses Moore** $5.85 Five dollars & 85 cts for fuel Sub dist No. 3. **Jackson Coonts** seven dollars & 50 cts for fuel furnished sub dist No. 5. **Minnie Rogers** Eight & 30 cts for Making fires & two boxes crayon Belington School. **John Ward** thirty cents for Broom & tin cup furnished Belington School. **O.H. Shanabarger** 8.00 making fires Wolf Run School. **W. S. Hayes** making fires Sub dist No. 1

Ordered that the Sect write to B. E. of Philippi dist for Enumeration grade of teacher salary of teacher & coal at fire building Mt. Liberty School.

Ordered that the Board of Education allow a subscription school to be taught in School House of sub dist No.7 or Ten Mile

Ordered that the Board adjourn till settlement with sheriff unless called together by president.

Geo McCutcheon Sect

At a meeting of the Board of Education Barker district Barbour County, West Virginia held at Belington at **John Ward**s Store the **20th day of June 1888** present **W. S. Phares** president **John Ward** & Dr. **D. S. Talbott** Commis the object of the meeting being to settle with Sheriff. Settlement is made with the following result

To amt due dist on last settlement	182.69
To State School fund	807.14
To Dist Levy	<u>98.45</u>
	1088.28

238 School Board Minutes

No.		
1	H. J. Price	28.00
2	S. H. Mclane	28.00
3	Hattie Jenkins	28.00
4	Cora Dunham	28.00
5	Maggie J. Obrien	28.00
6	James Coffman	28.00
7	O. H. Shanabarger	22.00
8	U. S. Hayes	28.00
9	Minnie Rogers	22.00
10	H. J. Price	28.00
11	S. H. Mclane	28.00
12	Maggie J. Obrien	28.00
13	James Coffman	28.00
14	U. S. Hayes	28.00
15	Cora E. Dunham	28.00
16	O. H. Shanabarger	22.00
17	O. H. Shanabarger	22.00
18	S. H. Mclane	28.00
19	Hattie Jenkins	28.00
20	Hattie Jenkins	28.00
21	James Coffman	28.00
22	Maggie J. Obrien	28.00
23	H. J. Price	28.00
24	H. J. Price	28.00
25	Cora E. Dunham	28.00
26	S. H. Mclane	28.00
27	Minnie Rogers	22.00
28	O. H. Shanabarger	22.00
29	Cora E. Dunham	28.00
30	Maggie Obrien	28.00
31	U. S. Hayes	28.00
32	U. S. Hayes	28.00
33	Hattie Jenkins	28.00
34	Minnie Rogers	22.00
35	Minnie Rogers	22.00
36	James Coffman	28.00

Delinquent	1.42
Commission	4.85
Transfer	49.10
On settlement	1015.37

James A. Williamson S. B. C. made with B. E. of Barker dist to Dist

Levy	687.25
To money collected on lands sold last year & claimed	2.34
	689.39

List of orders on building fund

Geo P. McCutcheon	15.00
Geo P. McCutcheon	10.00
L. N. Viquesney	89.89
Daniel Chenoweth	1.25
W. S. Shurtliff	9.80
Adph Moore	9.00
R. M. Godwin	44.00
Guy V. Ward	1.00
Layfayette Corrick	3.25
Daniel Day	1.87
W. S. Phares	5.75
Alph Moore	8.55
L. B. Lovett & Bro	4.05
William England	7.00
Jackson Hillyard	4.25
A. H. Andrews & Co.	238.66
S. L. Howell	8.70
S. R. Moore	6.64

James Poling will be in their order settlement

H. J. Price	8.00
Hattie Jenkins	8.00
U. S. Hayes	8.00
O. H. Shanabarger	8.00
Minnie Rogers	8.00
John Ward	.30
Cora Dunham	8.00
Jackson Coonts	7.50
Ulysses Moore	5.85
James Coffman	8.00

240 School Board Minutes

A. Right & sons	2.80
Maggie J. Obrien	8.00
S. H. Mclane	8.00
W. S. Shurtliff	2.00
Baker & Swick	2.84
Commission	34.05
John Cade	1.00
Isaac Coonts	2.35
T. T. Elliott	6.00
D. S. Talbott	6.00
Mistake on Miss Rogers order	.30
	611.68

Delinquent	6.16
Transfer	5.44
Order No. 33 not in this settlement	2.34
Due dist	69.15
	689.59

Notice in this settlement there was 21x28 dollar orders & 4x22 dollar orders leaving 7.28 Order & 4x22 dollar order 2 to come in settlement. On teachers fund only 403.57 was paid on ½ of State fund. Give Sheriff credit at next settlement order No.33 Baker & Swick as it was not settled on this settlement Bal due dist on Building fund of 69.15

      Received of the Board of Education of Barker dist Barbour County West Va. this the 20th day of June 1888 an order on **J. W. Robinson** Ex Sheriff of Barbour Co. West Va. for Four hundred and three dollars and 57/100 dollars for collection.
      J. A. Williamson S. B. E.

Amt today levy on for 1888 is as following
Total value of real Estate is $132177.65 cents
Total value of personal property is 63807.00
Amount of State School fund is $842.51 cents

July 1st, 1888
      I have been notified by the Clk of County Court that the Sheriff is charge all with $6.38 from sale of delinquent lands the clk did not notify me till after settlement.
      Geo McCutcheon

Total amt of property & real Estate   195984.65
                                                                            .40
                                                                    7839386.00

At a meeting of the Board of Education held on the **2d day of July 1888** at **John Ward**s Store present **W. S. Phares** president **John Ward** & Dr. **D. S. Talbott** Commissioners the following business transacted

Ordered that the Levys be laid as follows 14 cts on the $100.00 for Teachers fund and 40 cts on the 100.00 for Building Fund.

                              Trustees appointed

1. **Hayes Cauley**
2. **Wm. Bolton** 3 years **H. C. Rosenberger** & **Daniel Day** will expire the 20th day of June 1890
3. **Jethro Bennett** 3 years
4. **Lewis Price**
5. **Solomon Wilson**
6. **John Price**
7. **F. B. Durrett**
8. **Lewis Cauley**
9. **W. R. Moore**

                     Geo McCutcheon Secty

At a meeting of the Board of Education held on the **20th day of August 1888** at **John Ward**s Store present **John Ward** & Dr. **D. S. Talbott** Commissioners the following business transacted the meeting being to receive bids for a School House to be built at Belington bids were conferred and Contract awarded to **T. T. Elliott** to Build School House his bid being 550.00 Five hundred & fifty dollars.

           After which Board adjourned
                   Geo McCutcheon Sect

School Board Minutes

At a meeting of the Board of Education held on the **11**[th] **day of Sept 1888** at **John Ward**s Store present Dr. **D. S. Talbott & John Ward** Commissioners the following business transacted
    Trustees appointed as follows
No. 2   **H. C. Rosenburger** 3 years
No. 2   **John R. Phares** 2 years
No. 10 **T. T. Elliott** 3 years
No. 10 **John C. Dunham** 2 years
No. 11 **R. A. McCutcheon** 1 year
    Contracts for Necessaries Coal house & Flue were awarded or let to **T. T. Elliott** for Forty nine dollars & fifty cents 49.50
    Painting sold to **Wirl Buckey** at twenty dollars & seventy five cents 20.75
    On motion Board adjourned
        Geo McCutcheon Sect

1888 Contracts between Teachers & Trustees filed

Sept 13	**W. S. Phillips** Sub Dist No. 4 grade of certificate No. 2 Hunters Fork
Sept 17	**Floyd Holden** Sub Dist No. 7 grade of certificate No. 1 Ten Mile
Sept 17	**S. H. Mclane** Sub Dist No. 2 grade of certificate No. 1 Belington Old School
Oct 6	**W. C. Moore**
Oct 6	**Cora E. Dunham** Sub Dist No. 5 grade of certificate No.1
Oct 6	**W. F. Jennings** Sub Dist No. 1 grade of certificate No. 2 Hillyard
Oct 6	**Alice Wallace** Sub Dist No. 3 grade of certificate No.9
Oct 6	**Olive Arnett** Sub Dist No. 2 grade of certificate No. 3
Jan 4	**Belle Swearingen** Sub Dist No. 10 grade of certifcate No. 1 Belington New School

School Board Minutes 243

At a meeting of the Board of Education held on the **6th day of Oct 1888** at **John Ward**s Store

George Currence was appointed a trustee for Sub Dist No. 8 (Mr. **Ray** was also appointed or at least he told me so)

2d It is agreed to purchase of **Thomas Kane** & Co. through their agent **E. G. Huffman** 20 doubles School desks for the sum of $76.00 one half to be paid for out of Levy of 1888 & one half out of the Levy of 1889.

Geo P. McCutcheon Sect

At a meeting of the board of Education held on the **5th day of Nov 1888** at **John Ward**s Store present **W. S. Phares** president **John Ward** & Dr. **D. S. Talbott** Commissioners the following business transacted

Divisions of New sub school dist as follows from **Rosenburger** line to **Talbotts** & **Newlon** line. **Talbott** & **Newlon** to be included in sub dist No.2 from **Newlons** line to **Shurtliffs** line with **John Booths** line, the line on Eastern comes of sub dist No. 2 to be changed as to include **John Booth, Nelson Boothe, Mary Boothe**, the line on **N. E. Comer** to be changed so as to include **John C. Dunham** & **Granville Godwin** in sub dist No. 10

On motion **J. W. Ward** was paid Eleven dollars for furnishing stove for school house No. 10

Guy V. Ward was paid Five dollars & 80 cts for Coal furnished sub dist No. 2

Arch Coberly was paid 40 cts for poker & damper furnished sub dist No.9

John T. Moss was paid one dollar & 58cts for crayon, thumb latch, Glass, broom, bucket &c for Sub dist No. 9

G. H. Gall was paid one dollar & 25 cts for 1 grade furnished Sub dist No. 7

James L. Ramsey was paid ninety dollars for Roofing, flooring, building flue & cfth school House No. 7

On motion Board adjourned to meet the 4th Saturday in Nov 1888 at 1 o'clock p.m.

Geo McCutcheon Sect

244 School Board Minutes

At a call meeting of the Board of Education held on the **10th day of November 1888** at **John Ward**s Store present **W. S. Phares** president **John Ward** Commissioner the following business transacted

On the deed for lot on which School house No. 10 stands as sub dist No. 10 was this day executed by **T. T. Elliott** & wife to the Board of Education of Barker dist

On motion it was ordered that **T. T. Elliott** be paid the sum of 550. Five hundred and fifty dollars for building school House No. 10 payments as follows one order for two hundred and seventy five dollars out of levy of 1888 and two order of $137.50 One hundred and thirty seven dollars and fifty cents each out of levy of 1889 said ordered was this day executed to **T. T. Elliott**.

On motion it was ordered that **T. T. Elliott** be also paid forty nine dollars & 50 cts one order of one half or 24.75 payable out of levy of 1888 and the other out of levy of 1889 said orders was this day executed to **T. T. Elliott** said orders being for Coal house, Necessaries, Brick flue & cfth for school house No. 10.

On motion it was ordered that **Laben Moore** be paid thirty dollars and 25 cts for roofing and daubing school House No.3

Ordered that **Jackson Hillyard** be paid two dollars and 25 cts for repairing Coal house in sub dist No. 1

Ordered and order Executed to **Wirt Buckey** for $20.75 for painting School House No.10

One order out of levy of 1888 for 10.38 or one half the amount and one out of levy of 1889 for the other half or Ten dollars and 37 cts.

On motion Board adjourned to meet the 4th Saturday in Nov at 1 oclock P.M.

T. T. Elliott was also given order for two dollars for iron received for stove pipe & 150 feet of Extra lumber for building platform

        Geo McCutcheon Sect

The Board gave me authority to pay **James Coffman** an order for 90.00 for Reframing school House No.7 which I did Nov. 6, 1888

        Geo McCutcheon Sect

At a call meeting of the board of Education of Barker district held at **John Ward**s Store the **13th day of November 1888** the following business transacted

On motion it is ordered that G. G. R. R. Co. be paid by order on sheriff Twelve dollars and 16 cents for freight on School desks freight of **Thomas Kane** & Co. Chicago Ill.

Ordered that **Geo McCutcheon** be paid two 25 cts witness fee in behalf of Barker dist against **Jacob Robinson** Ex Sheriff of Barbour Co

Ordered that **Thomas Kane** & Co. be paid thirty Eight & 40 cts ½ of payment on School seats

Ordered that Board adjourn to meet the 24th day of Nov. 1888.

Geo McCutcheon Sect

At a meeting of the Board of Education held on the **24th day of Nov 1888** at **John Ward**s Store present **W. S. Phares** pres & **John Ward** Commis the following business transacted

On motion it is ordered that **A. C. Harris** be paid thirty four dollars and 90 cts for Roofing Hunters Fork School House

Ordered that **Sylvester M. Poling** be paid Eleven dollars and 60 cent for building brick flue to School House No.9

Ordered that **John Ward** be paid Eighty cents 1 Broom & water Bucket furnished School House No. 2

Ordered that **T. J. Corley** be paid one dollar and 95 cts for cleaning of School lot Sub dist No. 1

Ordered that **Shurtliff & Right** be paid one dollar and eighty cents for mdse furnished Sub dist No. 4

Ordered that **L. B. Lovett** & Bro be paid three dollars and 50 cts for mdse furnished Schools Nos 9 & 3

Ordered that the Board adjourn to meet the 3d Saturday in January at 2 oclock

Geo P. McCutcheon Sect

School Board Minutes

Dec 12, 1888

An order was drawn on shelf to **Thomas Kane** & Co. for the remaining half of payments on School desks the order was for 38.40 in full to **Thomas Kane** & Co act.

   Geo McCutcheon Sect B. E.

At a meeting of the Board of Education of Barker district held at **John Ward**s Store the 19th day of Jan 1889 present **W. S. Phares** president & **John Ward** Commis the following business transacted

  Ordered that **Shurtleff & Right** be paid Two dollars and 85 cents for crayon, Hat hooke, Coal Hod, Cloak Hooks & cfth furnished sub dists No. 4, 7 & 10.

  Ordered that **A. Right** & son be paid two dollars for Coal Hod, Broom, Bucket, Shovel & cfth furnished sub No. 6

  Ordered that **Guy Elliott** be paid Six dollars & 50 cents for coal for Sub dist No. 10

  Ordered that **W. S. Davis** be paid thirteen dollars for 1 stove & stove pipe, 6 doz screws & pipe

  Ordered that **John C. Right** be paid Seventeen dollars and 75 cents for Building flue and furnishing fuel for School House No.6

  Ordered that **Guy V. Ward** be paid one dollar & 50 cts for hauling school desks and putting up coat hook in sub dist No. 10

  Ordered that **Geo McCutcheon** be paid two dollars and 75 cents for witness fee in behalf of Barker dist vs. **J. W. Robinson** Ex Sheriff of Barbour County

  Ordered that **L. B. Lovett** & Bro be paid seven dollars & 62 for shovel, grate & stove Barrell sub dist No. 3, 1 Broom sub dist 9 & 1 order of **Laben Bennett** assigned to **L. B. Lovett** & Bro for delivering and setting up stove sub dist No.3 also chalk, Lock & Glass for sub dist No.7

  On motion Board adjourned to meet the 3d Saturday in March at 2 oclock PM

   Geo McCutcheon Sect

Received a transfer from Valley dist from trustees **Jesse Teter, J. B. Simpson & J. A. Gaunt** for 3 children of **E. G. Huffman** to attend school sub dist No. 10 in Barker dist for the term of 3 months. Transfer dated the 18th of Jan 89
Geo McCutcheon

At a meeting of the Board of Education held on the **16th day of March 1889** at **John Ward**s Store present **W. S. Phares** pres and **John Ward** Commis the following business transacted

Ordered that **James H. Robinson** be paid Six dollars & 35 cents for fuel furnished Sub dist No.9

Ordered that **Elam T. Bennett** be paid nine dollars for furnishing coal sub dist No.4

Ordered that **Laben Moore** be paid Six and 10 cents for coal furnished Sub dist No.3

Ordered that **R. M. Bennett** be paid Eight dollars for building fires & sweeping house Sub dist No.3

Ordered that **Wm. England** be paid Ten dollars for furnishing 125 bu coal Sub dist No.5

Ordered that **Marion B. Shomo** be paid three dollars & 90 cents for making fires &cfth sub dist No.1

Ordered that **Joshua Bartlett** be paid Six dollars for repairs on School House No.8

Ordered that **Alice Wallace** be paid Eight dollars for building fires, sweeping house sub dist No.9

Ordered that **Joseph Hart** be paid the sum of Five dollars & 45 cts

Ordered that **W. S. Phillips** be paid Eight dollars for making fires in sub dist No.4

Ordered that **Cora E. Dunham** be paid Eight dollars for building fires & sweeping house sub dist No.5

Ordered that **L. B. Lovett** & Bro. be paid thirty cents for 1 box chalk & 2 panes of glass for sub dist No.1

Ordered that **W. C. Moore** be paid Eight dollars building fires sub dist No.6

Ordered that Glade district be paid & was paid Seventy

248 School Board Minutes

three dollars & 71 cents for transfers from the year of 1886 to 1888 or for school year ending June 30, 1889
    On motion board adjourned
          Geo McCutcheon Sect B. E.

For the school year ending June 30, 1889
    Statement of Settlement made the 12th day of June 1889 between **J. H. Williamson** Sheriff of Barbour County & Board of Education of Barker dist. Settlement was made with following results bal. Due Sheriff on Building fund   120.97
Bal due Sheriff on Teachers fund   305.01

Levy for the year of 1889
The total amount of real estate to Levy on for next year is 135163.35 the total amount of personal property 59286. Total amount of personal property & real estate 194449.35

Teachers Fund
    At a meeting of the Board of Education held on the **12th day of June 1889** at **L. B. Lovett** & Bro Store present **W. S. Phares** president & Dr. **D. S. Talbott** Commis. Settlement was made with Sheriff with following results **James A. Williamson** Sheriff from act with Barker dist

to State School fund		842.50
To Dist Levy		<u>293.95</u>
		$1136.45
	By Commission	14.60
	Delinquent	1.95
33	**Hattie Jenkins**	29.33
6	**W. C. Moore**	28.00

3	W. S. Phillips	22.00
7	Olive Arnett	22.00
1	Floyd Holden	28.00
2	Samuel H. Mclane	28.00
8	Wm T. Jennings	22.00
5	Alice Wallace	18.00
29	Cora E. Dunham	29.05
31	U. S. Hayes	29.26
10	W. C. Moore	28.00
17	Olive Arnett	22.00
13	S. H. Mclane	28.00
12	Floyd Holden	28.00
11	Alice Wallace	18.00
36	James Coffman	29.24
22	Cora E. Dunham	28.00
14	Cora E. Dunham	28.00
4	Cora E. Dunham	28.00
21	Samuel H. Mclane	28.00
23	Floyd Holden	28.00
32	U. S. Hayes	29.26
15	W. T. Jennings	22.00
19	F. Belle Swearingen	28.00
9	W. S. Phillips	22.00
18	W. E. Moore	28.00
29	Floyd Holden	28.00
26	Olive Arnett	22.00
20	Alice Wallace	18.00
28	Samuel H. McLean	28.00
24	Hattie Hollen	28.00
38	Hattie Hollen	28.00
25	W. C. Moore	28.00
31	Alice Wallace	18.00
32	W. F. Jennings	22.00
33	W. F. Jennings	22.00
35	Olive Arnett	22.00
36	F. Bell Swearingen	28.00
27	W. S. Phillips	44.00
34	Hattie Hollen	28.00
16	Hattie Hollen	28.00

250 School Board Minutes

30	Cora E. Dunham	28.00
49	Glade District	73.71
30	Maggie J. O'Brien	27.42
37	F. Bell Swearingen	28.00
39	F. Bell Swearingen	28.00
27	Minnie M. Rodgers	23.00
34	Minnie M. Rogers	23.00
35	Minnie M. Rogers	23.00
26	Sam'l H. McLean	29.10
28	O. H. Shanaberger	<u>22.88</u>
		1441.46

June 12, 1889
James A. Williamson Sheriff of Barbour County in account with Barker District

To District Levy	$783.93
To money collected on delinquent lands last year	2.34
To Balance due Barker District on last settlement	<u>69.15</u>
Total	$855.42

Orders No.

4	John T. Moss	1.58
20	H. C. Harris	34.90
15	George P. McCutcheon	15.00
36	George P. McCutcheon	10.00
13	Laben Moore	30.25
25	Shurtleff & Right	1.85
19	Thomas Kane & Co.	38.40
7	T. T. Elliott	275.00
18	Geo P. McCutcheon	2.25
11	T. T. Elliott	24.75
12	T. T. Elliott	2.00
17	G&G. R. Rd. Co.	12.16
10	W. S. Phares	6.00
12	John W. Ward	6.00
3	Arch Coberly	.40
25	L. B. Lovett & Bro	3.50
22	John Ward	.80
1	John Ward	11.00

2	G. V. Ward	5.80
21	Sylvester M. Poling	11.60
	Wirt Buckey	10.38
33	Baker & Swick	2.87
14	Jackson Hillyard	2.25
32	Guy V. Ward	1.50
	John Shank fee bill	1.25
	J. A. Williamson fee bill	.75
	J. A. Williamson	5.00
	I. V. Johnson	3.75
	delinquent	5.68
	commission	38.86
	by error of 1.30	1.30

Orders No. Building Fund

23	T. J. Corley	1.95
34	L. B. Lovett & Bro	7.62
30	W. S. Davis	13.00
6	James L. Ramsey	90.00
29	Guy Elliott	6.50
27	Shurtleff & Right	2.55
11	David Talbott	6.00
33	Geo. P. McCutcheon	2.75
31	John C. Right	17.75
28	A. Right & Son	2.00
51	S. H. McLean	8.00
48	W. E. Moore	8.15
52	W. R. Coonts	9.00
46	L. B. Lovett & Bro	.30
45	Cora Dunham	8.00
42	Alice Wallace	8.00
50	Floyd Holden	8.00
35	James H. Robinson	6.35
54	J. D. Chenoweth	9.95
24	D. W. Day	2.00
44	L. C. Phillips	8.00
40	Marion B. Shomo	3.90
43	Joseph B. Hart	5.45
53	John Finley	8.00

252 School Board Minutes

39	Wm. England	10.00
55	Guy Cade	8.00
37	Laben Moore	6.10
38	R. M. Bennett	8.00
	Twp executions	135.29
	John Shanks Fee bill	1.25

Building Fund
J. A. Williamson	.75
J. A. Williamson	5.00
I. V. Johnson	3.75
Delinquent	5.68
Commission	38.86
Settled at	$976.39
Amt. due	116.93

At a meeting of the Board of Education of Barker district held at **J. W. Ward**s store house on the **first day of July 1889** present **W. S. Phares** President, **John Ward** and **F. B. Durrett** commissioners

It was ordered that there be four months school for the year 1889. Trustee appointed in

District No.1	**Nixon Shomo**
District No.2	**Daniel W. Day**
District No.3	**George M. Booth**
District No.4	**James Coffman**
District No.5	**Samuel Coonts**
District No.6	**Isaac Poling**
District No.7	**B. B. Rhorabaugh** for 3 years
	Lewis Jones for 2 years
District No.8	**Columbus Finley**
District No.9	**Daniel Ice**

Levies for building purposes 40 cents on the $100. valuation. Teachers fund not levied on account of not knowing

amt. of State School fund. Teachers salaries
No. 1   Twenty eight dollars per month
No.2   Twenty two dollars pr month
No. 3   Eighteen dollars per month

Ordered that the Schools shall commence on the first Monday in November 1889.

Ordered that **H. C. Harris** be allowed nine dollars for cleaning school house lot No. 4

G. J. Stalnaker Secretary

At a meeting of the Bd of Ed. of Barker Dist. Barbour Co. W. Va. held on the **28 day of Oct. 1889** present **W. S. Phares** President, **John W. Ward** commissioner

It was ordered that **Guy V. Ward** be given an order on the sheriff of Barbour Co. W. Va. for $32.50 also two orders to **S. W. Fisher** for $182.50 each one payable out of the Levy of 1889 the other out of the Levy of 1890.

G. J. Stalnaker Secretary

At a meeting of the Bd. of Ed. of Barker Dist held at **J. W. Wards** store house on the **30 day of Nov 1889.** Present **J. W. Ward** and **F. B. Durrett** commissioners and **W. S. Phares** President. The following business was transacted

Ordered that **Albert Rhorabaugh** be allowed $7.50 for furnishing 125 bu. coal to sub Dist No.7

That **E. G. Chenoweth** be allowed $3.00 for making safe and bench for Mouse Run School house.

That **Nathan Kelley** be allowed $6.40 for furnishing 125 bu. coal to sub Dist No.9

That **W. S. Davis** be allowed $4.15 for furnishing recitation benches, coal hod, Broom, Bucket, Dipper, Shovel and two boxes crayon.

That **L. B. Lovett** & Bro. be allowed fifty cents for two boxes chalk and one broom.

That **Cicero Phillips** be allowed $4.00 for furnishing one Table for school house No.10

That **J. W. Ward** be allowed $1.27 for furnishing 3 doz. screws, 9 window light 10x12, 1 paper tacks and one joint 7in stove pipe in Sub Dist No.7

That **Jethro Moore** be allowed thirteen ($13.00) dollars for repairs to school house in sub Dist No.4

That **A. Right** & Sons be allowed $1.15 for Bucket, Broom, Box crayons, cup, stove pipe and dipper.

That **J. C. Right** be allowed $6.60 for repairs on school house in sub Dist No.6

That **Frederic Moore** be allowed $28.00 for 1 mo. Wages in sub Dist No.6

That **W. C. Moore** be allowed $28.00 one mo. Wages in sub Dist No.5

That **Alice Wallace** be allowed $22.00 for teaching one month in sub Dist No.9

Also ordered that **J. A. Viquesney** be and is employed to teach the Belington School in Sub Dist No.2 and that said School shall commence on Monday Dec. 2, 1889. Also that **John McCloud** be appointed Trustee in room of **H. C. Rosenberger**. Also that the President and Secretary are empowered to give Teachers Drafts when the Board is not is session. Also that the boundary line between sub Dist No. 10 and sub Dist No. 2 shall and is hereby changed so as to include **J. J. Newlon, D. S. Talbott** and **H. C. Rosenberger** in sub Dist No.10

Ordered that the Board meet at **J. W. Ward**s store house on the last Saturday of January 1890 at one oclock P.M.
    G. J. Stalnaker Scy

At a meeting of the Board of Ed. of Barker Dist. held at **J. W. Ward**s store house on the **21 day of December 1889** present **W. S. Phares** president and **J. W. Ward** & **F. B. Durrett** Commissioners

It was ordered that **Rezin Davis** be allowed an order for

$250., **Robt. Thompson** an order for $3.50, **G. V. Ward** an order for $5.95.

Also ordered that in as much as the Co. Supt. Has reversed the decision of the Bd. at their meeting of Nov. 30, 1889 in which they changed the boundary line of sub dist No. 10 & sub. Dist No.2. The boundary lines between sub Dist No. 10 & sub Dist No.2 be changed so as to include **J. J. Newlon** and **D. S. Talbott** in sub Dist No.10

Ordered that a meeting of said Bd. be held at **J. W. Ward**s Jan 25, 1890

G. J. Stalnaker Scy

At a meeting of the Board of Education of Barker Dist held at **J. W. Ward**s store house on the **25 of January 1890** present all of the members of said board.

It was ordered that **Emmett G. Chenoweth** be allowed an order for Four dollars. Also that **Samuel Price** be allowed an order for Four dollars also that **C. F. Fisher** be allowed an order for $1.85 also that **Cicero Phillips** be allowed an order for $2.75 also that **J. W. Ward** be allowed an order for Twenty five cents.

G. J. Stalnaker

At a meeting of the Bd. of Ed. of Barker Dist held at **J. W. Ward**s store house on the **25 day of June 1890** present **W. S. Phares** President **J. W. Ward** Commissioner

Settlement was made with the Sheriff with the following results

To State School Fund	613.24
To Dist Levy	546.38
To Rail R.	141.45
	1301.07

James A. Williamson	5.01
Inst on same	18.91

256 School Board Minutes

Trans to Philippi Dist		27.42
1	Frederic Moore	28.00
2	Wm. C	28.00
3	Alice Wallace	22.00
4	M. H. King	28.00
5	C. B. Wilmoth	22.00
6	Kate OConner	28.00
7	Calora L. Douglas	28.00
8	W. S. Philips	22.00
9	W. S. Philips	22.00
10	Frederic Moore	28.00
11	W. C. Moore	28.00
12	J. A. Viquesney	22.00
13	D. E. Phillips	28.00
14	M. H. King	28.00
15	Alice Wallace	22.00
16	C. B. Wilmoth	22.00
17	Calora L. Douglas	28.00
18	Alice Wallace	22.00
19	Frederic Moore	28.00
20	D. E. Phillips	28.00
21	D. E. Phillips	28.00
22	J. A. Viquesney	22.00
23	W. C. Moore	28.00
24	M. H. King	28.00
25	Kate OConner	28.00
26	Kate OConner	28.00
27	Calora L. Douglass	28.00
28	D. E. Phillips	28.00
29	Frederic Moore	28.00
30	W. S. Phillips	22.00
31	W. S. Phillips	22.00
32	C. B. Wilmoth	22.00
33	C. B. Wilmoth	22.00
34	W. C. Moore	28.00
35	M. H. King	28.00
36	Kate OConner	28.00
37	Alice Wallace	22.00
38	J. A. Viquesney	22.00

School Board Minutes 257

39	Calora L. Douglas	28.00	
40	J. A. Viquesney	22.00	
Delinquent			$1.46
Sheriffs Com			27.24
Total amt.			$1404.04

1	Geo. P. McCutcheon	11.00
2	J. H. Poling	37.50
3	G. V. Ward	32.90
4	S. W. Fisher	182.50
6	Albert Rhorbough	7.50
7	Jethro Moore	13.00
8	W. S. Davis	4.15
9	A. Right & Son	1.15
10	L. B. Lovett & Bro	.50
11	J. C. Right	6.60
12	J. W. Ward	1.27
13	Cicero Phillips	4.00
14	Nathan Kelly	6.40
15	E. G. Chenoweth	3.00
16	J. C. Findley	3.00
17	Rezin Davis	2.50
18	Robert Thompson	3.50
19	G. V. Ward	5.95
20	Emmett G. Chenoweth	4.00
21	Samuel Price	4.00
22	C. F. Fisher	1.85
23	Cicero Phillips	2.75
24	J. W. Ward	.25
25	Kate O Connor	8.02
26	Arthur Mc Clane	8.00
27	C. B. Wilmoth	8.00
28	D. E. Phillips	8.00
28	W. S. Phillips	8.00
29	Samuel Price	10.00
30	John Price	9.00
31	Hazel Cauley	6.00
32	P. B. Findley	6.45
33	S. W. Fisher	2.00

258 School Board Minutes

34	Nathan Kelley	2.00
35	M. H. King	8.15
36	E. G. Huffman	4.67
37	W. H. Row	2.00
37	Alice Wallace	8.00
38	W. C. Moore	8.00
39	J. W. Ward	.50
40	W. R. Coonts	12.05
41	W. M. Biby	3.00
42	J. C. Right	8.00
43	R. M. Bennett	8.80
44	Fred Moore	8.13
45	J. A. Viquesney	8.00
46	J. C. Willoughby	8.32
	Co. Supt to Geo. P. McCutcheon	15.00
36	E. T. Bennett	9.00
39	J. W. Ward	6.00
3	H. C. Harris	9.00
	Levy	780.65
	Commission	38.92
	Order J. A. Williamson June 12	120.97
	Interest	7.50
	Philippi Dist Trans	4.16
15	W. Buckey	10.37
38	Co. Sup. David Talbott	6.00
9	T. T. Elliott	137.50
26	Thos Kane	38.40
1	A. C. W. Stricker	2.24
1887	H. L. Ray	.70
1889	Holister Ray	.50
1888	T. T. Elliott	24.75
1889	W. S. Phares	6.00
1888	T. T. Elliott	137.50
5	G. H. Gall	1.25
41	Joshua Bartlett	6.00
	I. V. Johnson Fee Bill	4.35
Total		1062.51
Due Sheriff		281.86

Building Fund 281.86
Teacher Fund 102.97
Whole amt due Sheriff 384.83
On Settlement June 25, 1890
        G. J. Stalnaker Sec

Amt to levy for the Year 1890 $1358.60/100

    At a meeting of the Bd. of Ed. of Barker Dist held at **J. W. Wards** Store house on **Monday the 7 day of July 1890** present **W. S. Phares** President and **J. W. Ward** and **B. B. Durrett** Commissioners. The following business was transacted.
    Appointment of Trustees

Sub Dist		Term of
No. 1	**M. Hart**	3 years
No. 2	**J. R. Phares**	3 years
No. 3	**Wm. Biby**	3 years
No. 4	**John Moore**	3 years
No. 5	**Samuel Coonts**	3 years
No. 6	**Isaac Price**	2 years
No. 6	**J. B. Godwin**	3 years
No. 7	**Sam Jones**	3 years
No. 7	**S. E. Yoak**	2 years
No. 8	**Ben Holbert**	3 years
No. 9	**Lewis Harris**	3 years
No.10	**W. S. Davis**	3 years
No.10	**W. J. Thornhill**	3 years

    Ordered that the boundary line of Sub Dist No. 10 be and is hereby changed so as to include **D. S. Talbott** and **J. J. Newlon** in said Sub Dist (No.10)
    Ordered that the Teachers monthly wages (or salary) for the school year 1890 be and is hereby fixed at
        28 dollars per month for No. One Teachers
        22 dollars per month for No. Two Teachers
        18 dollars per month for No. Three Teachers
    Ordered that the Levy for building purposes (or building fund) be 40 cents on the 100 dollars Valuation of assessible

property and that 23 cents on the 100 dollars Valuation of assessable property of Barker Dist.

Sept 15, 1887
Jacob Hudkins Sheriff of Barbour Co. Dr.
Dr. to Dist Levy at 3 ½ mills on $24416458 $854.00   57 ½
To State School Fund for $888.00   67 1/4
Total Teachers Fund for 1877 & 1878 $1743.00   24 3/4

Sheriff Dr to Dist Levy for Building Fund $488.20

Jacob Hudkins Treasurer of Barbour County to Bd Ed
No. 1878 to State School Fund $1061.90. Also to levy for Teachers fund of 2 mills on $242600.29 $485.20
Dr to levy for Building fund on same at 2 ½ mills $606.50

NOTE: The following information was written on the inside back cover of the Barker District minute book.

      You do solemnly swear that the evidence you shall give in this case shall be the truth the whole truth & nothing but the truth so help you God.
      You do solemly swear that the Evidence you shall give in this controversy between **C. Phillips** the trustees of sub dist No.2 & **T. T. Elliott & John Phares** shall be the truth the whole truth nothing but the truth so help you God.

      Form of Oath for swearing in trustees
      You do solemnly swear you will discharge your duties as trustee in Sub dist No. ___ to the Best of your skill & Judgement so help you God.

TOWNSHIP OF BARKER
ENUMERATION OF YOUTH
1870

Dis No		Males White	Males Col'd	Females White	Females Col'd	Whole White	Whole Col'd	Total
1	William Wilson			4		4		4
	Samuel Latham			2		2		2
	Herod W. Blake	2		2		4		4
	Mary Himes	7				7		7
	George Matthew	1		5		6		6
	Harmon Steerman	1		1		2		2
	Frederick Thorn	3				3		3
	Simon Swick	3		1		4		4
	William Day	5		3		8		8
	Nelson Williamson	1				1		1
	John Yokum	1				1		1
	John Hewett	2		3		5		5
	Benoni Ware	1				1		1
	Joseph Wilson	1				1		1
	Adam Ware			1		1		1
		28		22		50		50

262 School Board Minutes

Dist No.		Males		Females		Whole		Total
		White	Col'd	White	Col'd	White	Col'd	
2	N. Yokum	3		3		6		6
	J. S. Skidmire	2		1		3		3
	Ellen Yoke			1		1		1
	R. G. Thorn			1		1		1
	Jacob Thorn	1		2		3		3
	Thomas N. Bartlett	2		1		3		3
	William Coberly	2		1		3		3
	Josiah Douglas	1		2		3		3
	Nimrod Champ	1		2		3		3
	A. Swick	1		5		6		6
	O. S. Zirkle	1		2		3		3
	J. R. Ware	1		5		6		6
	A.J. Williams			4		4		4
	B. H. Taylor	2				2		2
	James Booth	1		2		3		3
	John M. Shomo	5		3		8		8
	H. H. Coonts	3		2		5		5
	A. Vanscoy	1				1		1
	Rebecca George	1				1		1
		28		37		65		65

School Board Minutes

Dist No.		Males White	Col'd	Females White	Col'd	Whole White	Col'd	Total
3	Martin Hewes			3		3		3
	Marshall Stalnaker	3		2		5		5
	B. B. Wiseman	2		3		5		5
	Michael Conner	5				5		5
	Patrick King	1		1		2		2
	Jonas Lance	3				3		3
	Solomon George	2		1		3		3
	C. Ray			1		1		1
	Matthew O Conner	1		1		2		2
	G. C. Corley			1		1		1
	David G. McCauley	3				3		3
	Sarah E. Anderson			2		2		2
	Richard Booth			1		1		1
	B. B. Durrett	1		1		2		2
	Henry Wiseman	2		3		5		5
	Jesse L. Sandridge	2		1		3		3
	E. T. Talbott	3		1		4		4
	E. J. McCauley	2		1		3		3
	Joshua Proudfoot	1		1		2		2
	Patrick Bodkin	2		2		4		4
	Francis Hathaway	3		2		5		5
	Edgar Poling	3		2		5		5
	Matthew Edman	1		2		3		3

264 School Board Minutes

R. R. Talbott	1			1		1	
Jacob J. Thacker	1			1		1	
	42		32		74		74

Dist No.		Males		Females		Whole		Total
		White	Col'd	White	Col'd	White	Col'd	
4	Daniel Obrian	1		4		4		4
	Robert D. Kerr	4				4		4
	John Gost	2		2		4		4
	Andrew Monaghan	1		1		2		2
	Samuel Harris	2		1		3		3
	Patrick Judge	1		2		3		3
	Charles Eichler			1		1		1
	Lewis Zirkle	3		2		5		5
	Hisam Yeager	1		3		4		4
	Bridget McGinnes			1		1		1
	Jefferson Anderson	2		2		4		4
	William F. Hollen	2				2		2
	S. Monaghan	1				1		1
		20		19		39		39

Dist No.		Males White	Col'd	Females White	Col'd	Whole White	Col'd	Total
5	A. V. Wilmoth	1		4		5		5
	Margaret Tallman	1		1		2		2
	Charles H. Street	3		3		6		6
	James McGowan	2		5		7		7
	Martin Waters	4		1		5		5
	Jacob Sipe	3		2		5		5
	Harman Warner	3		1		4		4
	John Wigle	1				1		1
	John L. Sipe	1				1		1
	Conrad Carpenter	1		1		2		2
	Hiram Champ	2		2		4		4
	Mary A. Yeager	1		2		3		3
	Hugh Fineral	1		2		3		3
	James W. George	1		1		2		2
	Ephraim McCauley	1				1		1
	Daniel Carpenter			1		1		1
	Martin Teats	4		2		6		6
	Abraham Ware	1				1		1
	Charles Eichler			1		1		1
	James M. Bennett	1				1		1
	Noah J. Sipe			1		1		1
	George E. Anderson			1		1		1
		32		31		63		63

266 School Board Minutes

Dist No.		Males White	Males Col'd	Females White	Females Col'd	Whole White	Whole Col'd	Total
6	Jesse Teter	2		2		4		4
	Joseph Teter	3		2		5		5
	Thomas Monahon	1				1		1
	William Yeager	1		2		3		3
	David Foy	2		2		4		4
	J. W. Harper			1		1		1
	C. M. Groves			2		2		2
	A. B. Wilmoth	1		1		2		2
	James V. Skidmore	2		2		4		4
	William Gaunt	2		2		4		4
	Samuel Rucker	2				2		2
	Joseph Jones	1		1		2		2
	Hiram Rinehart	4		1		5		5
	Solomon Harris	1				1		1
	Fenelon Howes	2		1		3		3
	Oliver Teter	2		2		4		4
	Solomon Cade	2				2		2
	J. Bennett			1		1		1
	Judson Weese	1				1		1
	L. Weese	1				1		1
		30		22		52		52

Dist No.		Males White	Males Col'd	Females White	Females Col'd	Whole White	Whole Col'd	Total
7	Solomon Coffman			1		1		1
	Benjamin Howe	1				1		1
	Emile Viquesney	3		4		7		7
	D. J. Shomo	3		1		4		4
	A. J. Rowe	2		2		4		4
	Margaret Arbogast	1				1		1
	James Corley	3		1		4		4
	John Corley	2		3		5		5
	L. D. Steerman	1				1		1
	Jackson Hillyard	2		2		4		4
	George Stipe	2				2		2
		20		14		34		34

268 School Board Minutes

Dist No.		Males		Females		Whole		Total
		White	Col'd	White	Col'd	White	Col'd	
8	S. W. Stalnaker			1		1		1
	Granville Stalnaker	1		1		2		2
	Burr P. Newlon	3		3		6		6
	Elijah Pritt	1		2		3		3
	John Wright	1		1		2		2
	William M. Phillips	1		1		2		2
	John Hillyard	2		1		3		3
	George Phillips	3		2		5		5
	Chambers Mustoe			2		2		2
	James Mustoe	1				1		1
	Israel Coffman			1		1		1
	Harriet Booth			1		1		1
	William Cade	2		4		6		6
	Francis Thornhill	1		2		3		3
	William Elliott	1				1		1
	R. A. McCutcheon	2		2		4		4
	James Teter	3		2		5		5
	Eliza Shurtluff	1		2		3		3
	Martin Hillyard	1		3		4		4
	W. S. Phares	1		1		2		2
	John L. Hilkey	1				1		1
		26		32		58		

School Board Minutes 269

Dist No.		Males White	Males Col'd	Females White	Females Col'd	Whole White	Whole Col'd	Total
9	J. Delauder	2		2		4		4
	Barton Cross	2		4		6		6
	J. J. Ramsey	5		3		8		8
	Hannibal Poling	2		1		3		3
	William Cross	1		1		2		2
	B. Cross	1		1		2		2
	Simpson Cross	1				1		1
	John Cross	2				2		2
	Granville Moore			1		1		1
	Jethro Bennett	2				2		2
	William Moore	3		1		4		4
	Thomas Roberts	2		2		4		4
	William S. Moore	4		2		6		6
	C. Cross			1		1		1
	Levi Cross	3				3		3
	Thomas Williams	2		2		4		4
		32		21		53		53

270 School Board Minutes

Dist No.		Males White	Males Col'd	Females White	Females Col'd	Whole White	Whole Col'd	Total
10	Frederick Booth	2		3		5		5
	Henry Coonts	3		3		6		6
	James L. Ramsey			2		2		2
	Phillip Ramsey	3				3		3
	Lair D. Coonts	1		1		2		2
	David England			2		2		2
	Albert England	1		1		2		2
	Deborah Kelly	2		1		3		3
	Agnes Kelly	1				1		1
	Daniel Moore	3		1		4		4
	William G. W. Price	2		3		5		5
	James England	3		1		4		4
	Levi Fitzwater	2		1		3		3
	Jacob Delauder	2		3		5		5
	John M. Ramsey	1		3		4		4
	Adam Coonts	4		2		6		6
	Mary Poling			1		1		1
	John Hill			2		2		2
	Henry Ridgeway	2		4		6		6
	William England	4		2		6		6
		36		36		72		72

School Board Minutes 271

Dist No		Males White Col'd		Females White Col'd		Whole White Col'd		Total
11	Alpheus Smith			1		1		
	Daniel Ice	1		1		2		
	Israel Poling			2		2		
	Henry Payne	1		1		2		
	Dyer Kelley	1		4		5		
	Jasper Hoffman	1				1		
	David Sturm	1				1		
	Joseph Cassana			2		2		
	Martin Woolverton	1		2		3		
	Peter Poe	2		1		3		
	Caroline Boner	1		2		3		
	Elizabeth Hill	1				1		
	Phebe Ice			1		1		
	John Poling	1				1		
	Solomon Myers	2				2		
	Robert Moran	1		1		2		
	Daniel Moore	1				1		
		15		18		33		

Dist No.		Males		Females		Whole		Total
		White	Col'd	White	Col'd	White	Col'd	
12	Newton Chenoweth	3	1			3	1	
	John M. Corley	1		1		2		
	Wm. Sharps	1		1		2		
	John Finley	3		4		7		
	John A. Wagoner	2				2		
	David Thompson	1		1		2		
	James D. C. Thompson	3		2		5		
	Nehemiah Howell	4				4		
	Jefferson Phillips	1		3		4		
	Allen Wood	1		3		4		
	Jasper Poling	2				2		
	John D. Murphy	1		3		4		
	Randolph Coberly	2		1		3		
	Eli Everson	3		2		5		
	Jacob Shockey	1		5		6		
	F. C. Shockey			1		1		
	Ellis Wilmoth	3		2		5		
	Martin M. Poling	1		1		1		
	George Daugherty	1				1		
		34	1	30		64	1	

School Board Minutes 273

Dist No.		Males White	Col'd	Females White	Col'd	Whole White	Col'd	Total
13	William J. Right	3		3		6		6
	William R. Moore			5		5		5
	Balas England	1		3		4		4
	B. M. Wolverton	3		2		5		5
	George Gibson	3				3		3
	Henry England	1				1		1
	Isaac Price	4		4		8		8
	Silas R. Price	2		2		4		4
	John Price	1		3		4		4
	Elizabeth Yoke	2		2		4		4
	Albert Price			1		1		1
	Elizabeth Moore	2		2		4		4
	S. England			2		2		2
	Arnold Right	4		2		6		6
	Absalom Digman	1		3		4		4
		27		34		61		61

School Board Minutes

Dist No.		Males White	Males Col'd	Females White	Females Col'd	Whole White	Whole Col'd	Total
14	Levi T. Hollen	2		3		5		5
	Benjamin Jones	1				1		1
	Aretus Mclean	1		2		3		3
	W. W. Jones	3		2		5		5
	F. J. Jones	1				1		1
	Anthony S. Rohrbough	2		3		5		5
	Jacob Mclean			1		1		1
	Garrett Herron	2		1		3		3
	Elmore Daniels	3		4		7		7
	Lloyd Davis	2		1		3		3
		17		17		34		34

ENUMERATION OF YOUTH
1871

Not given

ENUMERATION OF YOUTH
1872

Dist No.		Males		Females		Whole		Total
		White	Col'd	White	Col'd	White	Col'd	
1		28		22				50
2	Anthony Swick	1		6				
	R. G. Thorn			1				
	T. N. Bartlett	2		1				
	Jacob Thorn	2		3				
	John Skidmore	2		2				
	James R. Ware	1		6				
	Able Vanscoy	1		1				
	Elizabeth George	1						
	Ellender Yeake			1				
	William Coberly	2		1				
	O. S. Zirkle	1		2				
	J. M. Shomo	5		2				
	Nimrod Champ	1		2				
	R. N. Taylor	3						
	James Booth	1		2				
	A. A. Coonts	3		2				
	Martin Champ	1		1				
	A. J. Williams	1		5				
		28		38				66
3	David G. McCauley	4						
	M. Edmond	1		2				

	Geo. Moore	1					
	Israel Poling	1	2				
	Mrs. Mary Davis		2				
	John Poling	1					
	Richard Boalton	3	2				
		22	32				54
12	John M. Corley	1	1	1			
	James D. C. Thompson	3	2				
	Thomas Holbert	3	2				
	Allen Wood	1	3				
	Ellis Wilmoth	4	2				
	Jefferson Phillips	1	4				
	Franklin Shockey		1				
	Eli Everson	2	2				
	Jacob Shockey	1	5				
	Geo. Daugherty	2	1				
	Nehemiah Howell	3	1				
	David Thompson	1					
	Sanford Poling	1	1				
	John A. Wagner	3	1				
	Coalman L. Jones	1					
	Randolph Coberly	3	1				
	Eugenia Murphy	1					
	Newton Chineworth	3					
	John Finley	2	4				
		36	31	1			68
13	William J. Right	4	4				

School Board Minutes 277

	B. M. Wolverton	3	2				
	William G. W. Price	1	3				
	G. R. Price	2	3				
	J. Price	2	4				
	William Price Sr.		1				
	J. Price	3	3				
	D. Kelly	2	1				
	A. Kelly	1					
	C. J. Schoonover	1	1				
	E. M. Moore	2	2				
	B. England	1	3				
	A. Digman	2	3				
	S. G. Digman	1					
	E. Yoak	2	1				
	J. B. Godwin	2					
	Wm. R. Moore	1	5				
	A. Right	4	3				
	J. England		1				
		34	40			74	
14	Lloyd Davis	2	1				
	John D. Ball	1					
	Levi J. Holland	2	3				
	W. W. Jones	2	1				
	Ben Jones	2					
	Reat. Mclane	3	2				
	Jacob Mclane	1					
	F. J. Jones	2					

278 School Board Minutes

	John L. Jones	3		3				
	A. S. Rohorbaugh	2		4				
	Garrett Herrion	2		2				
	Hiram Rhinehart	4						
		26		16				42

ENUMERATION OF YOUTH
1873

Dist No.		Males		Females		Whole		Total
		White	Col'd	White	Col'd	White	Col'd	
1		30		25				55
2		24		30				54
3		32		25				57
4	not given							
5		30		24				54
6		27		19				46
7		25		25				50
8		25		31				56
9		32		26				58
10		23		29				52
11		18		25				43
12		38		34	1			72
13	not given							
14		22		11				33

ENUMERATION OF YOUTH
1874

Dist No.		Males		Females		Whole		Total
		White	Col'd	White	Col'd	White	Col'd	
1		40		29				69
2		29		34				63
3		41		43				84
4		27		23				50
5		31		42				73
6		24		20				44
7		21		24				47
8		30		41	1			72
9		42		29				71
10		32		22				54
11		27		31				58
12		33		28	1			62
13		37		28				65
14		29		16				45

ENUMERATION OF YOUTH
1875

Dist No.	Males White	Males Col'd	Females White	Females Col'd	Whole White	Whole Col'd	Total
1	31		23				54
2	27		32				59
3	39		30				69
4	30		33				63
5	28		38				66
6	25		17				42
7	24		20				44
8	33	1	36	1			69
9	39		33				72
10	28		22				50
11	24		30				54
12	32	1	29				61
13	40		21				61
14	30		20				50

ENUMERATION OF YOUTH
1876

Dist No.		Males White	Col'd	Females White	Col'd	Whole White	Col'd	Total
1		38		38				76
2		30		24				54
3		40		32				72
4		34		34				66
5		29		40				69
6		26		18				44
7		24		21				45
8		25	1	26	1			53
9		30		29				59
10		27		26				53
11		27		34				61
12		33	1	32				66
13		34		17				51
14		32		21				53
15		24		26				50

ENUMERATION OF YOUTH
1877

Dist No.		Males White	Col'd	Females White	Col'd	Whole White	Col'd	Total
1		40		37				77
2		24		26				50
3		35		46				81
4		24		28				52
5		48		35				83
6		34		24				58
7		23		22				45
8		25	2	29	1			57
9		30		31				61
10		24		24				48
11		33		27				60
12		37	1	25				63
13		37		19				56
14		29		18				47
15		23		30				53

ENUMERATION OF YOUTH
1878

Dist No.		Males		Females		Whole		Total
		White	Col'd	White	Col'd	White	Col'd	
1	not given							
2	not given							
3	not given							
4	not given							
5		37		29				66
6	not given							
7		22		32				54
8		29	1	27	2			59
9		31		27				58
10		28		29				57
11		28		25				53
12		33		32				65
13		38		24				62
14	not given							
15		27		38				65

ENUMERATION OF YOUTH
BETWEEN SIX AND TWENTY ONE
1879

Sub Dist No.	Males	Females
1	36	32
2	not given	not given
3	45	36
4	not given	not given
5	29	35
6	not given	not given
7	25	30
8	29 (Col - 2)	27 (Col - 1)
9	29	25
10	26	29
11	32	31
12	30	28
13	33	23
14	30	25
15	28	41

ENUMERATION OF YOUTH
1880

None given

ENUMERATION OF YOUTH
BARKER DISTRICT BARBOUR COUNTY WEST VIRGINIA
1881

Sub Dist No.	Males	Females	Total
1	40	29	69
2	24	23	47
3	52	55	107
4	43	30	73
5	44	35	79
6	29	23	52
7	31	34	65
8	24	23	47
9	34	20	54
10	29	31	60
11	33	29	62
12	26	26	52
13	28	18	46
14	33	20	53
15	28	37	65
Total	498	433	931

Two colored males in Sub Dist. No.2
W. S. Shurtleff President
F. B. Durrett Sec.

ENUMERATION OF YOUTH
1882
Not given

ENUMERATION OF YOUTH
1883
Not given

ENUMERATION OF YOUTH
1884
Not given

ENUMERATION OF YOUTH
1885
Not given

ENUMERATION OF YOUTH
1886
Not given

ENUMERATION OF YOUTH
1887
Not given

ENUMERATION OF YOUTH
1888
Not given

ENUMERATION OF YOUTH
1889

March 5th 1889
The Enumeration of youth of School age between 6 years & 21 is 555 for the year ending June 30, 1889.
The enumeration of Belington New School Sub Dist. No. 10 is 29 Scholars. Cost of running School - teachers salary 4x28 = 112.00, coal 6.50

ENUMERATION OF YOUTH
1890
Not given

INDEPENDENT DISTRICT OF BELINGTON
1893-1899

At a meeting of the Board of Education of The Independent School District of Belington West Virginia held at **R. A. McCutcheon**s Old Store House in said Independent District on the **3d day of July 1893** at one o'clock P.M. **Fenelon Howes**, President, **R. A. McCutcheon** and **H. C. Rosenberger** Commissioners were present. After the following Oaths of Office were administered proceeded to business.

Oath of President
State of West Virginia County of Barbour to wit: I **Fenelon Howes** do solemnly affirm that I will support the Constitution of the United States and the Constitution of this State, and that I will faithfully discharge the duties of my office of President of the Board of Education of the Independent School District of Belington, W. Va. to the best of my skills and judgment, So help me God.
Sworn to and subscribed before me **R. A. McCutcheon** a Notary Public the 3 day of July 1893.
R. A. McCutcheon N.P.

Oath of Members
State of West Virginia, County of Barbour to wit: We **H. C. Rosenberger** and **R. A. McCutcheon** do solemnly affirm that we will support the Constitution of the United States, and the Constitution of this State and that we will faithfully discharge the duties of our office of Commissioners of the Board of Education of the Independent School District of Belington W. Va. to be Best of our skill and judgment. So help us God.
Sworn and subscribed before me **Fenelon Howes** a Notary Public in and for the County and State of West Virginia, the 3 day of July 1893.
Fenelon Howes N.P.

Ordered that there shall be 4 months School or more if there shall be money to run longer.
Ordered that salaries of Teachers be left to the discretion of the Board.
Ordered that the Levy for Tuition be 50 cents on the One

Hundred dollars Valuation of assessable property of The Independent School District of Belington W. Va and for building purposes 30 cents on the One Hundred dollars valuation of assessable property of said Independent School District.

Ordered that the schools shall commence on the first Monday in November 1893.

There being no further business, Board adjourned to meet on the 3d Saturday in August 1893 at **R. A. McCutcheon**s Old Store House at 1 O'clock P.M.
Fenelon Howes Pres.
G. J. Stalnaker Sec.

Office of the Board of Education of the Independent School District of Belington W. Va.

At a meeting of the Board held on the **19 day of August 1893**, present **Fenelon Howes**, President, and **R. A. McCutcheon** and **H. C. Rosenberger** members of the Board.

On motion of **R. A. McCutcheon** it is ordered that the Board of Education of Barker and Valley Districts be notified to meet and make settlement with this board within one week.

On motion of **R. A. McCutcheon** it is ordered that The Secretary be authorized to notify The Assessors of the Eastern and Western Assessment Districts of Barbour Co. and the County Clerk of said County to send this Board the amount of assessable property in our Independent School District by the 30 of August 1893 or sooner if possible.

On motion of **R. A. McCutcheon** it is ordered that the President be and is ordered that the President be and is hereby authorized to provide a Record Book for the Independent School District of Belington, W. Va.

On motion of **H. C. Rosenberger**, it is ordered that **Arthur McLean** the use of the School House in Belington to teach a subscription School, provided he return possession of House and keys at end of school or sooner if demanded by the Board.

On motion of **H. C. Rosenberger**, the Board does now adjourn to meet on the 30 day of August 1893 at 2 o'clock P.M.
Fenelon Howes Pres
G. J. Stalnaker Sec

School Board Minutes 291

Amount of Assessable Property in The Independent School District of Belington W. Va. for the Year 1893

Real Estate on Barker Side	$19262.00
Real Estate on Valley Side	5804.00
Personal Property on Barker side	11340.00
Personal Property on Valley side	3302.00
Rail Road Assessment of G&B R R	7436.14
Rail Road Assessment of W. Va. Central & Pennsylvania	<u>17705.80</u>
Total	64849.94
Order from Valley Dist. on acct. of Building Fund	$10.35
Order from Valley Dist on acct. of Tuition Fund	3.10
State School Fund	89.58
R. R. Tax as reported by Supt.	196.11

Office of the Board of Education of the Independent School District of Belington in the County of Barbour.

At a meeting of the Board, held on the **21st day of September 1893**, present **Fenelon Howes** President, and **H. C. Rosenberger** and **R. A. McCutcheon** members of the Board.

On motion it is ordered that **Edwin N. Locke** be employed as Principal Teacher in our said Independent District.

On motion of **H. C. Rosenberger**, it is ordered that the Store House belonging to **R. A. McCutcheon** be and is hereby rented at Eight dollars per month for the purpose of a school room for the advanced pupils.

On motion, it is ordered that Notices be posted proposing to purchase Two Hundred bushels of good coal, said purchase to be made on the 7 day of October 1893 at 2o'clock P.M. at **R. A. McCutcheon**s Store house.

On motion the board does now adjourn to meet on the 7 day of October 1893 at 2 o'clock P.M.

      Fenelon Howes Pres.
        G. J. Stalnaker Secretary

292 School Board Minutes

Office of the Board of Education of the Independent School District of Belington, in the County of Barbour.

At a meeting of the Board, held on the **7 day of October 1893**, present **Fenelon Howes** President and **H. C. Rosenberger** and **R. A. McCutcheon** members of the Board.

On motion of **R. A. McCutcheon** it is ordered that **Nora Hamilton** be and is hereby appointed and employed as teacher in the primary department for the term of four months commencing on the first Monday of November 1893.

On motion of **H. C. Rosenberger** it is ordered that **Warren Cade** be and hereby is awarded the contract of furnishing Two Hundred bushels of good coal he being the lowest bidder Viz. Six dollars and Seventy Five cents per 100 bushels, and that he shall deliver 100 bushels at the School house in Belington and 100 bushels at **R. A. McCutcheon**s Store House on or before the first Monday in November 1893.

On motion it is ordered that **John M. Good** be and is hereby employed to build a coal house and two privies for the sum of Twenty dollars.

On motion it is ordered that the Secretary be and is hereby authorized to notify the Board of Education of Valley District to make settlement with the Board of the Independent School District of Belington and apportion the amount of funds in their hands due the said Independent School District as the law requires, by the 20 day of October 1893, and also for said Board of Valley not to expend any of the money in their hands that would belong to the Independent School District of Belington according to said settlement.

On motion the Board does now adjourn <u>sine die</u>.

    Fenelon Howes Pres
     G. J. Stalnaker Secretary

Office of the Board of Education of The Independent School District of Belington in the County of Barbour.

At a meeting of the board on the **21 day of November 1893** present **Fenelon Howes** President and **R. A. McCutcheon** member of the board.

On motion of **R. A. McCutcheon** it is ordered that **I. M. Poling** be and is hereby allowed Order No. one on the Sheriff on Acct of the building fund for $12.00

On motion of **R. A. McCutcheon** it is ordered that **John M. Good** be and is hereby allowed Order No. 2 on the Sheriff for $20.00 chargeable to the Building Fund.

On motion of **R. A. McCutcheon** it is ordered that **Warren Cade** be and is hereby allowed Order No.3 on the Sheriff for $13.50 chargeable to the Building Fund.

On motion of **R. A. McCutcheon** it is ordered that **Fenelon Howes** be and is hereby allowed Order No.4 on the Sheriff for $29.17 chargeable to the building Fund.

On motion of **R. A. McCutcheon** it is ordered that **F. M. Howes** be and is hereby allowed Order No.5 on the Sheriff for $4.50 chargeable to the building Fund.

On motion the board does now adjourn to meet upon the 2 day of December 1893 at one o'clock P.M.

    Fenelon Howes Pres
     G. J. Stalnaker Sec.

Office of the Board of Education of the Independent School District of Belington in the County of Barbour.

At a meeting of the board held on the **2 day of December 1893**, present **Fenelon Howes** President and **R. A. McCutcheon** member of the Board.

On motion of **R. A. McCutcheon** it is ordered that **Gawthrop and Lake** be and is hereby allowed Order No.Six on the Sheriff for seventy one cents on account of the Building Fund.

On motion of **Fenelon Howes** it is ordered that **R. A. McCutcheon** be and is hereby allowed Order No.Seven on account of the Building Fund for Eight dollars.

On motion of **Fenelon Howes** it is ordered that **Howard McCutcheon** be and is hereby allowed Order No. Eight on the Sheriff on account of the Building Fund for Four dollars.

On motion of **R. A. McCutcheon** it is ordered that **H. Crites** be and is hereby allowed Order No. Nine on the Sheriff on account of the Building Fund for One dollar.

On motion of **R. A. McCutcheon** it is ordered that **L. B. Lovett** & Bro. be and is hereby allowed Order No. Ten on account of the Building Fund for fifty cents.

On motion of **R. A. McCutcheon** it is ordered that **Ed. N. Locke** a teacher be and is hereby allowed Order No. One on account of the Teachers Fund for Forty dollars.

On motion of **R. A. McCutcheon** it is ordered that **Nora Hamilton** a teacher be and is hereby allowed Order No. Two on the Sheriff, on account of the Teachers Fund for Thirty dollars.

On motion the Board does now adjourn to meet upon the 30 day of Dec 1893 at one o'clock P.M.

F. Howes Pres
G. J. Stalnaker Sec

Office of the Board of Education of the Independent School District of Belington in the County of Barbour.

At a meeting of the Board held on the **6th day of January 1894**, present **Fenelon Howes** President, **R. A. McCutcheon** and **H. C. Rosenberger** members of the Board.

On motion of Board, **E. N. Locke** was chosen Secretary protem of Secretary **Stalnaker**.

On motion it is ordered that **L. B. Lovett** & Bro. be and is hereby allowed order No. 11 on Sheriff of Barbour County on account of the Building fund for ($0.70) Seventy cents.

On motion of **H. C. Rosenberger** it is ordered that **R. A. McCutcheon** be and is hereby allowed order No. 12 on Sheriff of Barbour County on account of the Building fund for Eight dollars and Five cents.

On motion of the Board it is ordered that **Lemon Davis** be and is hereby allowed order No. 13 on Sheriff of Barbour County on account of the Building Fund for Two Dollars.

On motion of the Board it is ordered that **Howard McCutcheon** be and is hereby allowed order No. 14 on Sheriff on account of the Building fund for Two Dollars.

On motion it is ordered that **Ed. N. Locke** be and is hereby allowed Order No. 3 on Sheriff on account of the Teachers Fund for Forty Dollars.

On motion it is ordered that **Nora Hamilton** be and is hereby allowed order No. 4 on Sheriff on account of the Teachers Fund for

Thirty Dollars.

On motion the Board adjourned to meet on the 27th day of Jan 1894 at 1 o'clock P.M.

   Fenelon Howes Pres
   E. N. Locke Secty pro tem

Office of the Board of Education of the Independent School District of Belington in the County of Barbour.

At a meeting of the Board held on the **31st day of January 1894** present **Fenelon Howes** President and **R. A. McCutcheon** Commissioner of the Board.

On motion of **R. A. McCutcheon**, the following Orders were allowed Viz. Order No. 5 in favor of **Edwin N. Locke** for $40.00 chargeable to the Teachers Fund, Order No. 6 in favor of **Nora Hamilton** for $30.00 chargeable to the Teachers Fund. Order No. 15 in favor of **R. A. McCutcheon** for Eight dollars, chargeable to the Building Fund. Order No. 16 in favor of **Lemon Davis** for Two dollars chargeable to the Building Fund. Order No. 17 in favor of **Howard McCutcheon** for Two dollars & chargeable to Building Fund.

On motion the Board does now adjourn to meet on the 28 day of February 1894 at 1 o clock P.M.

   Fenelon Howes Pres
   G. J. Stalnaker Sec.

Office of the Board of Education of the Independent School District of Belington in the County of Barbour.

At a meeting of the Board held on the **24 day of February 1894**.

On motion of **R. A. McCutcheon** the following Orders were allowed Viz: Order No. 7 in favor of **Edwin Locke** for $40.00 Chargeable to the Teachers Fund. Order No. 8 in favor of **Nora Hamilton** for $30.00 Chargeable to the Teachers Fund.

Order No. 18 in favor of **R. A. McCutcheon** for $8.00 chargeable to the Building Fund. Order No. 19 in favor of **Howard McCutcheon** for $2.00 chargeable to the Building Fund. Order No. 20

in favor of **Lemon Davis** for $2.00 chargeable to the Building Fund.

On motion of **R. A. McCutcheon** it is ordered that the same Teachers **Edwin N. Locke** and **Nora Hamilton** be and are hereby employed to Teach one month from this data making in all 5 months at the same price they have been Teaching Viz. 40 & 30 dollars per month.

On motion of **H. C. Rosenberger** it is ordered that **Fenelon Howes** be and is hereby allowed Order No. 21 for $12.00 for one School Desk, chargeable to the Building Fund.

On motion the Board does now adjourn to meet on the 28 day of March 1894 at one O'clock P.M.

    F. Howes Pres
        G. J. Stalnaker Sec.

Office of the Board of Education of the Independent School District of Belington W. Va.

At a meeting of the Board held on the **24 day of March 1894**, present **Fenelon Howes** President, **R. A. McCutcheon** and **H. C. Rosenberger** members.

On motion of **R. A. McCutcheon** it is ordered that **Edwin Locke** be allowed order No. 9 for Forty dollars and **Nora Hamilton** be allowed Order No. 10 for Thirty dollars, both orders chargeable to the Teachers Fund of Belington Independent School District W. Va.

On motion of **H. C. Rosenberger** it is ordered that **R. A. McCutcheon** be allowed order No. 22 for $8.50 and **H. K. McCutcheon** for Two dollars Order No. 23, and **Lemon Davis** order No. 24 for $2.00 all of said orders chargeable to the Building fund of Belington Independent School Dist. of West Virginia.

On motion of **H. C. Rosenberger** it is ordered that **Edwin N. Locke** be employed as Principal and to teach the Belington Independent School for next year.

On motion of **R. A. McCutcheon** it is ordered that **Nora Hamilton** be employed to Teach in the primary department of the Independent School District of Belington W. Va. for next year.

On motion the Board does now adjourn to meet Sine die

    F. Howes Pres
        G. J. Stalnaker Sec

School Board Minutes 297

T. T. Elliott Sheriff of Barbour County in account with the Teachers Fund of The Independent School District of Belington West Virginia for the year ending June 30, 1894.

To amt. from State School Fund for year ending June 30, 1894 $89.58. To 50 cents Real Estate levied on a valuation of $233.27 (37969) (116.63) $66.63. To personal property amt. received from other sources for the year ending June 30, 1894. Amount received from Valley District $3.10. Rail Road Tax as reported by Co. Superintendent $196.11. Amt. Received from Barker District as per settlement $2.01. Total $480.64

By School orders paid to date.

Order	Dated	Drawn to	Amount
1	Dec. 2, 1893	**Ed. N. Locke**	40.00
2	Dec. 2, 1893	**Nora Hamilton**	30.00
3	Jan. 6, 1894	**Ed. N. Locke**	40.00
4	Jan. 6, 1894	**Nora Hamilton**	30.00
5	Jan. 31, 1894	**Ed. N. Locke**	40.00
6	Jan. 31, 1894	**Nora Hamilton**	30.00
7	Feb. 24, 1894	**Edwin Locke**	40.00
8	Feb. 24, 1894	**Nora Hamilton**	30.00
9	March 24, 1894	**Edwin Locke**	40.00
10	March 24, 1894	**Nora Hamilton**	30.00

By Commission at 5% on New levy for Teachers Fund   9.49
By Commission at 2 ½% on $196.11 R. R. Tax   4.90
By Commission delinquent list   8.41
By Commission Release by Co. Court   3.36
Total $376.16
Balance due District $104.48

T. T. Elliott Sheriff of Barbour County, in account with the Building Fund of The Independent School District of Belington, West Virginia for the year ending June the 30, 1894.

To 30 cents levied on a valuation of 437969 (13.90) $11390 To amt received from other sources. Order from Valley District 10.35. Order from Barker District 30.19. Total 159.66

By sundry Building Orders paid to date

School Board Minutes

Order	Date	Drawn to	Amount
1	Nov 21, 1893	I. M. Poling	12.50
2	Nov 21, 1893	John M. Good	20.00
3	Nov 21, 1893	Warren Cade	13.50
4	Nov 21, 1893	Fenelon Howes	29.17
5	Nov 21, 1893	F. M. Howes	4.50
6	Dec 2, 1893	Gawthrop & Lake	.71
7	Dec 2, 1893	R. A. McCutcheon	8.00
8	Dec 2, 1893	Howard McCutcheon	4.00
9	Dec 2, 1893	H. Crites	1.00
10	Dec 2, 1893	L. B. Lovett Bro	.50
11	Jan 6, 1894	L. B. Lovett Bro	.70
12	Jan 6, 1894	R. A. McCutcheon	8.05
13	Jan 6, 1894	Lemon Davis	2.00
14	Jan 6, 1893	Howard McCutcheon	2.00
15	Jan 31, 1893	R. A. McCutcheon	8.00
16	Jan 31, 1893	Lemon Davis	2.00
17	Jan 31, 1893	Howard McCutcheon	2.00
18	Feb 24, 1893	R. A. McCutcheon	8.00
19	Feb 24, 1893	Howard McCutcheon	2.00
20	Feb 24, 1893	Lemon Davis	2.00
21	Feb 24, 1893	F. Howes	12.00
22	March 24, 1893	R. A. McCutcheon	8.50
23	March 24, 1893	H. K. McCutcheon	2.00
24	March 24, 1893	Lemon Davis	2.00

By release of erroneous assessment		2.01
By delinquent list	3.16	
By Commission	<u>7.98</u>	
	168.28	
Balance due Sheriff	13.84	

I hereby certify that the foregoing book has been examined by me today and find them correct.
July 4, 1894   **G. C. Poling** Co. Supt.

Office of the Board of Education of Belington Independent School District in the county of Barbour.

At a meeting of the board held on the **2 day of July 1894** present **Fenelon Howes** president and **R. A. McCutcheon** and **H. C. Rosenberger** members of the board.

On motion **R. A. McCutcheon** it is ordered that for the year 1894 there shall be taught six months school and that they shall commence on the first Monday in September 1894.

On motion of **H. C. Rosenberger** it is ordered that the Teachers salaries shall be as follows that is Principal $40.00 and Assistant $30.00 per month.

On motion it is ordered that for the year beginning July 1st 1894 the Levy for (Tuition) or Teachers fund shall be 30 cents on the $100. and for Building purposes 40 cents on the $100. valuation of assessable property.

On motion the board does now adjourn to meet sine die
Fenelon Howes Pres

Office of the Board of Education of Belington Independent School Dist. in the County of Barbour.

At a meeting of the Board, held on the 1st day of October 1894, Present **Fenelon Howes** president and **H. C. Rosenberger & R. A. McCutcheon** members of the Board: The following claims were allowed and ordered paid Viz:

Fenelon Howes to cash advanced to the Educational Publishing Co., Toledo, Ohio for 30 ft of State Blackboard at 25c a sq ft. $7.50 and to Freight on same .89. Also, to cash advanced for same co. for 1 ½ Doz: Eracers 2.25 & postage on same .45   Total $11.09
H. K. McCutcheon
F. Howes Pres

On motion of **H. C. Rosenberger** it was ordered that **Waine Lee** be paid $5.80 for making school desks and repairing chairs.

Contracts with the teachers were completed and accepted. It was ordered that a meeting of the people of the Independent School District be called Saturday to nominate school officers for the ensuing year.

300 School Board Minutes

On motion the Board adjourned sine die.
R. A. McCutcheon Secy Pro tem

Office of the Board of Education of the Belington Independent School District.

At a meeting of the Board held on the **24 day of November 1894** present **F. Howes** President and **R. A. McCutcheon** commissioner.

On motion it is ordered that **E. Locke** be allowed an order for $40.00 and **Nora Hamilton** an order for $30.00 chargeable to the Tuition Fund.

On motion it is ordered that **Howard K. McCutcheon** be allowed an order for $14.00 and **R. A. McCutcheon** an order for $8.00 chargeable to the building fund.

On motion the Board does now adjourn to meet sine die.
H. K. McCutcheon
F. Howes Pres

Office of the Board of Education of the Independent School District of Belington, W. Va.

At a meeting of the Board held on the **21 day of December 1894** present **Fenelon Howes** President and **R. A. McCutcheon** and **H. C. Rosenberger** commissioners.

On motion of **R. A. McCutcheon** it is ordered that **Alpheus Moore** be charged the legal tuition as prescribed by school law for each of his 4 children attending school at Independent School District of Belington commencing on the 19 day of November 1894.

On motion of **R. A. McCutcheon** it is ordered that **I. N. Lock** be allowed an order No. 5 for $40.00 and **Nora Hamilton** Order No. 6 for $30.00 chargeable to the Tuition Fund.

On motion **H. C. Rosenberger** it is ordered that **H. K. McCutcheon** be allowed order for No.8 for $4.00 chargeable to the building fund.

On motion of **H. C. Rosenberger** it is ordered that **R. A.**

McCutcheon be allowed Order No. 9 for $8.00 chargeable to the Building Fund.
On motion the Board does now adjourn sine die.
   F. Howes Pres
    G. J. Stalnaker Sec.

  Office of the Board of Education of the Independent School District of Belington West Virginia.
  At a meeting of the Board held on the **22 day of February 1895**, present **H. C. Rosenberger** President protem and **R. A. McCutcheon** commissioners. The following business transacted
  On motion of **H. C. Rosenberger** the following Orders were allowed Order No. 9 in favor of **Ed. N. Locke** for $40.00 and Order No. 10 in favor of **Nora Hamilton** for $30.00 both chargeable to the Teachers Fund.
  On motion of **R. A. McCutcheon** it is ordered that the following orders chargeable to the Building Fund be allowed Order No. 12 for $1.88 in favor of **L. B. Lovett** & Bro. Order No. 13 for $8.00 in favor of **R. A. McCutcheon**. Order No. 14 for $4.00 in favour of **H. K. McCutcheon**.
  On motion the Board does not adjourn to meet sine die.
   F. Howes Pres
    H. K. McCutcheon Sec

  T. T. Elliott Sheriff of Barbour County, in account with the Teachers Fund of Belington Independent District for the year ending **June 30, 1895**. Dr.
  To balance due District on settlement for the year ending June 30, 1894 $104.48. To amount from State School Fund for the year ending June 30, 1895 $108.81. To 30 cents levied on a valuation of 55450 for the year ending June 30, 1895 $166.35. To G&B R. R. Tax $83.75. To W. Va. Central & Pittsburg $110.78. Total $514.17

302 School Board Minutes

Order No.		Amount
11	Ed. N. Locke	40.00
8	Nora Hamilton	30.00
7	Ed. N. Locke	40.00
9	Ed. N. Locke	40.00
1	Ed. N. Locke	40.00
2	Nora Hamilton	30.00
10	Nora Hamilton	30.00
3	Ed. N. Locke	40.00
5	Ed. N. Locke	40.00
6	Nora Hamilton	30.00
4	Nora Hamilton	30.00

By releases 1.20. By delinquent 19.05. By 5 % commission on net levy 8.31. By 2% commission R. R. Levy .54. Total $419.10. Balance due District 155.07.

T. T. Elliott Sheriff of Barbour County in account with the Building Fund of Belington Independent District for the year ending June 30, 1895. Dr.

To amount due Sheriff from settlement of year ending June 30, 1894 13.84. To 40 cents levied on a valuation of 551.22 for the year ending June 30, 1895. 220.49

Order No.		Amount
8	R. A. McCutcheon	9.00
3	G. J. Stalnaker	15.00
11	R. A. McCutcheon	8.00
1	G. J. Stalnaker	10.00
3	Waine Lee	5.80
6	R. A. McCutcheon	14.84
9	Howard McCutcheon	4.00
8	R. A. McCutcheon	8.00
7	L. B. Lovett & Bro	.95
5	Howard McCutcheon	4.00
4	Charles Newlon	18.72
9	R. A. McCutcheon	8.00
8	H. K. McCutcheon	4.00
2	F. Howes	11.09

10	H. K. McCutcheon	4.00
13	R. A. McCutcheon	8.00
14	H. K. McCutcheon	4.00
12	L. B. Lovett & Bro	1.88
9	H. C. Rosenberger	9.90
15	R. A. McCutcheon	8.00
16	Howard McCutcheon	4.00
7	F. Howes	9.00

By balance from last years settlement 13.94
By release of **W. W. Right** 1.20
By delinquents 9.84
By commission at 5% on net levy 11.02
Balance due District 15.31
To order No. 17 same to be charged to **J. W. Rosenberger** sheriff by B. E. $15.31

Amt. of Assessable property for the year ending June 30, 1895
Total value of personal property on Valley side 5744.00
Total value of personal property on Barker side 13525.00
Amt. of State school Fund $140.14
Balance due Dist. on settlement with Sheriff for yr ending June 30, 1895 on Tuition 155.07
Balance due Dist. on settlement with Sheriff for yr ending June 30, 1895 Building Fund $15.31
Total value of Real Estate on Eastern side 12522.00

      Office of the Board of Education of the Independent School District of Belington West Virginia.

      At a meeting of the Board held on the **2st day of July 1895**, present **Fenelon Howes**, president and **R. A. McCutcheon** and **H. C. Rosenberger** members of the board.

      On motion of **R. A. McCutcheon** it is ordered that the number of months schools to be taught this year shall be Five.

      On motion of **H. C. Rosenberger**, it is ordered that there may be three teachers employed for school year beginning July 1st 1895 and ending June 30, 1896.

      On motion of **H. C. Rosenberger** it is ordered that Teachers salaries for the present year be as follows Principal $40.00 pr. month First Assistant $30.00 pr. month and Assistant $20.00 pr. month.

On motion of **R. A. McCutcheon** it is ordered that School Levies for year beginning July 1st 1895 and ending June 30, 1896 shall be as follows: for Teachers Fund 40 cents on the One Hundred dollars valuation and for the Building Fund 40 cents on the one Hundred dollars valuation.

On motion of **H. C. Rosenberger** it is ordered that Schools shall commence on the first Monday in October 1895.

On motion the board does now adjourn to meet on the 12 day of July 1895 at one o'clock P.M.

H. K. McCutcheon Sec
F. Howes Pres

Office of the Board of Education of the Independent School District of Belington West Virginia.

At a meeting of the Board held on the **28 day of September 1895**, present **F. Howes**, president and **R. A. McCutcheon** and **H. C. Rosenberger** members of the board.

On motion of **H. C. Rosenberger** it is ordered that schools shall commence on Monday Oct 1st 1895 instead of the first Monday of October as heretofore ordered.

On motion of **H. C. Rosenberger** it is ordered that **John R. W. Cross** be allowed an order for forty cents payable out of the building fund.

On motion of **R. A. McCutcheon** it is ordered that **O. C. Davis** be awarded the furnishing of the Coal to run at 5 mo. school at this proposition of $1.60 per long Tun.

H. K. McCutcheon Sec
F. Howes Pres

Office of the Board of Education of the Independent School District of Belington West Virginia.

At a meeting of the Board held on the **7 day of October 1895**, present **Fenelon Howes**, president and **R. A. McCutcheon** and H.

C. Rosenberger members.

On motion of **R. A. McCutcheon** it is ordered that the Board buy a No. One Stove.

On motion it is ordered that the Teachers shall teach Algebra, Physical Geography, Retorick and Latin, in case any scholar wants to study any or all of said branches.

On motion it is hereby ordered that the board do hereby rent a room of **L. B. Lovett** at four dollars pr. month for 5 months as school room for primary department.

H. K. McCutcheon Secre.
F. Howes Pres

Office of the Board of Education of the Independent School District of Belington West Virginia.

At a meeting of the Board held on the **21 day of October 1895**, present **Fenelon Howes**, president and **R. A. McCutcheon** and **H. C. Rosenberger** members.

On motion of **H. C. Rosenberger** it is ordered that **Bulah Hume** a Teacher holding a No. 2 Teachers certificate be and is hereby employed to teach at 5 mo. school in said District for $22.00 pr. month and that **Nora Hamilton** a Teacher holding a No. One Teachers certificate be and is hereby employed to teach a 5 mo. school in said Dist. for the sum of Thirty dollars pr. month.

On motion of **H. C. Rosenberger** it is ordered that **F. Howes** be allowed an order for 414.10 for stove & freight.

On motion of **H. C. Rosenberger** it is ordered that **W. E. Trimble** be allowed an order for $1.20 payable out of Building fund of said Dist.

F. Howes Pres
H. K. McCutcheon Sec.

Office of the Board of Education of the Independent School District of Belington West Virginia.

At a meeting of the Board held on the **16 day of Nov. 1895**, present **Fenelon Howes**, president and **R. A. McCutcheon, H. C. Rosenberger** members.

On motion of **H. C. Rosenberger** it is ordered that **Beulah Hume** be allowed the sum of Twenty Five dollars per month for her services as Teacher in 3d department.

On motion of **H. C. Rosenberger** it is ordered that **J. B. Ware** be allowed order No. 1 for $40.00 **Nora Hamilton** order No. 2 for $30.00 and **Beulah Hume** order No. 3 for $25.00 payable out of the Teachers Fund of Belington Ind. District of Barbour Co. W. Va.

On motion of **R. A. McCutcheon** it is ordered that **Alpheus Moore** shall pay Belington Ind. Dist. 5 cents per day for each day his children attended School in this Ind. Dist. Whole number of days 306 making $15.30

On motion of **H. C. Rosenberger** it is ordered that **E. T. Cade** be allowed an order for $6.30 on the Sheriff of Barbour Co. W. Va. payable out of Building Fund.

On motion of **H. C. Rosenberger** it is ordered that **R. A. McCutcheon** be allowed an order for Eight dollars and **L. B. Lovett** an order for Six dollars payable out of Building Fund.

On motion the Board does now adjourn to meet in 4 weeks from today at 2 o'clock P.M.

    H. K. McCutcheon Sesc
    F. Howes Pres.

   Office of the Board of Education of the Independent School District of Belington West Virginia.

At a meeting of the Board held on the **14th day of December 1895**, present **Fenelon Howes**, president and **R. A. McCutcheon** and **H. C. Rosenberger** members.

The following business was transacted Viz:

On the teachers fund the following claims were allowed

To **J. B. Ware** for the 2d month	40.00
To **Nora Hamilton** for the 2d month	30.00
To **Bula Hume**	25.00

On the building the following orders were drawn

To **R. A. McCutcheon** for rent of room	8.00
To **Bert McCutcheon** for making fire &c	2.00

To **Max Shurtleff** for making fire &c	2.00
To **Clinton Taylor** for making fire &c	2.00
To **O. C. Davis** for coal delivery	21.21
To **D. B. Hankey** for lumber	4.00
To **L. B. Lovett** for rent of school room	6.00

On motion of **R. A. McCutcheon** that any one having contagious disease in the school should be excluded by the teacher.

On motion the board adjourned to meet in four weeks.

Nota Bene! Error. The dates of the Orders were Nov. the 14th instead of December the 14th 1895.

R. A. McCutcheon Clerk Protem
F. Howes Pres

Office of the Board of Education of the Independent School District of Belington West Virginia.

At a meeting of the Board held on the **January 17, 1896**, Present **Fenelon Howes**, president and **R. A. McCutcheon** member the following business transacted.

On motion of **R. A. McCutcheon** it is ordered that the following Orders drawn upon the Teachers Fund be allowed Order No. 7 to **J. B. Ware** for $40.00. Order No. 8 to **Nora Hamilton** for $30.00. Order No. 9 **Beulah Hume** for 25.00 and on Building Fund order No. 14 to **R. A. McCutcheon** for 8.00. Order No. 15 to **L. B. Lovett** for 6.00. Order No. 16 to **Burt McCutcheon** for $2.00. Order No. 17 **Max Shurtleff** for 2.00. Order No. 18 to **Clinton Taylor** for $2.00.

On motion the Board does now adjourn to meet on the 14 day of February 1896 at 4 o'clock P.M.

F. Howes Pres
H. K. McCutcheon Sec

Office of the Board of Education of the Independent School District of Belington, West Virginia.

At a meeting of the Board held on the **14 day of Feb'y, 1896**, present **F. Howes**, President and **R. A. McCutcheon** commissioner.

308 School Board Minutes

The following business was transacted, Viz:
On the teachers fund the following claims allowed

To **J. B. Ware** for 4 months	40.00
To **Nora Hamilton** for 4 months	30.00
To **Beulah Hume**	25.00

On the building fund the following claims were allowed

To **R. A. McCutcheon** for rent	8.00
To **Burt McCutcheon** for making fires &etc.	2.00
To **Max Shurtleff** for making fires &etc.	2.00
To **Clinton Taylor** for making fires &etc.	6.00
To **L. B. Lovett** for rent of room	6.00

On motion of **R. A. McCutcheon** it is ordered that the Secretary be and is hereby authorized to notify **Alpheus Moore** to pay $15.30 the amt. of Tuition due from him to the Bd. of Ed. of Belington Ind. District to the Sheriff of Barbour County West Virginia at once and take duplicate receipts for same and file one with said Board of Education.

On motion the Board does now adjourn to meet on the 10 day of March 1896 at 4 o'clock P.M.

    F. Howes Pres
      H. K. McCutcheon Sec.

Office of the Board of Education of the Independent School District of Belington, West Virginia.

At a called meeting of the Board held the **7th day of March, 1896,** the following business was transacted Viz: (Present **F. Howes,** President and **R. A. McCutcheon** member)

On the teachers fund the following orders were drawn

To **Nora Hamilton** for the 5th and last month	30.00
To **Bula Humes** for the 5th and last month	25.00

On the building fund the following orders were drawn

To **Max Shurtleff** for building fires etc.	2.00
To **Clinton Taylor** for building fires etc.	2.00

On motion the Board adjourned to meet March 10th 1896.

Office of the Board of Education of the Independent School District of Belington, W. V.

Pursuant to adjournment of the Board met Present **F. Howes**, Pres and **R. A. McCutcheon** member. Transacted the following business.

Ordered that **Mr. Moore** pay to the Sheriff tuition of $13.15 and take his receipt for the same and give to the President of our Board of Education.

Ordered that **J. B. Ware** be paid his salary Teachers fund 40.00

The following orders were drawn on the Sheriff Viz.

R. E. McCutcheon	Building Fund	3.00
R. A. McCutcheon	Building Fund	8.00
L. B. Lovett	Building Fund	6.80
F. M. Right & Co.	Building Fund	.60

On motion the Bd. adjourned (sine die)
H. K. McCutcheon Sec
F. Howes Pres

J. W. Robinson Sheriff of Barbour County by **B. B. Rohrbough** his deputy in account with the Teachers Fund of Belington Independent District for the year ending June 30, 1896.

To amt. due Dist. from settlement of 1895 $155.07. To amt. of State School fund 140.14. To 40 cents levied on the 4100. Of a valuation $61270.00 245.08. To 40 cents G&B R. R. 27.45. To WVC&P R. R. 78.80. To amt. Tuition from **Alpheus Moore** 13.15. Total $659.69.

Order No.	In favor of	Amount
11	**Nora Hamilton**	30
1	**J. B. Ware**	40
2	**Nora Hamilton**	30
3	**Beulah Hume**	25
4	**J. B. Ware**	40
6	**Beulah Hume**	25
5	**Nora Hamilton**	30
7	**J. B. Ware**	40

310 School Board Minutes

10	J. B. Ware	40
12	Beulah Hume	25
9	Beulah Hume	25
11	Nora Hamilton	30
8	Nora Hamilton	30
15	J. B. Ware	40
14	Beulah Hume	25
13	Nora Hamilton	30

By delinquent Real estate for West Side 2.40. By Delinquent Person Prop. West Side 2.65. By amt. improperly assessed 3.40. Exhoneration **D. W. Day** .44 Exhoneration **Abel Teter** 1.15

Com. on 235.04 at 5% 11.75. Com. on 106.25 R. R. T. 2.12 Amt. due Dist. 130.78

J. W. Robinson Sheriff of Barbour County West Virginia by **B. B. Rohrbough** his deputy in acct. with the building fund of Belington Ind. Dist. for the year ending June 30, 1896.

To amt. due Dist. from last settlement (yr end June 30, 1895) $15.31. 40 levied on 100 on a valuation of $61270. $245.08. G&B R. R. 27.45. WV.C&P $78.80.

Order No.	In Favor of	Amount
5	J. R. W. Cross	.40
4	Floyd Ware	18.00
26	H. C. Rosenberger	9.00
3	G. J. Stalnaker	10.00
9	G. J. Stalnaker	15.00
27	R. A. McCutcheon	9.00
2	G. C. Poling	16.50
2	Max E. Shurtleff	2.00
1	R. E. McCutcheon	2.00
5	R. A. McCutcheon	8.00
4	E. T. Cade	6.23
25	F. Howes	9.00
6	F. Howes	14.10
3	Walton Huffman	2.00
6	L. B. Lovett	6.00
11	O. C. Davis	21.21

10	Max Shurtleff	2.00
9	Clinton Taylor	2.00
7	R. A. McCutcheon	8.00
13	Lloyd B. Lovett	6.00
8	Bert McCutcheon	2.00
7	W. E. Trimble	1.20
12	D. B. Hankey	4.00
15	L. B. Lovett	6.00
17	Max Shurtleff	2.00
16	Bert McCutcheon	2.00
14	R. A. McCutcheon	8.00
1	S. M. Stancliff & Co.	29.90
25	D. L. Walcott	38.25
15	L. B. Lovett & Bro.	6.80
8	R. A. McCutcheon	8.00
13	R. E. McCutcheon	2.00
9	L. B. Lovett	6.00

Order No.	In favor of	Amount
14	F. M. Right	.60
16	R. A. McCutcheon	8.00
10	Bert McCutcheon	2.00
11	Max Shurtleff	2.00
19	Max Shurtleff	2.00
18	Clint Taylor	2.00
12	Clint Taylor	2.00
20	Clint Taylor	2.00

By delinquent Real Est. West Side	2.40
By Delinquent Personal Prop. West Side	2.65
By erronious assessment	3.40
Exhonerations **D. W. Day**	.58
Exhonerations **Abel Teter**	1.53
By 5% comm. On 235.04	11.75
By 2% comm. On 106.25	2.12
Total $327.62	
Balance due Dist.	39.02

School Board Minutes

Amt. of Assessable property in Belington Ind. Dist. for year 1896.
Personal property East side	14670.00
Personal property West side	6000.00
Total	20670.00
Real Estate East side	8811.00
Real Estate West side	2649.00
Real Estate West corporation	6075.00
Real Estate East corporation	24538.00
Amt. of G&B R.R.	7036.00
Amt. of WVa. & C&P	20485.00
Total	90264.00
Amt. of State School Fund	168.34

Amt. Due Dist. on Tuition from settlement with Sheriff 130.78
Amt. Due Dist. on Building Fund from settlement with Sheriff for year 1895 $39.02

      Office of the Board of Education of the Independent School District of Belington, Barbour County, West Virginia.
    At a meeting of the Board held on the **6 day of July, 1896,** Present **F. Howes,** President and **R. A. McCutcheon** and **H. C. Rosenberger** members.
    On motion of **H. C. Rosenberger**, it is ordered that the schools of this district shall be taught five months during the present school year.
    On motion of **H. C. Rosenberger** it is ordered that there be employed 3 Teachers to teach the schools of this district the present school year.
    On motion of **R. A. McCutcheon**, it is ordered that the salaries of teachers per month for the school year shall be as follows, for first rooms $50.00, for second $30.00, third $25.00
    It having been ascertained by the Board that it will be necessary to raise by levy, for the payment of teachers salaries for the current year in addition to the available funds on hand $200.88. On motion of **R. A. McCutcheon**, it is ordered that the tax of 30 cents on the one hundred dollars valuation of the real estate and personal property of the district be levied for that purpose.
    On motion of **H. C. Rosenberger,** it is ordered that the tax of

40 cents on the one hundred dollars valuation of the real estate and personal property of the district be levied for building purposes.

On motion of **R. A. McCutcheon** it ordered that **M. C. Lough** be employed as principal teacher and **Charles Wigle** as second Teacher and Miss **Lake** as third Teacher for the present school year.

On motion the Board does now adjourn sine die.

F. Howes Pres
H. K. McCutcheon Secre.

Office of the Board of Education of the Independent School District of Belington, Barbour County, West Virginia.

At a call meeting of the board held on the **21st of September, 1896**, Present **H. C. Rosenberger** and **R. A. McCutcheon** members. The following business was transacted, Viz:

The minutes of last meeting were read and approved.

The Resignation of **G. J. Stalnaker** as Secretary of the Board of Education was accepted and **H. K. McCutcheon** was appointed Secretary.

Miss **Jennette Lake** having tendered her Resignation as teacher for 3d room. On motion of **H. C. Rosenberger**, Miss **Bertha Douglas** was employed in her place.

On motion of **H. C. Rosenberger** an order was allowed **G. J. Stalnaker** for $10.00 on Building Fund.

On motion of **H. C. Rosenberger** the President **Fenelon Howes** was appointed to see to getting 300 Bu. of coal for the coming winter.

On motion the Board adjourned to meet on the 1st day of October at 1 o'clock P.M.

H. K. McCutcheon Sec.
R. A. McCutcheon Pres Pro tempore

Office of the Board of Education of the Independent School District of Belington, Barbour County, West Virginia.

At a call meeting of the board held on the **22d day of September, 1896**, Present **F. Howes**, President and **R. A.**

McCutcheon and **H. C. Rosenberger** Members. At a call meeting of the Board.

P. L. Lovett was appointed Depositary for Belington Independent School District.

On motion of **R. A. McCutcheon, P. L. Lovett**'s Bond for Two Hundred Dollars as Depositary, was received and approved.

On motion of **H. C. Rosenberger** the Board adjourned to meet Saturday September 26, 1896 at 1 o'clock P.M.

H. K. McCutcheon Sec.
F. Howes Pres.

Office of the Board of Education of the Independent School District of Belington, Barbour County, West Virginia.

At a call meeting of the board held on the **26 day of September, 1896**, Present **F. Howes**, Pres. and **R. A. McCutcheon**.

On motion of **R. A. McCutcheon** it was ordered that the schools begin Monday the 19th October 1896.

On motion Bd. adjourned Sine die
H. K. McCutcheon Sec.

Office of the Board of Education of the Independent School District of Belington, Barbour County, West Virginia.

At a meeting of the board held on the **8th day of October, 1896**, Present **F. Howes**, President and **R. A. McCutcheon** member.

On motion of **R. A. McCutcheon** it was ordered that contracts be entered into with **M. C. Lough, Jacob Wigle** and **Bertha Douglass** teachers.

On motion the Board adjourned Sine die.
H. K. McCutcheon Sec.

Office of the Board of Education of the Independent School District of Belington, Barbour County, West Virginia.

At a meeting of the board held on the **31st day of October, 1896**, Present **F. Howes**, President and **R. A. McCutcheon** and **H. C. Rosenberger** members. On motion of **R. A. McCutcheon** the following claims were allowed on Building fund

To **James Right**	3.00
To **Geo. M. Serpell**	8.35
To **W. E. Trimble**	.75

Adjourned to meet 14th November at 1 P.M.
        H. K. McCutcheon Sec.
        F. Howes Pres.

Office of the Board of Education of the Independent School District of Belington, Barbour County, West Virginia.

At a meeting of the Board held on the **14th day of November, 1896**, Pres **F. Howes**, Pres, **H. C. Rosenberger** & **R. A. McCutcheon** members.

On motion of **R. A. McCutcheon** the following orders were allowed on Teachers Fund

To **M. E. Lough**		50.00
To **Jacob Wigle**		30.00
To **Bertha Douglass**		<u>25.00</u>
		$105.00

On Building Fund

To **Maj. Howes**	Freight on coal	6.90
To **Burt McCutcheon**	Building fires	2.00
To **Jacob Wigle**	Building fires	2.00
To **Lee David**	Building fires	2.00
To **R. A. McCutcheon**	Rect.	<u>13.10</u>
		26.00

On motion of **H. C. Rosenberger** a transfer was ordered to Miss **Dolly Ward** from Belington Independent District to Barker Sub District. To continue as long as she attends school during this school year.

On motion of **H. C. Rosenberger** the Board adjourned to meet

School Board Minutes

Dec. 12 at 1 o'clock P.M.
> F. Howes Pres.
> H. K. McCutcheon

Office of the Board of Education of the Independent School District of Belington, Barbour County, West Virginia.

At a call meeting of the board held on the **15th Day of December,1896**, Present **F. Howes**, President and **R. A. McCutcheon** & **H. C. Rosenberger** mem.

On motion of **R. A. McCutcheon** the following orders were allowed

On the Teachers Fund

No. 19	**M. C. Lough**		50.00
No. 20	**Jacob Wigle**		30.00
No. 21	**Bertha Douglass**		31.00

On Building Fund

No. 26	**L. B. Lovett** & Bro.	Mdse.	2.28
No. 27	**R. A. McCutcheon**	Rect	8.00
No. 28	**R. A. McCutcheon**	Rect	5.00
No. 29	**Jacob Wigle**	Building fires	2.00
No. 30	**R. E. McCutcheon**	Building fires	2.00
No. 31	**Lee Davis**	Building fires	2.00
No. 32	**H. C. Rosenberger**	Hauling coal	3.50
No. 33	**James A. Right**	Carpenter work	1.25
No. 34	**M. C. Lough**	Erasers	.55

On Building Fund the following orders were also allowed for Text Books

Order No. 1	To Werner School Book Co.	12.00
Order No. 2	To **E. H. Butler** & Co.	13.25
Order No. 3	To Thompson Brown & cs	8.75
Order No. 4	To Christopher Sower & Co.	3.30
Order No. 5	To J. B. Lippincott & Co.	5.90
Order No. 6	To Ginn & Co.	15.25
Order No. 7	To D. C. Heath & Co.	15.00

On motion of **H. C. Rosenberger**, **Robb Dunham** was hired to Build Fires & sweep out in Room No. 3 for the remainder of the school in place of **Lee Davis**.

H. K. McCutcheon not having been sworn in was sworn in as Secretary.
On motion the Board does now adjourn Sine Die.
H. K. McCutcheon Sec
F. Howes

Office of the Board of Education of the Independent School District of Belington, Barbour County, West Virginia.

At a call meeting of the board held on the **16th day of January, 1897**, Present **F. Howes**, Pres. and **R. A. McCutcheon** & **H. C. Rosenberger** members.

On motion of **H. C. Rosenberger** the following orders were allowed on the Teachers Fund.

No. 22	M. C. Lough	50.00
No. 23	Jacob Wigle	30.00
No. 24	Bertha Douglass	28.00

On Building Fund

No. 35	Burt McCutcheon		2.00
No. 36	Robt. Dunham		2.00
No. 37	Jacob Wigle		2.00
No. 38	R. A. McCutcheon		8.00
No. 39	R. A. McCutcheon	Rent two rooms	5.00
No. 40	Chas. F. Teter		3.48

On motion the board does now adjourn Sine Die.
Fenelon Howes Pres.
H. K. McCutcheon Secre.

Office of the Board of Education of the Independent School District of Belington, Barbour County, West Virginia.

At a call meeting of the board held on **February, 1897**, Present **F. Howes**, President and **R. A. McCutcheon** member.

On motion the following orders were allowed

School Board Minutes

On Teachers Fund.
Order No. 25	M. C. Lough	50.00
Order No. 26	Jacob Wigle	30.00
Order No. 27	Bertha Douglass	28.00

On Building Fund
Order No. 41	R. A. McCutcheon	8.00
Order No. 42	R. A. McCutcheon	5.00
Order No. 43	Burt McCutcheon	2.00
Order No. 44	Jacob Wigle	2.00
Order No. 45	Robb Dunham	2.00

On motion the Board Adjourned to meet Dec. 12, 1897 at 3 o'clock P.M.

    H. K. McCutcheon Sec
    Fenelon Howes Pres.

Office of the Board of Education of the Independent School District of Belington, Barbour County, West Virginia.

At a call meeting of the board held on the **12th day of March 1897**, Present **F. Howes**, President and **R. A. McCutcheon** member.

On motion the following orders were allowed on Teachers Fund.

M. C. Lough	50.00
Bertha Douglass	28.00

On Building fund
R. A. McCutcheon	8.00
R. A. McCutcheon	5.00
R. E. McCutcheon	2.00
Robb Dunham	2.00
D. B. Hankey	2.40

On motion the Bd. adjourned to meet March 23d 1897 at 3 P.M.

    H. K. McCutcheon Secretary
    Fenelon Howes Pres.

Office of the Board of Education of the Independent School District of Belington, Barbour County, West Virginia.

At a call meeting of the board held on the **23d day of March 1897**, the following business was transacted

On motion the following orders were allowed

On Teachers Fund.

		Jacob Wigle	30.00
	On building fund		
No. 51	To **F. M. Right** & Co.		.55
No. 52	To **L. B. Lovett** & Bro.		.60
No. 53	To **Jacob Wigle**		2.00
No. 54	To **F. Howes**		1.40

Fenelon Howes Pres.
H. K. McCutcheon

B. B. Rhorbough, Deputy Sheriff of Barbour County in account with the Teachers Fund of Belington Independent District for the year ending June 30th 1897.

Due from Sheriff on last settlement 1896 $130.70. R. R. Tax for 1896 $87.60. State School Fund $168.37.

No. 29	Jacob Wigle	30.00
No. 28	M. C. Lough	50.00
No. 30	Bertha Douglas	28.00
No. 27	Bertha Douglas	28.00
No. 24	Bertha Douglas	28.00
No. 25	M. C. Lough	50.00
No. 26	Jacob Wigle	30.00
No. 23	Jacob Wigle	30.00
No. 22	M. C. Lough	50.00
No. 20	Jacob Wigle	30.00
No. 19	M. C. Lough	50.00
No. 21	Bertha Douglas	30.00
No. 18	Bertha Douglas	25.00
No. 16	M. C. Lough	50.00
No. 17	Jacob Wigle	30.00

By releases for 96 $2.52. Delinquent list 15.53. Commission on R. R. Money 1.75. Commission on Levy 12.54

320 School Board Minutes

    Balance due Sheriff
Amt. of receipts from all sources for Teachers Fund $637.71
Amt. of Sheriff credits $572.34
Balance due Dist. from Sheriff $65.37
    Not a correct statement.

    B. B. Rhorbough Deputy Sheriff of Barbour County in acct with the Building Fund of Belington Independent District for the year 1896. 6/20th/97
    Acct due Dist. from last settlement $39.02. Levy for 1896 $250.97. R. R. Tax for 96 $87.62. Acct. from Text Books Sold $20.49.

No.		Amount
52	L. B. Lovett & Bro.	.60
49	Robt. Dunham	2.00
51	F. M. Right & Co.	.55
48	R. E. McCutcheon	2.00
53	Jacob Wigle	2.00
47	R. A. McCutcheon	5.00
46	R. A. McCutcheon	8.00
50	D. B. Hankey	2.40
42	R. A. McCutcheon	5.00
44	Jacob Wigle	2.00
43	Bert McCutcheon	2.00
41	R. A. McCutcheon	8.00
36	Robb Dunham	2.00
32	H. C. Rosenberger	3.50
45	Robb Dunham	2.00
5	J. B. Lippincott & Co.	5.90
2	E. H. Butler & Co.	13.25
3	Thompson Brown & Co.	8.75
1	Werner Sch. Book Co.	12.00
7	D. C. Heath & Co.	15.00
6	Ginn & Co.	15.25
10	G. J. Stalnaker	15.00
35	Bert McCutcheon	2.00
37	Jacob Wigle	2.00

School Board Minutes 321

39	R. A. McCutcheon	5.00
38	R. A. McCutcheon	8.00
5	W. E. Trimble	.75
30	R. E. McCutcheon	2.00
28	R. A. McCutcheon	5.00
26	L. B. Lovett & Bro.	2.28
33	James A. Right	1.25
31	Lee Davis	2.00
27	R. A. McCutcheon	8.00
34	M. C. Lough	.55
30	Clay Rosenberger	9.00
29	Jacob Wigle	2.00
1	Viquesney and Yeager	1.70
4	Geo. M. Serpell	8.35
24	R. A. McCutcheon	13.10
3	James A. Right	3.00
23	Lee Davis	2.00
25	F. Howes	6.90
17	F. Howes	9.00
2	G. J. Stalnaker	10.00
22	Jacob Wigle	2.00
21	Bert McCutcheon	2.00
16	R. A. McCutcheon	9.00

Total by vouchers $248.55
Total amt. charged for 96 $398.98
By releases Sheriffs credits $286.69
By delinquents for 96 $20.60
By Commission on R. R. Tax $1.75
Balance due Dist $112.29
Balance due Sheriff on Settlement $280.57

 Amount of Assessable Property in Belington Independent District for 1897. Personal Property East Side $4,130.00. Personal Property West Side $15,575.00. Total $19,705.00. Real Estate East and Real Estate West 45,271.00. Total 64976.00.

 Acct of G&B R. R. 7056.00. Acct of W.Va. Central 20830.00. Acct of R. C. & B. 3000.00. Total 95862.00.

 Amounts from the sale of Delinquent Lands. Teachers Fund $3.40. Building Fund $5.50.

School Board Minutes

Office of the Board of Education of the Independent School District of Belington, Barbour County, West Virginia.

At a meeting of the Board held on the **5th day of July 1897**, Present **R. A. McCutcheon & H. C. Rosenberger** members.

H. C. Rosenberger qualified as member of Bd. of Ed. for Ensuing Term.

On motion it was ordered that The Levies for the conduct of the Free Schools of the District for the year beginning the 1st day of July 1897 be made for the Respective Funds at the following rates. For Teachers Fund 50¢ on the $100 valuation
For Building Fund 40¢ on the $100 valuation
    On motion the Board adjourned Sine Die.
        Fenelon Howes Pres
        H. K. McCutcheon

At a meeting of the Board of Education of Belington Ind. Dist. held **July 23 1897** at their office: The president **F. Howes & H. C. Rosenberger & R. A. McCutcheon** present.

The following business was transacted.

B. B. Rhorbough Sheriff of Barbour County in account with the Teachers fund of Belington Independent District for the year ending June 30th 1897. Due from Sheriff on last settlement 1896 $130.78.

Personal property on E. Side 16170.00. Personal property on W. Side 2412.00. Real Estate E. Side 37299.00. Real Estate W. Side 8072.00. Total $63953.00

B&O R. R. Tax assessment 7056.00. WVa Cen. R. R. 20830.00. R. C&C 3000.00. Total amt of taxable property $94,839.00. Tax on same at 30 cts on $100 is 168.34. State School fund Total $452.85

Orders paid		Amount
No. 29	**Jacob Wigle**	30.00
No. 28	**M. C. Lough**	50.00
No. 30	**Bertha Douglas**	28.00
No. 27	**Bertha Douglas**	28.00
No. 24	**Bertha Douglas**	28.00
No. 25	**M. C. Lough**	50.00

No. 26	Jacob Wigle	30.00
No. 23	Jacob Wigle	30.00
No. 22	M. C. Lough	50.00
No. 20	Jacob Wigle	30.00
No. 19	M. C. Lough	50.00
No. 21	Bertha Douglas	31.00
No. 18	Bertha Douglas	25.00
No. 16	M. C. Lough	50.00
No. 17	Jacob Wigle	30.00
Total		540.00

  By releases for 1896 $2.52
  Delinquent list 15.53
  Add for delinquent
  Commission on R. R. Tax 6.17
  Commission on Levy 11.88
  Total 18.05
  Due from Sheriff June 30, 1897 $102.37
    Fenelon Howes Pres
    July 28th 1897

  B. B. Rohrobough Deputy Sheriff of Barbour County in account of the building fund of Belington Ind. School Dist. for the year ending June 30, 1897. Balance due the District from last settlement $39.02. Personal property on E. Side 16170.00. Personal property on W. Side 2412.00. Real Estate E. Side 37299.00. Real Estate W. Side 8072.00. B&O assessment 7056.00. W Va C. assessment 20830.00. C&C assessment 3000.00. Total 94839.00 at 40 cts on the 100.00 val. = 379.35. From textbooks sold 20.49. Total 438.86.

Orders Paid

No.		Amount
52	L. B. Lovett	.60
49	Robt. Dunham	2.00
51	F. M. Right & Co.	.55
48	R. E. McCutcheon	2.00
53	Jacob Wigle	2.00
47	R. A. McCutcheon	5.00
46	R. A. McCutcheon	8.00
50	D. B. Hankey	2.40

324   School Board Minutes

42	R. A. McCutcheon	5.00
44	Jacob Wigle	2.00
43	Bert McCutcheon	2.00
41	R. A. McCutcheon	8.00
36	Robt. Dunham	2.00
32	H. C. Rosenberger	3.50
45	Robt. Dunham	2.00
5	J. B. Lippincott & Co.	5.90
2	E. H. Butler 7 Co.	13.25
3	Thompson & Barron & Co.	8.75
1	Werner School book Co.	12.00
7	D. C. Heath & Co.	15.00
6	Ginn & Co.	15.25
10	G. J. Stalnaker	15.00
35	Bert McCutcheon	2.00
37	Jacob Wigle	2.00
39	R. A. McCutcheon	5.00
38	R. A. McCutcheon	8.00
5	W. E. Trimble	.75
30	R. E. McCutcheon	2.00
28	R. A. McCutcheon	5.00
26	L. B. Lovett & Bro.	2.28
33	J. A. Right	1.25
31	Lee Davis	2.00
27	R. A. McCutcheon	8.00
34	M. C. Lough	.55
30	H. C. Rosenberger	9.00
29	Jacob Wigle	2.00
1	Viquesney & Yeager	1.70
4	Geo. M. Serpell	8.35
24	R. A. McCutcheon	13.10
3	J. A. Right	3.00
23	Lee Davis	2.00
25	F. Howes	6.90
17	F. Howes	9.00
2	G. J. Stalnaker	10.00
22	Jacob Wigle	2.00
21	Bert McCutcheon	2.00
16	R. A. McCutcheon	9.00

Total by vouchers $248.55. By releases 3.25. By delinquent list 20.60. Comm. on R. R. Tax 6.17. Comm. on levy 11.59. $17.76. Due from Sheriff June 30, 1897 149.58. Sheriff claims too much differences by $3.74.
    Fenelon Howes Pres.

July the 1st, 1897
    Assessed valuation of Property of the Independent School Dist of Belington W. Va. Commencing July the 1st, 1897. Valuation of Real Estate Ind. Dist is 45271.00. Personal property is 19705.00. B&O R. R. Is 7056.00. W. Va. Central is 20830.00. R. C. & C. is 3000.00. Total amt. $95862.00
    State School fund 163.04. Tax on 95862 at 40 c per 100 per $100. Due from Sheriff on last settlement $383.44.

    Belington Independent School District **July 23d 1897**. The Board of Education composed by **Major Howes** President and **H. C. Rosenberger & R. A. McCutcheon** members met and transacted the following business - Viz: Corrected the errors of the last settlement with the sheriff **B. B. Rohrobough** per his deputy **Geo. M. Right** and appointed

Miss **Jennie Simons** for the 3d room	Salary $30.00
Jacob Wigle for the second room	Salary $35.00
W. E. Tomblyn for the first room	Salary $40.00

    Mr. **H. C. Rosenberger** resigned his office as a school commissioner.
    School shall commence Oct. 25th 1897.
    Fenelon Howes Pres.

326 School Board Minutes

Office of the Board of Education of the Independent School District of Belington W. Va.

At a meeting of the Board held on the **23d Day of Oct. 1897** Present **F. Howes** President **R. A. McCutcheon** member.

On motion of **R. A. McCutcheon** it was ordered that a Bowl for stove in second school room be purchased.

On motion of Mr. **C. Philips** was duly sworn in as member of Bd Education of Belington Independent School Dist.

On motion an order was allowed on the Building Fund in favour of **R. C. Bristow** $6.85

On motion the Board adjourned to meet Friday Nov. 19th 1897 at 4 P.M.

H. K. McCutcheon Sec
Fenelon Howes Pres.

Office of the Board of Education of the Independent School District of Belington W. Va.

At a meeting of the Board held on the **19 day of November, 1897** Present **F. Howes** President, **Cicero Philips & R. A. McCutcheon** members.

On motion of **R. A. McCutcheon** it was ordered that the Following Drafts be drawn

On the Teachers Fund.

W. E. Tomblyn	40.00
Jacob Wigle	35.00
Jennie Simons	30.00
On the Building Fund	
Jacob Wigle	2.00
Robt. Dunham	2.00
Walton Huffman	2.00
R. A. McCutcheon rent	13.00
Cicero Philips	4.15

On motion of **C. Philips** a transfer was ordered to **Roy Greathouse** from Belington Ind. Dist. to upper Belington School Dist.

On motion the Board adjourned Sine Die.
H. K. McCutcheon Sec.

Major F. Howes, Belington, West Virginia - The following is a true statement of the Rail Road tax which you should have been credited with in Belington Independent District, and also the amount for which I drew my order to the sheriff, **B. B. Rhorabough**, March the 18th 1897.

W. Va. Central & Pittsburg R. R. Co.	140.23
Roaring Creek & Belington	21.00
Grafton & Belington	48.43
Total	209.66

Very truly yours
Chas. I. Zirkle, Co. Supt.

Belington, W. Va. Dec. 7th 1897
I certify that the above is a true copy of a letter received by **Major Howes** President of Belington Ind. School District from **C. I. Zirkle** County Supt of Free Schools.
R. A. McCutcheon Member of the Board of Belington Independent School Dist.

Office of the Board of Education of the Independent School District of Belington West Virginia.
At a meeting of the Board held on the **17th of December, 1897** Present **F. Howes** President, **Cicero Philips & R. A. McCutcheon** members.
On motion the following orders were allowed
On Teachers Fund

W. E. Tomblyn	50.00
Jacob Wigle	35.00
Jennie Simons	30.00

328 School Board Minutes

On Building Fund

Jacob Wigle Janitor		2.00
R. E. McCutcheon Janitor		2.00
Robt Dunham Janitor		2.00
D. B. Hankey Rent		5.00
R. A. McCutcheon Rent		8.00
E. M. Ware carpenter work		.75
L. B. Lovett & Bro. Sundries		1.96
C. Philips Table		2.25
R. A. McCutcheon Sprinkler		.50
C. W. Burk Coal 1 Ton		1.90

On Building Fund the following orders were allowed for School Books. Viz:

Christopher Sower Co. (Duplicate)	3.30
J. B. Lippincott & Co.	5.80
Ginn & Co.	5.30
D. C. Heath & Co.	4.58
American Book Co	37.52

On motion Bd. adjourned to meet Jan. 15, 1897.

Fenelon Howes Pres

H. K. McCutcheon Sec.

Office of the Board of Education of the Independent School District of Belington West. Va.

At a meeting of the Board held on the **15 day of January 1898.** Present **F. Howes** President **Cicero Philips** and **R. A. McCutcheon** members.

On motion the following orders were allowed

On Teachers Fund

Jacob Wigle	35.00
Jennie Simons	30.00

On Building Fund

Jacob Wigle Janitor	2.00
R. E. McCutcheon Janitor	2.00
R. W. Dunham	2.00

Clinton Taylor   Janitor One day **Hankey**   .25
R. A. McCutcheon   Rent   8.00
D. B. Hankey   Rent   5.00
Elam T. Cade   Carpenter work   2.75
Cicero Philips   Carpenter work   2.75
Cicero Philips   Freight on seats   10.20
J. A. Robinson   Stove pipe   .80
Chas. C. Wentz   Erasers   3.50
Favorite Desk and Seating Company   101.80
On motion Board adjourned to meet January 22d 1898.
   Fenelon Howes President
   H. K. McCutcheon Secretary

  Office of the Board of Education of the Independent School District of Belington West Virginia.
  At a meeting of the Board held on the **22 day of January 1898.**
  Pr. of **Tomblyn**s School a week behind. Order was drawn on Teachers Fund
  W. E. Tomblyn   45.00

  Office of the Board of Education of the Independent School District of Belington West Va.
  At a meeting of the Board held on the **11 day of February, 1898.** Present **F. Howes** President and **R. A. McCutcheon** member.
  On motion the following orders were allowed.
On Teachers Fund
39 **Jennie Simons**   30.00
40 **Jacob Wigle**   35.00
41 **W. E. Tomblyn**   45.00
Building Fund
83 **D. B. Hankey**   Pop.Lbr. 1.80
84 **R. C. Bristow**   5.00

330 School Board Minutes

85	R. A. McCutcheon Rent	8.00
86	R. E. McCutcheon Janitor	2.00
87	R. W. Dunham Janitor	2.00
88	E. Ware & Son Mdse	1.47
89	Jacob Wigle	2.00

On motion the Board Adjourned to meet March 11, 1898.
H. K. McCutcheon

Errorless
Personal Property East Side   15035.00
Personal Property West Side   3475.00
Real Estate East Side 2nd Dist 6665.00
Real Estate East Side Corporation 29648.00
Real Estate West Side 2nd Dist. 2912.00
Real Estate West Side Corporation 10770.00
B&O R. R. 2nd Dist   7809.00
B&O R. R. Corporation   8000.00
W. Va. C. R. R. Ind. Dist   20000.00
W. Va. C. R. R. Corporation   15000.00
R. C. & B. R. R. 2nd Dist   3000.00
R. C. & B. R. R. 2nd Dist Corporation   3000.00

Office of the Board of Education of the Independent School District of Belington West Virginia.

At a meeting of the Board held on the **11 day of March 1898**. Present **F. Howes** President **Cicero Philips** and **R. A. McCutcheon** members.

On motion the following orders were allowed on Teachers Fund

42	**Jacob Wigle**	35.00
43	**Jennie Simons**	30.00
45	Secty Bd. of Ed. Barker Dist.	5.78

Building Fund

90	**Robinson** Roofing Co.	.40
91	**Jacob Wigle**	2.00
92	**R. E. McCutcheon**	2.00

School Board Minutes 331

93	Robt. W. Dunham	2.00
94	R. A. McCutcheon	8.00
95	D. B. Hankey	5.00

State School Fund   193.20
W. Va. C.& Pittsburg R. R.   175.50
Grafton & Belington   68.53
Roaring Creek & Belington   26.32

Assessed Valuation of Property in Belington Ind. Dist.
Personal Property East Side   15035.00
Personal Property West Side   3475.00
Real Estate East Side   37299.00
Real Estate West Side   8072.00
Rail Roads   30886.00
Total   947.67

B. B. Rhorbough S. B. C. in account with the Teachers Fund of The Belington Independent Dist. Belington, W. Va. for the year ending June 30, 1898.

To Balance due Dist on settlement for the year ending June 30th 1897   68.69
To amt. due from State School Fund for the year ending June 30th 1897   163.04
Assessed valuation of P. Property in Ind Dist E. Side 4130.00
Assessed valuation of Personal property in Ind. Dist. West Side 155575.00
Assessed valuation Real Estate 45271.00
Assessed valuation G&B Div. R. R.   7056.00
Assessed valuation W. Va. C. R. R.   20830.00
Assessed valuation R. C. & B. R. R.   3000.00
Total   95862.00
Amt. Brot down 231.73
Total $711.04

B. B. Rhorbough S. B. C. in acct with Teachers Fund of Belington Ind. Dist Belington W. Va. for the year ending June 30, 1898.

Order No.		Amount
31	W. E. Tomblyn	40.00
32	Jacob Wigle	35.00
33	Jennie Simons	30.00
34	W. E. Tomblyn	50.00

School Board Minutes

35	Jacob Wigle	35.00
36	Jennie Simon	30.00
37	W. E. Tomblyn	45.00
37	Jacob Wigle	35.00
38	Jennie Simon	30.00
39	W. E. Tomblyn	45.00
40	Jacob Wigle	35.00
39	Jennie Simon	30.00
44	W. E. Tomblyn	45.00
42	Jacob Wigle	35.00
43	Jennie Simons	30.00
45	Secretary Barker Dist. (Valley Ward)	5.78

Delinquent list on Teachers Fund $6.56
Releases 23.60
Commission on R. R. Tax 6.17
Commission on Pres. & Real Prop. 32.14
Total of Orders 555.78
Total of Commission of Delinquents 624.25
Balance Due District $86.79
   B. B. Rhorbough S. B. C.

B. B. Rhorbough S. B. C. in acct. with Building Fund of The Belington Ind. District Belington W. Va. for the year ending June 30, 1897.
  Do. Bal. Due Dist. from last year 149.58
  Assessed valuation of Personal Property E. Side 4130.00
  Assessed valuation of Personal Property W. Side 15575.00
  Assessed valuation Real Estate 45271.00
  Assessed valuation G&B Dir. 7056.00
  Assessed valuation W. Va. & C. 20830.00
  Assessed valuation R. C. & B. 3000.00
  Amt. Brot. Down 149.58
  By error in Bal due from last year 3.36
  Total 529.66

B. B. Rhorbough S. B. C. in act. With Building Fund of The

Belington Independent School Dist Belington W. Va. for the year ending June 30, 1898.

Order No.		Amount
56	Jacob Wigle	2.00
57	Robt. Dunham	2.00
58	Walton Huffman	2.00
59	R. A. McCutcheon	13.00
60	Cicero Philips	4.15
62	Jacob Wigle	2.00
63	R. E. McCutcheon	2.00
70	Robt. Dunham	2.00
64	D. B. Hankey	5.00
65	R. A. McCutcheon	8.00
61	E. M. Ware	.75
66	L. B. Lovett & Bro.	1.96
66	C. Philips	2.25
69	R. A. McCutcheon	.50
68	C. W. Burk	1.90
71	Jacob Wigle	2.00
72	R. E. McCutcheon	2.00
73	R. W. Dunham	2.00
76	C. Taylor	.25
81	R. A. McCutcheon	8.00
82	D. B. Hankey	5.00
77	E. T. Cade	2.75
78	C. Philips	2.75
80	C. Philips	10.20
74	J. A. Robinson	.80
75	Chas. C. Wentz	3.50
79	Fav. Desk & Seating Co.	101.80
83	D. B. Hankey	1.80
84	R. C. Brislow	5.00
85	R. A. McCutcheon	8.00
86	R. E. McCutcheon	2.00
87	R. W. Dunham	2.00
88	E. Ware & Son	1.47
89	Jacob Wigle	2.00
90	Robinson Roof Co.	.40
91	Jacob Wigle	2.00

334 School Board Minutes

92	R. E. McCutcheon	2.00
93	R. W. Dunham	2.00
94	R. A. McCutcheon	8.00
95	D. B. Hankey	5.00
40	C. P. Teter	3.48
54	F. Howes	1.40
7	F. Howes	9.00
	H. C. Rosenberger	9.00
	R. A. McCutcheon	9.00
55	H. K. McCutcheon	15.00
	H. K. McCutcheon	10.00
	R. C. Brislow	6.85
	J. B. Lippincott & Co.	5.80
	D. C. Heath	5.30
	Ginn & Co.	4.58
	American Book Co.	37.52
96	S. H. Williamson	5.60

Delinquent list on Bldg Fund 5.19
Releases 16.36
Commission on R. R. Tax 6.17
Commission on Pers. & Real Property 32.14
Total amt of orders Bldg Fund 352.76
Bal. Due Dist. $115.04
Money from sale of School Books 43.81
Total Bal due District $158.85
    B. B. Rohrbough S. B. C.

    Office of the Board of Education of the Independent School District of Belington West Virginia.
    At a meeting of the Board held on the **4th of July, 1898.** Present **F. Howes** President **Cicero Philips** and **R. A. McCutcheon** members.
    On motion order was drawn in favor of **H. K. McCutcheon** for $10.00.
    On acct. of Error in acct of Real Estate & Personal Property as

given in by Co. Clerk.
The Board adjourned to meet Saturday July 9, 1898.
H. K. McCutcheon Secr'y

Office of the Board of Education of the Independent School District of Belington West Virginia.

At a meeting of the Board held on the **9th day of July 1898.** Present **F. Howes** President **Cicero Philips** and **R. A. McCutcheon** members.

On motion it was ordered that Five months of School be taught with Three Teachers provided, a room can be secured for Third Teacher.

On motion of **R. A. McCutcheon** it was ordered that the salaries of teachers per month be

For Principal	$45.00
!st Asst.	$40.00
2nd Asst.	$30.00

On motion it was ordered that contracts be entered into with **W. E. Tomblyn, Jacob Wigle** and **Agnes Welch.**

On motion it was ordered that Schools begin on the 30th day of October 1898 continuing Five months.

On motion it is ordered that a Tax of 40 cents on the One Hundred Dollars valuation of Real Estate & Personal Property of the Dist. be levied for Building purposes.

On motion it is ordered that a Tax of 40 cents on the One Hundred Dollars Valuation of Real Estate & Personal Property of the Dist. be levied for Teachers Fund.
H. K. McCutcheon Sec'y

Office of the Board of Education of the Independent School District of Belington W. Va.

At a meeting of the Board held on the **2d day of September, 1898.** Present **F. Howes** President, **Cicero Philips** member.

On motion of **C. Philips**, Miss **Jennie Simons** was hired as

teacher for 3d room.
    No further business, Board adjourned Sine Die.
        H. K. McCutcheon Sec.

    Office of the Board of Education of the Independent School District of Belington W. Va.
    At a meeting of the Board held on the **23 day of September, 1898.** Present **F. Howes** President **Cicero Philips** and **R. A. McCutcheon** members.
    On motion it was ordered that the question concerning the issuing and selling if necessary of Bonds on the Belington Independent School District for the amt. of $4500.00 payable Twenty years from date of issue at 5% interest. (In no event to exceed six percent) Interest payable annually be submitted to the voters of said district November 8th 1898 at the General Election.
    On motion of **R. A. McCutcheon** it is ordered that Doors be purchased (with locks for same) & put on the coal houses belonging to the Ind. School District and that the out houses belonging to Ind. School Dist. be cleaned.
        H. K. McCutcheon Sec.

    Office of the Board of Education of the Independent School District of Belington on the **23d day of September 1898** of which all the members had due notice: It is ordered that a vote be taken at the voting place in Belington of the qualified voters of Belington Independent School District on the 8th day of November 1898 at the general election, to ascertain whether the Board of Education of said District shall be authorized and empowered to issue bonds for the purpose of erecting a Public School Building for the use of the said Independent district in the town of Belington at a cost not exceeding $4500.00 including the lot on which the said house is to be built.
    Said bonds to be of interest at the vote of 5% (in no event to exceed six percent) the interest to be paid on the said bonds annually and the bonds themselves to be payable in Twenty years from this date

and that a copy of this order be posted by the Secretary of this Board at three of the usual public places in the Independent School District of Belington and at the front door of the Court House of Barbour County for four weeks before the said election.

    President
    Bd. Of E. Belington Ind. District
    H. K. McCutcheon Secretary
    B. of E. Belington Ind. District

  Office of the Board of Education of the Independent School District of Belington West Virginia.
  At a meeting of the Board held on the **1st day of October 1898**. **F. Howes** President, **R. A. McCutcheon** and **Cicero Philips** members.
  On motion the following orders were allowed on Building Fund.

Order No.		Amount
100	**E. G. Huffman**	4.75
101	**F. P. Rease**	18.90

  No further business the Board adj. Sine Die.
    H. K. McCutcheon Secretary

  Office of the Board of Education of the Independent School District of Belington West Virginia.
  At a meeting of the Board held on the **28th day of October 1898**.
  Present **F. Howes** Pres. **R. A. McCutcheon & Cicero Philips** Members.
  On motion the following orders were allowed
On Teachers Fund

46	**W. E. Tomblyn**	45.00
47	**Jacob Wigle**	40.00
48	**Jennie Howes**	30.00

On Building Fund

17	Robb Dunham	2.00
18	**Robt. E. McCutcheon**	2.00
19	**R. A. McCutcheon** Rent & Etc	8.25
20	**F. Howes** D. B. H. Rent & Etc	6.60
21	**Jacob Wigle**	2.00
22	**C. Philips** Desk	2.20

    No further business Board Adj. Sine Die.
        H. J. McCutcheon

    Office of the Board of Education of the Independent School District of Belington West Virginia.
    At a meeting of the Board held on the **14th day of November 1898.** Present **F. Howes** President **R. A. McCutcheon** and **Cicero Philips** members.
    On motion of **R. A. McCutcheon** it is ordered that the Board of Education of the Independent School District take Legal steps to the issuing of Bonds and placing them on the docket for the purpose of building a School House in the Independent School District of Belington Barbour County, West Virginia.
    Board adjourned Sine Die.
        H. K. McCutcheon Secretary

Nov. 14 Order #102   **E. T. Cade**   2.50

    Office of the Board of Education of the Independent School District of Belington, Barbour County.
    At a meeting of the Board held on the **25 day of November 1898.** Present **Cicero Philips** and **R. A. McCutcheon** members. (Note in margin of minute book: Called meeting by Prest. who excused himself on acct headache & was absent. **R. A. McCutcheon**)
    On motion the following orders were allowed

On Teachers Fund

49	W. E. Tomblyn	45.00
50	Jennie Howes	30.00
51	Jacob Wigle	40.00

On Building Fund

23	John A. Robinson	1.25
24	R. A. McCutcheon	8.00
25	R. A. McCutcheon	2.00
26	Jacob Wigle	2.00
27	R. W. Dunham	2.00

On motion of **R. A. McCutcheon** it was ordered that the Board of Education of Belington Independent School District contract with a printer to print Fifty blank Bonds taking the Philippi School Bonds as a sample. That the Bonds be sold to the higher bidder with the interest not to exceed six per cent per annum or at lower rates if possible and place the sum realized from the sale of said School Bonds in the Tygarts Valley Bank of Philippi, West Virginia to the credit of the Building Fund of the Belington Independent School District of Belington W. Va. subject to the order of the Board of Education of the school district aforesaid.

That the Board of Education aforesaid is hereby authorized to employ a good architect to draw plans and specifications for a Public Brick School house to be built in Belington, taking as a model the Philippi public Brick School house with some variations and that the Board of Education pay the expenses incurred. The Clerk of Board to correspond with printer and architect and report.

That we ascertain what a lot large enough for school purposes say ½ to 3/4 of an acre will cost near the Luzerne Hotel.

Also to see what the land say, 3/4ths of an acre can be secured adjoining the lot up on which the old school house now stands and if Serpell will give Forty to Fifty feet Street back of said School lot or a continuation of Howard Street.

Cicero Phillips President Pro tem
Howard K. McCutcheon Secretary

Office of the Board of Education of the Independent School District of Belington, Barbour County, West Virginia.

School Board Minutes

At a meeting of the Board held on the **16th day of December 1898.** Present **F. Howes** President **Cicero Phillips** and **R. A. McCutcheon** members.

On motion of **R. A. McCutcheon, Melville Peck** was appointed counsel for the Belington Independent School District from this date until the 30th of June 1899.

On motion of **R. A. McCutcheon** is ordered that the Bonds be issued and sold as soon as needed.

On motion Board adjourned, Sine Die.
    H. K. McCutcheon Secty

Office of the Board of Education of the Independent School District of Belington, Barbour County, West Virginia.

At a meeting of the Board held on the **19th day of December 1898.** Present **Cicero Phillips** and **R. A. McCutcheon** members. **Cicero Phillips** Acting President.

On motion of **R. A. McCutcheon** the deeds of **T. T. Elliott** and **J. N. B. Crim** were accepted.

On motion the Board adjourned, Sine Die.
    Cicero Phillips Protem
    H. K. McCutcheon Secty

Office of the Board of Education of the Independent School District of Belington, Barbour County, West Virginia.

At a meeting of the Board held on the **December 24, 1898.** Present **F. Howes** President and **R. A. McCutcheon** member.

On motion the following orders were allowed
On Teachers Fund

52	**W. E. Tomblyn**	45.00
53	**Jacob Wigle** issued late	40.00
54 & 55	**Jennie Howes** last duplicate	30.00

Building Fund

28	R. E. McCutcheon	2.00
29	R. W. Dunham	2.00
30	Jacob Wigle	2.00
31	Maj. F. Howes	5.00
32	R. A. McCutcheon	8.00

Board adj. Sine Die.

H. K. McCutcheon Secty

Office of the Board of Education of the Independent School District of Belington, Barbour County, West Virginia.

At a meeting of the Board held on the **January 28th 1899.** Present **Cicero Phillips** and **R. A. McCutcheon** members. **R. A. McCutcheon** President Pro Tem.

On motion the following orders were allowed.

On Teachers Fund

56	W. E. Tomblyn	45.00
57	Jacob Wigle	40.00
58	Jennie Howes	30.00

On Building Fund

35	Sam. Holt	2.00
36	John Right	2.00
33	R. A. McCutcheon	8.00
34	R. E. McCutcheon	2.00
37	R. W. Dunham	2.00
38	Jacob Wigle	2.00
39	Brooks & Jackson	.60
40	F. Howes	5.00

For Books

9	Thompson Brown & Co.	2.80
10	J. B. Lippincott & Co.	4.80
11	American Book Co.	27.48
12	D. C. Heath & Co.	17.68
13	Eldridge & Co.	9.00
14	Ginn & Co.	17.86

15   E. H. Butler & Co.   6.90

 On motion of **Cicero Phillips** it was ordered that the Board of Education of Belington Ind. Dist. advertise in two papers for bids for the erection of a Brick School house after the plan of the Philippi Public school building with some necessary changes.

 On motion of **Cicero Phillips** the specifications of Washington City as far as they applied to the proposed Building, was accepted.

 On motion of **Cicero Phillips** nine Bonds were ordered made of Five Hundred Dollars each to be proposed by **M.Peck** and advertised. Interest to be at Six per cent.

    R. A. McCutcheon Pres Pro Tem
    H. K. McCutcheon Secy

 Office of the Board of Education of the Independent School District of Belington, Barbour County, West Virginia.

 At a meeting of the Board held on the **February 11, 1899.** Present **Cicero Phillips** and **R. A. McCutcheon** members.

 Minutes of last meeting were read and approved.

 On motion it was ordered that the sale of Bonds be advertised in two papers for Four weeks as follows. Viz:

    Bond Sale

 Sealed Bids will be received by the Secretary of the Board of Education of the Independent School District of Belington at the Office of the Secretary in the principals room in Belington, Barbour County, West Virginia, from this date until 12 o'clock on the Twenty first day of March 1899 for one or more of the nine Bonds of $500.00 each to be issued by said Board to erect a public school Building in said town. Bonds in coupon form, to be six percent per annum, payable annually and the bonds themselves to be payable after four years and within twenty years. The favorable bids for district will be accepted, yet all may be rejected. Bonds to be dated and issued as the money is needed, but none later than May 15, 1899.

 Board of Education by
   President
    H. K. McCutcheon Secretary
    Feb. 11, 1899

Sealed bids will be received from 17th of February 1899 to March 21st for one or more of Nine Bonds of $500.00 each.

On motion the claims of the Philippi Republican $4.78 and Belington Independent $2.28 advertising were allowed.

On motion the Board adjourned Sine Die.

    Robt. A. McCutcheon President Pro tempore
    H. K. McCutcheon Sec'y

Office of the Board of Education of the Independent School District of Belington, Barbour County, W.Va.

At a meeting of the Board held **March the 2nd 1899** Present **Cicero Phillips** and **R. A. McCutcheon** members, and **F. Howes** the President. The following business was transacted. Viz:

The following orders were audited and allowed

Out of Teachers fund

Mrs. **Virginia Howes**	30.00
Jacob Wigel	40.00
W. E. Tomblyn	45.00

On the Building Fund, the following orders were ordered. Viz:

Jacob Wigel	2.00
Robert Dunham	2.00
R. Emmett McCutcheon	2.00
L. B. Lovett & Bro	1.80
R. A. McCutcheon for room rent	8.00
R. A. McCutcheon for one Seal	2.50
F. Howes for rent	5.00
E. Ware & Son	1.54

On motion of **R. A. McCutcheon** duly seconded, the Board of Education of the aforesaid District of Belington, agree to stop all proceedings in regard to letting contract of school house building until the injunction case before the circuit court is settled in regard to said building.

On motion of **R. A. McCutcheon** one Seal, with the words "Created by an act of the Legislature February the 25th 1893, Barbour County, West Virginia" was adopted." Cost $2.50

On motion, adjourned Sine Die.

344 School Board Minutes

R. A. McCutcheon, Secy pro tem

At a meeting of the Board held **March 21st 1899**. Members being all duly notified. **R. A. McCutcheon** acting President.

On motion of **Cicero Phillips**, the following orders were allowed on Building Fund.

51   Philippi Republican   Printing Bond Sale $4.59
52   Belington Independent Printing Bond Sale $4.59

On motion of **Cicero Phillips** it was ordered that Judge **W. T. Ice** be retained by the Board of Education as assistant counsel in the Injunction case of **F. P. Rease** against the Board of Education of the Independent School District of Belington and that he be allowed a fee of Forty Dollars and expenses for his services to be reduced in proportion as **Melville Peck** will be able to aid in the services of making the defense of the Board in said cause.

On motion of **Cicero Phillips** it was ordered that the Board now proceed to open and consider the sealed Bids made for the Bonds of the Board pursuant to notice duly published and posted and that two sealed bids had been made Viz: The First National Bank of Grafton by **L. Mallone** Vice President, bid the sum of Forty Six hundred and thirty five Dollars, for all of the Nine Bonds to be issued, or 103 for any of said Bonds and that Serpell Bros. Per **Geo. M. Serpell** bid for said Bonds nine in number the sum of Forty six hundred and Eighty Dollars which bids are in writing and filed with the Secretary of the Board. The **Serpell** bid being for the Delivery of the Bonds after April 1st 1899. Upon consideration whereof it is ordered by the Board that the Bid of **Serpell** Bros. for the nine Bonds be accepted to be delivered between April 1st and June 15th, 1899 the said **Serpell** Bros to have ten days notice of the time when any of the said Bonds are to be cashed.

On motion of **Cicero Phillips** it was ordered that if enumeration of the school children of the Independent School District, is not in before the 25th of March some suitable person be hired to take it.

No further business before the Board, on motion the Board adjourned Sine Die.

R. A. McCutcheon President, Pro Tem

H. K. McCutcheon Secretary

Office of the Board of Education of the Independent School District of Belington, Barbour County, West Virginia.
At a meeting of the Board held **April 29, 1899.** Present **F. Howes,** President **C. Phillips** and **R. A. McCutcheon** members.
On motion the following orders were allowed on Building Fund

Geo. M. Serpell	2.70
R. A. McCutcheon	3.70
Cicero Phillips	2.70
Geo. M. Kittle Taking Depositions	10.85
S. A. Moore (Gran. E. Taft)	1.25

On motion it was ordered that Bill of **W. T. Ice** be tabled until next meeting.

R. A. McCutcheon	2.25
C. Phillips	2.25

On motion the Board adjourned Sine Die.
H. K. McCutcheon, Sec.

Office of the Board of Education of the Independent School District of Belington, Barbour County, West Virginia.
At a meeting of the Board held **Saturday May 6, 1899.** Present **F. Howes,** President, **Cicero Phillips** and **R. A. McCutcheon** members.
On motion of **R. A. McCutcheon** plans and specifications No. One with amendments to be added if needed, were accepted.
On motion of **R. A. McCutcheon** it was ordered that **Geo. M. Kittle** be employed to revise the plans and specifications.
On motion of **R. A. McCutcheon** it was ordered that sealed bids for the erection of a Brick School House to be built in the Independent School District of Belington, W. Va. be received up until noon Thursday, May 18th 1899.
On motion it was ordered that the Secretary notify all the

parties that have made bids of the date set.
On motion the Board adjourned Sine Die.

Office of the Board of Education of the Independent School District of Belington, Barbour County, West Virginia.

At a meeting of the Board held on **Wednesday, May 17, 1899.** Present **F. Howes,** President **R. A. McCutcheon** and **Cicero Phillips** members.

On motion it was ordered that the action of the Board of Ed. of May 6th so far as it related to the accepting of plans and specifications known as Plans and Specifications #1 be and is hereby rescinded and in place of it we do now receive and accept Plans and Specifications #4 known as the Shackleford plan and specifications heretofore - and that the services of **Geo. Kittle** as voted in minutes of meeting of Board of May 6th be now dispensed with.

Board adjourned to meet Thursday, May 18th 1899 at 1 P.M.
Fenelon Howes Pres
H. K. McCutcheon Secretary

Office of the Board of Education of the Independent School District of Belington, Barbour County, West Virginia.

At a meeting of the Board held on **Thursday, May 18th, 1899** at One oclock P.M. Present **F. Howes,** President, **R. A. McCutcheon** and **Cicero Phillips** members.

Minutes of last meeting were read and approved.

On motion of **R. A. McCutcheon** it was ordered that the Secretary open and read the sealed bids made for the construction of Brick School House, pursuant to notice duly published and posted and it appearing that Three sealed bids had been made. Viz:

Charles L. Hickman of Clarksburg   Bid $3785.00
Samuel L. Holt of Philippi   Bid $3749.41
Shackleford & Son of Grafton   Bid $4114.00

On motion it was ordered that **Sam. T. H. Holt**'s bid be accepted.

It was ordered that payments be made to the contractor as follows:
$100.00 when excavation is completed
$300.00 when foundation is completed
$300.00 when brick work if commenced
$400.00 when first story is complete
$500.00 when Brick work is complete
$700.00 when slate roof is on
$500.00 when plastering is completed

The residue $949.41 to be paid when keys to the building are turned over to the Board of Education.

The building to be completed by November 1st 1899.

On motion of **Cicero Phillips** it was ordered that the Bond to be given by **Holt** be One Thousand Dollars ($1000) & Mrs. **S. Holt** accepted as security.

On motion Board adjourned Sine Die.

Howard K. McCutcheon, Secretary

Office of the Board of Education of the Independent School District of Belington, Barbour County, West Virginia.

At a meeting of the Board held **Tuesday, June 13th, 1899.** Present **F. Howes,** President **R. A. McCutcheon** and **Cicero Phillips** members.

Minutes of last meeting read and approved with exception of clause relating to Bond as given by **S. T. H. Holt** of $1000.00 which is hereby made $7500.00

Bond of **S. T. H. Holt** with Mrs. **S. T. H. Holt** and **Alston P. Dayton** sureties accepted.

On motion of **Cicero Phillips** it was ordered that the Building Committee be appointed **W. S. Shurtleff, H. C. Rosenberger** and **J. M. Taylor** are appointed as Building Committee. **F. Howes** President of Board protested against **W. S. Shurtleff, H. C. Rosenberger** and **J. M. Taylor** as Building Committee as named in article of agreement.

On motion of **C. Phillips** it was ordered that the Secretary of the Board of Education, Belington Independent, School Dist. inform **M. Peck** the Board's attorney to bring suit against **F. P. Rease** and his sureties for $1000.00 damages sustained in injunction Suit of **F. P. Rease** vs. Board of Education.

On motion of **R. A. McCutcheon** it was ordered that the claim of Attny **W. T. Ice** which was tabled at meeting of Board April 29th 1899. On motion of **C. Phillips** it was again tabled.

On motion Board adjourned Sine Die.

Howard K. McCutcheon Sec'ty

Office of the Board of Education of the Independent School District of Belington, Barbour County, West Virginia.

At a meeting of the Board held **Thursday June 15, 1899.** Present **F. Howes** President, **R. A. McCutcheon** and **Cicero Phillips** members.

Minutes of last meeting read and approved excepting clause in which Pres. **F. Howes** protests against Building Committee.

On motion of **Cicero Phillips** it is ordered that two Bonds of Five Hundred Dollars ($500.00) each to be issued today and drawing interest from today, and two Bonds of Five Hundred dollars ($500.00) each be issued July 1st 1899 drawing interest from July 1st 1899. **Serpell** Bros. to have Ten Days notice of any issue of Bonds after July 1st 1899.

The money delivered from the sale of these Bonds to be deposited in the First National Bank of Grafton West Virginia, subject to the order of the Board of Education of the Independent School District of Belington, Barbour County, West Virginia.

President **Howes** leaving before adjournment, **Cicero Phillips** acted President.

On motion Bill of Atty **M. Peck** for services rendered and expenses incurred in injunction suit as per Bill rendered $40.65 was allowed.

Bill of **H. K. McCutcheon** Secty, for Stamps and Stamped Envelopes used for Bond $1.50 allowed.

Balance of the Bonds to be issued as needed by the Board of Education, **Serpell** Bros to have Ten days notice before the issuing of the same.

H. K. McCutcheon Secty

Office of the Board of Education of the Independent School District of Belington, Barbour County, West Virginia.

At a meeting of the Board held **Wednesday, June 28th, 1899.** Present **F. Howes,** President, **R. A. McCutcheon** and **Cicero Phillips** members.

Minutes of last meeting were read and approved.

On motion of **R. A. McCutcheon** the claim of Judge **W. T. Ice** was taken from the table and on motion, allowed.

Order   **W. T. Ice** Fee $48.25

On motion of **R. A. McCutcheon** a check was ordered drawn on the First National Bank of Grafton, West Virginia for $100.00 in favor of **T. T. Elliott** for School house lot, after which Board settled with Sheriff account of settlement.

    H. K. McCutcheon Secretary

B. B. Rhorabough S. B. C. in account with Teachers Fund of the Belington Independent School District, Belington, West Virginia for the year ending June 30th 1899.

Balance due Dist. from last year $86.79
Assessed val. of Pers. Property E. Side $15035.00
Assessed val. of Pers. Property W. Side $3475.00
Assessed val. of Real Estate E. Side $36313.00
Assessed val. of Real Estate W. Side $13682.00
R. R. Tax B&O, G&B Div, W. Va. Central, Roaring Ck & Belington
Total charges on Teachers Fund $740.45

B. B. Rhorbough S. B. C. in account with Teachers Fund of Belington Independent School District of Belington, West Virginia for the year ending June 30th 1899.

Order No.		Amount
46	W. E. Tomblyn	45.00
47	Jacob Wigle	40.00
48	Jennie Howes	30.00
49	W. E. Tomblyn	45.00
50	Jennie Howes	30.00
51	Jacob Wigle	40.00
52	W. E. Tomblyn	45.00
53	Jacob Wigle	40.00
54-55	Jennie Howes	30.00

350 School Board Minutes

56	W. E. Tomblyn	45.00
57	Jacob Wigle	40.00
58	Jennie Howes	30.00
59	Jennie Howes	30.00
60	Jacob Wigle	40.00
61	W. E. Tomblyn	45.00

Delinquent list on Teachers Fund $2.64
Releases 10.90
Commission on R. R. Tax 3.73
Commission on Pers. & Real Propert 12.52
Balance Due District $125.66

B. B. Rhorabough S. B. C. in account with Building Fund of the Belington Independent School District of Belington W. Virginia.

Assessed valuation of Personal property East Side $15035.00
Assessed valuation of Personal property West Side $3475.00
R. R. Tax, B&O, G&B Div., W Va Central, Roaring Creek, Belington
Amount due Dist from last year $158.85
Charges   619.31
Receipts from Sale of Books **P. L. Lovett**   39.98
Total Charges   659.29

B. B. Rhorabough in account with Building Fund of the Belington Independent School District of Belington West Virginia.

Order No.		Amount
100	E. T. Huffman	4.75
101	F. P. Rease	18.90
17	Robt Dunham	2.00
18	R. E. McCutcheon	2.00
19	R. A. McCutcheon	8.25
20	F. Howes	6.60
21	Jacob Wigle	2.00

22	E. Phillips	2.20
102	E. T. Cade	2.50
23	John A. Robinson	1.25
24	R. A. McCutcheon	8.00
25	R. E. McCutcheon	2.00
26	Jacob Wigle	2.00
27	R. W. Dunham	2.00
28	R. E. McCutcheon	2.00
29	R. W. Dunham	2.00
30	Jacob Wigle	2.00
31	F. Howes	5.00
32	R. A. McCutcheon	8.00
33	R. A. McCutcheon	8.00
34	R. E. McCutcheon	2.00
35	Sam Holt	4.00
36	John Right	2.00
37	R. W. Dunham	2.00
38	Jacob Wigle	2.00
39	Brooks & Jackson	.60
40	F. Howes	5.00
9	Thompson Brown & Co.	2.80
10	J. B. Lippincott & Co.	4.80
11	American Book Co.	27.48
12	D. C. Heath	17.68
13	Elridge & Co.	9.00
14	Ginn & Co.	17.86
15	E. H. Butler & Co.	6.90
16	R. W. Dunham	2.00
17	R. E. McCutcheon	2.00
18	Jacob Wigel	2.00
20	R. A. McCutcheon	8.00
21	R. A. McCutcheon	2.50
49	L. B. Lovett & Bro.	1.80
	F. Howes	5.00
50	E. Ware and Son	1.54
51	Philippi Republican	4.59
52	Belington Independent	4.59
	Geo. M. Serpell	2.70
54	R. A. McCutcheon	3.70

352 School Board Minutes

57	Cicero Phillips	2.70
56	Geo. M. Kittle	10.85
	S. A. Moore	1.25
58	R. A. McCutcheon	2.25
59	C. Phillips	2.25
61	H. K. McCutcheon	1.50
	W. T. Ice	48.25
97	L. B. Lovett & Bro.	.85
1	R. A. McCutcheon	9.00
98	H.K. McCutcheon	10.00
3	C. Phillips	9.00
2	F. Howes	9.00
1	H. K. McCutcheon	15.00
41	Republican	4.78
42	Independent	2.28
	F. Howes	5.00
60	M. Peck	40.65
Orders not presented		13.35
Delinquent list		12.64
Releases		10.90
Com. on $250.47 @ 5%		12.52
Com. on R. R. Tax		3.73
Total charges		$437.04
Total amt. due District on Building Fund		$222.25
	F. Howes	

Office of the Board of Education of the Independent School District of Belington.

At a meeting of the board held on **July 3, 1899** at 1 o'clock P.M. Present **F. Howes** president **S. L. Brooks** and **Cicero Phillips** members.

Blackburn Ware was elected by the board as their secretary.

Minutes of previous meeting were read and adopted.

The levies for the fiscal year beginning July 1st '99 were laid. Levy for building fund at 40 cents on the $100.00 valuation of property. Levy for teachers fund at 45 cents on the $100.00 valuation of property.

It was agreed by the Board that four teachers be employed for the ensuing winter and the term of school be fixed at 5 months.

It was moved and seconded and duly carried that the selecting of the teachers and fixing their salaries be deferred till the next meeting.

It was moved and seconded and duly carried that the suit now pending before **W. G. Keys** a Justice for Barbour County in which the Board of Education of the Independent School District of Belington is plaintiff and **F. P. Rease** &c defendants be withdrawn and dismissed by said Board and it is hereby ordered that a copy of this order be furnished **M. Peck**, the attorney heretofore appointed by said Board and one to **C. M. Murphy** prosecuting attorney for Barbour County and they and each of them be and are hereby directed and ordered to withdraw said action or have same dismissed on motion of plaintiff.

It appearing from the records of the meetings of said Board that at a meeting of said Board held on June 13, 1899 that the bond of **S. T. H. Holt** principal and Mrs. **S. T. H. Holt** and **A. G. Dayton** sureties with his contract annexed was accepted and approved, and that said agreement on which said bond was given contained the names of **W. S. Shurtleff, H. C. Rosenberger** and **J. M. Taylor** as building committee and the board desiring to rescind and annul so much of said order of June 13th as relates to the appointment of retaining of said **W. S. Shurtleff, H. C. Rosenberger** and **J. M. Taylor** as such building committee, and to correct said agreement and said board by striking out the above named committee and inserting in their stead the names of **F. P. Rease, John Right** and **James E. Forney** who are hereby appointed the building committee for said board and **S. T. H. Holt.** Holt principal in said bond and party to said agreement being present in person and Mrs. **S. T. H. Holt** and **A. G. Dayton** being present by agent and all parties consenting to the changes aforesaid, it was therefore moved and seconded and duly carried that the aforesaid order be and the same is hereby rescinded as aforesaid that **F. P. Rease, John Right** and **James E. Forney** be and the same are hereby appointed a building committee for said board and that with the consent of said board and the assent of **S. T. H. Holt** principal and Mrs. **S. T. H. Holt** and **A. G. Dayton** sureties the said agreement and the said bond be and the same are hereby corrected as aforesaid and that said agreement and said bond be and the same are hereby accepted by said board and approved as corrected.

S. T. H. Holt the contractor for the building of the school

354 School Board Minutes

house in said Ind. District being present gave his consent to the said board allowing them to change the location of said school house, to any the said board might select, reserving the right however to be allowed any necessary expenses over and above which he would incur by building said house on the old school house lot and agreeing to make a reasonable reduction in case his work is made easier by building on some other lot.

H. K. McCutcheon was allowed an order for $10.00 for services as secretary of Board.

Board adjourned to meet at call of any members.

    F. Howes President
    J. Blackburn Ware Secretary

Office of the Board of Education of the Independent School District of Belington.

At a meeting of the board held on **July 8, 1899** at 2:30 P.M. of which meeting all members had notice according to law. Present **F. Howes** president, **S. L. Brooks** member.

Minutes of previous meeting were read and approved.

It was moved, seconded, and duly carried that the teachers salaries for the coming winter be fixed as follows:

Principal	$45.00 per month
1st Assistant	$38.00 per month
2nd Assistant	$33.00 per month
Primary	$33.00 per month

The board then proceeded to consider the applications for the school and after due consideration select the following as teachers for the ensuing year.

Principal	**M. S. Blair**
1st Assistant	**W. B. Shanabarger**
2nd Assistant	Miss **Lucy B. Wood**
Primary	Miss **Tillie R. C. Bernhardt**

On motion the board adjourned to meet at call of any member.

    F. Howes President
    J. Blackburn Ware Secretary

Office of the Board of Education of the Independent School District of Belington.

At a meeting of the board held on the **2nd day of September, 1899** at 5 o'clock P.M.

Present **F. Howes** president **S. L. Brooks** and **Cicero Phillips** members.

Minutes of previous meeting were read and adopted

On motion duly seconded and carried it was ordered that all orders heretofore made if any such were made, by said Board locating the new school house to be built in said district upon any particular lot be and the same are hereby rescinded and annulled and the said Board with the consent of **S. T. H. Holt** contractor, heretofore given and entered of record proceeding to locate said school house in the most healthy and desirable location, as will best accommodate all the inhabitants of said district, do the order by motion duly made and seconded and carried, that said house be and the same is hereby located on the west side of the Tygarts Valley river in said district on lots Nos 1, 2, 3, & 4 in section 3 of block 16 adjoining the 2 acre tract of land owned by **Fenelon Howes** and being near the residence of **William Hill** and being the same four lots donated by the T. V. M. & G. Co. to the Board of Education of said district for educational purposes. The deed making said conveyances is filed in this office and is hereby referred to and made a part of this record, and said Public school house to be built for said district upon said lots is to be built according to plans and specifications known as plans No. 4 heretofore adopted by said Board, and under the supervision of **F. P. Rease, John Right** and **James E. Forney** the Building Committee heretofore appointed by said Board and under and according to the contract heretofore made between said Board and said **Holt** which here with the consent of both parties is made applicable to said location as herein made.

On motion the Board adjourned.

    F. Howes President
   J. Blackburn Ware Secretary

Office of the Board of Education of the Independent School District of Belington.

At a meeting of the board held on the **7th day of Sept. 1899**

356   School Board Minutes

at 8 o'clock A.M. at the residence of **F. Howes**. Present **F. Howes** president **S. L. Brooks** and **Cicero Phillips** members.

Minutes of previous meeting were read and adopted.

The claims of **H.K. McCutcheon, R. A. McCutcheon** and **Cicero Phillips** as witnesses in case of Board against **F. P. Rease & S. L. Brooks** and the claim of **W. G. Keys**, Justice for costs in same, were presented and on motion made second and carried were tabled till the next meeting.

It was moved and seconded that **S. T. H. Holt** be paid $100.00 for making the excavation for the school building. **Cicero Phillips** demanded that the yeas and nays be spread upon the record and as the names of said members were called, the following vote was cast and on said question **S. L. Brooks** "Yea", **Cicero Phillips** "Nay", **F. Howes** "Yea" said motion is duly carried and so ordered.

The Board adjourned to meet at calling.
   F. Howes
    J. Blackburn Ware   Secretary

  Office of the Board of Education of the Independent School District of Belington.

At a meeting of the board held on the **11th day of September, 1899** at 10:30 A..M. Present **F. Howes** president **S. L. Brooks** and **Cicero Phillips** members.

Minutes of previous meeting were read and adopted.

On motion made and duly seconded and carried the following order was made: Process having been served upon the Board in an injunction awarded the plaintiff **James Coffman** suing on behalf of himself and other against the Board, it is ordered that proceedings as therein enjoined be stayed, and that this Board do make defense to said injunction by answer or such other judicial proceedings as may be proper and that **J. Hop Woods** and **A. G. Dayton** attorney at law be employed by the Board as assistants to **C. M. Murphy**, Prosecuting Attorney of this County as Counsel for the Board therein and that such reasonable fees and expenses be paid them therefore as shall hereafter be agreed and ordered.

The answer to the above named injunction prepared by the above named Attorneys was read before the Board and on motion made and duly seconded and carried it was adopted as the answer of said Board to said bill and **F. Howes** the President of said Board after making affidavit to said answer as required by law, was authorized to attach the seal of said Board upon said answer.

The Board on motion adjourned to meet at call of President.
Fenelon Howes Pres
J. Blackburn Ware Sect.

Office of the Board of Education of the Independent School District of Belington.

At a meeting held at the residence of **F. Howes,** president in said district, at 4:40 P.M. on **Oct. 9, 1899** of which all members had notice according to law. Present **F. Howes** president and **S. L. Brooks** member.

Minutes of previous meeting were read and approved.

On motion made and duly seconded and carried, it was ordered that **S. T. H. Holt** be paid $300.00 per contract for school house foundation.

On motion made and duly carried it was ordered that **F. Howes** be empowered to contract for the digging of a well on the school house lot on which the school house is being built.

On motion the Board adjourned.
Fenelon Howes Pres.
J. Blackburn Ware Sect.

Office of the Board of Education of the Independent School District of Belington.

At a meeting held at the residence of **F. Howes** on the **18th day of Oct. 1899** at 1 P.M. of which all members had notice according to law. Minutes approved. Present **F. Howes** president and **S. L. Brooks** member.

On motion made, seconded, and carried, it was ordered that

358 School Board Minutes

Mr. **Holt** be paid $300.00 the third payment under his contract.
 On motion made and duly carried, **R. A. McCutcheon** was allowed $230. **H. K. Mcutcheon** $230. **Cicero Phillips** $230. witness fee in suit of Board v. **F. P. Rease** &c and $225. costs in same to **W. G. Keys** J. P.
 On motion made, duly carried **S. D. Robinson** was allowed an order for $13.30 for tiling for well on school house lot.
 On motion Board adjourned.
  F. Howes Pres.
   J. Blackburn Ware Sect.

 Office of the Board of Education of the Independent School District of Belington.
 At a meeting held on the **15th day of Nov. 1899** at 4 P.M. at the residence of **F. Howes**, of which all members had notice according to law. Present **F. Howes** president and **S. L. Brooks** member. Minutes were read and approved.
 On motion made and duly seconded and carried, it was ordered that **S. T. H. Holt** be paid $400.00 the fourth payment under his contract.
 On motion made, seconded and carried **E. T. Cade** was allowed an order of $5.70 for work done fixing school house.
 On motion made and seconded and duly carried, it was ordered that **T. T. Elliott** be paid $300.00 for payment in full of old school house lot.
 Board adjourned.
  J. Blackburn Ware Secretary

 Office of the Board of Education of the Independent School District of Belington.
 At a meeting held at the residence of **F. Howes on the 25th day of Nov. 1899** at 10 A.M. Present **F. Howes** and **S. L. Brooks** member.
 Minutes of previous meeting were read and approved.

On motion duly carried, **M. S. Blair** was allowed order for $45.00, **W. B. Shanabarger** $38.00, **Tillie R. C. Bernhardt** $33.00, **Lucy B. Wood** $33.00, wages for first months teaching. On motion **J. R. Cade** was allowed $2.00, **W. B. Huffman** $2.00, **Charles Hankey** $4.00 for building fires for first month.

On motion the Randolph and Barbour Supply Co. was allowed an order for $14.95 for school supplies.

On motion made seconded and carried, **A. G. Dayton** was allowed $50.00 counsel fee in case of **Coffman** vs. Board, same amount allowed to **J. Hop Woods** for counsel fees in same case.

On motion Board adjourned.
    F. Howes Pres.
    J. Blackburn Ware Secretary

Office of the Board of Education of the Independent School District of Belington.

At a meeting held on **December 4, 1899** at 1:00 P.M. at the residence of **F. Howes** of which all members had notice according to law. Present **F. Howes** president and **S. L. Brooks** member.

Minutes of previous meeting were read and approved.

On motion made and carried the remaining five bonds of $500.00 each were issued and delivered to **Geo. M. Serpell**, bearing interest from this date.

On motion **S. T. H. Holt** was allowed an order for $500.00 the fifth payment made under his contract.

On motion made and carried, **R. A. McCutcheon** was allowed an order for $8.00 for one months rent for school house, same order to **D. B. Hankey** for rent for **Hankey** Building for one month.

On motion Board adjourned.
    F. Howes Pres.
    J. Blackburn Ware Secretary

School Board Minutes

Office of the Board of Education of the Independent School District of Belington.

At a meeting held in said office on **Dec. 22, 1899** at 3:30 P.M. of which all members had notice according to law. Present **F. Howes** president and **S. L. Brooks** member.

Minutes of previous meeting were read and approved.

On motion made seconded and duly carried **S. T. H. Holt** was allowed an order for $700.00 the sixth payment under his contract.

Teachers allowed orders for second month of school. Order allowed to **D. B. Hankey** for $8.00 for rent. Order allowed to **R. A. McCutcheon** $8.00 for rent. Orders allowed to **J. B. Cade** $2.00, **W. B. Huffman** $2.00 and **Charles Hankey** $4.00 for building fires.

On motion made and duly carried it is ordered that **F. Howes**, President, be empowered to contract for seats for school house, and **S. L. Brooks** be authorized to insure the school building for $3000.00 and the furniture at $300.00

Board adjourned.
        F. Howes Pres.
        J. B. Ware Secretary

School Board Minutes

(Note: The minute book for The Independent School District of Belington also contained minutes for the first three board meetings of 1900)

Office of the Board of Education of the Ind. Dist.

At a meeting of the Board of Education of said district at the house of **F. Howes**, on the **8th day of January, 1900** of which all members had notice according to law. Present **F. Howes** president and **S. L. Brooks** member.

Minutes of previous meeting were read and approved.

On motion made and duly carried **John A. Robinson** was allowed $57.72 for spouting and gutter way on school house to be paid as follows: $14.50 to be paid by order on sheriff $43.32 to be paid by check on school bonds.

On motion an order was allowed to **P. P. Rease** for $260. for coal.

On motion the following orders were allowed for books purchased by board. To American Book Co. $14.12 to D. C. Heath &C $7.60 to **E. H. Butler** & Co. $8.40

S. L. Brooks was allowed an order of $33.00 to pay for insurance policy on school building.

On motion made and duly carried it was ordered that the president and secretary issue orders to teachers upon presentment of monthly summary and end of each month, without a meeting of the Board, also to issue orders for fire building and rent, at same time and without meeting of board.

On motion Board adjourned.

F. Howes Pres.

J. Blackburn Ware Secretary

Office of the Board of Education of the Independent School District of Belington.

At a meeting of said Board held in the office of **Maj. Howes** on the **27th day of Jan. 1900** of which all members had notice according to law. Present **F. Howes** president and **S. L. Brooks** member.

Minutes of previous meeting were read and approved.

Orders were issued to **Lucy B. Wood** and **Tillie R. C. Bernhardt** for 3rd month teaching.

Orders issued to **W. B. Huffman** for $2.00 and to **Charles Hankey** for $4.00 for building fires. Order of $8.00 issued to **D. B. Hankey** for 3rd months rent for house.

On motion made and duly carried a check was issued to **J. H. Ryland** for $44.24 for freight on school house furniture.

Board adjourned.

    F. Howes Pres.
      J. Blackburn Ware Secretary

Office of the Board of Education of the Independent School District of Belington.

At a meeting of said Board held in the office of **F. Howes** on the **21st day of February 1900**, of which all members had notice according to law. Present **F. Howes** president and **S. L. Brooks** member.

Minutes of previous meeting were read and approved.

On motion made and duly carried, that whereas **S. T. H. Holt** has completed the school house for said district according to his contract with said board and said Board having duly inspected the same and believing it to be a good workman like job, it is ordered that the same be and the same is hereby accepted by said Board, and the residue owing to said **Holt** paid. Amt. paid $1389.28 check for same having been issued Feb 14, 1900.

On motion made and duly carried it was ordered that a check be drawn on bond issue in favor of **Thomas Kane** & Co. for $248.76 for school house furniture.

On motion made and duly carried it was ordered that a check be drawn on bond issue in favor of Randolph and Barbour Supply Co. for $56.89 for stoves and sundries for school house.

On motion made and duly carried an order was allowed to **S. L. Brooks** of $9.72 for lumber furnished.

On motion made and duly carried an order was allowed **E. Ware** & Son for $14.85 for window blinds furnished for school house.

School Board Minutes 363

On motion made and duly carried **R. A. McCutcheon** was allowed an order for $4.00 for rent.

On motion made and duly carried the following orders were allowed:

To **J. R. Cade** $1.00 for building fires
To **Charles Hankey** $3.00 for building fires
To **D. B. Hankey** $6.00 for rent
To **W. B. Huffman** $2.00 for building fires
To **W. B. Shanabarger** $38.00 for 4 months teaching
To **Peter Reed** 80¢ for serving two summons in case of Board vs. **Brooks** &c.

F. Howes Pres.
J. Blackburn Ware Secretary

INDEX

A

Anderson, George, E. 265
Anderson, Jefferson 264
Anderson, Sarah E. 263
Anderson, T. J. 13
Andrews, A. H. 214, 220, 224, 230, 239
Arbogast, John 166, 175
Arbogast, Margaret 267
Arnett, Olive 242, 249

B

Baker (&Swick) 251
Baker, C. O. 228
Baker, E. O. 170, 231
Baker, J. M. 17, 25, 27, 28, 46
Baker, John M. 84
Baker, John W. 61
Baker, R. M. 88, 96, 97
Baker, W. B. 213, 217, 219, 221, 223, 228, 229, 230, 231
Baker, W. W. 219
Ball, J. D. 200
Ball, John D. 11, 233, 277
Barte, H. 191, 194, 195, 197, 201, 202, 203, 215, 216, 218, 223, 226, 227
Barte, Henry 85, 115, 117, 121, 125, 127, 128, 133, 135, 138, 146, 147, 189, 191, 192, 193, 199, 201, 203, 205, 208, 211, 212, 214, 222, 225
Bartee 152
Bartee,H. 152, 153, 163, 164, 165, 167, 168, 200, 202
Bartee Henry 129, 141, 143, 144, 145, 146, 151, 155, 156, 158, 159, 167, 168, 190, 200, 233
Bartlet, Joshaway 231
Bartlett, A. G. 193, 194, 195, 196, 197, 198, 199
Bartlett, J. W. 188, 217
Bartlett, Josh 217
Bartlett, Joshua 116, 216, 221, 228, 247, 258
Bartlett, T. N. 275

Bartlett, Thomas 91
Bartlett, Thomas N. 262
Barty, H. 229
Baughman, G. W. 133, 134, 139, 141, 144, 147, 148, 149, 150
Baughman, Geo. W. 148
Bennett, E. T. 142, 149, 258
Bennett, Elam T. 247
Bennett, F. B. 127
Bennett, J. 266
Bennett, James M. 265
Bennett, Jethro 40, 194, 198, 211, 213, 241, 269
Bennett, L. C. 53, 55, 133, 136, 139, 141, 145, 147, 148, 149, 152, 153, 154, 155, 156, 159, 160, 162
Bennett, Laben 246
Bennett, Luther C. 161
Bennett, R. M. 178, 247, 252, 258
Bennett, S. C. 157
Berlin 114
Berlin, F. 114
Bernhardt, Tillie R. C. 354, 359, 362
Bibey, J. N. 217, 221
Bibey, W. M. 182, 187, 189
Bibey, William 173, 223
Bibey, William M. 171
Bibey, Wm. M. 176, 177, 178
Bible, W. M. 132
Biby, W. M. 85, 98, 116, 180, 182, 183, 185, 186, 206, 258
Biby, William M. 179
Biby, Wm. 259
Biby, Wm. M. 85, 210
Blake, C. M. 205, 206, 207, 209, 210
Blake, C. W. 209
Blake, Herod W. 261
Blair, M. S. 354, 359
Boalton, Richard 276
Bodkin, Patrick 263
Bolton, Richard M. 121
Bolton, W. M. T. 185
Bolton, Wm. 105, 241
Boner, Caroline 271
Bonner, J. N. 89

Bonner, S. S. 176
Bonner, Sampson S. 51
Booth 85
Booth, Fred 35
Booth, Frederick 270
Booth, George 233
Booth, George M. 252
Booth, Harriet 268
Booth, J. G. 175
Booth, J. Y. 86, 108, 124, 132, 166
Booth, James 10, 91, 262, 275
Booth, John 45, 57, 186, 189, 199, 207, 210, 243
Booth, Richard 263
Boothe, Mary 243
Boothe, Nelson 243
Bosley, Wm. H. 61
Bowman, L. C. 53
Bowman, Thomas W. 29
Brislow, R. C. 333, 334
Bristow, R. C. 326, 329
Brooks 363
Brooks (& Jackson) 341, 351
Brooks, S. L. 352, 354, 355, 356, 357, 358, 359, 360, 361, 362
Browning, James 149
Buckey, E. 103, 117, 119, 120, 123, 130, 131, 132, 168, 175
Buckey, W. 258
Buckey, Wirl 242
Buckey, Wirt 244, 251
Burdett, B. F. 177, 181
Burk, C. W. 328, 333
Butler, E. H. 316, 351, 361
Byrd, Wm. E. 231
Byrd, Wm. E. (Dr.) 72, 226

C

C, William 256
Cade, E. T. 176, 186, 205, 206, 210, 306, 310, 333, 338, 351, 358
Cade, Elam T. 329
Cade, Guy 252
Cade, J. B. 360

368 School Board Minutes

Cade, J. M. 204, 210
Cade, J. R. 359, 363
Cade, Jno. M. 220
Cade, John 116, 128, 231, 240
Cade, John M. 215, 227
Cade, Solomon 266
Cade, Warren 292, 293, 298
Cade, William 268
Cade, Wm. 95
Campbell, L. H. 215, 220
Canfield, David 227, 231
Carpenter, Conrad 265
Carpenter, Daniel 265
Carter, C. B. 40, 116, 121, 152, 161, 172, 184, 202, 223, 225, 227, 231
Carter, J. R. 134, 150
Cassana, Joseph 271
Cauley, Hayes 241
Cauley, Hazel 257
Cauley, J. M. 98, 128
Cauley, John 213
Cauley, John M. 187
Cauley, Lewis 241
Champ, Hiram 265
Champ, Martin 275
Champ, Nimrod 52, 54, 262, 275
Champ, Thomas 80
Chenoweth, Daniel 233, 234, 239
Chenoweth, E. G. 253, 257
Chenoweth, Emmett G. 255, 257
Chenoweth, J. D. 251
Chenoweth, Newton 177, 272
Chineworth, J. D. 86
Chineworth, Newton 276
Chinworth, John 80
Chinworth, Newton 58
Coberley, James 197, 198, 199
Coberley, R. 199
Coberly, Arch 243, 250
Coberly, Haymond 35
Coberly, James 142, 149, 181, 188, 193, 194, 196

Coberly, Jas. 185, 187
Coberly, Randolph 11, 38, 57, 100, 111, 119, 128, 132, 170, 175, 177, 184, 189, 272, 276
Coberly, William 262, 275
Coffman 359
Coffman, Israel 268
Coffman, James 103, 104, 107, 111, 152, 153, 154, 155, 156, 158, 165, 173, 174, 175, 185, 187, 188, 194, 195, 196, 197, 198, 199, 205, 206, 207, 209, 210, 213, 216, 218, 219, 220, 221, 233, 237, 238, 239, 244, 249, 252, 356
Coffman, Jas. 159, 160, 161, 162, 164, 168, 169, 187
Coffman, Samuel 24, 47
Coffman, Solomon 10, 76, 109, 171, 173, 176, 177, 178, 179, 180, 182, 183, 185, 186, 187, 189, 267
Comer, N. E. 243
Conberley, Randolph 172
Conner, Michael 263
Coonts, A. A. 275
Coonts, Adam 47, 67, 116, 117, 270
Coonts, H. H. 262
Coonts, Henry 270
Coonts, Isaac 55, 228, 240
Coonts, Jackson 237, 239
Coonts, James 189
Coonts, Lair D. 270
Coonts, S. D. 200
Coonts, Samuel 252, 259
Coonts, Samuel D. 223, 233
Coonts, W. R. 196, 199, 211, 251, 258
Coontz, Adam 34, 39
Corder, A. D. 75
Corder, A. T. 78, 80
Corder, W. W. 83
Corley, A. W. 46
Corley, Archibald W. 44
Corley, C. 177, 179
Corley, Cornelius 92, 164, 165
Corley, E. 176
Corley, G. C. 56, 263
Corley, G. W. 47, 180
Corley, George W. 25

Corley, Hayes 225
Corley, Hezakiat 96
Corley, J. M. 154, 161, 189
Corley, J. W. 178, 199
Corley, James 267
Corley, John 179, 183, 267
Corley, John M. 11, 13, 27, 272, 276
Corley, L. W. 140, 161
Corley, Lewis 116, 213
Corley, S. W. 189
Corley, T. J. 245, 251
Corley, William 119, 131
Corrick, Layfayette 239
Corrick, M. V. L. 234
Crim, J. N. B. 340
Crislip, W. A. 47
Crislip, Wm. A. 44
Crites, H. 293, 298
Cross, B. 269
Cross, Barton 228, 231, 269
Cross, C. 269
Cross, E. P. 103, 104, 108, 111, 123, 126, 131, 132
Cross, J. R. 165
Cross, J. R. W. 310
Cross, John 269
Cross, John R. W. 304
Cross, Laben 207, 210
Cross, Levi 10, 14, 40, 46, 57, 67, 85, 86, 189, 190, 191, 192, 193, 194, 195, 197, 199, 200, 201, 202, 203, 210, 211, 269
Cross, S. S. 151
Cross, Salathiel 224, 231
Cross, Simpson 172, 183, 200, 269
Cross, William 65, 66, 150, 168, 172, 179, 185, 192, 198, 223, 269
Cross, Wm. 99, 116, 127, 128, 175, 183
Currance, Geo. W. 217
Currence, George 243
Currents, George 200

D
Dadisman, Flora 206, 208, 209

Daniels, Elmore 274
Daugherty, Geo. 276
Daugherty, George 272
Daugherty, Malisa A. 135
Daugherty, Martin B. 135
David, Lee 315
Davis, Lee 316, 321, 324
Davis, Lemon 294, 295, 296, 298
Davis, Lloyd 11, 18, 29, 34, 36, 43, 48, 119, 274, 277
Davis, Mary 276
Davis, O. C. 304, 307, 310
Davis, Rezin 254, 257
Davis, Slage 131
Davis W. S. 170, 246, 251, 253, 257, 259
Day, Aaron 44, 48
Day, D. W. 251, 310, 311
Day, Daniel 175, 233, 234, 239, 241
Day, Daniel W. 252
Day, Dan'l 167
Day, William 154, 161, 167, 175, 261
Day, Wm. 17
Dayton, A. G. 353, 356, 359
Dayton, Alston P. 347
Delauder, J. 269
Delauder, Jacob 270
Denton, Lorenzo 109, 214
Derrett, B. B. 35
Derrett, John 21
Digman, A. 277
Digman, Absalom 273
Digman, George 11, 73
Digman, S. G. 277
Douglas 313
Douglas, Calora L.. 256, 257
Douglas, Josiah 262
Douglass, Bertha 314, 315, 316, 317, 318, 319, 322, 323
Douglass, Calora L. 256
Drummond, R. A. 157
Drummond, R. J. 152, 153, 154, 155, 156, 159, 160, 162, 164, 166, 168, 170, 173, 174, 175
Drummond, W. J. 13, 15

Drummond, Wm. J. 16
Dunham, Cora 234, 237, 238, 239, 242, 251
Dunham, Cora E. 247, 249, 250
Dunham, J. A. 37, 47, 50, 53, 74, 78, 81, 93, 96, 97, 98, 105, 107, 110, 112, 113, 177, 180, 181, 185, 186, 187, 196, 198, 199, 206, 207, 209, 210, 216, 219, 220, 223, 228, 229, 230, 231
Dunham, Jacob A. 61, 92
Dunham, John 85, 171, 183
Dunham, John C. 242
Dunham, R. Jona 161, 170
Dunham, R. W. 328, 330, 333, 334, 339, 341, 351
Dunham, Robb 316, 318, 320, 338
Dunham, Robert 85, 343
Dunham, Robt. 317, 320, 323, 324, 326, 328, 333, 350
Dunham, Robt. W. 331
Durrett, B. B. 103, 109, 259, 263
Durrett, F. B. 55, 72, 75, 78, 81, 87, 90, 95, 96, 102, 106, 108, 112, 122, 125, 130, 135, 138, 142, 145, 147, 148, 149, 150, 151, 152, 154, 156, 158, 162, 164, 165, 167, 168, 170, 172, 176, 241, 254, 171, 184, 199, 252, 253, 285
Durrett, G. B. 129
Durrett, J. B. 153
Durrett, J. H. 151, 152, 153, 155, 163, 165, 167, 168, 169, 175
Durrett, John H. 156, 158, 159
Durrett, R. B. 195

E

Edman, Matthew 35, 263
Edmond, M. 275
Edmond, Matthew 10
Edmonds, M. 64, 115
Edmund, M. 67
Eichler, Charles 264, 265
Elbon, Joseph 115, 128
Elliott 211
Elliott, A. H. 48
Elliott, D. F. 66
Elliott, F. T. 115

Elliott, Guy 246, 251
Elliott, T. T. 151, 193, 201, 203, 205, 208, 210, 211, 212, 214, 215, 216, 218, 219, 220, 222, 223, 224, 225, 226, 227, 228, 229, 232, 236, 240, 241, 242, 244, 250, 258, 260, 297, 301, 302, 340, 349, 358
Elliott, William 268
England, Albert 50, 154, 161, 184, 270
England, B. 277
England, Balas 273
England, David 270
England, Henry 273
England, J. 277
England, James 11, 40, 61, 77, 109, 189, 270
England, John 50
England, S. 273
England, William 131, 132, 140, 151, 154, 161, 207, 210, 221, 230, 235, 239, 270
England, Wm. 109, 217, 224, 247, 252
England, Wm. Jr. 120, 124
Everson, Eli 272, 276
Evrit, I. L. 79
Evrit, Ira L. 79
Evrit, J. L. 81

F

Findley, Columbus 223, 252
Findley, J. C. 257
Findley, John 166
Findley, P. B. 257
Fineral, Hugh 265
Finley, Ira 191
Finley, J. C. 191
Finley, John 172, 175, 177, 251, 272, 276
Fink, Hamilton 146, 161
Fisher, B. W. 135
Fisher, C. F. 232, 255
Fisher, C. T. 217, 221
Fisher, S. W. 253, 257
Fitzgerld, J. W. 49

Fitzwater, Levi   170, 175, 181, 270
Forney, James E.   353, 355
Fornish, G. V.   53
Foy, David   266
Funk, Hamilton   116

G

Gainer, S. C.   51
Gall, E. D.   200, 211
Gall, G. H.   243, 258
Ganer, J. C.   191
Ganer, Solomon   79
Ganer, Solomon C.   96
Gant, W. A.   93
Gaunt, J. A.   247
Gaunt, W. A.   74, 78, 80, 81, 88, 90, 91, 95, 105, 107, 108, 111, 113
Gaunt, William   266
Gawthrop (& Lake)   293, 298
George, Abraham   140
George, Abram   150
George, Elizabeth   275
George, J. W.   61
George, James W.   10, 14, 21, 22, 27, 29, 30, 81, 265
George, Jas. W.   38
George, R. G.   130
George, R. T.   115, 149, 153
George, R. Taylor   161
George, Rebecca   262
George, Simpson   116
George, Solomon   263
Gest, John   140
Ghost, Christian   80
Gibson, George   273
Glascock   214, 215, 218, 219, 220, 223
Godwin, G. B.   40, 140
Godwin, Granville   234
Godwin, J. A.   79
Godwin, J. B.   41, 42, 43, 45, 51, 52, 53, 54, 55, 56, 57, 58, 59, 61, 62, 64, 65, 66, 67, 68, 69, 70, 71, 72, 74, 75, 77, 78, 81, 82,

83, 84, 85, 86, 87, 89, 90, 91, 92, 93, 95. 97, 98, 99, 100, 101, 102, 103, 104, 106, 110, 113, 114, 115, 117, 118, 121, 124, 125, 127, 128, 129, 131, 132, 135, 138, 140, 141, 143, 144, 145, 146, 147, 149, 150, 151, 153, 161, 182, 189, 191, 192, 193, 194, 195, 197, 199, 200, 201, 202, 203, 204, 205, 208, 210, 211, 214, 220, 222, 227, 231, 259, 277
Godwin, J. M. 75, 81, 82, 85, 87, 88, 93, 95, 120, 121, 122, 124, 126, 127, 129, 131, 132, 133, 137, 141, 145, 148, 149, 152, 153, 155, 156, 159, 162, 173, 175
Godwin, Jacob B. 40, 51, 56, 67, 87, 101, 161
Godwin, John M. 72, 93, 130, 157, 158, 161
Godwin, R. M. 102, 234, 239
Godwin, W. G. 127, 149, 202, 216, 221
Good, J. M. 88, 103
Good, John M. 292, 293, 298
Gost, John 40, 150, 264
Greathouse, Roy 326
Gribble, V. N. 9
Gross, Joseph P. 76
Groves, C. M. 47, 266
Groves, Charles M. 19
Groves, Chas. M. 25

H

Hall, E. 84
Halls, Jas. 215
Hamilton, Nora 292, 294, 295, 296, 297, 300, 301, 302, 306, 307, 308, 309, 310
Hankey 329, 359
Hankey, Charles 359, 360, 362, 363
Hankey, D. B. 307, 311, 318, 320, 323, 328, 329, 331, 333, 334, 359, 360, 362, 363
Harper, J. W. 10, 266
Harper, John W. 35
Harris, A. C. 245
Harris, Alice 204, 205, 206, 207, 208, 209, 210, 220
Harris, H. C. 18, 250, 253, 258
Harris, Lewis 259
Harris, M. E. 119, 122, 125, 129, 164, 166, 168, 170, 173, 174, 194,

　　　　195, 196, 197, 198
Harris, Samuel   264
Harris, Solomon   142, 150, 266
Hart, Joseph   247
Hart, Joseph B.   251
Hart, M.   233, 259
Hart, Milton   115, 203
Hartman, A. J.   20, 25, 26, 46

Hartman, S. P.   153, 156, 159, 160, 162
Hartman, S. T.   152, 155
Harvey, (Dr.)   115
Hathaway, A. J.   122, 126, 129, 130, 149, 152, 156, 157, 162, 169,
　　　　174, 175
Hathaway, Andrew J.   163
Hathaway, F.   45, 56
Hathaway, Francis   10, 21, 22, 26, 27, 29, 30, 32, 35, 38, 40, 41, 42,
　　　　51, 115, 120, 130, 140, 150, 263
Hathaway, J.   147, 148
Hathaway, J. M.   163
Hathaway, Jonathan   60, 63, 64, 71, 73, 74, 76, 79, 80, 107, 111, 112,
　　　　113, 123, 125, 126, 131, 139, 141, 143, 144, 147, 150, 152,
　　　　153, 155, 157, 158, 163, 169, 173, 174
Hawkins   194
Hawkins, J. H.   210
Hawkins, T.   193
Hawkins, T. H.   196, 202, 203, 206, 210
Hawkins, T. N.   194, 199, 205
Hayes, U. S.   238, 239, 249
Hayes, W. S.   237
Heatherly, F. E.   192
Heatherly, J. C.   182, 188
Heatherly, J. E.   192, 199, 209, 211, 222, 232
Heatherly, James E.   191, 208, 220
Heatherley, J. E.   198
Heilliard, John A.   130
Helpeinstein, W. H.   198
Herrion, Garrett   278
Herron, Garrett   274
Hewes, Martin   263
Hewett, John   261

Hickman, Charles L. 346
Hilkey, J. L. 15, 38, 48
Hilkey, John L. 9, 10, 12, 13, 16, 17, 18, 20, 21, 22, 26, 27, 29, 30,
    31, 32, 33, 34, 35, 36, 37, 39, 42, 43, 44, 46, 47, 268
Hilkey, Maggie E. 16
Hilkey, Margaret E. 24, 29
Hill, Delilah 135
Hill, Elizabeth 271
Hill, Jacob 135
Hill, John 270
Hill, Olive 135
Hill, William 355
Hillard, J. A. 129
Hilliard, J. B. 65
Hilliards, Jackson 58
Hillyard, E. 63
Hillyard, J. A. 119, 123, 125, 126, 131, 146, 159, 164, 168, 170, 174,
    175
Hillyard, J. B. 161, 175
Hillyard, J. R. 153, 154, 166
Hillyard, Jackson 35, 54, 171, 179, 180, 215, 228, 231, 235, 239,
    244, 251, 267
Hillyard, John 34, 268
Hillyard, M. 226, 231
Hillyard, Martin 188, 193, 225, 226, 231, 268
Hillyard, W. J. 178
Himes, Mary 261
Hoffman, E. G. 166, 181
Hoffman, Jasper 271
Holbert, B. 189
Holbert, Ben 259
Holbert, G. W. 199
Holbert, Thomas 116, 128, 150, 276
Holden, Floyd 242, 249, 251
Hollan, J. S. 220
Holland, L. T. 71
Holland, Levi J. 277
Hollen, Hattie 249
Hollen, J. S. 215
Hollen, L. T. 89, 184, 188, 201, 210
Hollen, Levi T. 25, 30, 57, 61, 274

Hollen, S. T.   104
Hollen, W. J.   81
Hollen, William F.   264
Holler, J. W.   172, 183
Holt   347, 353, 362
Holt, S.   347
Holt, S. T. H.   347, 353, 355, 356, 357, 358, 359, 360, 362
Holt, Sam.   341, 351
Holt, Sam. T. H.   346
Holt, Samuel L.   346
Hoover, Simon   142, 150
House, F.   121
House, Joseph   68, 72
Howe, Benjamin   267
Howel, David M.   52
Howell, D. M.   53, 61
Howell, David M.   17, 45
Howell, G. T.   206, 210
Howell, Nehemiah   272, 276
Howell, S. L.   235, 239
Howes   154, 348
Howes, F.   35, 56, 178, 294, 296, 298, 299, 300, 301, 302, 303, 304,
       305, 306, 307, 308, 309, 310, 312, 313, 314, 315, 316, 317,
       318, 319, 321, 322, 324, 326, 327, 328, 329, 330, 334, 335,
       336, 337, 338, 340, 341, 343, 345, 346, 347, 348, 349, 350,
       351, 352, 354, 355, 356, 357, 358, 359, 360, 361, 362, 363
Howes, F. M.   77, 155, 156, 158, 159, 163, 164, 165, 166, 172, 184,
       293, 298
Howes, Fenelon   13, 15, 16, 17, 19, 32, 41, 266, 289, 290, 291, 292,
       293, 294, 295, 296, 298, 299, 300, 303, 304, 305, 306, 307,
       313, 317, 318, 319, 322, 323, 325, 326, 328, 329, 346, 355,
       357
Howes, Jennie   337, 339, 340, 341, 349, 350
Howes, Jos.   32
Howes, Joseph   20, 32, 38, 40, 48, 58
Howes, M.   151, 152, 153
Howes, Maj.   315, 361
Howes, Maj. F.   9, 11, 33, 341
Howes, Major   325, 327
Howes, Major F.   327

Howes, Major Fenelon 9
Howes, Virginia 343
Hudkins, Jacob 132, 158, 159, 173, 191, 192, 260
Hudkins, T. N. 191
Huffman 114
Huffman, E. G. 175, 188, 194, 195, 198, 207, 210, 243, 247, 258, 337
Huffman, E. T. 350
Huffman, W. B. 359, 360, 362, 363
Huffman, Walton 310, 333, 326
Hume, Beulah 306, 307, 308, 309, 310
Hume, Bulah 305
Humes, Bula 306, 308
Hunt, J. F. 127, 130, 131
Hunt, J. H. 123
Hunt, John F. 118, 129

I

Ice, Daniel 35, 47, 76, 128, 131, 192, 198, 225, 227, 229, 2231, 252, 271
Ice, Dan'l 44
Ice, Phebe 271
Ice, S. E. 225
Ice, W. T. 121, 345, 348, 349, 352
Ice, William T. 131
Ice, Wm. T. 109, 199

J

Jackson (& Brooks) 341, 351
Jarvin, W. D. H. 214, 220
Jenkins, Hattie 234, 235, 238, 239, 248
Jennings, W. F. 242, 249
Jennings, W. T. 249
Jennings, Wm. T. 249
Johnson, I. V. 251, 252, 258
Johnson, J. D. 211
Johnson, J. V. 218, 222

Johnson, Robert 121
Jones, B. 150
Jones, B. L. 132
Jones, B. S. 120, 134, 165, 175
Jones, Ballard 61, 65, 140, 153, 161, 185
Jones, Ben. 277
Jones, Benjamin 274
Jones, C. L. 52
Jones, Coalman L. 276
Jones, F. J. 274, 277
Jones, J. D. 178
Jones, John L.. 278
Jones, Joseph 266
Jones, Lewis 172, 252
Jones, Sam 259
Jones, W. W. 82, 85, 91, 93, 95, 97, 98, 99, 102, 104, 106, 152, 274, 277
Jones, Wm. B. 77
Jones, Wm. M. 61, 62, 64, 65, 68, 84
Jones, Wm. W. 58, 59, 64, 65, 66, 67, 71, 74, 78, 81, 83, 84, 86, 87, 90, 99, 100, 101, 110
Judge, Patrick 264

K
Kade, E. T. 165
Kane, Thomas 201, 203, 210, 243, 245, 246, 250, 362
Kane, Thos. 258
Keiser, Henry 115
Kelley, Dyer 184, 271
Kelley, Nathan 155, 162, 253, 258
Kelley, S. R. 195, 198
Kelly, A. 277
Kelly, Agnes 270
Kelly, D. 277
Kelly, Deborah 270
Kelly, Dyar 65
Kelly, Dyer 11
Kelly, Nathan 257
Kelly, Nathan E. 65

Kerr, Emmett   154
Kerr, G. W.   175
Kerr, L. D.   46, 115, 120, 132
Kerr, L. H.   166
Kerr, L. N.   81
Kerr, Luther H.   64, 153, 161
Kerr, R. D.   10, 81, 84
Kerr, R. E.   136, 139, 142, 143, 147, 148, 150, 151, 152, 155, 157, 159, 160, 161, 162, 164, 165, 168, 169, 173, 174
Kerr, Robert D.   264
Kettle, Noah   151
Keys, W. G.   353, 356, 358
Keys, Wm. P.   11
Keyser, Henry   151
King, M. H.   256, 258
King, Patrick   263
Kittle, Geo.   346
Kittle, Geo. M.   345, 352
Knotts, James   32, 80
Kunst, Isaac   231

L

Lake   313
Lake (& Gawthrop)   293, 298
Lake, I. M.   23
Lake, J. M.   18, 48
Lake, Jennette   313
Lance, Jonas   263
Lanham, B.   50
Lanham, V.   53
Latham, Samuel   261
Lee, Waine   299, 302
Lock, I. N.   300
Locke, E.   300
Locke, E. N.   294, 295
Locke, Ed. N.   294, 297, 301, 302
Locke, Edwin   295, 296, 297
Locke, Edwin N.   291, 295, 296
Lough, M. C.   313, 314, 316, 317, 318, 319, 321, 322, 323, 324

Lough, M. E.   315
Lovett   214, 218, 219, 220, 223
Lovett, L. B.   224, 226, 227, 228, 229, 231, 232, 235, 239, 245, 246,
        247, 248, 250, 251, 253, 257, 293, 294, 298, 301, 302, 303,
        305, 306, 307, 308, 309, 310, 311, 316, 319, 320, 321, 323,
        324, 328, 333, 343, 351, 352
Lovett, Lloyd B.   311
Lovett, P. L.   314, 350

M
Madden, F. P.   62
Madden, Martin   136, 139, 142, 143, 147, 148, 149
Madden, Thomas   67, 69, 71, 72, 74, 80, 82, 83, 88, 92, 94, 105, 108,
        110, 111, 112, 119, 120, 124, 125, 126, 130, 131, 132, 150
Maddin, Thomas   129, 130
Mallone, L.   344
Marteney, Perry   133, 151
Marteny, Pansy   83
Mathew, Amos   124
Mathew, J. C.   63
Matlick, E. C.   207, 208, 210
Matlick, Effie C.   204, 206
Matthew, Amos   132
Matthew, George   261
Mattic, E. C.   209
Mc Cauley   153
Mc Cauley, D. G.   137, 157
Mc Cauley, David G.   162, 263, 275
Mc Cauley, E. J.   158, 160, 263
Mc Cauley, Ephraim   265
Mc Cauley, John   225
Mc Cauley, L. G.   150
Mc Clain, Jacob   184
Mc Cloud, John   254
Mc Colley, E.   176
Mc Cutcheon, Bert   306, 311, 320, 321, 324
Mc Cutcheon, Burt   307, 308, 315, 317, 318
Mc Cutcheon, Geo.   212, 213, 214, 216, 218, 222, 223, 224, 225, 226,

       227, 228, 229, 230, 232, 233, 234, 235, 236, 237, 239, 240,
       241, 242, 243, 244, 245, 246, 247, 248, 250, 251
Mc Cutcheon, Geo. P.   257, 258
Mc Cutcheon, H. J.   338
Mc Cutcheon, H. K.   296, 298, 299, 300, 301, 302, 303, 304, 305, 306,
       307, 308, 309, 313, 314, 315, 316, 317, 318, 319, 322, 326,
       327, 328, 329, 330, 334, 335, 336, 337, 338, 340, 341, 342,
       343, 345, 346, 348, 349, 352, 354, 356, 358
Mc Cutcheon, Howard   293, 294, 295, 298, 302, 303,
Mc Cutcheon, Howard K.   300, 339, 347, 348
Mc Cutcheon R. A.   12, 13, 15, 16, 20, 32, 34, 35, 36, 37, 38, 39, 40,
       41, 42, 43, 44, 45, 47, 48, 50, 56, 57, 58, 59, 60, 61, 64, 65,
       67, 68, 71, 72, 73, 74, 76, 78, 80, 81, 82, 83, 84, 85, 86, 87,
       89, 90, 91, 92, 93, 95, 97, 98, 99, 100, 101, 102, 103, 104,
       105, 106, 109, 110, 111, 113, 115, 120, 123, 127, 131, 132,
       134, 137, 138, 140, 141, 142, 143, 149, 150, 151, 152, 153,
       154, 156, 157, 158, 161, 162, 167, 168, 171, 172, 175, 176,
       179, 181, 183, 186, 187, 192, 193, 194, 195, 197, 199, 200,
       201, 202, 203, 205, 208, 211, 213, 214, 215, 217, 220, 221,
       242, 268, 289, 290, 291, 292, 293, 294, 295, 296, 298, 299,
       300, 301, 302, 303, 304, 305, 306, 307, 308, 309, 310, 311,
       312, 313, 314, 315, 316, 317, 318, 320, 321, 322, 323, 324,
       325, 326, 327, 328, 329, 330, 331, 333, 334, 335, 336, 337,
       338, 339, 340, 341, 342, 343, 344, 345, 346, 347, 348, 349,
       350, 351, 352, 356, 358, 359, 360, 363
Mc Cutcheon, R. E.   309, 310, 311, 316, 318, 320, 321, 323, 324,
       328, 330, 333, 334, 341, 350, 351
Mc Cutcheon, R. Emmett   343
Mc Cutcheon, Robt. A.   343
Mc Cutcheon, Robt. E.   338
Mc Gee, William F.   19
Mc Gee, Wm. F.   28, 31, 39, 54
Mc Ginnes, Bridget   264
Mc Gowan, James   265
Mc Guiness, Patrick   10, 151
Mc Lane, Jacob   55, 134, 172, 221
Mc Lane, S. H.   206, 210, 231
Mc Lane, S. J.   223
Mc Lane, Thomas   121
Mc Lean, Arthur   290
Mc Lean, Jacob   44, 48, 213

Mc Lean, S. H.   251
Mc Lean, Sam'l H.   250
Mc Lean, Samuel H.   249
Mclane, Andes   86
Mclane, Hanning   188
Mclane, Jacob   116, 277
Mclane, Reat.   277
Mclane, S. H.   229, 230, 238, 240, 242, 249
Mclane, Samuel H.   249
Mclean, Aretus   274
Mclean, Jacob   216, 274
Mclean, S. H.   227, 237
Mclean, Samuel H.   234
Meoss, J. I.   134
Meoss, J. T.   196, 199
Mertin   45
Meshane, J.   150
Modisett, A. B.   44
Modistet, A. B.   46
Monaghan, Andrew   264
Monaghan, S.   264
Monahon, Thomas   266
Moon, W. C.   221
Moon, W. R.   221
Moore   43, 309
Moore, A.   149, 216, 221
Moore, A. B.   119, 122, 126, 129, 148, 149, 163, 164, 171
Moore, Alph   234, 239
Moore, Alpheus   116, 120, 132, 172, 184, 185, 189, 192, 198, 204, 210, 213, 235, 300, 306, 308, 309
Moore, D.   45
Moore, Daniel   11, 13, 16, 19, 21, 22, 26, 27, 29, 30, 32, 34, 35, 36, 37, 38, 40, 41, 270, 271
Moore, Dan'l   42
Moore, E. M.   166, 175, 277
Moore, Elizabeth   273
Moore, Fred   231, 258
Moore, Frederic   254, 256
Moore, Frederick   228
Moore, Geo.   276
Moore, Granville   269

Moore, Isaiah   175
Moore, Isiah   166
Moore, Jethro   254, 257
Moore, John   18, 19, 233, 259
Moore, Laben   10, 35, 104, 116, 134, 149, 154, 161, 171, 183, 224, 230, 244, 247, 250, 252
Moore, Marcus   154
Moore, Marquis   161
Moore, Nora   105, 107, 112, 165, 167, 168, 169, 173, 174
Moore, Nova   163
Moore, S. A.   345, 352
Moore, S. R.   236, 239
Moore, W. C.   216, 223, 228, 229, 230, 231, 242, 247, 248, 249, 254, 256, 258
Moore, W. E.   249, 251
Moore, W. R.   127, 149, 151, 172, 184, 228, 231, 241
Moore, W. S.   104
Moore, William   269
Moore, William R.   273
Moore, William S.   269
Moore, Wm. R.   11, 35, 117, 213, 216, 277
Moore, Ulysses   237, 239
Moran, Robert   271
Moran, Samuel   185, 187, 188, 198
Moran, Thomas   96, 125
Moran, Thos.   111
More, C. M.   62, 63, 66
More, Charles M.   66
Moss, J. T.   177, 188, 211, 218
Moss, John T.   155, 162, 243, 250
Moss, Jno. T.   221
Murphy, C. M.   194, 197, 198, 201, 210, 353, 356
Murphy, Eugenia   276
Murphy, John D.   272
Mustoe, C.   68, 82, 84
Mustoe, Chambers   35, 58, 59, 61, 62, 64, 66, 71, 74, 78, 83, 268
Mustoe, James   268
Myers, Solomon   271

N

Nestor, M. L. 69
Newlen, B. P. 183
Newlen, J. J. 183

Newlon 243
Newlon (& Stalnaker) 9
Newlon, B. J. 221
Newlon, B. P. 59, 150, 171, 177, 180, 194, 198, 204, 210, 215, 217, 221, 223, 225
Newlon, Bur P. 16, 19
Newlon, Burr P. 46, 268
Newlon, Charles 302
Newlon, J. J. 171, 189, 195, 198, 204, 206, 210, 222, 223, 225, 227, 231, 254, 255, 259
Newlon, W. F. 217, 221

O

O Brien, Anna 194, 213
O Brien, Annie 219
O Brien, Daniel 137, 161
O Brien, Hannah 137, 141, 142, 144, 147, 148, 151, 159, 161
O Brien, M. 152
O Brien, M. N. 155, 157, 160, 162
O Bryan, Melville 115
O Conner, Kate 256, 257
O Conner, Matthew O. 263
Obrian, Daniel 264
Obrien, Anna 197, 198, 208, 219, 220
Obrien, Hannah 136
Obrien, Maggie 234, 238
Obrien, Maggie J. 238, 240, 250
Oldaker, M. V. 17, 31
Oldaker, Martin V. 24, 46

P

Pain, Nathan 57, 100
Pane, Nathan 45
Panes, Nathan Second 46
Panin, Nathan 85
Parks, Benjamin 77
Parks, W. L. 76
Parks, W. S. 179, 184
Parks, Wm. L.. 61, 67, 98
Parks, Wm. S. 177
Patton, M. 231
Payne, Henry 271
Peck, M. 224, 342, 347, 348, 352, 353
Peck, Melville 340, 344
Phares, J. R. 259
Phares, John 260
Phares, John R. 242
Phares, Seymour 185
Phares, W. S. 10, 204, 232, 233, 234, 235, 236, 237, 239, 241, 243, 244, 245, 246, 247, 248, 249, 250, 252, 253, 255, 258, 259, 268
Pharis, W. S. 195, 198, 210
Philips, C. 326, 328, 333, 335, 338
Philips, Cicero 326, 327, 328, 329, 330, 333, 334, 335, 336, 337, 338
Phillips, A. 216, 221
Phillips, B. F. 62, 64, 94, 96, 102, 104, 108, 110
Phillips, C. 151, 152, 153, 164, 260, 345, 347, 348, 352
Phillips, Cicero 124, 131, 163, 165, 167, 221, 233, 236, 254, 255, 257, 339, 340, 341, 342, 343, 344, 345, 346, 347, 348, 349, 352, 355, 356, 358
Phillips, D. E. 256, 257
Phillips, E. 351
Phillips, George 268
Phillips, George M. 52
Phillips, Jefferson 272, 276
Phillips, L. C. 251
Phillips, Monroe 140, 161, 164, 165, 167, 169, 173, 174, 175
Phillips, S. R. 105, 106, 110, 111, 113, 139, 144, 147, 152, 155, 157, 162, 164, 169, 173, 174, 175, 177, 178, 180, 181, 185, 187, 188, 217
Phillips, Sallie R. 159, 160, 165, 213, 219, 221, 273

Phillips, Simeon 68
Phillips, W. S. 242, 247, 256, 257
Phillips, William M. 268
Poe, David 60, 63, 65
Poe, Peter 271
Poe, S. B. 116, 121, 123, 128, 132, 188
Poe, W. M. 103, 140, 150
Poling, A. J. 225, 231
Poling, Abraham 189
Poling, Edgar 263
Poling, G. C. 298, 310
Poling, Hannibal 269
Poling, I. M. 292, 298
Poling, Israel 271, 276
Poling, J. H. 257
Poling, J. M. 216
Poling, J. N. 205, 210
Poling, J. S. 152, 153, 159, 160, 177, 179, 181
Poling, J. W. 216, 221
Poling, James 151, 155, 172, 202, 227, 233, 239
Poling, James W. 173, 176
Poling, Jas. 166, 184
Poling, Jas. S. 157
Poling, Jasper 272
Poling, John 271, 276
Poling, Josiah 196, 199
Poling, Martin M. 272
Poling, Mary 270
Poling, N. 216
Poling, Sanford 184, 276
Poling, Sylvester M. 245, 251
Potter, W. C. 62, 65, 66
Potter, Wm. C. 68
Price, A. 184
Price, Albert 116, 128, 149, 154, 161, 172, 178, 273
Price, G. R. 277
Price, H. J. 234, 238, 239
Price, Isaac 11, 67, 82, 85, 216, 221, 233, 259, 273
Price, J. 277
Price, John 15, 241, 257, 273
Price, John L. 215

Price, Lewis   18, 19, 213, 241
Price, Samuel   255, 257
Price, Silas R.   273
Price, William G. W.   270, 277
Price, William Sr.   277
Price, Wm. G. W.   11
Prise, John   189
Pritt, Elijah   268
Proudfoot, Joshua   16, 26, 95, 115, 120, 263
Proudfoot, Joshue   80
Proudfoot, Thomas   130

R

Ramsey, J. J.   10, 47, 162, 269
Ramsey, J. L.   243
Ramsey, J. M.   47, 89, 98, 105, 117, 154, 161, 172, 208, 227, 231
Ramsey, J. Morgan   161
Ramsey, J. N.   69, 116
Ramsey, J. S.   108
Ramsey, J. W.   204, 205, 206, 209, 210, 223, 229, 230, 231
Ramsey, Jas.   168
Ramsey, James   175
Ramsey, James L.   251, 270
Ramsey, John J.   28, 54, 157
Ramsey, John M.   11, 28, 270
Ramsey, John W.   228
Ramsey, P.   128
Ramsey, Phillip   115, 117, 118, 121, 125, 127, 133, 135, 141, 145, 146, 189, 270
Ramsey, S.   194
Ramsey, Samuel   198
Ray, C.   263
Ray, H. L.   229, 232, 258
Ray, Holister   258
Ray, L. H.   217
Rease, F. P.   337, 344, 347, 348, 350, 353, 355, 356, 358
Rease, P. P.   361
Recter, H. P.   128

Recter, N. P.   115
Rector, H. P.   127, 150, 180, 183
Reed, Peter   353
Reger, Albert   162
Reger, W. F.   47
Rhinehart, Hiram   278
Rhinehart, John W.   41
Ridgeway, Henry   128, 270
Ridgway, Charles   134, 149
Ridgway, Henry   116, 151, 189
Right (& Shurtleff)   178, 180, 182, 185, 188, 190, 198, 245, 246, 250, 251
Right, A.   11, 37, 47, 60, 77, 86, 193, 198, 216, 221, 224, 227, 228, 231, 237, 240, 246, 251, 254, 257, 277
Right, A. F.   124, 133
Right, A. R.   134, 149, 185, 194, 198
Right, Arnold   15, 273
Right, F. M.   309, 311, 319, 320, 323
Right, G. M.   164, 173, 175, 176, 178, 179, 181, 186, 187, 189, 193, 196, 197, 198, 199
Right, Geo. M.   166, 325
Right, Geo. W.   170
Right, Geor. M.   185
Right, George M.   174
Right, I. F.   129, 131, 136, 137, 144, 147, 148, 160
Right, Isaac F.   129, 155
Right, J.   130
Right, J. A.   324
Right, J. C.   65, 116, 162, 172, 178, 184, 202, 254, 257, 258
Right, J. F.   122, 125, 131, 138, 139, 149, 150, 152, 157, 159, 160, 162
Right, James   315
Right, James A.   316, 321
Right, John   86, 116, 131, 134, 150, 176, 177, 178, 179, 180, 182, 183, 184, 185, 186, 187, 188, 231, 171, 172, 225, 341, 351, 353, 355
Right, John C.   156, 246, 251
Right, L. E.   120, 132
Right, Marion   105
Right, R. M.   109
Right, W. J.   116, 127, 149, 151, 172, 176, 183,186

Right, W. W.   164, 166, 170, 173, 175, 176, 178, 179, 180, 194, 195, 197, 198, 199, 213, 217, 219, 221, 303
Right, William J.   273, 276
Right, Wm. J.   9, 11, 12, 13, 15, 16, 19, 20, 103, 112
Rinehart, Himan   116
Rinehart, Hiram   36, 266
Rinehart, James   151
Rineheart, Hiram   10
Rhorabaugh, A. S.   89
Rhorabaugh, Albert   253
Rhorabaugh, B. B.   252
Rhorabough, A.   223
Rhorabough, A. F.   226
Rhorabough, Albert   102
Rhorabough, B. B.   179, 181, 327, 349, 350
Rhorbough, Albert   257
Rhorbough, B. B.   319, 320, 322, 331, 332, 334, 349
Roahrbough, B. B.   177
Roberts, Thomas   269
Robinson   330, 333
Robinson, F. N.   66
Robinson, J. A.   329, 333
Robinson, J. F.   182
Robinson, J. H.   94, 97, 177, 180, 181, 189
Robinson, J. N.   66
Robinson, J. W.   219, 220, 222, 230, 232, 240, 246, 309, 310
Robinson, Jacob   245
Robinson, James H.   247, 251
Robinson, John A.   339, 351, 361
Robinson, S. D.   358
Rodgers, Minnie M.   250
Rogers   236
Rogers, Minnie   233, 237, 238, 239
Rogers, Minnie M.   250
Rohorbaugh, A. S.   278
Rohr, Lucy   213, 219
Rohrabaugh, Nathan   53
Rohrbough, Anthony S.   274
Rohrbough, B. B.   309, 310
Rohrobough, B. B.   323, 325
Rorabugh, A. H.   231

Rorhabaugh, A. S.   27
Rosenberger, Clay   321
Rosenberger, H. C.   203, 213, 241, 242, 254, 289, 290, 291, 292, 294, 296, 299, 300, 301, 303, 304, 305, 306, 310, 312, 313, 314, 315, 316, 317, 320, 322, 324, 325, 334, 347, 353
Rosenberger, J. W.   303
Rosenburger   243
Row, A. D.   187
Row, A. J.   10, 178, 180, 186
Row, Jackson   200
Row, W. H.   258
Rowe, A. J.   267
Roy, H. L.   221
Rucker, Samuel   121, 266
Ryland, J. H.   362

S

Sandridge, Jesse L.   263
Schoonover, C. J.   277
Schoonover, R. E.   47
Schoonover, W. J.   109
See, L. M.   19, 40
See, Lavenia M.   15
See, Lavin M.   24
See, M. S.   47
Serpell   344, 348
Serpell, Geo. M.   315, 321, 324, 344, 345, 351, 359
Shackleford   346
Shaffer, B. F.   155, 158, 162
Shaffer, G. W.   164, 173, 175
Shaffer, Geo. W.   167, 169
Shaffer, George W.   174
Shanabarger, O. H.   234, 237, 238, 239
Shanabarger, W. B.   354, 359, 363
Shanaberger, O. H.   250
Shanaberger, S. A.   199
Shank, John   251, 252
Sharps, Wm.   272

Shires, S. E.   170
Shockey, Bell   135
Shockey, F. C.   137, 150, 196, 199, 272
Shockey, Francis   11
Shockey, Franklin   276
Shockey, Harriet   135
Shockey, Jacob   272, 276
Shockey, John W.   135
Shockey, Rebecca   135
Shockey, Sarah M.   135
Shockey, William E.   135
Shomo, C. E.   79
Shomo, Chas.   228
Shomo, D. J.   171, 176, 180, 267
Shomo, G. M.   108
Shomo, G. N.   134, 149
Shomo, G. W.   63
Shomo, George N.   76
Shomo, Hubert   109, 111
Shomo, J.   68
Shomo, J. J.   179
Shomo, J. M.   275
Shomo, J. W.   25
Shomo, John M.   262
Shomo, Marion B.   247, 251
Shomo, Nixon   44, 225, 252
Shomo, Thomas   65
Shomore, J. W.   46
Shomore, Nixon   47
Showmore, Chas.   231
Shurtleff (& Right)   178, 180, 182, 185, 188, 190, 198, 246, 250, 251
Shurtleff, Eliza   268
Shurtleff, Max   307, 308, 311
Shurtleff, Max E.   310
Shurtleff, W. A.   140
Shurtleff, W. S.   90, 93, 94, 95, 102, 105, 108, 109, 110, 118, 123, 124, 125, 126, 129, 130, 131, 133, 136, 137, 138, 141, 146, 147, 148, 150, 151, 152, 153, 154, 155, 156, 158, 159, 162, 163, 164, 165, 167, 168, 170, 171, 172, 176, 177, 178, 179, 180, 182, 183, 184, 185, 186, 187, 188, 189, 204, 210, 215, 217, 224, 230, 285, 347, 353

394 School Board Minutes

Shurtleff, W. Scott   158
Shurtliff   243, 245
Shurtliff, W. S.   90, 220, 221, 226, 227, 228, 231, 234, 237, 239, 240
Simon, Jennie   332
Simon, Perry   176
Simonds   128
Simons, Andrew   44
Simons, Jennie   325, 326, 327, 328, 329, 330, 331, 332, 335
Simpson, J. B.   247
Simpson, Jas.   115
Sipe, Daniel   117, 131
Sipe, Geo. E.   165
Sipe, George, E.   176
Sipe, H. C.   153
Sipe, Jacob   10, 17, 29, 31, 46, 52, 61, 85, 91, 97, 127, 131, 157, 162, 265
Sipe, John L.   265
Sipe, N. C.   67, 78, 79, 80, 159, 164, 166, 169, 173, 174, 175
Sipe, N. E.   176
Sipe, Nancy C.   39, 46, 52, 56, 157
Sipe, Nannie   152
Sipe, Noah I.   24
Sipe, Noah J.   265
Sipe, Nomi C.   66
Skidmire, J. S.   262
Skidmore, J. S.   80
Skidmore, J. W.   108
Skidmore, James V.   266
Skidmore, John   275
Smith, Abie J.   229, 230
Smith, Allie J.   223
Smith, Alpheus   271
Smith, J. R. W.   11, 35, 153
Smith, John R. W.   161
Stalnaker   294
Stalnaker (& Newlon)   9
Stalnaker, A. W.   152, 153, 154, 155, 157, 159, 160, 161, 162
Stalnaker, G.   116, 128
Stalnaker, G. J.   125, 126, 129, 133, 136, 138, 142, 147, 148, 151, 218, 221, 253, 254, 255, 259, 290, 291, 292, 293, 294, 295, 296, 301, 302, 310, 313, 320, 321, 324

Stalnaker, G. T. 149
Stalnaker, Garison 123
Stalnaker, Garrison 129
Stalnaker, Granvill 103
Stalnaker, Granville 10, 67, 268
Stalnaker, I. W. 34
Stalnaker, Marshall 263
Stalnaker, S. W. 268
Stancliff, S. M. 311
Steerman, Harman 23, 35
Steerman, Harmen 86
Steerman, Harmon 261
Steerman, J. B. 163
Steerman, J. M. 124, 132, 151
Steerman, L. D. 267
Steerman, William 124, 131
Steerman, Wm. 115, 137, 149
Stewart, A. P. 54
Stipe, George 267
Street, C. F. 64, 82
Street, C. H. 42, 50, 55, 59, 63, 65, 74, 75, 76, 77, 80, 87, 89, 90, 96, 148
Street, C. N. 68, 69, 88, 145
Street, C. V. 56, 81, 82, 87, 92, 94, 98, 101, 102, 105, 107, 110, 130, 174
Street, Caroline V. 74
Street, Charles H. 15, 265
Street, Charles N. 68
Street, Susan 104
Street, V. H. 95
Street, W. A. 75, 76, 78, 80, 82, 83, 88, 89, 90, 92, 93, 103, 104, 108, 111
Street, Wm. A. 83
Strickler, A. C. W. 258
Sturm, David 271
Swearingen, Belle 242
Swearingen, F. Bell 249, 250
Swearingen, F. Belle 249
Swick (& Baker) 240, 251
Swick, A. 262
Swick, Anthony 275

Swick, Eugene 143, 149
Swick F. L. 62, 64, 66, 67, 71, 72, 73, 75, 79, 80, 82, 89, 101
Swick F. S. 99, 131
Swick, Simen 86
Swick, Simon 10, 58, 64, 69, 115, 151, 163, 261

T
Tahney, Patrick 92
Talbot, D. S. 222
Talbott, A. C. 175
Talbott, Alexander 118, 166
Talbott, D. S. 171, 183, 212, 213, 214, 218, 223, 225, 226, 227, 229, 232, 233, 234, 235, 236, 237, 240, 241, 242, 243, 248, 254, 255, 259
Talbott, David 251, 258
Talbott, E. P. 141, 149
Talbott, E. T. 263
Talbott, Edward S. 73
Talbott, Geo. E. 166
Talbott, George E. 175
Talbott, J. W. 44, 45, 48, 49, 114, 130, 218
Talbott, James W. 38, 48, 49
Talbott, Jas. W. 38, 48
Talbott, R. B. 46
Talbott, R. R. 10, 24, 264
Talier, Albert 127
Tallman, H. M. 46
Tallman, F. M. 38, 56, 79
Tallman, Margaret 265
Tallman, R. L. 51, 55, 60, 63, 65, 75, 80, 82, 105, 112, 113, 115, 122, 126, 129, 130, 132, 136, 138, 141, 147, 148, 150, 152, 153, 156, 158, 173
Tallman, R. S. 121, 136, 159, 160, 162
Tallman, R. T. 129
Tallman, Robt. L. 16, 23, 26, 28
Taook, G. H. 151
Taylor, A. L. 213, 219, 220, 223, 229, 230, 231
Taylor, A. P. 230

School Board Minutes 397

Taylor, B. H. 262
Taylor, C. 333
Taylor, Clint 311
Taylor, Clinton 307, 308, 311, 329
Taylor, J. M. 347, 353
Taylor, J. W. 37, 43, 47
Taylor, R. N. 275
Taylor, V. F. 18, 23, 31, 46
Taylor, V. L. 230
Teats, Martin 265
Teter, A. H. 102
Teter, Abel 61, 73, 88, 89, 97, 103, 109, 118, 131, 134, 150, 166, 175, 310, 311
Teter, B. F. 150
Teter, C. F. 90, 93, 96, 105, 107, 112, 118, 119, 125, 129, 132, 138, 143, 145, 147, 148, 149, 159, 161, 206, 210, 215, 220
Teter, C. H. 89
Teter, C. P. 334
Teter, Chas. F. 317
Teter, D. P. 142
Teter, E. F. 150
Teter, G. M. 131
Teter, Ida M. 185, 187
Teter, J. 125
Teter, J. B. 115, 150
Teter, J. M. 125
Teter, James 268
Teter, Jesse 10, 21, 22, 30, 115, 153, 161, 163, 247, 266
Teter, Jos. 34, 45, 69
Teter, Joseph 21, 22, 26, 27, 29, 30, 31, 32, 34, 36, 37, 38, 39, 41, 42, 43, 44, 45, 48, 50, 51, 52, 53, 55, 56, 57, 58, 59, 61, 62, 66, 67, 68, 70, 71, 72, 74, 78, 81, 82, 83, 84, 85, 86, 87, 89, 90, 91, 92, 95, 97, 98, 99, 100, 102, 104, 106, 110, 113, 114, 115, 116, 117, 118, 121, 124, 127, 128, 129, 132, 133, 134, 135, 138, 140, 141, 143, 144, 145, 146, 147, 149, 150, 190, 218, 232, 266
Teter, Joseph Jun/Jr. 21, 22, 35, 36, 41, 84
Teter, M. V. 121, 125, 129, 130, 143, 145, 148, 164, 167, 168, 169, 173, 174, 175
Teter, Oliver 266
Teter, T. B. 137

Teter, V. F. 95
Teter, W. W. 44, 48, 50, 51, 55, 61, 63, 66, 87, 91, 93, 96, 97, 107, 109, 111, 112
Tobott (Dr.) 200
Thacker, D. 151
Thacker, J. D. 156, 162, 170, 175
Thacker, J. S. 52
Thacker, Jacob J. 264
Thacker, Jacob S. 60
Thacker, S. 90
Thomas, James H. 103
Thompson, David 272, 276
Thompson, Frank 225, 231
Thompson, Hezekiah 192
Thompson, James D. C. 272, 276
Thompson, Robert 255, 257
Thorn, Frederick 261
Thorn, Geo. 10, 16
Thorn, George 35
Thorn, Jacob 262, 275
Thorn, R. G. 19, 101, 111, 262, 275
Thornhill, Francis 268
Thornhill, W. J. 259
Throop, G. H. 142
Tomblyn 329
Tomblyn, W. E. 325, 326, 327, 329, 331, 332, 335, 337, 339, 340, 341, 343, 349, 350
Tompson, James 151, 155
Tompson, Jas. 165
Trimble, W. E. 305, 311, 315, 321, 324

V
Valentine, F. D. 165, 175, 200
Valentine, G. W. 217, 221
Valentine, J. R. 207, 210
Vanscoy, A. 262
Vanscoy, Able 275
Vickcaney, Benjamin 67
Viquesney 321, 324

Viquesney, E. 10
Viquesney, Emile 267
Viquesney, J. A. 254, 256, 257, 258
Viquesney, L. N. 234, 239

W

W, J. A. 222
Waggle, John 124, 130
Wagner, J. A. 189
Wagner, John 172
Wagner, John A. 276
Wagoner, J. A. 99
Wagoner, John A. 272
Waid, J. W. 191
Walcott, D. L. 311
Wallace, Alice 242, 247, 249, 251, 254, 256, 258
Ward, Dolly 315
Ward, G. V. 251, 255, 257
Ward, Guy V. 234, 239, 243, 246, 251, 253
Ward, J. 210
Ward, J. W. 175, 178, 204, 210, 243, 252, 253, 254, 255, 257, 258, 259
Ward, John 232, 233, 234, 235, 236, 237, 239, 241, 242, 243, 244, 245, 246, 247, 250, 252
Ward, John W. 166, 250, 253
Ware, Abraham 265
Ware, Adam 261
Ware, Benoni 261
Ware, Blackburn 352
Ware, E. 330, 333, 343, 351, 362
Ware, E. M. 328, 333
Ware, Elahue 43
Ware, Elihue 51, 115
Ware, Floyd 310
Ware, J. B. 306, 307, 308, 309, 310, 360
Ware, J. R. 262
Ware, J. Blackburn 354, 355, 356, 357, 358, 359, 361, 362, 363
Ware, James R. 275

Ware, Nora   110
Warner, Harman   265
Warner, Harmon   175
Warner, Henry   120
Waters, Martin   265
Weaver, William H.   85
Weaver, Wm. H.   57
Weese, Judson   266
Weese, L.   266
Weese, W. F.   47
Welch, Agnes   335
Wentz, Chas. C.   329, 333
Werner, Harmon   166
Werner, Henry   132
Werner, Richard   10, 35
White, F. M.   60, 61, 62, 64, 67, 73, 76, 86, 88, 89, 91, 94, 96
Wigel, Jacob   343
Wigle, Charles   313
Wigle, Jacob   314, 315, 316, 317, 318, 319, 320, 321, 322, 323, 324,
          325, 326, 327, 328, 329, 330, 331, 332, 333, 335, 337, 338,
          339, 340, 341, 349, 350, 351
Wigle, John   265
Williams, A. J.   10, 69, 86, 262, 275
Williams, Thomas   9, 10, 269
Williams, Thos.   9
Williamson   23
Williamson, J. A.   218, 231, 232, 240, 251, 252, 258
Williamson, J. H.   248
Williamson, James A.   239, 248, 250, 255
Williamson, Nelson   261
Williamson, S. H.   334
Willmoth, Alice   147, 148
Willmoth, Daniel E.   85
Willmoth, F. C.   209
Willoughby, J. C.   258
Wilmoth   211
Wilmoth, A. B.   115, 266
Wilmoth, A. J.   10, 22, 26, 27, 32, 35, 41, 42, 45, 50, 51, 52, 53, 55,
          56, 57, 65, 91, 92
Wilmoth, A. M.   179, 181, 188, 209, 210, 218, 221
Wilmoth, A. V.   31, 35, 98, 99, 109, 115, 118, 265

Wilmoth, Alice   136, 141, 159, 177, 185, 187, 213, 219
Wilmoth, Alice M.   207, 220
Wilmoth, C. B.   256, 257
Wilmoth, Daniel C.   100, 109, 214
Wilmoth, Ellis   272, 276
Wilmoth, F. C.   186, 187, 188, 207, 209, 210, 218, 221
Wilmoth, Flora   220, 230, 232
Wilmoth, Flora C.   219, 223, 229, 230
Wilmoth, Florence   185, 187, 206
Wilmoth, Florence C.   213
Wilmoth, Florence E.   204
Wilmoth, Isaac W.   109
Wilson, Alpheus   115
Wilson, Celia   13, 28, 47
Wilson, Iasiah   115
Wilson, Joseph   175, 261
Wilson, Josiah   137, 150, 167
Wilson, Jossiah   134
Wilson, Lewis   44, 54, 135, 149
Wilson, Sol   216
Wilson, Solomon   35, 99, 116, 128, 189, 213, 221, 241
Wilson, William   261
Wilson, Wm. P.   10
Wiseman, B. B.   263
Wiseman, Henry   263
Wolverton, B. M.   273, 277
Wood, Allen   35, 54, 214, 272, 276
Wood, Dinah   223, 230
Wood, Lucy B.   354, 359, 362
Woods   45
Woods, J. Hop   356, 359
Woods, Samuel   199
Woolverton, B. M.   15
Woolverton, Martin   271
Wright, John   268

Y
Yeager (&Viquesney)   321
Yeager, Hiram   46

Yeager, Hisam 45, 264
Yeager, Hysam 10, 35
Yeager, Joseph C. 73
Yeager, Mary A. 265
Yeager, Nisam 57
Yeager, William 266
Yeager, Wm. L.. 39, 46
Yeake, Ellender 275
Yoak, E. 277
Yoak, S. E. 232, 259
Yock, Solomon 102
Yoke, Elizabeth 273
Yoke, Ellen 262
Yoke, S. E. 225, 231
Yokum, John 261
Yokum, N. 262

Z

Zerkle, Jacob 40
Zerkle, Oliver 43
Zirkle 54
Zirkle, C. I. 327
Zirkle, Chas. I. 327
Zirkle, Lewis 96, 111, 264
Zirkle, O. S. 262, 275